The Contemporary Conflict Resolution Reader

The Contemporary Conflict Resolution Reader

TOM WOODHOUSE, HUGH MIALL,
OLIVER RAMSBOTHAM AND
CHRISTOPHER MITCHELL

polity

First published in 2015 by Polity Press

Polity Press
65 Bridge Street
Cambridge CB2 1UR, UK

Polity Press
350 Main Street
Malden, MA 02148, USA

ISBN-13: 978-0-7456-8676-9
ISBN-13: 978-0-7456-8677-6(pb)

A catalogue record for this book is available from the British Library.

Typeset in 9.5 on 13 pt Swift
by Toppan Best-set Premedia Limited
Printed and bound in the UK by TJ International Ltd, Padstow, Cornwall

The publisher has used its best endeavours to ensure that the URLs for external websites referred to in this book are correct and active at the time of going to press. However, the publisher has no responsibility for the websites and can make no guarantee that a site will remain live or that the content is or will remain appropriate.

For further information on Polity, visit our website: politybooks.com

Contents

Part I   Foundations

Part II Conflict Theories and Analysis

Part III   Praxis (1) Conflict Prevention and Nonviolence

Part IV   Praxis (2) Mediation, Negotiation and Reconciliation

Part V Praxis (3) Peacebuilding

Part VI   Challenges and Future Directions

Sources and Acknowledgements

Thanks to all who have inspired us to take this on and who have provided invaluable help along the way. To our editors at Polity for their expertise and guidance – Louise Knight who first had the idea of the Reader and creatively urged us on to complete it; and Pascal Porcheron, who coordinated everything expertly, especially the references. To Rachel Thorne for her tireless work securing permission for use of the pieces in this reader; Sarah Dancy, for her excellent copyediting; and Jen Woodhouse for pointing out the importance of the hermeneutics of meaning-recollection. We are especially grateful to the authors whose work we have selected for their contributions to the field and in some cases for help in securing permissions.

We are grateful to the following for permission to reproduce copyright material:

Richer Resources Publications for material excerpted from Immanuel Kant, *On Perpetual Peace: A Philosophical Sketch*, translated by Ian Johnston, pp. 13–25, Vancouver Island University, Nanaimo, BC, Canada, 2012, copyright © 2012 Richer Resources Publications. SAGE for material excerpted from 'The Value for Conflict Resolution of a General Discipline of International Relations', by Quincy Wright in *Journal of Conflict Resolution*, 1(1), March 1957, pp. 3–8; published by SAGE Publications, Inc., copyright © 1957, SAGE Publications. Transcend International for material excerpted from 'Conflict Transformation by Peaceful Means (the Transcend Method)', by Johan Galtung, http://www.transcend.org; reproduced by kind permission. SAGE for material excerpted from 'Solving Conflicts: A Peace Research Perspective', by Johan Galtung, *Journal of Peace Research*, pp. 37–45, 56, published by SAGE Publications, Inc., copyright © 1990, Peace Research Institute Oslo. Simon & Schuster Inc. for material excerpted from *The Functions of Social Conflict*, by Lewis A. Coser, Free Press, pp. 33–38, copyright © 1976 by The Free Press, © renewed 1984 by Lewis A. Coser; reprinted with the permission of Simon & Schuster Publishing Group; all rights reserved. Harvard University Press for material excerpted from 'Bargaining, Communication, and Limited War', in *The Strategy of Conflict*, by Thomas C. Schelling, pp. 54–59, Cambridge, MA: Harvard University Press, copyright © 1960, 1980 by the President and Fellows of Harvard College; copyright © renewed 1988 by Thomas C. Schelling. Syracuse University Press for material excerpted from *Building a Global Civic Culture: Education for an Interdependent World*, by Elise Boulding, pp. 3–7, 1990; reproduced by permission. John Wiley & Sons for material excerpted from *Handbook of Conflict Resolution: Theory and Practice*, by Morton Deutsch and Peter Coleman, pp. 11–12, 2000; reproduced through Copyright Clearance Center. Palgrave Macmillan for material excerpted from *The Structure of International Conflict*, by Christopher R. Mitchell, pp. 281–284, 309–311, published 1989 by Palgrave Macmillan; reproduced with permission of Palgrave Macmillan. Taylor & Francis Books UK for material excerpted from 'Extending the Reach of Basic Human Needs: A Comprehensive Theory for the Twenty-First Century', by D. J. D. Sandole in *Conflict Resolution and Human Needs: Linking Theory and Practice*, edited by Kevin Avruch and Christopher Mitchell, 2013, pp. 23–24, copyright © 2013, Routledge; reproduced by permission of Taylor & Francis Books UK. University of California Press for material excerpted from *Ethnic Groups in Conflict*, 2nd ed., by Donald L. Horowitz, pp. 628–633, University of California Press, 2001, copyright © 2001, The Regents of the University of California. Polity Press for material excerpted from Preface, *New and Old Wars*, 2nd ed., by Mary Kaldor, Polity Press, pp. vii–xi, 2006; reproduced by permission of Polity Press and the author. Taylor & Francis Books for material excerpted from 'Special Issue: The Economic Functions of Violence in Civil Wars', by David Keen in *The Adelphi Papers* 38(320), 1998, pp. 9–13, copyright © The International Institute for Strategic Studies; reproduced by permission of Taylor & Francis Ltd, www.tandfonline.com on behalf of The International Institute for Strategic Studies. Professor Frances Stewart for material excerpted from *Horizontal Inequalities: A Neglected Dimension of Development*, by Frances Stewart, WORKING PAPER 1, pp. 2–7; reproduced by kind permission. Cambridge University Press for material excerpted from *Dynamics of Contention*, by Doug McAdam, Sidney Tarrow and Charles Tilly, pp. 17, 39–45, copyright © Cambridge University Press, 2001; reproduced by permission of Cambridge University Press and the authors. The Center for Leadership at Columbia College for material excerpted from 'A Nested Theory of Conflict', by Maire A. Dugan, published in *A Leadership Journal: Women in Leadership – Sharing the Vision*, pp. 12–18, July 1996; reproduced by permission. The Institute of Peace for material excerpted from 'An Integrated Framework for Building Peace', by John Paul Lederach, in *Building Peace: Sustainable Reconciliation in Divided Societies*, pp. 79–85, Washington, DC: Endowment of the United States Institute of Peace, 1997; reproduced by permission. Professor Richard E. Rubinstein for material excerpted from *Conflict Resolution: Dynamics Process & Structure*, by Richard E. Rubinstein, edited by Ho-Won Jeong, pp. 173–177, 190–195, 1999; reproduced by kind permission. Taylor & Francis Books for material excerpted from *Theories of Violent Conflict: An Introduction*, by Jolle Demmers, pp. 122–127, 132–135, copyright © 2012, Routledge, 2012; reproduced by permission of Taylor & Francis Books UK. Cambridge University Press for material excerpted from 'Ethnicity, Insurgency, and Civil War', by James D. Fearon and David D. Laitin, from *American Political Science Review*, 97(1), February 2003, pp. 75–76, copyright © American Political Science Association, published by Cambridge University Press; reproduced by permission of Cambridge University Press and the authors. Swiss Agency for Development and Cooperation (SDA) for material excerpted from *Conflict Analysis Tools*, by Simon A. Mason and Sandra Rychard, pp. 2–3, 10, December 2005; reproduced by permission. Swisspeace for material excerpted from FAST Analytical Framework Angola, May 2007, http://www.swisspeace.ch/fileadmin/user_upload/Media/Projects/FAST/Africa/Angola/Angola_AF_May_2007.pdf; reproduced by permission. Berghof Foundation for material excerpted from *A Systemic Approach to Conflict Transformation: Exploring Strengths and Limitations*, edited by Daniela Körppen, Beatrix Schmelzle and Oliver Wils; no. 6, pp. 19–29, copyright © 2008, Berghof Research Center for Constructive Conflict Management, www.berghof-handbook.net; reproduced by permission. Rowman & Littlefield Publishing Group for material excerpted from *Constructive Conflicts*, 2nd ed., by Louis Kriesberg and Bruce W.

Dayton, pp. 78–80, 85, 91–92, 1998, Rowman & Littlefield; reproduced by permission. Lynne Rienner Publishers, Inc., for material excerpted from *Breaking the Cycles of Violence: Conflict Prevention in Intrastate Crises*, by Janie Leatherman, William DeMars, Patrick D. Gaffney and Raimo Väyrynen, chapter 2, copyright © 1999 by Kumarian Press; used with permission of Lynne Rienner Publishers, Inc. Yale University Press for material excerpted from *Ethnic Conflict and Civic Life*, by Ashutosh Varshney, pp. 5–12, 2002, Yale University Press; reproduced by permission. Berghof Foundation for material excerpted from 'Nonviolent Resistance and Conflict Transformation in Power Asymmetries', in *Advancing Conflict Transformation*. Carnegie Corporation of New York for material excerpted from Carnegie Corporation of New York, Executive Summary, pp. xvii–xix, xxxvii, 1997, Carnegie Commission on Preventing Deadly Conflict; reproduced by permission. The Albert Einstein Institute for material excerpted from *From Dictatorship to Democracy: A Conceptual Framework for Liberation*, by Gene Sharp, pp. 7–8, 30–37, 1993, The Albert Einstein Institution, Boston; the full text is available and free sale and for free download at www.aeinstein.org. European Centre for Minority Issues (ECMI) for material excerpted from 'Conflict Prevention in the Baltic States: The OSCE High Commissioner on National Minorities in Estonia, Latvia and Lithuania', edited by Rob Zaagman, pp. 62–63, Flensburg: European Centre for Minority Issues, 1999; reproduced by permission. Brookings Institute Press for material excerpted from 'Chill Out: Why Cooperation is Balancing Conflict Among Major States in the Arctic', by Andrew Hart et al., May 2012, http://www.brookings.edu/research/reports/2012/05/30-arctic-cooperation-jones; reproduced by permission. Taylor & Francis Group LLC Books for material excerpted from *Negotiation Games: Game Theory to Bargaining and Arbitration*, by Stephen J. Brams, pp. 169–175, 1990, Routledge, copyright © 1990; reproduced through Copyright Clearance Center. The Navajivan Trust for material excerpted from *Nonviolence in Peace and War*, by M. K. Gandhi, vol. 2, Navajivan Publishing House, pp. 171–175, 1949; reproduced by permission. *The Berghof Handbook II*, edited by Beatrix Austin, Martina Fischer and Hans J. Gießmann, copyright © 2011 Berghof Research Center for Constructive Conflict Management, www.berghof-handbook.net; reproduced by permission. SAGE Publications for material excerpted from *Understanding Conflict Resolution: War, Peace and the Global System*, 2nd ed., by Peter Wallensteen, copyright © SAGE Publications Ltd, 2013; reproduced by permission of SAGE Publications, London, Los Angeles, New Delhi and Singapore. Taylor & Francis Group LLC Books for material excerpted from *Making Peace*, by Adam Curle, Tavistock Publications, pp. 15–18, 1971; reproduced by permission. William Zartman for material excerpted from *International Mediation in Theory and Practice*, by Saadia Touval and I. William Zartman, Westview, pp. 8–10, 1995; reproduced by kind permission. SAGE for material excerpted from 'Readiness Theory and the Northern Ireland Conflict', by Dean G. Pruitt in *American Behavioral Scientist*, 50(11), July 2007, pp. 1520–1541; published by SAGE Publications, Inc., copyright © 2007, SAGE Publications. The Institute of Peace for material excerpted from 'Why Orphaned Peace Settlements are More Prone to Failure', in *Managing Global Chaos: Sources of and Responses to International Conflict*, edited by C. Crocker et al., pp. 533–534, 1996, Washington, DC: Endowment of the United States Institute of Peace; reproduced by permission. Cornell University Press for material excerpted from *The Mediation Dilemma*, by Kyle Beardsley, pp. 6–7, 2011, copyright © 2011 by Cornell University; used by permission of the publisher, Cornell University Press. European Centre for Conflict Prevention for material excerpted from 'The Meaning of Reconciliation', in *People Building Peace: 35 Inspiring Stories from Around the World*, edited by Paul van Tongeren, pp. 37–45, 1999; reproduced by permission. The Random House Group Limited and Houghton Mifflin Harcourt Publishing Company for material excerpted from *Getting to Yes*, by Roger Fisher, William Ury and Bruce Patton, pp. xxv–xxvi, 10–15, published by Hutchinson, copyright © 1981, 1991 by Roger Fisher and William Ury; reprinted by permission of The Random House Group Limited and Houghton Mifflin Harcourt Publishing Company; all rights reserved. Springer for material excerpted from *From Identity-Based Conflict to Identity-Based Cooperation: The ARIA Approach in Theory and Practice*, by Jay Rothman, pp. 12–15, New York: Springer, copyright © 2012, Springer Science + Business Media New York; reproduced through Copyright Clearance Center. The Community Relations Council for material excerpted from *Approaches to Community Relations Work*, CRC Pamphlet No. 1, by Mari Fitzduff, Community Conflict/NI Peacebuilding, 1991; reproduced by permission. Bloomsbury Publishing Plc for material excerpted from *In the Middle: Non-official Mediation in Violent Situations*, by Adam Curle, edited by Tom Woodhouse, pp. 9–10, 21–29, 1986, Berg, copyright © Adam Curle, 1986 Berg, an imprint of Bloomsbury Publishing Plc. Bloomsbury Publishing Plc for material excerpted from *Peacemaking in a Troubled World*, by Adam Curle, edited by Tom Woodhouse, pp. 20–25, 1991, Berg, copyright © Adam Curle, 1991 Berg, an imprint of Bloomsbury Publishing Plc. Mediation UK for material excerpted from *Training Manual in Community Mediation Skills*, Mediation UK, 1995 and *Conflict Mediation Workbook*, Durham University Global Security Institute, 2013. Elsevier for material excerpted from *Disputes and Negotiations: A Cross-Cultural Perspective*, by Philip H. Guilliver, pp. 234–243, 1979, Academic Press Inc., copyright © Elsevier, 1979. Taylor & Francis Group for material excerpted from 'Explaining Conflict Transformation: How Jerusalem Became Negotiable', by Cecilia Albin in *Cambridge Review of International Affairs*, 18(3), October 2005, pp. 339–355, copyright © 2005 Routledge. Taylor & Francis Books UK for material excerpted from *Dilemmas of Statebuilding*, by Roland Paris and Timothy D. Sisk, pp. 1–3, 11–12, 313–314, 2009, copyright © 2009, Routledge; reproduced by permission of Taylor & Francis Books UK. Rand Corporation for material excerpted from 'America's Role in Nation Building from Germany to Iraq', by J. Dobbins et al., pp. xix, xxii–xxv, RAND, 2003; and 'UN's Role in Nation-Building: From the Congo to Iraq', by J. Dobbins et al., pp. xv–xxi, RAND 2005; reproduced through Copyright Clearance Center. SAGE Publications for material excerpted from 'Hybrid Peace', by Roger Mac Ginty, *Security Dialogue*, 41(4), pp. 291–412; published by SAGE Publications, Inc., copyright © 2010, Peace Research Institute Oslo. Berghof Foundation for material excerpted from 'Transitional Justice: The Emergence of a Paradigm', by Martina Fischer, *The Berghof Handbook for Conflict Transformation*, copyright © Berghof Foundation, www.berghof-handbook.net; reproduced by permission. Dan Smith for material excerpted from 'Towards a Strategic Framework for Peacebuilding: Overview Report on the Joint Utstein Study of Peacebuilding', by Dan Smith, pp. 25–28, 2004, Peace Research Institute Oslo for Norwegian Ministry of Foreign Affairs; reproduced by kind permission. SAGE Publications for material excerpted from *The Potential Complementarity of Mediation and Consultation within a Contingency Model of Third Party Intervention*, by R. J. Fisher and L. Keashly, *Journal of Peace Research*,

28(1), 1991, pp. 29–42, copyright © 1991, Peace Research Institute Oslo. International Alert for material excerpted from *A Code of Conduct: Conflict Transformation Work*, pp. 4–6, 12–13, copyright © International Alert, London. European Centre for Conflict Prevention for material excerpted from 'Women Take the Peace Lead in Pastoral Kenya, Back to the Future'; the story is largely based on the article 'Citizen's Peace – Peacebuilding in Wajir, North Eastern Kenya', by Dekha Ibrahim Abdi, published in *People Building Peace: 35 Inspiring Stories From Around the World*, edited by Paul van Tongeren, 1999; reproduced by permission. John Wiley and Sons for material excerpted from 'Governing (in) Kirkuk: Resolving the Status of a Disputed Territory in post-American Iraq', by Stefan Wolff, in *International Affairs*, 86(6), November 2010, pp. 1361–1379, Blackwell Publishing, copyright © 2010 Stefan Wolff, International Affairs, The Royal Institute of International Affairs. Penguin Books Ltd and Penguin Group (USA) LLC for material excerpted from the preface of *The Better Angels of Our Nature: The Decline of Violence in History and Its Causes*, by Steven Pinker, pp. xxi–xxvi, Allen Lane, 2011, copyright © 2011 by Steven Pinker; used by permission of Penguin Books Ltd Viking Penguin, a division of Penguin Group (USA) LLC. Taylor & Francis Books UK for material excerpted from *Climate Change and Armed Conflict: Hot and Cold Wars*, by James R. Lee, pp. 165–170, 2009, copyright © 2009, Routledge; reproduced by permission of Taylor & Francis Books UK. Berghof Foundation for material excerpted from 'Revisiting Change and Conflict: On Underlying Assumptions and the De-Politicisation of Conflict Resolution A Response', by Vivienne Jabri, copyright © Berghof Foundation, www.berghof-handbook.net; reproduced by permission. Pluto Press for material excerpted from *From Pacification to Peacebuilding*, by Diana Francis, pp. 64–66, 2010; reproduced by permission. The Institute of Peace for material excerpted from *Culture and Conflict Resolution*, by Kevin Avruch, Washington, DC: Endowment of the United States Institute of Peace, pp. 16, 97–98, 1998; reproduced by permission. Palgrave Macmillan for material excerpted from *The Palgrave International Handbook of Peace Studies: A Cultural Perspective*, edited by Wolfgang Dietrich, Josefina Echavarría Alvarez, Gustavo Esteva, Daniela Ingruber and Norbert Koppensteiner, published 2011 by Palgrave Macmillan; reproduced with permission of Palgrave Macmillan. Tavaana E-Learning Institute for Iranian Civil Society for material excerpted from 'Ushahidi: From Crisis Mapping Kenya to Mapping The Globe', http://tavaana.org/en/content/ushahidi-crisis-mapping-kenya-mapping-globe; reproduced with permission. Palgrave Macmillan for material excerpted from 'Cosmopolitanism after 9/11', by David Held, in *International Politics*, edited by Michael Cox, 47(1), 2010, pp. 52–61, published by Macmillan Publishers Ltd; reproduced with permission of Palgrave Macmillan.

In some instances we have been unable to trace the owners of copyright material and we would appreciate any information that would enable us to do so.

The publishers would also like to acknowledge use of extracts taken from the following publications which either appear in the public domain or where no copyright holder could be traced:

Lewis F. Richardson, *The Mathematical Psychology of War* (Mimeo; 1919). K. Boulding, *Conflict and Defense; A General Theory*. New York: Harper Torch Books, 1962. J. Burton, *Conflict and Communication*. London: Macmillan, 1969. A. Rapoport, *Conflict in Man-Made*

Environment. Harmondsworth: Penguin, 1974. E. Azar, *The Management of Protracted Social Conflict; Theory and Cases*. Aldershot: Dartmouth, 1990. C. R. Mitchell, *The Structure of International Conflict*. London: Macmillan, 1981 (extracts from chapters 11 and 12, 'Managing Conflict' and 'Peacemaking'). The Dayton Agreement. The General Framework Agreement for Peace in Bosnia and Herzegovina (available online at http://www.ohr.int/dpa/default.asp?content_id=380). Northern Ireland documents (extracts from E. Mallie and D. McKittrick, *The Fight for Peace: The Secret Story Behind the Irish Peace Process*. London: Heinemann, 1996, and public domain source: http://cain.ulst.ac.uk/events/peace/docs/fd22295.htm).

Bibliographic Sources

Part I Foundations

1 Kant, I. (2003) *On Perpetual Peace: A Philosophical Sketch*, trans. T. Humphrey. Indianapolis: Hackett Publishing Company (extract from pp. 12–16).
2 Quincy Wright, P. (1957) 'The Value for Conflict Resolution of a General Discipline of International Relations', *Journal of Conflict Resolution* (March) 1/1 (extract from pp. 3–8).
3 Richardson, Lewis F. *The Mathematical Psychology of War* [Mimeo; 1919].
4 Boulding, K. (1962) *Conflict and Defense: A General Theory*. New York: Harper Torch Books (extract from pp. 1–7).
5 Burton, J. (1969) *Conflict and Communication*. London: Macmillan (seven extracts from pp. xv, 62, 72, 73–4, 100–3).
6 Galtung, J. (2000) 'Conflict Theory and Practice', The *Transcend Manual,* Disaster Management Training Programme. New York: United Nations (extract from p. 1).
7 Galtung, J. (1989) 'The Middle East Conflict', *Solving Conflicts: A Peace Research Perspective.* Honolulu: University of Hawaii Institute for Peace (extract from pp. 37–45, 56).
8 Rapoport, A. (1974) *Conflict in Man-Made Environment*. Harmondsworth: Penguin (extracts from chapter 16, 'A Taxonomy of Conflicts').
9 Azar, E. (1990) *The Management of Protracted Social Conflict; Theory and Cases*. Aldershot: Dartmouth (extract from pp. 5–17).
10 Coser, L. (1956) *The Functions of Social Conflict*. London: Routledge (extract from pp. 33–38).
11 Schelling, T. (1960) *The Strategy of Conflict*. Cambridge, MA: Harvard University Press (extract from pp. 54–59).
12 Boulding, E. (1990) *Building a Global Civic Culture; Education for an Interdependent World*. New York: Syracuse University Press (extract from pp. 3–15).
13 Deutsch, M. (2000) 'A Brief History of Social Psychological Theorizing about Conflict', in M. Morton Deutsch and P. Coleman, eds. *Handbook of Conflict Resolution Theory and Practice*. San Francisco: Jossey Bass (extract from Introduction, pp. 11–12).

Part II Conflict Theories and Analysis

14 Mitchell, C. R. (1981) *The Structure of International Conflict*. London: Macmillan. (extracts from chapters 11 and 12, pp. 275–311).
15 Sandole, D. (2013) 'Extending the Reach of Basic Human Needs: A Comprehensive Theory for the Twenty-First Century', in K. Avruch and C. Mitchell, eds., *Conflict Resolution and Human Needs: Linking Theory and Practice*. London and New York: Routledge Studies in Peace and Conflict Resolution (extracts from pp. 21–39).
16 Horowitz, D. (1985) *Ethnic Groups in Conflict*. Berkeley: University of California Press (extracts from pp. 141–143, 628–633).
17 Kaldor, M. (2006) *New and Old Wars: Organized Violence in a Global Era*. Cambridge: Polity (extract from pp. vii–xi, preface 2nd ed.).

18 Keen, D. (1998) 'The Economic Functions of Violence in Civil Wars', *Adelphi Paper* 320. Oxford: OUP for International Institute for Strategic Studies (extract from pp. 9–13).

19 Stewart, F. (2001) 'Horizontal Inequalities: A Neglected Dimension of Development', Working Paper 1. Centre for Research on Inequality, Human Security and Ethnicity (CRISE), Queen Elizabeth House, University of Oxford (extract from pp. 1–7).

20 McAdam, D., Tarrow, S. and Tilly, C. (2001) *Dynamics of Contention*. Cambridge: Cambridge University Press (extracts from pp. 17, 39–44).

21 Dugan, M. (1996) 'A Nested Theory of Conflicts', *A Leadership Journal: Women in Leadership* 1. Center for Leadership, Colombia College (extracts from pp. 12–18).

22 Lederach, J. P. (1997) *Building Peace: Sustainable Reconciliation in Divided Societies*. Washington, DC: United States Institute of Peace Press (extract from pp. 79–85).

23 Rubinstein, R. (1999) 'Conflict Resolution and the Structural Sources of Conflict', in H. W. Ho-Won Jeong, ed., *Conflict Resolution: Dynamics, Process and Structure*. Farnham: Ashgate (extracts from pp. 173–176, 190–195).

24 Demmers, J. (2012) 'Telling Each Other Apart: A Discursive Approach to Violent Conflict', in J. Demmers, *Theories of Violent Conflict*. London: Routledge (extract from pp. 122–135).

25 Fearon, J. D. and Laitin, L. (2003) 'Ethnicity, Insurgency, and Civil War', *American Political Science Review* 97/1 (extract from pp. 75–90).

26 Mason, S. A. and Rychard, S. (2005) *Conflict Analysis Tools*. Swiss Agency for Development and Cooperation (SDC), Conflict Prevention and Transformation Division (COPRET). Bern: SDC. Available online at http://www.sdc.admin.ch/en/Home/Documentation/Advanced_Search?action=search.

27 Swisspeace (2007) FAST Conflict Analytical Framework applied to Angola. Swiss Peace Foundation: Bern. Available online at http://www.swisspeace.ch/fileadmin/user_upload/Media/Projects/FAST/Africa/Angola/Angola_AF_May_2007.pdf.

28 Norbert Ropers (2008) *Systemic Conflict Transformation: Reflections on the Conflict and Peace Process in Sri Lanka*. Berlin: Berghof Foundation (extract from pp. 13–16). Available online at http://www.berghof-handbook.net/uploads/download/dialogue6_ropers_lead.pdf.

Part III   Praxis (1): Conflict Prevention and Nonviolence

29 Kriesberg, L. and Dayton, B. (1998) *Constructive Conflict: From Escalation to Resolution*. Lanham, MA: Rowman and Littlefield (extracts from 2nd ed., chapters 3 and 4, pp. 80–92).

30 Leatherman, J., Väyrynen, R., Demars, W., and Gaffney, P. (1999) *Breaking Cycles of Violence, Conflict Prevention in Intrastate Conflicts*. Boulder, CO: Kumarian Press (extracts from pp. 36–39, 46–50).

31 Varshney, A. (2002) *Ethnic Conflict and Civic Life: Hindus and Muslims in India*. New Haven, CT: Yale University Press (extract from pp. 5–12).

32 Dudouet, V. (2008) 'Nonviolent Resistance and Conflict Transformation in Power Asymmetries', in B. Austin, M. Martina and H. J. Gießmann, eds., *Advancing Conflict Transformation. The Berghof Handbook II*. Berlin: Berghof Research Center for Constructive Conflict Management (extracts from section 3.1, pp. 6–8, and section 3.2c, pp. 11–12).

33 *Report of the Carnegie Commission on Preventing Deadly Conflict* (1997) Executive Summary. Carnegie Corporation of New York (extracts from pp. xvii–xix, xxxvii).

34 Sharp, G. (2010) *From Dictatorship to Democracy*. Boston: Albert Einstein Institute (extracts from pp. 7–8, 30–37).

35 Zaagman, R. (1999) Conflict Prevention in the Baltic States: The OSCE High Commissioner on National Minorities in Estonia, Latvia and Lithuania, European Centre for Minority Issues, Flensburg. Extracts from 'Statement of the High Commissioner on National Minorities (HCNM), Mr Max van der Stoel (Tallinn, 12 July 1993)' (p. 62) and 'HCNM Letter of 19 December 1998 to President Lennart Meri of Estonia' (pp. 65–670).

36 Hart, A., Jones, B. and Steven, D. (2012) 'Chill Out: Why Cooperation is Balancing Conflict Among Major States in the New Arctic', *Managing Global Order*. Washington, DC: Brookings Institute. Available at http://www.brookings.edu/research/reports/2012/05/30-arctic-cooperation-jones.

37 Brams, S. (1990) *Negotiation Games*. London: Routledge (extract from 'The Use of Threat Power in Poland, 1980–81', pp. 169–174.)

38 Gandhi, M. K. (1949) *Nonviolence in Peace and War*, vol. II. The Navajivan Trust. Jivanji Dahyabbai Desai, Navajivan Press, Ahmedabad (extracts from pp. 171–173, 174–175).

Part IV   Praxis (2) Mediation, Negotiation and Reconciliation

39 Wallensteen, P. (2007) *Understanding Conflict Resolution*. London: Sage (extracts from pp. 47–51, 2nd ed.).

40 Curle, A. (1971) *Making Peace*, London: Tavistock, (extracts from pp. 15–18).

41 Touval, S., and Zartman, W. eds. (1985) *International Mediation in Theory and Practice*. Boulder: Westview (extract from pp. 8–10).

42 Pruitt, D. (2007) 'Readiness Theory and the Northern Ireland Conflict', *American Behavioural Scientist* (July) 50/11 (extract from pp. 1524–1538).

43 Hampson, F. O. (1996) 'Why Orphaned Peace Settlements are More Prone to Failure', in C. Crocker et al., eds, *Managing Global Chaos: Sources of and Responses to International Conflict*. Washington, DC: United States Peace Institute (extract from pp. 533–535).

44 Beardsley, K. (2011) *The Mediation Dilemma*. New York: Cornell University Press (extract from pp. 6–7).

45 Assefa, H. (1999) 'The Meaning of Reconciliation', in P. van Tongeren, ed., *People Building Peace: 35 Inspiring Stories from Around the World*. Utrecht: European Centre for Conflict Prevention (extract from pp. 37–45).

46 Fisher, R. and Ury, W., with Patton, B. eds. (2012) *Getting to Yes: Negotiating Agreement Without Giving In*. New York: Random House (extract from pp. xxvi–xxxvi, 10–15).

47 Rothman, J., ed. (2012) *From Identity-Based Conflict to Identity-Based Cooperation: The ARIA Approach in Theory and Practice*. New York: Springer (extract from pp. 12–15).

48 Fitzduff, M. (1991) *Approaches to Community Relations Work*. CRC Pamphlet No. 1. Belfast: Community Relations Council. Available at http://cain.ulst.ac.uk/issues/community/fitzduff.htm.

49 Curle, A. (1991) 'Peacemaking Public and Private', in T. Woodhouse, ed., *Peacemaking in a Troubled World*. Oxford: Berg (extract from pp. 20–25).

50 Curle, A. (1986) *In the Middle*. Leamington Spa: Berg (extracts from pp. 9, 10, 21–29).

51 Mediation UK (1995) *Training Manual in Community Mediation Skills*, 'What is Active Listening'.

52 Use of Language by Mediators: Exercises (1-page sheet, adapted from Lambeth Neighbourhood Mediation Training).

53 Gulliver, P. (1979) *Disputes and Negotiations*. Waltham, MA: Academic Press (extracts from pp. 234–251).

54 Albin, C. (2005) 'Explaining Conflict Transformation: How Jerusalem became Negotiable', *Cambridge Review of International Affairs* 18/3 (extract from pp. 339–353).

55 The Dayton Agreement. The General Framework Agreement for Peace in Bosnia and Herzegovina. Available online at http://www.ohr.int/dpa/default.asp?content_id=380.

56 Northern Ireland Documents (extracts from E. Mallie and D. McKittrick, *The Fight for Peace: The Secret Story Behind the Irish Peace Process*. London: Heinemann (1996), pp. 375–381; the Framework Document is available online at http://cain.ulst.ac.uk/events/peace/docs/fd22295.htm).

Part V   Praxis (3) Peacebuilding

57 Paris, R. and Sisk, T. (2009) 'Understanding the Contradictions of Postwar Peacebuilding', in R. Paris and T. Sisk, eds, *The Dilemmas of Statebuilding: Confronting the Contradictions of Postwar Peace Operations*. Abingdon: Routledge (extract from pp. 1–13).

58 Dobbins, J., McGinn, H., Crane, K., Jones, S., Rathmell, A., Swanger, R. and Timilsina, A. (2004) *The US Role in Nation-Building: From Germany to Iraq*. Santa Monica: RAND Corporation (extract from Executive Summary, pp. xix–xxv) and Dobbins, J., Jones, S., Crane, K., Rathmell, A., Steele, B., Teltschik, R., Timilsina, A. (2005) *The UN's Role in Nation-Building: From Congo to Iraq*. Santa Monica: RAND Corporation (extracts from pp. xv–xx).

59 Mac Ginty, R. (2010) 'Hybrid Peace: The Interaction between Top-Down and Bottom-Up Peace', *Security Dialogue* (August) 41/4 (extract from pp. 392–403).

60 Fischer, M. (2011) 'Transitional Justice and Reconciliation: Theory and Practice', in B. Austin, M. Fischer and J. Giessmann, eds, *The Berghof Handbook II*. Opladen: Barbara Budrich Publishers (extract from pp. 407–413).

61 Smith, D. (2004) *Towards a Strategic Framework for Peacebuilding: Getting Their Act Together*. Oslo: International Peace Research Institute (extract from pp. 27–28).

62 Fisher, R. and Keashly, L. (1991) 'The Potential Complementarity of Mediation and Consultation within a Contingency Model of Third Party Intervention', *Journal of Peace Research* 28/1 (extract from pp. 35–39).

63 International Alert (1998) *Code of Conduct for Conflict Transformation Work*. London: International Alert (extracts from pp. 4–6, 12–13).

64 van Tongeren, P., Brenk, M., Hellema, M. and Verhouven, J., eds. (1999) *People Building Peace – 35 Inspiring Stories from Around the World*. Utrecht: European Centre for Conflict Prevention (extract from pp. 243–249. This is largely based on Dekha Ibrahim Abdi's own account *Citizen's Peace – Peacebuilding in Wajir, North Eastern Kenya*).

65 Wolff, S. (2010) 'Governing (in) Kirkuk: Resolving the Status of a Disputed Territory in post-American Iraq'. *International Affairs* 86/6 (extract from pp. 1361–1379).

Part VI   Challenges and Future Directions

66 Pinker, S. (2011) *The Better Angels of our Nature: The Decline of Violence in History and Its Causes*. London: Penguin (extract from pp. xxi–xxvi).

67 Lee, J. (2009) *Climate Change and Armed Conflict*. London: Routledge (extract from pp. 165–170).

68 Jabri, V. (2006) *Revisiting Change and Conflict: On Underlying Assumptions and the De-Politicisation of Conflict Resolution*. Berlin: Berghof Handbook Dialogue No. 5 (extract from pp. 69–75).

69 Francis, D. (2010) *From Pacification to Peacebuilding: A Call to Global Transformation*. London: Pluto Press (extract from pp. 64–66).

70 Avruch, K. (1998) *Culture and Conflict Resolution*. Washington, DC: US Institute of Peace Press (extracts from pp. 16, 97–8).

71 Dietrich, W., et al., eds. (2011) *The Palgrave International Handbook of Peace Studies: A Cultural Perspective* (extracts from pieces by Karlheinz Koppe, Aurangzeb Haneef, Kam-por Yu, Grimaldo Rengifo V and Kofi Asare Opoku, pp. 32, 125, 247, 374–375, 418–419).

72 'Ushahidi: From Crisis Mapping in Kenya to Mapping the Globe'. Available at http://tavaana.org/en/content/ushahidi-crisis-mapping-kenya-mapping-globe/.

73 Held, D. (2010) 'Cosmopolitanism after 9/11', *International Politics* 47/1 (extract from pp. 52–55).

Debating Conflict Resolution: Texts, Voices and Narratives

Tom Woodhouse, Hugh Miall, Oliver Ramsbotham and Christopher Mitchell

Why this Reader?

We published the first edition of *Contemporary Conflict Resolution* in 1999 and followed this with a second in 2005 and a third in 2011. A fourth edition is pending and there are translations of the book in Japanese and Spanish. We are gratified that our book has played a role in the development of conflict resolution studies in colleges and universities worldwide, and that it has been well received not only in the academies but also by policymakers and peace workers. In the years since we wrote the first edition, the panorama of conflict and conflict resolution has continued to change and we have revised the content of the book accordingly. We decided that the time had arrived to complement the content of *Contemporary Conflict Resolution* by producing a Reader to enable all who use the book to continue to deepen their knowledge of the theoretical and practical aspects of conflict resolution. We are delighted that Chris Mitchell, whose publications have been seminal in the development of the field and have inspired many academics to teach and research in conflict resolution, accepted our invitation to join us in editing it.

Our aim in producing this book was to select a set of inspiring texts which will give readers a good overview of the field, from its origins to current work. Together, *Contemporary Conflict Resolution* and the Reader will provide a strong framework for study and preparation for research in the area of conflict and conflict resolution. The Reader includes some of the classic statements of conflict resolution by the progenitors of the field, as well as exciting examples of recent work on ways in which the field is changing to meet new challenges.

Besides the more standard academic sources, the Reader provides examples of conflict analysis frameworks and their application to cases, case studies of mediation and negotiation, exercises in the use of skills for mediators, texts of peace agreements, codes of conduct of conflict resolution organizations and examples of cyber-conflict resolution. The Reader draws together extracts from journal articles, books and official texts, together with examples of grey literature of a kind that readers may not find it easy to track down. The aim is to balance striking and inspiring academic pieces that convey the excitement of the field with material illustrating its practical implications.

We present the material in six parts. Each part has an introduction which explains the significance of the readings in relation to the part's topic and each reading has a brief editorial commentary to introduce the authors. Parts III to V, which cover praxis, categorize the readings into three types: *reflective pieces* (theory and conceptualization), *guides to practice* (the operational end of conflict resolution, with examples of organizations and policies at work in real world situations) and *case studies*. The *toolbox* feature at the end of each part offers further resources to allow you to explore beyond the readings presented, with an emphasis on policy and practice. Part VI serves both as a survey of future challenges and a general conclusion to the Reader.

The first extract in this Reader is Immanuel Kant's *On Perpetual Peace*, written in 1795. Kant was a precursor of conflict resolution, providing a justification in philosophy for the core values that academics and practitioners in conflict resolution later came to espouse – the idea of a *foedus pacificum*, an international order and a cosmopolitan culture marked by a humanitarian care for strangers. The penultimate extract in the Reader was downloaded in 2014 and describes the Ushahidi conflict mapping platform, which uses mobile phone technology to map real time incidents in order to provide an early warning indicator for conflict prevention. We have edited the readings in order to select the text from the original source that has most relevance to the theme of the part in which the reading appears. We see one of the functions of this Reader as a tool that might inspire users to further research. If a text inspires you or if you wish to pursue the references cited in the text, we advise you to seek out the full text of the original. The bibliographic sources of the readings can be found on pp. xvii–xxi.

Omissions from the primary material as originally published are indicated by ellipses. All other editorial interventions appear within square brackets.

Guide to Contents

Part I deals with the way in which social conflict became a systematic focus for academic study, with the foundations laid in the 1950s and 1960s, as a reaction to the Second World War and the bipolar nuclear confrontation of the Cold War. The readings presented here represent the work of what might be called the 'parents of the field'. They reflect the sense of innovation and excitement of a new field and the diverse backgrounds of those who came to define it – economists, mathematicians, sociologists, psychologists, political scientists and former diplomats.

Most of the readings in this part fall within the category of reflective pieces, as founders of the field began the challenge of defining methodologies and building theories about the nature of human conflict. The earliest piece is by one of the precursors, Immanuel Kant, whose *On Perpetual Peace* was published in 1795. We end Part I with a piece by Morton Deutsch covering the significance of Darwin, Marx and Freud for the new field. In between, we present a selection of readings, by P. Quincy Wright, Lewis F. Richardson, Kenneth Boulding, John Burton, Johan Galtung, Anatol Rapoport, Edward Azar, Lewis Coser, Thomas Schelling and Elise Boulding.

Part II presents a range of contemporary theories of conflict and some guides to conflict analysis. The first is by Chris Mitchell, whose work represents one of the best attempts to draw the multidisciplinary work of the founders into a more integrated framework to explain the structure of international conflict. Other reflective readings follow from Dennis Sandole, Donald Horowitz, Mary Kaldor, David Keen, Frances Stewart, Doug MacAdam, Sidney Tarrow and Charles Tilly, Marie Dugan, John Paul Lederach, Richard Rubinstein, Jolle Demmers, James Fearon and David Laitin. Most of these deal with theories about the nature and dynamics of intrastate ethnic civil wars and contentious politics that have characterized the bulk of conflicts occurring since 1950. Guides to practice and case studies are represented by three readings that deal with tools and models for conflict analysis, from the Swiss Agency for Development and Cooperation, Swisspeace, and the Berghof Foundation in Germany.

Part III is the first of three praxis themed sections. We use the word *praxis* to describe the reflexive, dynamic and two-way relationship between academic theory and the work of practitioners of conflict resolution. One of the first objectives of conflict research was to show how research and theory could lead to policy whereby violent conflict might be prevented by developing tools, techniques and institutions to manage conflict constructively and nonviolently. The readings in this part are selected to exemplify three approaches towards this objective. The first is for conflict parties to limit the means with which they pursue conflict to constructive methods (Kriesberg, Brams). The second approach is to develop international and domestic conflict prevention capacity (Leatherman et al., Carnegie Commission, Hart et al., Varshney). The third approach, an extension of the first, is to use nonviolence (Gandhi, Sharp, Duduoet).

Part IV covers mediation, negotiation and reconciliation, which account for much of the core work of conflict resolution. These ways of working in conflict are not determined by any fixed method, formula or blueprint, and practitioners take various approaches. The readings in this part illustrate this with seven reflective pieces covering differing analyses and approaches to third-party roles; seven guides to practice, from Fisher and Ury's classic *Getting to Yes*, to the listening skills needed by mediators; and four case studies, covering Tanzania, Jerusalem, the Dayton Agreement and the peace agreements which settled the conflict in Northern Ireland.

Just as conflict prevention became a major preoccupation of conflict resolvers from the 1990s, and especially as a response to the genocides in Rwanda and Srebrenica, peacebuilding, covered in Part V, has now become a central focus for both theory builders and policymakers. To a significant degree, this reflects the relative success of third parties in securing peace agreements in many of the world's major conflicts. Once peace agreements are reached, the challenge is to make them sustainable through long-term peacebuilding. The extraordinary experiment in peacebuilding is the theme of this part. Six reflective pieces are presented, illustrating the range of perspectives in the literature about the objectives and ideologies embedded in peacebuilding. These are followed by two 'guide to practice' pieces, showing the diversity of roles that peacebuilders can engage with as 'third-siders', and the ethical codes of which they must be aware. Two case studies from northeast Kenya and Kirkuk in post-conflict Iraq illustrate approaches to peacebuilding from below and above.

In the final part, we revisit themes set out in the introduction and look ahead to the ways in which conflict resolution may need to adapt to new conflicts, learn from its failures and respond to new challenges. In this spirit, readers are invited to see themselves as fellow-participants in a joint venture that no one person, organization, culture, gender or part of the world can claim as its own.

Part VI concludes the book by considering four questions. Have levels of violent conflict gone down since the Second World War? If so, has this had anything to do with a greater level of international endorsement of the aim of conflict resolution – to transform actually or potentially violent conflict into nonviolent processes of change – and expertise in bringing this about? Where are the continuing 'frontiers of failure'? How are these now being addressed, and what more needs to be done? Eight readings have been selected to represent varying responses to these four questions. Guides to practice appear in the Toolbox section, including an account of the use of future imaging workshops as developed by Elise Boulding, now a grandparent of the field. Our final invitation is to suggest that once you have completed this Reader you might organize a future imaging workshop and explore your own ideas about future challenges and responses.

How to Use This Reader

We have chosen readings to illustrate the range and diversity of approaches to understanding conflict and its resolution, and, in Parts III–V, the selected texts and resources have also been organized in four categories (reflective pieces, guides to practice, case studies, and tools) in order to emphasize the interplay between theory and practice in the development of conflict resolution. We recommend that the texts should not be taken as closed sources of unchallengeable knowledge, but as stimulants to further critical reflection, theorizing and praxis. In this way, they can support a process of reflective and participatory learning whose goal is the creative development and enhancement of knowledge.

Using the Reader to stimulate critical reflection for 'second-order learning'

Reflective learning refers to the ability to reflect on your experience and, drawing on appropriate concepts and ideas, develop insights that can lead to change – whether these are changes in behaviour, attitudes or in aspects of your academic or professional work as a conflict resolver. This draws from an educational philosophy which suggests that subjective experience is central in the learning process. But the important question is whether we actually learn from experience. To do this, we need tools to help us understand and evaluate experience in order that we can draw useful lessons about it and make plans for change. There is an intimate relationship, therefore, between experience and reflection, theory and practice – the praxis which we refer to in Parts III, IV and V. Figure 1 (based on Kolb's Experiential Learning Cycle) is one way to conceptualize the reflective process.

Without theory, reflections may not lead towards insight into practice. At the same time, theory divorced from experience can remain too abstract. In relation to Kolb's

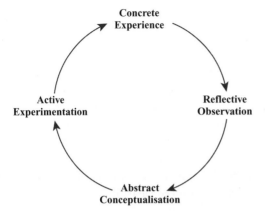

Source: D. A. Kolb, *Experiential Learning Experience as a Source of Learning and Development*. New Jersey: Prentice Hall, 1984

Figure 1 *Kolb's Experiential Learning Cycle*

Learning Cycle, many of the selections in the Reader are examples of abstract conceptualization in the form of reflective pieces. Drawing on theory, practitioners (and conflict parties pursuing constructive conflict behaviour) can be seen to engage in active experimentation, and this leads in turn to concrete experiences (and sometimes failures) from which reflective observation can draw new lessons and concepts. In the classroom, active experimentation can be generated by simulation and role play scenarios developed from the case studies or from the guides to practice. For example, group work exercises can be generated by tutors or self-designed by students to explore how conflict prevention, or problem-solving, or mediation, or peacebuilding initiatives might be used. Students might debate the merits of the different approaches to conflict resolution taken by some of the key founders and theorists (Kenneth Boulding, Elise Boulding, Johan Galtung, John Paul Lederach, Adam Curle, and so on), or move beyond the texts to discover new theories or skills not represented here. The excitement of working in the field of conflict resolution comes from the capacity to develop critically and respond creatively, as the nature of conflict changes. The key is to understand the innovation that comes from praxis – the challenge of making knowledge work in the applied pursuit of nonviolent conflict resolution.

Learning in this way generates a capacity for what John Burton called 'second order learning', (which is referred to in chapter 2 of *Contemporary Conflict Resolution* and for generating new 'modes of knowing' as defined by Elise Boulding). Burton, along with Ronald Fisher, Herb Kelman and others, developed problem-solving both as a *research tool* for conflict resolution (to observe the dynamics of parties in conflict) and as *a method* of conflict resolution. However, it was also seen by Burton as a potent method of generating new thinking about the phenomenon of conflict and human behaviour. Burton here was influenced by some of the concepts in general systems theory, especially the idea of first- and second-order learning. In systems theory, attention is given to the role of social learning and culture in the way in which social systems change. Some familiarity with this is necessary to understand the concept (rather than just the technique) of problem-solving.

The theory holds that although social systems 'learn' through their members, who individually adjust their world views according to experience, sociocultural systems also have underlying assumptions which make the system as a whole more resistant to change than their individual members. These underlying assumptions are defined as 'default values' which, because they are so commonly used, become regarded as immutable, and actors in the system tend to forget that they can exercise choices in order to attain goals. When problems occur, they are addressed by reference to the 'default values', and this kind of reaction is termed first-order learning.

However, in systems theory, orderly and creative transformation of social systems requires a capacity for second-order learning, which requires a willingness to challenge assumptions. Ideological orientations to social change are regarded as the antithesis of second-order learning, because ideologies are claims to ultimate truth achieved with a predefined set of ends and means, the challenging of which is seen as heretical. For systems theorists, the key innovation was to use the idea of second-order learning to convert conflict to cooperation through a participative design process called facilitated problem-solving.

The best way to use this Reader is to see it as a resource to convert traditional learning into a participatory process, akin to Rapoport's 'participative design process'. In our chapter on 'Conflict Resolution, the Media and the Communications Revolution' in *Contemporary Conflict Resolution*, we look at the way in which information and communication technologies can enhance networked patterns of research and learning through the emergence of modes of cyber-conflict resolution.

Having stressed the importance of critical reflection, before we conclude this introduction we need to be alert to two more areas of concern. First, critics of conflict resolution from the outside question the whole validity and utility of the field; and second, critics from within raise concern about excluded voices. Following the principles of critical reflection and participatory learning, it is important for readers to be aware of whose voices form the narrative of conflict resolution and which voices need to be added. For conflict resolution to be authentic and effective, it must be global and inclusive. Another word of warning is necessary here. Like all social scientists, students and practitioners of conflict resolution must be aware of the consequences of their work and its impact on other people – especially on the most vulnerable, who are often the victims of conflict. For this reason the precautionary principle, the idea that actions should be measured by their possible negative as well as their desired positive impacts, should always be borne in mind.[1] Conflict resolution has an ethical and moral dimension, expressed in Mary Anderson's idea of 'do no harm' when engaging in humanitarian work.[2] A chapter in *Contemporary Conflict Resolution* deals with the ethics of intervention in conflict, and in Part V of this Reader, we present extracts from the Code of Conduct developed by International Alert, providing a guide to ethical decisions which must be taken before engagement.

The 'Hermeneutics of Suspicion': Critiques and Disagreements

Conflict resolution must be subject to the same exposure to critical scrutiny as any other social or political science. Proponents of conflict resolution have often disagreed vigorously with each other about methods and theories (see, for example, Galtung and Boulding's 'friendly quarrels' in the *Journal of Peace Research*).[3] Theories and ideas should not be taken at face value but exposed to the 'hermeneutics of suspicion' – the idea developed by critical theorists that apparently objective academic theories may conceal undeclared values and ideologies. Indeed, critiques of conflict resolution have appeared in the academic literature during the past few years. In essence, the thrust of these criticisms amount to serious questions about the capability of 'outsiders' (and especially those intervening from the West) to influence and secure peace processes by negotiation and agreement. It has been argued that attempts at impartial intervention can actually fuel and prolong war and its miseries. Linked to this kind of criticism is the idea that the Western model of conflict resolution (promoted through the United Nations, for example) is fundamentally flawed. This is so because it is inadequate both in its analysis of the causes and dynamics of contemporary armed conflict, and in the prescriptions that follow from this analysis. Or worse, conflict resolution, wittingly or unwittingly, is part of a hegemonic liberal peace project controlled by the 'Global north' to control and contain zones of conflict in order to stabilize and preserve existing power structures. These critiques are reflected in our readings (see, for example, Mac Ginty on 'Hybrid Peace', Reading 59) and can provide a good resource to reflect on and debate the validity or otherwise of foundational conflict resolution theory. Despite such critiques, we believe that in principle the idea of conflict resolution is ultimately sufficiently broad to encompass the global conflicts to which the critics refer.

Missing Voices: Texts, Voices, Narratives and Soundscapes

We also need to be aware of the limitations as well as the value of the texts. We might call this the hermeneutics of 'meaning-recollection' – that is, the responsibility of the conflict resolver, as theorist and practitioner, to tell the story of people affected by violence. Look beyond the text to become aware of voices, stories, narratives and chronicles which reflect the idea that many voices are, by definition, excluded from texts or cannot be expressed in textual form. There are oral traditions expressed through the arts, storytelling and culture in what John Paul Lederach has called the 'soundscape of healing and reconciliation', where 'language has significance beyond the scope of definitional meaning'.[4]

There are many voices that confirm the continued importance of conflict resolution, and there is widespread agreement that it matters. As a reminder that conflict resolution reaches far back into human history, we can recall the words of Aristotle from the fourth century BC, which have a very contemporary ring: 'It is not enough to win a war; it is more important to organize the peace.' Nevertheless, despite its longevity, in concluding this introduction, we need to be reminded that the narrative of conflict resolution continues to discover that there are many voices still outside the text and discourse, and that there are what Wolfgang Dietrich has called 'many peaces' which must be included. We include some of these voices in Reading 71, and for now leave the final word to Leymah Gbowee, winner, with Ellen Johnson Sirleaf, of the Nobel Peace Prize in 2011:

> Organizations like the UN do a lot of good, but there are certain basic realities they never seem to grasp…Maybe the most important truth that eludes these organizations is that it's insulting when outsiders come in and tell a traumatized people what it will take for them to heal. You cannot go to another country and make a plan for it. The cultural context is so different from what you know that you will not understand much of what you see. I would never come to the US and claim to understand what's going on, even in the African American culture. People who have lived through a terrible conflict may be hungry and desperate, but they are not stupid. They often have very good ideas about how peace can evolve, and they need to be asked.
>
> That includes women. Most especially women…
>
> To outsiders like the UN, these soldiers were a problem to be managed. But they were our children.[5]

Notes

1 World Commission on Effects of Scientific Knowledge and Technology, *The Precautionary Principle*, Paris: UNESCO, 2005.

2 M. Anderson, *Do No Harm: How Aid Can Support Peace – or War*. Boulder, CO: Lynne Reinner, 1999. On research ethics and methods, see also M. Smyth and G. Robinson, *Researching Violently Divided Societies: Ethical and Methodological Issues*. New York: United Nations, University Press, 2001; D. Druckman, *Doing Research; Methods of Inquiry for Conflict Analysis*. Thousand Oaks, CA: Sage, 2005.

3 K. Boulding, 'Twelve Friendly Quarrels with Johan Galtung', *Journal of Peace Research* 1/14 (1977): 75–86.

4 J. P. Lederach and A. J. Lederach, *When Blood and Bones Cry Out: Journeys through the Soundscape of Healing and Reconciliation*. Oxford: Oxford University Press, 2011, p. 226.

5 Leymah Gbowee, *Mighty Be Our Powers: How Sisterhood, Prayer, and Sex Changed a Nation at War*. Beast Books, 2013 (online).

Part I
Foundations

There can be a great deal of discussion about when, exactly, social conflict became a systematic focus for academic study. From the Classical world, and even earlier,[1] individual thinkers and writers have considered the nature of war and possible methods of achieving peace between, as well as justice within, societies. Thucydides' *The Peloponnesian War* was still considered essential reading in international relations courses in the 1960s (although perhaps now one could substitute Donald Kagan's magnificent reconsideration of that contemporary account of the long struggle between Athens and Sparta).[2] Hobbes and Machiavelli still form basic readings in courses on political theory. As Harry Hinsley has emphasized, theoretical writings on 'the pursuit of peace' have a very long pedigree.[3]

However, a good case can be made for the argument that the foundations for the academic study of conflict analysis and resolution were laid in the 1950s and 1960s, partly because of the impact of the Second World War – with its incalculable destruction and its 56 million dead – and partly because of the threat of the Cold War. As a reaction to that history and those dangers, many scientists and social scientists began to feel that much systematic and careful research needed to be carried out, not just on topics such as threats, arms races, the psychology of charismatic leaders, or the manipulation of power, but on the whole process by which conflicts arose, became coercive and destructive or might successfully be resolved without resort to violence.

This first set of writings, therefore, presents a selection from individual scholars and analysts from that era, who might well be called the 'parents of the field'.[4] Many of those represented in this part were 'individuals' in the sense that they often carried out their work in isolation from the intellectual mainstream of their time, and often with little hope of the familiar signs of academic reward – praise, professorships, prizes and sometimes even publication. In presenting a selection of their work, we are partly emphasizing a number of key themes that this early generation of scholars initially opened up, setting the field off in certain key directions, many of which remain central to this day – the nature of social conflict, its sources, different types of conflict, how people in conflict behave and feel, and how they might best prevent or alternatively cope with conflict in a constructive manner. We are also pointing out the diverse disciplinary backgrounds of this first generation of 'conflict researchers' who launched the new field in spite of much disdain and many obstacles – economists, mathematicians, sociologists, psychologists, political scientists, former diplomats. We are all standing on their shoulders.

Notes

1 R. Cohen and R. Westbrook, eds., *Armana Diplomacy; The Beginnings of International Relations*. Baltimore, MD: Johns Hopkins University Press, 2000.
2 D. Kagan, *The Peloponnesian War*, 4 vols. New York: Cornell University Press, 1969–84.
3 E. H. Hinsley, *Power and the Pursuit of Peace*. Cambridge: Cambridge University Press, 1963.
4 See the Toolbox at the end of this Part I.

1

On Perpetual Peace: A Philosophical Sketch

Immanuel Kant

Immanuel Kant was one of a series of major and minor philosophers – Rousseau, James Mill, William Penn – who, throughout recent history, grappled with the problem of war between separate, sovereign 'nations' whose rulers recognized no superior authority, nor any restraint of their actions other than their own national interests and their capability of achieving them, through force of arms if necessary. Such writers can justifiably be seen as the forerunners of the twentieth-century scholars who tried to found the field of conflict and peace research on a more 'scientific' basis. Many of the ideas the latter inherited came from the writings of individuals such as Kant, striving to provide some rationale for a more peaceful world. In this extract from his plea for 'perpetual peace', Kant discusses the whole issue of national rights and the need for a league of separate nations to produce a civilized and permanent peace.

* * * *

Second Definitive Article of Perpetual Peace the Law of Nations Shall Be Based on a *Federation* of Free States

Nations, as states, could be judged like human individuals who, in their state of nature (i.e., in their independence from external laws) inflict injuries on each other by the very fact that they live in close proximity to each other. Every nation can and should, for the sake of its own security, demand from the others that they should combine with it under a constitution similar to one in a civil state, in which each of them can have its rights protected. This would be an *alliance of nations*. However, it would not have to consist of a single state made up of these nations, for that would create a contradiction, since every state involves a relationship between *those above* (the ones who make the laws) and *those below* (the ones who obey, namely, the people), and many nations in a single state would amount to only a single nation, a situation which contradicts what we are assuming (for here we have to take into account the *right of nations* with respect to each other, to the extent that they exist as so many separate nations and are not to be fused into a single state).

We look with profound contempt on the attachment of savages to their lawless freedom, on the way they would rather fight each other constantly than subject themselves to the restraint of laws which they themselves establish, and thus on their preference for a wild freedom over a rational one, and we consider them a crude, uncivilized, and brutal degradation of humanity. Thus, one would think that civilized peoples (each one united in its own state) would hurry to come out of such a depraved condition as soon as possible. But instead of this each state considers its majesty (the majesty of a people is a meaningless expression) arises directly from its not being subject to any external legal compulsion, and the glory of its ruler stems from the fact that without his even having to place himself in any danger, many thousands stand at his command prepared to be sacrificed for some cause which is of no concern to them. The difference between the European savages and those in America consists for the most part in the fact that, while many American tribes have been totally devoured by their enemies, those in Europe know a better way of using the people they have conquered than making a meal of them: they prefer to have them increase the number of their subjects and thus the quantity of instruments for still more wide-ranging wars.

Given the viciousness of human nature, which reveals itself openly in the unrestrained relations of nations with each other (whereas in a lawful civil condition the constraints of government keep it heavily veiled), one could well be amazed that people have not yet been able to banish the word *right* entirely from the politics of war as pedantic and that no state has as yet been so bold as to advance this opinion in public. For Hugo Grotius, Pufendorf, Vattel, and others (all of them merely tiresome comforters) are always sincerely cited as *justification* for an outbreak of war, although their legal codes, whether treated in a philosophical or diplomatic manner, have not and cannot have the slightest *legal* force (because the states as such do not stand under any common external compulsion), and there is not a single example of a state which was ever moved to give up what it planned to do by means of arguments, even those armed with the testimonies of such important men. However, this homage which every state pays to the concept of rights (at least verbally) shows that there exists in human beings an even greater moral predisposition, although it may be asleep at the moment, at some point to become masters of the evil principle in them (for they cannot deny its existence). And they have the same hope for others. If they did not, the word *right* would never be mentioned by states who wish to attack each other, unless merely as a joke, like that Gallic prince who remarked: "The privilege that nature has given the strong over the weak is that the weak are to obey them."

The ways in which states prosecute their rights can never involve a judicial process, as they could if there were an external tribunal. Their only resort is war. But even with war and a favourable outcome in victory, the question of rights will not be determined. A peace treaty may well bring this particular war to an end, but not the condition of war (people can always find a new pretext, which we cannot declare obviously unjust, because in this situation everyone is a judge in his own cause). Nevertheless, the principle which holds that, according to natural rights, human beings in lawless circumstances "should move out of this condition" does not, thanks to the rights of nations, apply precisely to states, because, as states, they already have an internal legal constitution and thus have developed beyond the point where others can, according to their concept of right, forcefully bring them under a wider legal constitution.

However, reason, on the throne of the loftiest moral-giving power, absolutely denounces war as a legal procedure and, by contrast, makes the condition of peace an immediate obligation. But without a compact of nations among themselves, peace cannot be founded or secured. Hence, it requires a special form of *alliance*, which one could call an *alliance for peace* (*foedus pacificum*). This would not be the same as a *peace treaty* (*pactum pacis*), for, while the latter seeks merely to end *a particular* war, the former seeks to put an end to *all* wars forever....

Third Definitive Article for Perpetual Peace the Rights of Human Beings as Citizens of the World Shall Be Restricted to the Conditions of Universal Hospitality

The issue here, as in the previous article, is not one of philanthropy, but of right, and here *hospitality* (*Wirtbarkeit*) means the right of a stranger who arrives in the land of someone else not be treated by him in a hostile manner. The latter can turn the stranger away, if this can be done without bringing about his death, but so long as the new arrival acts peacefully, he cannot treat him as an enemy. The stranger cannot claim the *rights of a guest* (which would require a special charitable compact of friendship to make him for a certain period a member of the household) but rather the *rights of a visitor*. All human beings share in a right to present themselves to society, by virtue of their right to a common possession of the surface of the earth, on which, since it is a globe, people cannot be scattered for infinite distances but finally have to put up with living in close proximity to each other. But no one originally had more right to a particular place on earth than anyone else. Uninhabitable parts of this surface, like the sea and deserts, divide this human community, but in such a way that a ship or a camel (the ship of the desert) makes it possible for people to approach each other over these unclaimed regions and thus to make use of their right to the surface of the earth, which men share in common, for potential social interaction. The absence of hospitality along the sea coasts (for example, the Barbary Coast), the habit of plundering ships in nearby seas or of making slaves of stranded sailors or those in deserts – where people (for example, the Arab Bedouins) believe that their proximity to the nomadic races gives them the right to rob them – is thus contrary to natural law, that is, the privilege of those visiting a foreign land, a right which does not extend further than the conditions which make it possible for them to *attempt* to interact with the original inhabitants. In this way, distant parts of the world can enter into peaceful relations with each other. These relations may end up becoming publicly governed by law, and thus the human race will finally be able to bring a cosmopolitan constitution closer to realization....

The greater or lesser social interactions among the nations of the earth, which have been constantly increasing everywhere, have now spread so far that a violation of rights in one part of the earth is felt everywhere. Hence, the idea of a cosmopolitan right is not a fantastic, hysterical way of imagining rights, but a necessary completion of the unwritten code of both national and international law for the public rights of human beings generally and so for perpetual peace. Only under the conditions of international law can we flatter ourselves that we are continually approaching such a peace.

2

The Value for Conflict Resolution of a General Discipline of International Relations

P. Quincy Wright

Quincy Wright was a major figure in the group of distinguished political scientists who made the reputation of the University of Chicago in the 1930s and 1940s. He is chiefly known for his massive, comparative work *A Study of War*, which he and his graduate students completed in 1942 and which surveyed all wars that had taken place in the period since 1815. This pioneering work was more than impressive, given that it was completed well before the advent of computers that could store and analyse massive amounts of data. Moreover, it led directly to later studies such as J. David Singer and Melvin Small's Correlates of War Project (founded in 1963) and the University of Uppsala's Conflict Data Program (UCDP), which began in the 1970s. This article, from the very first edition of *Journal of Conflict Resolution*, is interesting in that it seems to assume that conflict resolution will inevitably form part of an international relations discipline, when the subsequent study of conflict actually became concerned with far more than interstate wars and other purely interstate matters.

*   *   *   *

Forms and Causes of Conflict

"Conflict" is a term of broad connotation with applications in the physical, biological, philosophical, and social worlds. Conflicts of material bodies and of animals of the same or different species, as well as conflicts of ideological, philosophical, or religious systems, may all provide approaches to the study of conflict between persons or social groups. The latter type of conflict, however, is the central interest in the study of "Conflict Resolution"; and, of all such conflicts, international conflict, often resulting in war, is (1) the most dangerous to mankind; (2) the most typical of social conflicts; (3) the most comprehensive of all other forms of conflict; and (4) the most thoroughly examined in the literature dealing with conflict.

That international conflict in the age of nuclear fission and fusion is dangerous to all men and to all societies few will question. War has always been a peril to human happiness, though it has sometimes facilitated progress. Today general war with modern instruments would be a catastrophe with few, if any, mitigations. There can be little doubt of the tendency of international conflict to generate war and, as Clausewitz pointed out, for wars to spread and to become absolute or total (3, 13, 14). The peaceful coexistence of inconsistent economic, political, social, and ideological systems becomes increasingly difficult to maintain as the world shrinks and as the rate of shrinkage accelerates. Such inconsistencies seen to demand resolution, and efforts at resolution breed conflicts, which in turn increase tension and the probability of war, especially if efforts are made to effect such resolution as rapidly as the accelerating rate of historic change seems to make necessary (14).

Social conflict has been attributed to the effort of social entities to maintain autonomy. This self-centeredness or *hybris*, seeking to bend the world to the purposes of the individual or group, thereby identifying those purposes with the will of God, has been called by Toynbee the "cardinal sin," though he recognizes that the struggle for survival, of which it is an implication, is the essence of life itself (9). Karl Deutsch explains this source of social conflict as the practice of giving weight to external communications only after they have been appraised by the internal communications system, relating the values and drives which constitute the individuality of the organism or society. In such appraisal, he writes, there is "a propensity to prefer self-reference symbols to information from the outside world" (5), often resulting in disaster for the entity (13). Yet, without some such preference, there is no autonomy and no life. The antinomy between the effort to do what is right according to the conscience of the ruler, the culture of the society, the law of the state, or the interests of the people and to do what is necessary according to information available concerning the power and policies of other states, the opinions of other societies, the universal law of nations, or the general interests of mankind fills the "realist" school of international politics with profound pessimism. To do what is right according to internal symbols, dispositions, and communications – that is, to preserve autonomy, independence, or sovereignty – may be to commit suicide. Deutsch notes that religious insight suggests a moderation of autonomy and self-interest by consideration of the interests of others and of the society of which all are members, exemplifying the virtues of humility, faith, reverence, and love, but only, according to Toynbee, at the expense of suffering, thus saving one's life by losing it (5, 9).

Though autonomy may be at the heart of all social conflict, it can be most easily studied in international conflicts, both because the sovereign states are, par excellence, the social entities seeking autonomy (11) and because in the sovereign state the decision-making process is most open to observation, at least if the government is constitutional and democratic.

Conflict, as noted, may be physical, biological, or philosophical, as well as social. International conflicts may exhibit all these characteristics. War is fought on the military, economic, propaganda, legal, and political fronts. Armies, like physical entities moving toward one another, seek to occupy the same place at the same time, each attempting to annihilate or capture the other. Generals, like game players, seek to devise and carry out strategies which will outcalculate the enemy's responses with a minimum of cost and risk of defeat and a maximum probability of victory. Governments seek to control economic goods and services in order to starve or bankrupt the enemy and to provide essential materials for themselves. They communicate symbols to the home population, to neutrals, and to enemies, each government seeking to convince all that its ideals, goals, and values are right and the enemy's wrong and that in any case it is going to win and the enemy to lose. On the legal front, each government argues in the court of world opinion the rightness and justice of its cause and conduct, and the violations of international law by the enemy. On the political front, diplomats of each side seek to induce neutral governments to be benevolent or to participate on their side and to induce the enemy to abandon its futile efforts. Thus analogies from every form of conflict – party politics, industrial strife, litigation, revolution, insurrection, prize fights, football, and chess – can throw light on the subject of international conflict. The study of war can contribute to the study of all forms of conflict (13, 14).

From the point of view of developing a science of conflict resolution, international conflict is especially important because it has been so widely studied. A unified discipline of international relations is only beginning to emerge, but its components – international politics and diplomacy, international law, international organization, international economics, the art of war, international communications and propaganda, and international education – are well-established disciplines, each with a voluminous literature which gives special emphasis to the causes and methods of solution of international conflicts. The disciplines of political geography, political demography, international ethics, and the technology, sociology, and psychology of international relations are less centered on the problem of conflict; but each seeks to conceptualize the field of international relations utilizing a particular body of data, so that both conflict and cooperation among states can be better understood (16).

The extensiveness of this literature and its division into disciplines, each developing a special point of view or concentrating upon a particular type of data, make synthesis a desideratum for the study of conflict resolution, because that subject cuts across all the disciplines (16).

A Discipline of International Relations

A unified discipline of international relations would differ from the study of the decision-making process or the foreign policy of particular states in that it would be universal in scope. It would seek to formulate propositions of predictive value for the world as a whole and propositions of control value useful for realizing the most widely recognized goals, such as those stated in the United Nations Charter and the Universal Declaration of Human Rights. It would differ from the particular international disciplines in that it would not limit itself to a particular method, to a particular body of data, or to the needs of a particular profession. Such a comprehensive discipline, both universal and interdisciplinary, in order to avoid the character of an encyclopedia or of a diffuse eclecticism, would, however, have to be developed from a definite point of view or frame of reference for organizing data and methods. That point of view might be *theoretical*, seeking a conceptualized description and history of international relations by locating governments and peoples in a multidimensional field defined by geographic and analytical co-ordinates.

Scrutiny of the location of states in the *geographic* field, with indication of the transportation and communication distances and the barriers, natural and artificial, between them, would suggest the relative frequencies of controversy and the relative vulnerabilities to attack and, consequently, the probability of conflict to be expected within different pairs of states. The relative permanence of boundaries in past history; the abundance of trade across them; the distribution of resources and population and of forms of culture, economy, and polity at a given moment could also be indicated, suggesting the "natural" boundaries of states and the probability of conflict through attempts to modify "unnatural" boundaries. The directions of movement in time in the field could be illustrated by the study of trends of change in these variables (16). The relations among the strategic, ideological, political, psychological, and other aspects of "distance" between states and among rates of change in these variables might, with proper analysis, suggest with greater precision the probability of co-operation or conflict between the members of each pair of states (13).

By locating states in an analytical field defined by co-ordinates, each indicating an aspect of capability or of value, the political orientation and long-run goals of states could be indicated (16). The relation between the location of the government, the constitution, the culture, and the people of each state in the field might suggest the probable direction of movement through time of each state in the field, on the assumption that in democracies the opinion of the people draws the government toward itself, while in anarchies the reverse is true. Scrutiny of this field might suggest the policies and actions of governments to be anticipated from these changing relations, as well as the changes in the character of the field as a whole, defined by those relations, whether toward some sort of order or toward anarchy (16).

Such a field analysis, providing the basis for synthesizing the characteristics and tendencies of each state, for comparing the relations between the members of different pairs of states, and for appraising trends of change in the state of international relations as a whole, might suggest general conditions and special circumstances breeding conflict and might even throw light on the nature and type of intervention likely to influence the course of conflict toward peace or war.

A general discipline of international relations might also adopt a *practical* point of view, seeking formulations for realizing the most generally accepted values, such as international peace with justice, national self-determination with international stability, human freedom with order, general prosperity with equal opportunities. If these values are all treated as absolute goals, they tend to conflict with one another. Efforts to realize national conceptions of justice and to maintain self-determination or autonomy are likely to disrupt peace and stability. The reconciliation of individual freedom, national independence, and social order, which has been the dominant problem of national governments, is no less a problem when transported to the international order. Rising prosperity tends to augment disparities between the rich and the poor in each state, and also between rich states and poor states, tending, in practice, toward inequality of opportunity. The problem, in dealing with these values, is therefore one of balance rather than of establishing and maintaining a hierarchy of means and ends. Measurement is therefore the essence of the problem. Formulas and models stating the relations of relevant variables and statistical series indicating the fluctuations of these variables in time and space might serve as guides to national foreign policy and international regulatory action designed to achieve balanced progress toward all these goals. Such materials should be the content of a discipline of international relations from the practical point of view (4).

Conflict Resolution and a Discipline of International Relations

The resolution of international conflicts can proceed through the continuous regulation of international relations by national governments or international agencies so as to prevent tensions from arising and aggravating disputes and situations among nations. Such resolution can also proceed through the application of appropriate methods of negotiation, inquiry, mediation, conciliation, arbitration, judicial settlement, utilization of regional agencies, or resort to the United Nations for recommendation and the co-ordination of measures to prevent aggression. A unified discipline of international relations would assist in both these types of activity (15). Such a discipline would also provide a basis for evaluating the applicability of any of the special disciplines of international relations to a given dispute or situation, and it would furthermore provide a basis for more specialized study of international conflict, whether treated as a function of the entire field of international relations, as a function of the relations of the states in a particular situation or controversy, as a function of the properties or characteristics of each government or nation involved in the situation, or as a function of the procedures or policies adopted to deal with a particular conflict situation.

This is not the place to elaborate further the possible approaches to the development of such a discipline. The present writer has attempted to do so in his volumes entitled *A Study of War* and *The Study of International Relations* and in his essay entitled "Criteria for Judging the Relevance of Researches on the Problem of Peace." The rising interest in education on international affairs has stimulated many writers and organizations to study the development of such a discipline. Attention may be called to the studies by Sir Alfred Zimmern (17, 18), S. H. Bailey (1, 2), Edith Ware (10), Charles A. W. Manning (8), Grayson Kirk (7), Geoffrey Goodwin (6), Howard Wilson (12), and others under the stimulus of the Institute of International Intellectual Cooperation, UNESCO, the Carnegie Endowment for International Peace, the New York Council on Foreign Relations, and the Royal Institute of International Affairs (16). Approaches to such a discipline through the medium of history have been attempted by Arnold J. Toynbee in his *Study of History*; by James T. Shotwell in *The Economic and Social History of the World War*, which he edited; and by the UNESCO Commission on a World History. Many of the papers presented at various sessions of the Conference on Science, Philosophy, and Religion have thrown light on the problem of creating such a discipline. It is to be anticipated that *Conflict Resolution* will, in successive numbers, contribute to the development of such a discipline and that, in turn, the developing discipline will contribute to the just and peaceful resolution of international conflicts.

References

1. Bailey, S. H. *International Studies in Great Britain*. London: Royal Institute of International Affairs, 1937.
2. Bailey, S. H. *International Studies in Modern Education*. London: Royal Institute of International Affairs, 1938.
3. Clausewitz, Carl von. *On War*. London, 1911.
4. de Sola Pool, Ithiel. *Symbols of Internationalism*. Stanford, Calif: Stanford University Press, 1951.
5. Deutsch, Karl W. "Self-referent Symbols and Self-referent Communication Patterns." In Bryson, Lyman, *et al.* (eds.), *13th Symposium on Science, Philosophy, and Religion: Symbols and Values, an Initial Study*. New York: Harper & Bros., 1954.
6. Goodwin, Geoffrey (ed.). *The University Teaching of International Relations: Proceedings of the International Studies Conference, Windsor, 1950*. London: Basil Blackwell, 1951.
7. Kirk, Grayson. *The Study of International Relations in American Colleges and Universities*. New York: Council on Foreign Relations, 1947.
8. Manning, Charles A. W. *The University Teaching of Social Sciences, International Relations*. Paris: UNESCO, 1954.
9. Toynbee, Arnold J. *An Historian's Approach to Religion*. London: Oxford University Press, 1956.
10. Ware, Edith E. *The Study of International Relations in the United States*. New York: Carnegie Endowment for International Peace, 1939.
11. Watkins, F. M. *The State as a Concept of Political Science*, p. 71. New York, 1934.
12. Wilson, Howard E. *Universities and World Affairs*. New York: Carnegie Endowment for International Peace, 1952.
13. Wright, Quincy. *A Study of War*, pp. 292, 297, 300 ff., 330. Chicago: University of Chicago Press, 1942.
14. Wright, Quincy. *Problems of Stability and Progress in International Relations*, pp. 150 ff. Berkeley: University of California Press, 1954.
15. Wright, Quincy. "Criteria for Judging the Relevance of Researches on the Problem of Peace." In Wright, Q., Cottrell, W. F., and Boasson, C., *Research for Peace*. Published for the Institute for Social Research, Oslo. Amsterdam: North-Holland Publishing Co., 1954.
16. Wright, Quincy. *The Study of International Relations*. New York: Appleton-Century-Crofts, 1955.
17. Zimmern, Sir Alfred. "Education for World Citizenship." In *Problems of Peace*, 5th series. Geneva: Institute of International Relations, 1931.
18. Zimmern, Sir Alfred. *University Teaching of International Relations: Proceedings of the International Studies Conference, Prague, 1938*. Paris: International Institute of Intellectual Cooperation, 1939.

3

The Mathematical Psychology of War

Lewis F. Richardson

Lewis Fry Richardson was, as the name suggests, a Quaker. He was also a distinguished mathematician, meteorologist, teacher, psychologist and, from 1926, Fellow of the Royal Society. Being a Quaker, he was also a conscientious objector during the First World War, which did not prevent him experiencing the effects of twentieth-century warfare as a member of the Friends Ambulance Service on the Western Front between 1916 and 1918, where he served alongside the French army as an ambulance driver. However, it did prevent him from ever obtaining a teaching post in a university, so much of his writing about war remained virtually unpublished until the very end of his life, when one of his sons took the manuscripts of *Statistics of Deadly Quarrels* and *Arms and Insecurity* to the University of Michigan, where the early group of conflict and peace researchers there, including Kenneth Boulding, helped to arrange publication. Richardson's work involved applying both statistical and mathematical techniques to the analysis of such topics as the frequency of wars and the dynamical aspects of conflicts. As can be seen in this brief extract from one of his early unpublished papers, he was interested in processes in which the actions of one side in a conflict brought about reactions from the other side, which, in turn, caused the first to increase its own original efforts. Much subsequent work in the field, especially on spiralling arms races, have their origins in this pioneering mathematical approach.

* * * *

I. Introduction

The death-grip of opposing forces which the war developed out of the comparatively mild rivalries of peace, demands our best efforts to understand it.

The view here put forward is that the warlike striving of either side is largely, though not entirely, an instinctive reaction to the stimulus of the warlike striving of the opposing side. By an instinct is here meant an inborn tendency to perceive a certain state of affairs, and thereupon to feel in a particular way, and to act towards a corresponding end. A tendency, that is to say, which one might easily follow without considering it; and to resist which, if one judged it desirable to resist, would require an effort of will.

We may make this view of the matter more definite by putting it into symbols. Let A_E be the warlike activity of the Entente, A_G the warlike activity of the Germanic alliance.

Then the instinctive tendency which has been referred to above, may be expressed by two such equations as the following, in which t is the time, k_E and k_G are positive constants, and d is the operator of the differential calculus so that dA_E/dt means the rate of increase of A_E with time.

$$\frac{dA_E}{dt} = k_E A_G \tag{1}$$

$$\frac{dA_G}{dt} = k_G A_E \tag{2}$$

In other words, a war, once set afoot, is continued and augmented by the tendency to mutual reprisals.

4
Conflict and Defense: A General Theory

Kenneth Boulding

Formally, Kenneth Boulding is always first described as 'an economist', but this is a wholly inadequate way of characterizing such a multifaceted person: educator, peace activist (whose activism on occasions included chaining himself to flagpoles in front of university administrative buildings), poet, Quaker, general systems theorist, wit, conflict theorist. In this last role, his influence is everywhere. He wrote pioneering works using economic techniques to enlighten understanding of complex social phenomena – conflict, power, dynamics, sustainability – which were central to the early development of conflict and peace research and helped to found such pillars of the field as the *Journal of Conflict Resolution* and the International Peace Research Association.

*   *   *   *

Conflict is an activity that is found almost everywhere. It is found throughout the biological world, where the conflict both of individuals and of species is an important part of the picture. It is found everywhere in the world of man, and all the social sciences study it. Economics studies conflict among economic organizations – firms, unions, and so on. Political science studies conflict among states and among subdivisions and departments within larger organizations. Sociology studies conflict within and between families, racial and religious conflict, and conflict within and between groups. Anthropology studies conflict of cultures. Psychology studies conflict within the person. History is largely the record of conflict. Even geography studies the endless war of the sea against the land and of one land form or one land use against another. Conflict is an important part of the specialized study of industrial relations, international relations, or any other relations.

The question, therefore, arises, "Is there a general phenomenon of conflict, and, therefore, a general theory of conflict, that applies in all these areas, or is the type of conflict that is studied in one area quite different from that studied in another?" It seems reasonable to suppose that conflict does exhibit many general patterns, that the patterns of conflict in industrial relations, international relations, interpersonal relations, and even animal life are not wholly different from one another, and that it is, therefore, worth looking for the common element. On the other hand, we should be surprised if there were no differences; the pattern of conflict in international relations, for instance, is not the same as in industrial or interpersonal relations. Just as it is important to perceive the similarities in different situations, so it is important to perceive the differences. These differences cannot be perceived, however, without a general theory to serve as a standard of comparison. It is my contention that there is a general theory of conflict that can be derived from many different sources and disciplines. In developing this theory, I shall first show the essential similarities in all conflict situations in a series of models of broad application. Then, in applying these to various special conflict situations, the differences among these situations will be more clearly revealed in terms of divergences from the general models.

There are two broad types of general model of any system – the static (including comparative statics) and the dynamic, or process, which takes sequences of events specifically into account. For both these types of model of conflict, however, there is the following general framework of concepts:

1. *The Party.* A conflict is a situation that involves at least two parties, so that the first concept must be that of a party. A party is a *behavior unit*, that is, some aggregate or organization that is capable of assuming a number of different positions while retaining a common identity or boundary. A behavior unit may be a person, a family, a species of animals or artifacts, a class of ideas, a theory, or a social organization such as a firm, a nation, a trade union, or a church. The mere aggregate of people called Smith, however, is not a behavior unit, simply because this aggregate does not behave as a unit. It makes sense to say that John Smith does something; it makes no sense to say that Smiths do something, simply because Smiths have no sufficiently common or organized characteristic. Under some circumstances, a crowd may be a behavior unit, because crowds sometimes do things as crowds. It might even make sense to say that all titmice or all Philadelphia Biddles are a behavior unit, if certain circumstances make all titmice or all Biddles react in much the same way. The test that decides whether an aggregate is a behavior unit, then, is whether it can be the subject in a sentence with a verb of action. Not all behavior units are parties to conflict, though most of them probably are. A behavior unit becomes a party when it becomes involved in conflict with another behavior unit. A party is something that cannot actually exist in the singular – they must come at least in pairs.

2. *Behavior Space.* Before we can proceed to a formal definition of conflict we must examine another concept, that of behavior space. The *position* of a behavior unit at a moment of time is defined by a set of values (subset, to be technical) of a set of variables that defines the behavior unit. These variables need not be continuous or quantitatively measurable. The different values of a variable must, however, be capable of simple ordering; that is, of any two values it must be possible to say that one is "after" (higher, lefter, brighter than) the other. Thus, for a person we might have the variable "angry." We might specify five grades of anger, say, speechless with anger, very angry, moderately angry, a little peeved, not angry at all. At any one time, a person must occupy one of these positions. We can, of course, specify as many grades as we wish. In the case of a quantity like height or weight, there may be in theory an infinite number of grades. In practice, even here we have only a finite number: if we measure

weight only in pounds, for instance, an adult person will have one or two hundred possible positions of this variable; even if we measure it in ounces, there are only two or three thousand possible positions. We see that there is no essential difference, therefore, between a quantity, which we think to measure exactly, and a quality. A quantity merely has a larger number of grades.

The *history* of a behavior unit is the record of the positions it has occupied at successive moments of time. We can think of a position as a single frame of a movie reel. The history, then, is the successive frames of the reel. History, however, stops at the present; all possible future positions of the behavior unit are what we mean by its behavior space. Back from the present, the history of the behavior unit unfurls as a single reel; forward from the present, there is not a single reel but a great many different possible future reels. It is this set of future positions that comprises the behavior space. There is not an infinite number of such reels because the set of potential positions is limited by the existence of *laws*. A law is a stable relationship between positions at different dates. Thus, if we have a body falling in a vacuum under a constant acceleration of 32 feet per second, the law of its movement tells us that there is only one possible place for it to be at each moment. It will have fallen 16 feet by the end of the first second, 64 feet by the end of the second second, and so on. This is an extreme case in which there is only a single set of future positions. In the case of complex systems like human and social systems, we cannot define the future positions uniquely. Nevertheless there are limits. I am sure I shall not be on the moon tomorrow, I am pretty sure I shall not be in New York, and, in fact, I am pretty sure I shall be right here where I am today, which is where I plan to be. There is a possibility, however, that my plans might change – the death of a relative, an urgent matter of business, and so on. I might be able to range these possible futures in order of their present likelihood, starting with the highly probable and going down to the impossible. This is the usual form of laws in social science.

3. *Competition.* Competition in its broadest sense exists when any potential positions of two behavior units are mutually incompatible. This is a broader concept than conflict, as we shall see, in the sense that, whereas all cases of conflict involve competition, in the above sense, not all cases of competition involve conflict. Two positions are mutually incompatible if each excludes the other, that is, if the realization of either one makes impossible the realization of the other. Thus, suppose we have two populations of different biological species, A and B. If an expansion of A makes an expansion of B impossible, and vice versa, we have a case of simple mutual competition. The intensity of competition depends on the likelihood of each behavior unit moving into the incompatible area. Thus we might have a situation in which an expansion of A would preclude an expansion of B, but, for some reason, an expansion of A is very unlikely. In that case, the competition will be weak. In an extreme case, we may have potential competition, where if A expanded, B would diminish but where there is no actual competition because A does not, in fact, expand.

4. *Conflict.* Conflict may be defined as a situation of competition in which the parties are *aware* of the incompatibility of potential future positions and in which each party *wishes* to occupy a position that is incompatible with the wishes of the other. Our

definition of conflict includes two little words, "aware" and "wishes," each of which is laden with philosophical dynamite. The nature of awareness is very obscure. Nevertheless, there is a clear difference between, say, the competition of land forms and the competition of animals, men, and societies. One can even postulate a condition of competition among animals or men that would not involve conflict, because there would be no awareness of the competitors. Thus, suppose we had two species of insects, one of which fed by day and the other by night on the same food supply. They might be in intense competition, in the sense that an increase in the number of one would force a diminution in the number of the other, but they might be totally unaware of each other's existence. Similarly, the world of man is so complex that many individuals and groups may be in competition and yet be quite unaware of the fact. Even where people are aware of potential conflict, there may be no actual conflict if there is no desire on the part of one party to occupy a region of its behavior space from which it is excluded by the other. Thus it is impossible for two people to sit on top of a flagpole at the same time. In this area, there is competition between them, and if they are aware of this, there is potential conflict. If, however, neither party has any desire to sit on the flagpole or even if only one party has this desire, the conflict will not become actual.

In an actual conflict situation, then, there must be awareness, and there must also be incompatible wishes or desires. If the concept of awareness raises philosophical difficulties, the concept of desire is haunted by the ghosts of agelong disputes about free will and determinism. We can escape them only by a heroic process of abstraction by which we hope to achieve a workable theory of behavior. The particular abstraction that we use is the idea of a *value ordering*. We suppose that the relevant parts of a party's image of its potential positions can be ordered on a scale of better and worse; that is, of any two positions, we can say either that one is better than the other or that they are equally good. This is what is called a *weak* ordering. A *strong* ordering is one in which we can always say of any two positions which is better and in which there are no two positions to which the party is indifferent. Weak orderings are probably less likely to lead to conflict than strong orderings. A pliable, good-natured person has many positions that are of about equal value to him; if he is excluded from one he simply goes to another without any sense of loss. An inflexible, opinionated person whose orderings tend to be strong, and who always knows quite positively which of two positions he prefers, is likely to run into conflict if his best position happens to be occupied by someone else.

We suppose, then, that there is an *ordered set* of positions of a behavior unit. This need not cover all conceivable positions; we do not bother to order very remote possibilities. In a conscious or unconscious form, however, the ordering is likely to extend over a range of positions in the vicinity of the present position. Thus I could say with some certainty that I would prefer a raise in salary to no raise at all or that I prefer a vacation and no new car to a new car and no vacation. This ordered set is pretty certain to extend beyond the set of possible positions, which is defined by the *boundary of possibility*.

The boundary of possibility is the next important concept. It defines certain limitations on the positions I could occupy, say, tomorrow, imposed by various physical, psychological, legal, and financial restrictions. I could not, for instance, be in Australia, simply because planes do not travel that fast. This is a physical limitation. I could not be in London, even though this might be physically possible, because my passport has expired, or even if I had a valid passport, because I cannot afford the trip. It would not be too difficult to draw on a map of the world my possibility boundary – a line that divides the world into two regions, one containing all the places to which I can go and the other containing all the places to which I cannot go. The same concept can be applied to my general behavior space. Thus I cannot, at any rate, tomorrow, be a very different person from what I am, but I can be a little different; there is a rough boundary here between possible and impossible changes in my personality or general conduct.

The *behavior* of a behavior unit consists in its moving to the best position possible, i.e., the point within its possibility boundary that is higher than any other on the value ordering. This principle is illustrated, in terms that will be familiar to economists, in Fig. 1. Here we suppose the plane of the paper represents the behavior space of an individual located at A. Each point on the paper, or *field*, represents a certain state of the universe that is within the purview of the individual at A. We neglect here the problem of the various ways in which these can be ordered: if there are only two variables in the behavior system, the plane can then express any combination of these by a set of Cartesian coordinates. We do not limit ourselves to this condition, however; since there is an infinite number of points on the plane, there is no reason why each one should not represent a state of a multidimensional universe. We order the field only to the extent that we suppose a line (the heavy line in the figure) represents the boundary of possibility, so that all points inside the line represent states of the universe that are possible or available to the behavior unit at A and that all points outside the line represent states that are not. We then suppose that the value ordering of the field can be represented by a surface (a *welfare function* or *utility function*) in the third dimension, such that any point R that is a higher point on this surface than another point S is better than S. On the plane, this surface can be represented by a series of contours, or indifference curves (dotted in the figure), that join all points of equal value in the value ordering, that is, to which the behavior unit is indifferent. This can only be done if the ordering is a weak ordering. In the figure, the best point that A can reach is the point C, where the

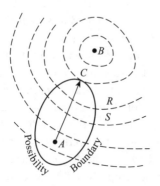

Figure 1

possibility boundary touches its highest indifference curve. In Fig. 1, we suppose that *B* is the point of *bliss*, the best conceivable state of the universe. This, however, is outside the possibility boundary, so that the behavior unit can only get to *C*.

...

This is a view of behavior that is derived fundamentally from the economist's theory of *rational behavior*.

5
Conflict and Communication
John Burton

Burton's early career as an Australian diplomat representing a middle-sized, non-European power with little coercive potential made him intensely sceptical about 'realist' theorizing and underpinned many of his innovative ideas about coping with conflicts. In these very early extracts from his extensive work, he first introduces the distinction between disputes and deep-rooted conflicts, arguing for resolution rather than compromise settlements, and promotes the advantages of conflict prevention as a strategy for avoiding many destructive conflicts.

* * * *

Resolution of conflict is a process that comes from the decision-making of the parties. It involves a reappraisal of values and alternatives and costs, and the appropriate international institution is one that facilitates this process. It is critical also of traditional diplomatic practices. International studies have tended to be conducted separately from contemporary diplomatic practice, and, on the other hand, the practice of diplomacy has been little influenced by research. No such watertight compartments are now possible. Diplomacy is becoming as much exposed to scientific scrutiny as is any branch of social policy, despite traditions of secrecy that are maintained. In conditions of controlled communication, in which scholars have opportunities to pose questions that seem significant to them on the basis of their theories, in which parties are endeavouring to explain their behaviour, relevant influences are revealed.

...

The main differences in function of the third party arise out of the difference in objective. Traditional mediation seeks agreements by compromises, or by persuading the parties that their best interests would be served by ceasing violence and arriving at a settlement. It is a negotiating framework. Controlled communication, on the other hand, endeavours to establish a condition in which the parties see their relationships as posing a problem to be solved. Both sides are assumed to have been acting in ways which appear to them, in the light of the knowledge they have, and the circumstances in which they operate, to be in their best interests. Neither is more right nor wrong than the other. Even if an aggressive initiative has been wholly with one side, even if there appears to have been a blatant case of unprovoked aggression, there is still a problem: the apparent aggression was stimulated by some circumstances, and it is in the interest of the suffering party to help solve the problem. The role of the third party is to establish a condition in which all the parties join with it in defining, identifying and solving the problem.

...

Abstract models help parties to observe the basis of conflict, and in particular to discern the processes and effects of escalation. Their own accusations and counter-accusations about atrocities and provocations come to be perceived within this frame-work of behavioural responses and escalation processes, thus making possible a less subjective interpretation of events. Once the past is reperceived and the violence explained, the future can be considered within a less fearful framework. The effect on the parties of an awareness of the processes of perception is a striking feature of this controlled communication. In short, the parties are helped not by the third party as such, but by the ordinary academic tools of analysis, to stand back from their conflict, and to understand its origins and its manifestations. Once each party is in a position to perceive the problem from a behavioural point of view of the other, communication is effectively controlled, and tends to become constructive.

...

Parties to a conflict have most rigid ideas about the character and motives of their opponents. They have usually experienced many years of conflict and their selections from past history and their moral judgements justify, confirm and reinforce their atti-tudes. To a third party their images of their opponents appear distorted; no man could so consistently be irrational, immoral and untrustworthy as one party is perceived to be by the other. That there is distortion is even clearer when it is discovered that each party has the same favourable image of itself and its behaviour, and the same unfavourable and treacherous one of the other. The initial problem is to demonstrate that these mirror images exist, that each party is making identical accusations about the other on the same kind of evidence. If the third party argues the case of one party, or in any way tries to demonstrate that an image or an interpretation of events is false, he prejudices his relationships with that party. Both sides must find out for themselves that their percep-tions and interpretations may be false.

Demonstrations of the possibility of false visual perceptions help to make the point, without in any way requiring the third party to enter into the debate.

...

Figure 1 may be interpreted as a very old lady or as a young girl. One set of political events and behavioural patterns can be interpreted as aggressive, or in some other way, according to the processes of perception that take place within the observer. In this case the observer can flash from one interpretation to another. What needs to be demon-strated is that all observation is preconditioned by experience – and by prejudice.

...

In these ways parties to a conflict can be persuaded that the assumptions they make about the behaviour of others are a consequence of their experiences, which are based upon perceptions, which themselves are conditioned by their attitudes and expectations in the environment in which they are observing and making judgements. The processes that lead to reinforcement and certainty can by these means be explained, at least

Figure 1 *Which is it – an old woman with chin sunk in wrap, or the heroine of an early twentieth-century romantic novel, her chin in air?*

sufficiently to suggest that all evidence must be tested by some means to ensure that it is being correctly interpreted.

...

Conflict Avoidance

So far we have been concerned with the use of controlled communication in the analysis and resolution of conflict, and in continuation of this, the promotion of functional cooperation between parties. It is in the context of resolving conflict that the technique is most clearly defined, and in which it can be compared with traditional means of peaceful settlement of disputes.

Conflict avoidance is a far more challenging objective because it involves prediction – prediction of likely conflicts, and prediction of future conditions in which they will take place. It could be argued that conflict avoidance is already an important objective of the day-to-day decision-making of administrations, and of the art of diplomacy generally. It could also be claimed to be one of the longer-term objectives of many international institutions, such as the Economic and Social Council and its associated agencies. It is the ultimate end of research institutions that seek to trace the sources of conflicts and to understand their nature. However, no government, international institution or research organisation has developed techniques designed to anticipate and to avoid particular international conflicts. Traditional means of peaceful settlement of disputes are relevant to particular problems after they have arisen, and to events leading up to them. It is difficult to envisage any circumstances in which they could be employed to anticipate and to avoid possible future conflicts among states and nations.

Conflict avoidance is of two different kinds. One is in respect of likely or anticipated conflicts – those that reasonably can be anticipated because of some observed changes that will in the future alter local relationships, as when the influence of a great power declines in a particular region. The other is in respect of the maintenance of peaceful relationships among states that are already in a close working relationship and do not anticipate the development of tensions. Controlled communication, with its emphasis upon analysis by parties of their own relationships, upon the perceptions that parties have of each other and alternatives available in adjusting to perceived conditions, is as applicable to the peaceful relationships of states as to relationships among states that are, or are likely to be, in conflict. It can be employed, therefore, not only in conflict resolution and in the avoidance of conflicts that can reasonably be anticipated if no steps are taken to avoid them, but also in the maintenance of peaceful relationships even when no source of conflict is currently suspected. It can have a prophylactic as well as a therapeutic function. As such it lends itself to institutionalised forms of regional and international organisation designed to promote peaceful relations and to deal with conflicts if they should arise.

To a limited degree the informal meetings of the British Commonwealth of Nations were an institution that fulfilled these combined functions. In many respects it was a controlled communication exercise in which tensions between members could be brought to the surface in the presence of other members who in some instances could act as a third party. No agenda, no minutes, no publicity, secret discussions and conditions conducive to free expression of attitudes, opportunities to alter attitudes and perceptions, and the absence of bargaining or negotiation were all features of the Prime Ministers' meetings. They lacked the insights and knowledge now available to specialists in the field of world politics, and increased numbers, less informality and a greater number of issues to be handled in the short time available for meetings have helped to destroy their effectiveness.

Whether employed for conflict resolution or conflict avoidance, controlled communication takes the same basic form. It is the parties that are required to project into the future, to define the problems that might occur, to check perceptions and assumptions, to examine their own internal conditions that could spill over into wider conflict, and finally to examine alternative means by which, through functional cooperation or otherwise, possible conflicts might be avoided. The third party has the role of injecting new information about possible trends in world society, the environment in which states will be responding, the changes that are likely to take place in values within the states concerned because of similar changes taking place elsewhere, changing industrial structures and the way in which these will alter international relations generally, and other relevant environmental conditions. In particular, the third party has the function of bringing to attention domestic problems that governments sometimes find more convenient not to consider, and not to admit exist.

The role of the third party in conflict avoidance is more active than in conflict resolution. It is only a third party that can take initiatives to determine parties and issues in relation to possible future conditions of conflict. Governments do not look many years ahead, and they are not likely to take initiatives in researching into or in solving future problems. This is the role of those studying problems of conflict, aware of theorising in this area, examining profiles of states that have and have not been engaged in conflicts, familiar with longer-term trends in world society, and prepared to predict continuation of some of these, and who can with some degree of credibility point to possible future sources of conflict and argue which policies should be avoided or should be encouraged if a condition of peaceful relations is to be maintained. This is a role traditionally filled by academics; it is one that could now be filled by recruited members of foreign offices and international institutions, thus including a 'third party' within decision making at national and international levels.

6

Conflict Theory and Practice

Johan Galtung

It is quite impossible to do justice to the influence that Johan Galtung has had – and continues to have – on the whole field of peace and conflict research since the 1950s. Starting with the establishment of PRIO (the Peace Research Institute Oslo) in the late 1950s and the founding of the *Journal of Peace Research* in 1964, moving through becoming the first Professor of Peace Studies at the University of Oslo in the 1970s and continuing through his many global professorial appointments thereafter, Galtung has been a theoretical and practical force in the study and application of ideas from conflict and peace research for many decades. His work for TRANSCEND (an online peace university) has enabled him to retain his intellectual independence; his practical work as a peacemaking and peacebuilding consultant has kept his work firmly based in the realities of intractable conflicts; and his extensive writings have challenged and stimulated several generations of students. The extracts here presented are, we hope, relatively unfamiliar but represent two sides of Galtung's work – the first a succinct statement about his key ideas regarding conflict formation and transformation and the second an example of the connection between his theoretical ideas and their use in generating real alternative solutions to real conflicts.

* * * *

Conflict Theory and Practice: A Perspective

Nonviolence
(physical and verbal violence)
Behavior

B

A **C**

Attitude
(hatred, distrust,
apathy)
Empathy

Contradiction
(blocked, stymied)
Creativity

A **conflict** has its own life cycle; almost like something organic. It appears, reaches an emotional, even violent climax, then tapers off, disappears – and often reappears. There is a logic: – individuals and groups (such as nations and states) have goals:

- goals may be incompatible, exclude each other, like two states wanting the same land, or two nations wanting the same state;
- when goals are incompatible a **contradiction**, an issue, is born;
- any actor/party with unrealized goals feels frustrated and more so the more basic the goal, like basic needs and basic interests;
- frustration **may** lead to aggression, turning inward as **attitudes** of hatred, or outward as **behavior** of verbal or physical **violence**;
- hatred and violence **may** be directed toward the holders of the goals standing in the way, but it is not always that "rational";
- violence is intended to harm and hurt (including oneself), and **may** breed a spiral of counter-violence as defense and/or **revenge**;
- that spiral of hatred and violence becomes a meta-conflict (like meta-stasis relative to cancer), over the goals of preserving and destroying.

In this way, a conflict may almost get eternal life, vexing and waning, disappearing and reappearing. The original, root, conflict recedes into the background like when Cold War attention focused mostly on such means of destruction as nuclear missiles.

Conflicts may combine, in series or parallel, into complex conflict formations with many parties and many goals, because the same parties and/or the same goals are involved. The elementary conflict formation with **two** parties pursuing **one** goal is rare, except for pedagogical purposes, or as the polarized products of hatred and violence leading to simplified conflict formations. The normal conflict has **many** actors, **many** goals and **many** issues, is complex, not easily mapped, yet that mapping is essential.

Life-cycle of a conflict

The **life-cycle** of a conflict may be divided into three phases, before violence, during violence and after violence, separated by outbreak and cease-fire. This does not imply that violence is unavoidable, or that conflict = violence/destruction.

7
The Middle East Conflict

Johan Galtung

Let us start with the beginning, literally speaking, with Genesis 15:18:

> So that day Jehovah made this covenant with Abram: "I have given this land to your descendants from the Wadi-el-Arish to the river Euphrates. And I give to them these nations: Kenites, Kenizzites, Kadmonites, Hittites, Perizzites, Rephaim, Amorites, Canaanites, Girgashites, Jebusites."

And we continue, Genesis 17:5–14:

> "What's more," God told him, "I am changing your name. It is no longer Abram ('Exalted Father'), but Abraham ('Father of Nations') – for that is what you will be. I have declared it. I will give you millions of descendants who will be from many nations. Kings shall be among your descendants! And I will continue this agreement between us generation after generation, forever, for it shall be between me and your children as well. It is a contract that I shall be your God and the God of your posterity. And I will give all this land of Canaan to you and them, forever. And I will be your God.
>
> "Your part of the contract," God told him, "is to obey its terms. You personally and all your posterity have this continual responsibility: that every male among you shall be circumcised; the foreskin of his penis shall be cut off. This will be the proof that you and they accept this covenant. Every male shall be circumcised on the eighth day after birth. This applies to every foreign-born slave as well as to everyone born in your household. This is a permanent part of this contract, and it applies to all your posterity. All must be circumcised. Your bodies will thus be marked as participants in my everlasting covenant. Anyone who refuses these terms shall be cut off from his people; for he has violated my contract."

A strong statement, indeed. A metaphor with both Chosen People and Promised Land in it, a metaphor that has served as an archetype not only for Judaism but also for Christianity and Islam, in other words for the three semitic religions that together may be said to define the Occident. This First Covenant with Abraham is crystal clear, especially if we accept the interpretation of Wadi-el-Arish as the Nile.[1] And the First Covenant is then confirmed in the Second Covenant, with Moses on Mt. Sinai, set down in Exodus for everybody to read.[2]

A myth, some might say. And I would say it is the kind of raw material out of which history is made. The reality of this myth is proven by its tenacity, close to 4,000 years by now.

Let us then look at the other side. Professor Ismail Zayid of Dalhousie University in Halifax, Nova Scotia, Canada, writes in *The Guardian Weekly:*[3]

> Zionist re-writing of the history of Palestine is not a novelty, but your correspondents compound falsification with absurdity. Credible historians, including Arnold Toynbee, assert that the Palestinian Arabs of today are the descendants of the cumulative stock of the Canaanites, Philistines, Jebusites

and others who inhabited Palestine, since the dawn of history and long before the Hebrew tribes invaded the Land of Canaan (Palestine).

Professor Maxime Rodison of the Sorbonne in Paris, and himself Jewish, states: "The Arab population of Palestine was native in all the senses of the word and their roots in Palestine can be traced back at least forty centuries." H. G. Wells wrote, sixty years ago: "If it is proper to 'reconstitute' a Jewish state (in Palestine), which has not existed for two thousand years, why not go back another thousand years and reconstitute the Canaanite state? The Canaanites, unlike the Jews, are still there."

The reader will notice that there is some overlap between the nations mentioned in that particular area of the world: the Canaanites, the Jebusites. And Philistines = Palestinians.

Is it possible to know such things? I do not think that is even the correct question, not knowing the correct answer. Even if it is a myth, this is the kind of raw material out of which history is made. Whether the evidence presented can stand up to tests of modern historiography may be less important. The important point is an intense feeling of belongingness, of *homeland*.

Four thousand years of human history. This is a long span of time, and if there is one thing I have learned myself by working for twenty-five years now, off and on, as a peace researcher on this extremely complicated and intractable conflict, it is the following: the roots of the solution, if there are any, are found in the future, not in the past. It is my experience that it is not in any way helpful to try to survey these 4,000 years in order to score points as to who did more injustice to whom, who lived longest, where, in the largest numbers, and so on. Rather, I will extract three simple axioms from the past, and let them guide my search for a possible solution in the future. After having done that I will more or less say good-bye to the past, and invite everybody to share with me these visions, not so much different from visions many others might have, in the search for a viable future in the Middle-East.

Axiom 1: *The right to live in that area is an inalienable right both for Arabs and for Jews.* In other words, I take both justifications as quoted above not only as sufficient evidence for that inalienable right, but also as equal evidence. And that leads me immediately to

Axiom 2: *No viable peace can be obtained in the area except by according equal rights and duties to Arabs and Jews.* In other words, any solution based on concepts of "undivided Israel" or "undivided Palestine" to the exclusion of Arabs and Jews, respectively, is doomed in advance, even if the exclusion does not mean expulsion, leaving alone extermination, but any type of secondary citizenship. No security would ever be found within any such form. Whatever kind of peace in the sense of "absence of violence" that can be obtained will be of only short duration and at the expense of tremendous levels of repression, probably also exploitation, and in most cases direct violence or threats of direct violence. In other words, the peace spoken about is only absence of overt violence, it is not "peace" in any real sense, and certainly not security. To mix two metaphors: the peace of the cemetery, on top of a volcano. That is, until an *intifadah* (shaking off), like the present uprising in the occupied territories, shatters the illusions of acquiescence with the occupation December 9, 1987.

To these axioms should then be added a third:

Axiom 3:　*Axioms 1 and 2 do not pertain only to the structure of a peaceful and viable solution, but also to any process leading to a viable solution.* In other words, any peace process is doomed to fail unless the two parties, here only described as "Arabs" and "Jews" (in alphabetical order), are accorded equal rights and duties in the process. Stated more succinctly and with a very clear address to the Camp David "peace process" (that never was one according to axiom 3): accords arrived at over the heads of one of the parties concerned cannot be part of a viable peace process, and will hardly lead to any viable peace structure.[4]

At this point let me be more specific. Let it first be said that the area I am thinking of is not much different from the area described in Genesis 15:18, with the interpretation mentioned, but somewhat smaller. I am thinking particularly of mandated Palestine administered by Britain after the First World War, until it was divided (by Churchill) in 1922 into Cis-Jordania (roughly equal to the area today controlled by Israel) and Trans-Jordania (roughly equal to the area today controlled by the Hashemite Kingdom of Jordan).

In that area, what I refer to as the "Middle East conflicts" are a complex web of three conflicts: (1) between Jews and Arabs over state formation in Israel/Palestine (roughly speaking the same as Cis-Jordania); (2) the conflict between the Jewish state and surrounding Arab states; and (3) the conflict over who shall be the conflict manager for the region – the United States, the two superpowers in conjunction, the United Nations, all three, or "none of the above." To this could then be added a fourth conflict between superpowers and possibly also other outside powers with special interests in the area.

However, at the nucleus of this complex we find the conflict between Arabs and Jews over state formation, in other words the conflict between Israelis and Palestinians over Israel/Palestine. Even if conflicts nos. 2 and 3 were adequately solved to the satisfaction of all the parties involved, the solution would hardly be viable unless conflict no. 1 was also solved. From that it does not follow that if conflict no. 1 is solved, conflicts nos. 2 and 3 will be solved automatically. But it does not seem unreasonable to claim that there is more clearly a causal flow in that direction than from nos. 2 and 3 to no. 1. The uprising has brought out this point very clearly, and even if the Israelis should manage to dampen, even extinguish, these heavy manifestations of the underlying conflict, the Israelis will clearly be living on borrowed time. After a lull a new eruption, then a new lull, a new eruption, and so on and on.

And then, what? The Israelis used to have five options in the area: *status quo* with more or less local autonomy, annexation 1, annexation 2, expulsion, and Palestinian state formation. *Annexation 1* would mean inclusion of the occupied territories in Gaza and the West Bank, giving to the Palestinians status as first-class citizens (with the possible exception of ministerial ranks, access to classified defense information and defense production information, and such areas). *Annexation 2* would mean inclusion of the same territories, but giving to the Palestinians only some kind of secondary class citizenship (among other reasons because of the "demographic time bomb"), like living where they are but voting in Jordan. But with an ongoing *intifadah*, the status quo is untenable, hence annexation 2 seems to be out. And the spread of the Palestinian revolt to areas inside the green line seems to indicate that annexation 1 is also out, and not only for demographic reasons.

What is left then would be "expulsion" and "Palestinian state formation." Roughly speaking these are the two options available but (so far) not articulated openly by the major Israeli parties, the Likud bloc and the Labor Party. What looks like efforts to maintain *status quo* barely conceals this incompatibility. If any actor in the area is a house divided against itself it must be Israel. And the rift seems to deepen with the growth of the orthodox parties.

The expulsion scenario would evict Palestinians to an area farther away from land they rightfully regard as theirs – the occupied territories of Gaza and the West Bank (and the Golan Heights) with a possible capital in East Jerusalem, and territory inside the green line. The scenario is tempting, of course, from an "undivided Israel" point of view because it would transform what today is an intra-state conflict into a set of inter-state conflicts that can be handled according to the conventional rules of the Westphalia "international system," with balance of power, strategic studies, occasional wars, and so on. But from a Palestinian point of view any such "solution" is totally unacceptable. All of this is totally incompatible with axioms 1 and 2 above; not to mention the international reaction.

The Palestinian state formation scenario would then be the only viable option of the four mentioned, but that in itself does not say very much in a solution-poor conflict. The question is what *kind* of state or states in the area, not only what kind of borders, and to explore that theme in more depth let me return to the axioms.

The options indicated by the extremists in the Middle-East, "undivided Israel" and "undivided Palestine," can serve the useful analytical purpose of identifying three other options, as indicated in Figure 1.

Option 1 is a 0–0 solution with neither the Arabs, nor the Jews, two nations, having any state in the area. Of course, this is what the Ottoman Empire was about, this is what the British Mandate was about, and today there are two clear successor possibilities

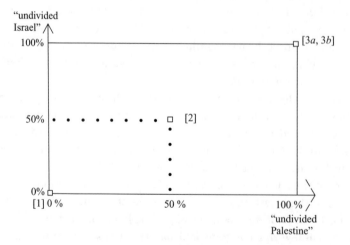

Figure 1 *Solving the Middle East Conflict: Three Options*

within this first option. One possibility is a border zone, or for that matter the whole area, put under clearly defined United Nations peace-keeping control, abrogating the right not only of the Palestinians but also of the Israelis to have a state with ultimate control of violence inside the territory and monopoly on foreign policy, including the exercise of violence outside. It is also possible to imagine that the present U.S.-Soviet detente might reach a high point in a shared willingness to control, jointly, the whole area as a superpower condominium. In other words, it is fairly clear what option 1 would mean in practice in the near future. But taken alone it is a clear nonstarter.

Option 2 is a 50–50 solution, which would mean that both parties have the right to a state in the area. In other words, back to a partition plan. There would be an Israeli state, and also a Palestinian state, giving to the Palestinian the same rights as those given to the Israelis of having a government, a parliament, a passport, and a flag. The Palestinian area would comprise all, or most, of the territories occupied in 1967, with a capital in East Jerusalem. In other words, "territories for peace" – as expressed repeatedly by the Arab side (Fez resolution 1987, Hussein-Arafat proposal 1985, Amman resolution 1987, and the agreement to give guarantees to all the states in the Middle East; culminating in the Algiers-Geneva-Stockholm resolutions late 1988). That 5 million Palestinians cannot make a living in that area is obvious. Nor can Israel house the total Jewish diaspora, but that is not an argument against the existence of Israel as a state with which Jews can identify.

It may certainly be objected that this solution was tried and failed in 1948. The Arab states around that central area attacked the newborn Israeli state. But before that the Jews had tried to seize as much of UN-allocated Arab Palestine as possible, including the massacre at Deir Yassin, 18 miles outside the borders allocated to a Jewish state before the British withdrawal (Plan Dalet). The argument could be that the same two scenarios might be enacted again.

Militarily, axiom 2 would, of course, rule out any effort to restrict forever the range of military weapons more severely in one of the states than in the other. Any such asymmetry is a way of communicating that one of the states is less trustworthy than the other. In other words, it is an asymmetric stigmatization, and unacceptable in any intense conflict for equal rights. If Israel does not like the idea of Palestine having any army at all, then the Palestinians might with equal justification say the same about Israel. If one of them is supposed to be disarmed, so also the other. If one of them is supposed to be transarmed, that is, possessing only means of defensive or nonprovocative defense, and no heavy weapons, so should the other. If one of them insists on a nuclear arsenal, so could the other. Again, the only viable lasting solution, including solution to the problem of security, is found in symmetry, and among those options defensive defense is by far the most stabilizing. However, detailed argumentation for this option lies outside the scope of this presentation. It should be noted that a Palestinian state would itself decide its relation to Jordan: open or latent enmity, coexistence, cooperation, confederation, federation, fusion. I do not see much basis for a prediction here, nor for knowing whether the last three possibilities would "Palestinize" Jordan or "Jordanize" Palestine.

Option 3 brings in a new element: the idea of transcending the conflict by bringing Arabs and Jews closer to each other (not Arabs and Arabs), on an equal basis, making "undivided Palestine" and "undivided Israel" compatible. Of course, total compatibility in the sense of the classical nation-state (one nation, one state) is impossible with (at least) two nations inhabiting the area. But there are at least two good possibilities within option 3: option 3a and option 3b.

Option 3a would bring in an additional element: a confederation, based on cantons, some Arab, some Jewish, in the area roughly corresponding to Cis-Jordania, or, better still, the whole area encompassed by the original mandate. A Swiss model, in other words, with open borders permitting the flow of persons, goods, services, and information inside,[5] but limiting, at least to start with, investment and settlement. If the Israelis could settle everywhere, they would be too strong economically and otherwise; if the Palestinians could settle everywhere, they would be too strong demographically (considering birth rates, and diaspora).

Since the confederation scenario is not often mentioned, let me be more specific. In such a scenario, there would be Arab cantons inside what today is known as Israel, for instance around Nazareth. There might also be Jewish cantons on the West Bank. In fact, one such canton might be exchanged for the other. Cantonization of all or parts of present Jordan (with at least 60% of the population being Palestinians) might be a part of the scenario. Cantons, and not necessarily only Palestinian, in present-day Sinai might be another part. Needless to say, all of this would depend on the ability of the actors in the area to convince each other and others that everybody would gain from a scheme of this kind. Jordan and Egypt might have to make some concessions.

Obviously, (all of) Jerusalem would be capital and federal territory, and the same principles would apply to Jerusalem as to the rest. The sum total of all the cantons would be known neither by the name of Israel nor by the name of Palestine, possibly by the two names hyphenated, possibly by a third name evocative of both or neither. There would certainly be a high level of internal government for the Arab cantons and for the Jewish cantons. But the sum total of Arab cantons would not be a Palestinian state in the sense defined above, nor would the sum total of Jewish cantons be identical with Israel of today or the successor state of Israel. But they would be sufficiently close for identification and cultural consistency. Palestinian law would apply in Arab cantons and Israeli law in Jewish cantons; disputes involving both would be settled by an overriding legal system. Neither would have a right to have an independent army. But the confederation as such might have an army for defense purposes, obviously with a defensive military doctrine.[6]

Option 3b is the image of the future often put forward by the Palestinian side, for instance by Al-Fatah: a secular state where Jews and Arabs (and Christians and others) live side by side. The area might roughly correspond to Cis-Jordania. In this vision there is an expression of the much higher ability of Moslems to accommodate Jews and Christians than vice versa. Islam has a concept of the religions of the *Kitab* (Old Testament); the other two exclude Islam with the concept of the Judeo-Christian faith. Catholic Spain (1492) evicted both Moslems and Jews; the Jews could settle for centuries in a number of Moslem countries (the "Oriental Jews") without being treated the way they were treated by Christians – Catholic, Protestant, Orthodox. Moreover, PLO was already an organization accommodating all three, together with secular Palestinians.

...

And, finally, is this plan realistic? In the sense of being immediately acceptable to all parties included, certainly not. In the sense of being at least as realistic as other plans, certainly yes. The three conflicts are simply intractable; a "situation" (to use very noninflammatory U.N. language) for which the British with their tendency to move people (in South Africa, East Africa, Trinidad, Fiji, Falkland/Malvinas, Gibraltar, Ulster, to mention some places) will have to take much of the blame. But they are not totally beyond solution.

We cannot stay with these conflicts forever. History has to move on. And the experience is rather unambiguous: only an equitable solution is a viable solution.

Notes

1 However, in Numbers 34 very concrete borders are given. And Numbers 33:50–56 give an almost exact formula for present-day Israeli policies: "You must drive out all the people living there and destroy all their idols." "You will be given land in proportion to the size of your tribes." "If you refuse to drive out the people living there, those who remain will be as cinders in your eyes and thorns in your sides. And I will destroy you as I had planned for you to destroy them."

2 Whereas the First Covenant is more geopolitical, the Second Covenant is more moral – with the Ten Commandments, for instance.

3 March 13, 1988. Also see Genesis 10:15–18.

4 For an analysis of this from a moderate Arab point of view, see Fayez A. Sayegh, Senior Consultant, Ministry of Foreign Affairs, Kuwait, *Camp David and Palestine; A Preliminary Analysis*, New York, October 1978.

5 Inside Israel, and in the world at large, Joseph Abileah, former concert master of the Haifa Symphony Orchestra, has very actively promoted the confederation idea. For an early presentation of my own version, see "The Middle East and the Theory of Conflict," *Essays in Peace Research*, vol. V (Copenhagen: Ejlers, 1980), pp. 77ff. (originally published in the *Journal of Peace Research*, 1971.)

6 See my *There Are Alternatives* (Nottingham: Spokesman, 1984), chapter 5, for some details about how and why this type of defense is particularly compatible with confederate decentralization. Is it to be ruled out completely that one day Israelis and Palestinians might have a joint interest in defending their joint country against attacks from neighboring states? In other words, a joint IDF-PLO force against attacks from anybody?

8

Conflict in Man-Made Environment

Anatol Rapoport

Rapoport's original background was as a mathematician (although he first trained as a concert pianist) and this often reveals itself in his quest for clear definitions, useful classifications and well-defined relationships in the social world as a basis for sound theory building. He was part of the early efforts to meld general systems theory with conflict research, and his first work in the field – *Fights, Games and Debates* (1960) – provided a simple taxonomy of classes of conflict which these later extracts seek to extend and illustrate with historical examples.

*   *   *   *

A Taxonomy of Conflicts

Human conflicts can be classified in several ways: according to the nature of the participants; according to the issues, if any; according to the means employed, etc. Participants may be individuals, small groups (families, companies, gangs), large groups (ethnic, racial, political), nations, or blocs (NATO, SEATO, Warsaw Pact). The issues may be rights or privileges, control over resources, political power, or, in extreme cases, the very existence of the participants as systems. The means may range from persuasive arguments to physical annihilation.

A systematic taxonomy of this sort could be represented by a three-dimensional table (participants versus issues versus means) where the cells would be filled with examples of each type – for example, a war between two states fought for, say, control of territory, with armies as means. Such an exercise would be of doubtful theoretical value and might actually be misleading by giving the impression that conflicts can be neatly pigeonholed into readily recognizable categories. In most cases, the issues of conflicts are mixed and vague, and the means are not independent of the issues and the participants. The participants may seem to be recognizable, but only because certain conventional labels have been affixed to them. For instance, there is said to be racial conflict in the United States. Yet, it is certainly not true that every person labeled 'white' is in conflict with every person labeled 'black'. 'Racial conflict' is a label given to one vaguely defined class of events which give the impression that two racial groups are aligned against each other.

The matter is no clearer with regard to issues. In a political campaign and in an international war, the 'issues' are usually announced and widely publicized. In many cases, however, the stated issues cannot be taken seriously, because they are too often used for the purpose of rallying support rather than to define goals to be achieved. Typically, the words used to describe the issues have no clear referents.

Nor do the three aspects of conflict mentioned exhaust the list. One can well examine conflicts in their historical role and with regard to their genesis and their impact on the course of history. Marx, as we have seen, viewed class conflict in this way; to him, instances of it appeared as manifestations of the same on-going historical process, even though the participants and the issues kept changing in different historical settings.

In offering a classification of conflicts here, the categories used will relate to the sort of *systems* involved. The nature of the systems in conflict, I believe, determines the interactions between them, and, hence, the nature of the conflict and its psychological, sociological, and historical import. In what follows, then, the theoretical approach to conflict will lean frankly toward the systemic view.

The classification will be guided also by relating a type of conflict to the way it is resolved. 'Conflict resolution' is an unfortunate term because it connotes reconciliation. There ought to be a more general term designating the cessation of conflict, whether by conciliation, disengagement, or destruction of one, or both, or all of the participants, and it is in this general sense that I mean the phrase 'the way it is resolved'. Therefore, when 'conflict resolution' is mentioned, it will be specified whether 'resolution' is meant in the wide sense of cessation, or in the narrower sense of reconciliation.

First, the distinction will be made between exogenous and endogenous conflicts. *Endogenous* conflicts are to be understood as those wherein the conflicting systems are parts of a larger system that has its own mechanisms for maintaining a steady state, which may include mechanisms for controlling or resolving conflict between the subsystems. Thus, when two citizens of a State engage in conflict, the State (the larger system) usually has at its disposal ways of preventing the conflict from exceeding certain bounds (such as resort to violence) and, in addition, institutions for resolving the conflict (courts etc.). On the other hand, when two States are in conflict, there may be no super-system to exercise control or resolve conflict. In that case, we speak of an *exogenous* conflict. (As will be seen, whether a conflict is the one or the other may not always be easy to decide. Even an inter-nation war may have some characteristics of an endogenous conflict. A civil war is an example of the ambiguity.)

A second distinction will be made between symmetric and asymmetric conflicts. In *symmetric* conflict, the participants are roughly similar systems and perceive themselves as such. Thus, two individuals in a fight, say, man and wife, or two comparable nations at war, are typical examples of symmetric conflict. In *asymmetric* conflict, the systems may be widely disparate or may perceive each other in different ways. A revolt or a revolution is an example of an asymmetric conflict. The system revolted against 'perceives' itself as defending order and legitimacy; the insurgents 'perceive' themselves as an instrument of social change or of bringing a new system into being. Asymmetric conflicts may be either endogenous or exogenous. Political opposition to a regime is an example of the former type; colonial conquest of 'backward' peoples is of the latter.

An additional distinction, closely related to that between symmetric and asymmetric conflicts, is that between issue-oriented and structure-oriented conflict. An *issue-oriented* conflict is resolved when the issue is settled; the resolution does not involve a change in the structures of either of the conflicting systems or in the super-systems of which they are components. A *structure-oriented* conflict is not resolved unless the structure of either system or of the super-system changes.[1] The European wars of the eighteenth century were typical examples of issue-oriented conflicts. They were also symmetric. However, an asymmetric conflict may also be issue-oriented: for example, a civil suit involving a citizen and a state, or a strike where the labor union and the management are widely disparate systems. A revolution is always a structure-oriented conflict. If it is successful, a structural change occurs in the society affected; if it is crushed (in which case, it is usually called a rebellion), the revolutionary organization (a system) is usually destroyed.

Finally, we shall examine competition. The actors are typically several small systems, each in conflict with every other. Economic competition and struggles for power among individuals in organizations are typical examples. These conflicts are also symmetric but are distinguished by many participants, each pursuing his own 'interests'.

This taxonomy, like most, is no more than a formalization of idealized conceptions. In nature, there are no pure types separated by sharp boundaries, except possibly chemical elements (and even these are found upon closer examination to be mixtures of isotopic variants). The purpose of any taxonomy is to bring some order into our thinking. On occasions we see an instance of a conflict that can be distinctly categorized. In Chapter 17, specific examples are discussed. Here, for illustration, the Third Punic War can be cited as an instance of a clearly exogenous conflict, since there was no agency that could control, regulate, or resolve (in the narrow sense) the conflict between Rome and Carthage. The 'resolution' of this conflict in our extended sense of the word was the complete destruction of Carthage. On the other hand, the wars between the European states in the eighteenth century, though appearing to be exogenous, were not so entirely. Although the states were formally sovereign, not subject to external regulating power, there were internal constraints on the goals pursued and, consequently, on the means employed. The 'community of states' was a system of sorts, perpetuated in the interests of the rulers. But the preservation of the system was effected through the principle of 'balance of power', which precluded complete victory in the sense of the annihilation of any of the member states.

...

Similar ambiguity may blur the distinction between symmetric and asymmetric; and between issue-oriented and structure-oriented conflicts. The French Revolution was at first the culmination of a struggle against the established order (absolute monarchy). The intervention of monarchical powers stimulated the formation of a revolutionary citizens' army, which under Napoleon became an instrument of the French State. Thereupon the war became symmetric. It was, however, still structure-oriented, since Napoleon's goal was the transformation of the political structure of Europe.

In the early decades of the labor movement in industrialized countries, the conflict between workers and employers was not symmetric, since the coercive power of the State was largely at the disposal of only the employers. The conflict was in part structure-oriented, even when it was short of revolutionary (for example, the Chartists sought to introduce far-reaching changes into the social and political structure of England). When labor unions became legalized and powerful, conflicts became accordingly more symmetric and eventually entirely issue-oriented.

...

In addition to the taxonomy outlined above, I shall now offer another, based on the classification of conflicts as fights, games, and debates. The distinction here is among the various ways of perceiving the opponent.

In a fight, the opponent is perceived most clearly as an 'enemy', as one who threatens one's own autonomy simply by being present or existing. The 'normal' reaction to such a threat is an attempt to remove the perceived enemy from one's environment, by destroying him, cautioning him, or putting him to flight. (One's own flight from the presence of an enemy is, of course, an avoidance of a fight.) Attention is focused on the enemy, and actions are guided by strong emotional impulses which frequently block rational analysis. Animals as well as humans engage in fights and, of course, do not engage in rational analysis. Their actions are for the most part reactions to stimuli provided by 'the enemy' and are seldom, if ever, modified by learning; the actions persist as long as the stimuli emanating from the enemy persist. If these disappear, as for example, when the enemy flees, the fight ceases. In men, memory and learning impinge on practically all behavior patterns, so that the psychological correlates of a fight may by no means disappear when the enemy is no longer physically present. So as long as the conflict is dominated primarily by the enemy as a noxious stimulus, either present or remembered, we can speak of fights, even in human situations.

A game is characterized by an analysis of a *situation* and of *other situations* foreseen as outcomes of *decisions*, both one's own and those of an opponent. The distinction between an enemy and an opponent is crucial. Whereas the enemy is defined by associated emotions and attitudes (for example, as someone who is hated or feared), the opponent in a game is not. The attitude toward the *person* of the opponent may be neutral or even entirely friendly. The focus of attention is not on the presence of noxious stimuli in the person of the opponent but on the *situation*, which the opponent partially controls. It is desired to bring about another situation, but the outcomes of one's actions are determined only partially by one's own decisions. The decisions of the opponent also influence the outcomes. Consequently, rational analysis is an indispensable feature of game behavior. The elimination of the opponent is not a central issue; the opponent is constrained by the rules of the game just as oneself is. A more desirable situation can be brought about by adopting a *strategy*, that is, a plan of action contingent on what the opponent can do in following his own interest.

The type of conflict just described is, of course, typical of so-called games of strategy – chess, bridge, etc. The opponent in such a game is not typically a personal enemy who must be eliminated or constrained in order to safeguard one's autonomy. In fact, the opponent is more often a personal friend. The opponent *cooperates* in keeping the game going, and the process of playing the game is typically a pleasant experience. The pleasure of the experience derives from the struggle itself. Since victory in this case is meaningful only if the rules of the game are adhered to, the player's resources are mobilized toward rational analysis. The task is to bring about a desirable situation (to 'win') *within* the constraints imposed by the rules of the game, among which is the fact that the opponent is trying to frustrate one's efforts. The opponent is therefore a *necessary* feature of the environment and of the satisfaction derived from it.

A *debate* is a conflict of ideas. In *Fights, Games, and Debates*[2] I defined the objective of this type of conflict as *converting* the opponent to one's own way of perceiving or evaluating the environment; that is, of turning the opponent into a confederate. Debates are essentially exchanges of verbal stimuli. It is, of course, true that most exchanges (conventionally called debates) are not directed toward converting the opponent. For example, two attorneys confronting each other in a courtroom are not trying to convince *each other* of the justice of their respective cases. They are trying to convince someone else, in particular the judge or the jury. Similarly, debates in legislative bodies are not usually undertaken with the view of convincing political opponents. Typically they serve the purpose of demonstrating to the debaters' supporting constituencies that their representatives are espousing their causes. Debates directed by opponents at each other rather than at a third party are rare. Nevertheless, it will serve some purpose here to single out the debate as a conflict where the object is to convince rather than to eliminate the opponent (as in a fight) or to outwit him (as in a game).

In short, the fight is dominated by affective components of conflict, the game, by rational ones, and the debate, by ideological ones.

It is tempting to draw a parallel between these components and the Freudian components of the psyche – the Id, the Ego, and the Superego. The Id, represented as the pleasure-principle determinant of action, stands for the here and now, a force that guides action along the gradient of increasing pleasure or of decreasing pain, without regard for consequences. The Ego, representing rationality, guides the action along lines perceived as leading to more desirable situations, that is, in the problem-solving mode. The Superego, representing the imperatives imposed by the culture – that is, by the symbolic environment – is the manifestation of ideological commitments. Both the Id and the Superego offer resistance to rational analysis, the former, by pressure of immediate desires, the latter, by guilt associated with challenging the imposed imperatives.

It should be clear that, as in the preceding taxonomy, the three types of conflict singled out are idealizations. Only among animals are conflicts (if manifested in combats) all purely fight-like. A game of strategy or an ideological conflict are both entirely outside the scope of the psychic repertoire of non-humans. In human beings, on the other hand, conflicts are typically mixtures of these three, war being an outstanding example. In war, the enemy is typically very much a real enemy to be destroyed or constrained. There is, nevertheless, a strategic aspect of war, presenting problems that invite rational analysis and a strategic mode of action. Many wars (although not all) have also been pervaded by ideological issues. It is only for the purpose of analysis that I have separated the affective, the rational, and the ideological components of human conflict.

Notes

1 For a discussion of this aspect of conflict, see, for example, J. Galtung, 'A Structural Theory of Aggression', *Journal of Peace Research*, 1964, No. 2, pp. 95–119.

2 A. Rapoport, *Fights, Games, and Debates* (Ann Arbor: University of Michigan Press, 1960), Part III.

9

The Management of Protracted Social Conflict

Edward Azar

Edward Azar grew up in a small village in Lebanon but finished his formal education with a PhD from Stanford. He entered the field of conflict analysis as part of the 'events data' movement of the 1970s and 1980s which sought to discern important action–reaction patterns between states within large datasets which were open to quantitative analysis. Between 1982 and 1987 he established a highly productive intellectual partnership at the University of Maryland with John Burton, which involved theorizing about protracted social conflict and practical interventions into conflicts such as those in Sri Lanka and in Lebanon. The extract below is from Azar's seminal work on conflicts in postcolonial societies.

* * * *

I. Introduction

Conflict is an inseparable part of social interactions. Conflict cannot take place without involvement of two or more parties. Mutually incompatible goals among parties amidst a lack of coordinating or mediating mechanisms give birth to conflict. In this broad sense, conflict is a generic social phenomenon involving individuals, societies, states, and their collectivities. In the 1950s, several scholars attempted to group various forms of conflicts (family, community, political, class) under one ontological entity: social conflict. Even interstate wars and other external conflictual behaviors were interpreted as subsets of social conflicts. Thus, the study of conflicts was framed by multidisciplinary and holistic approaches (see Boulding: 1956; Coser: 1956; Janowitz: 1964; Simmel: 1955).

Over the last three decades, however, the study of wars, crises and conflicts has gradually become compartmentalized and differentiated. *First*, a tendency has emerged to understand conflicts through a rather rigid dichotomy of internal and external dimensions. While sociologists, anthropologists, psychologists and others have been preoccupied with internal or domestic conflicts (civil wars, insurgencies, revolts, coups, protests, riots, revolutions *etc.*), external conflictual behavior (interstate wars, crises, invasions, border conflicts, blockades, *etc.*) has become an exclusive domain of investigation by international relations scholars. Some have attempted to link these internal and external dimensions of conflict. A number of scholars have traced domestic sources of external conflictual behavior by focusing on domestic political structures (Kissinger: 1969; Rosenau: 1966; Rummel: 1963), domestic conflicts or disorders (Rummel: 1973; Wilkenfeld: 1973), and population pressures and resource bases (Choucri and North: 1975; Pirages: 1976). On the other hand, several sociologists have identified external-systemic factors as independent variables responsible for domestic conflicts. Eisenstadt and Rokkan (1973), Paige (1968), and Skocpol (1979) have drawn a conclusion that domestic conflict, revolutionary crises, or regime breakdown can be accounted for by looking into the pattern and structure of intrusion by international political, economic and military systems into the domestic realm.

The *second* important development is the field theoretic approach to conflict analysis following Quincy Wright (1942). Kenneth Waltz has emphasized the importance of multiple-level causation of conflict and the utility of analyzing interstate conflict in terms of the contrasting images of man, state and society (Waltz: 1959). The study of domestic conflict has also been dominated by theories addressing different levels of causation, organized around concepts such as cognitive frustration-aggression, structural-functional deformity, inter-group competition, or the intrusion of systemic factors. By coupling this multilevel understanding of causation with functional issue areas, conflicts are further sub-categorized into psychological, social, political, economic, and military conflicts.

Finally, apart from this internal-external polarization and functional differentiation of conflict types, students of conflict appear to share consensual knowledge of the behavioral dynamics of conflicts. However, regardless of source and type, conflicts are generally conceived as such only when they are *overt and violent*. *Covert*, *latent* or *non-violent* conflicts are seldom regarded as appropriate objects of study. Moreover, conflicts are understood from an organic cycle perspective. Every conflict is thought to go through a cycle of genesis, maturity, reduction, and termination. The termination of violent acts is often equated with the state of peace (Yaniv and Katz: 1980).

The field is full of good ideas, but more knowledge is needed. Indeed, we need to study more systematically the type of conflict that does not fit exactly into the above classifications, a type which we have called 'protracted social conflict' (Azar *et al.*: 1978; Azar and Cohen: 1981; Azar: 1986). For example, many conflicts currently active in the underdeveloped parts of the world are characterized by a blurred demarcation between internal and external sources and actors. Moreover, there are multiple causal factors and dynamics, reflected in changing goals, actors and targets. Finally, these conflicts do not show clear starting and terminating points.

II. Protracted Social Conflict: Genesis, Dynamics and Outcomes

A. Genesis

The genesis component of our model identifies a set of conditions that are responsible for the transformation of non-conflictual situations into conflictual ones. In addition, it traces the pattern of causal relations among these conditions which give rise to a specific protracted social conflict. On the following page is an illustration (diagram 1.1) of the

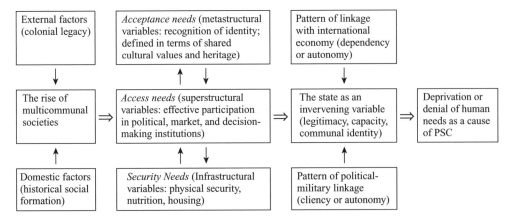

Diagram 1.1 *Genesis and Dynamics of Protracted Social Conflict (PSC)*

relationship between four clusters of variables (communal content, needs, governance and the role of the state, and international linkages) which are preconditions for protracted social conflict.

1. Communal content

Perhaps the most significant factor related to a protracted social conflict is the communal content of a society. If a society is characterized by multicommunal composition, protracted social conflicts are most likely to arise. (We use the term *community* as a generic reference to politicized groups whose members share ethnic, religious, linguistic or other cultural 'identity' characteristics.)

There are two factors which are responsible for the rise of politically active multicommunal societies. The first is colonial legacy. Application of the principle of 'divide and rule' by colonialists produced a unique political landscape in many parts of the world where a state artificially incorporated a multitude of communal groups (such as occurred in Lebanon, Israel, Malaysia) or a nation became divided into two or more states (*e.g.*, Korea). The second factor is a historical pattern of rivalry and contest among communal actors. Multicommunal societies, whether formed through the colonizing process or through intercommunal struggle, are characterized by disarticulation between the state and society as a whole, with the state usually dominated by a single communal group or a coalition of a few communal groups that are unresponsive to the needs of other groups in the society. Imposed integration or incorporation of distinctive and often conflictual communities into one political entity retards the nation-building process, strains the social fabric and eventually breeds fragmentation and protracted social conflict (see Alcock: 1972; Azar: 1986, 1979; Kriesberg: 1982; Osgood: 1979; Pruitt and Rubin: 1986).

2. Human needs

We assume that individuals strive to fulfill their developmental human needs through the formation of identity groups. A community is an identity group. The most obvious ontological need is individual and communal physical survival and well-being. Individual or communal survival is contingent upon the satisfaction of material needs. In the world of physical scarcity, these basic needs are seldom *evenly* or *justly* met. While one group of individuals may enjoy satisfaction of those needs in abundance, others do not. Grievances resulting from need deprivation are usually expressed collectively. Failure to redress these grievances by the authority cultivates a niche for a protracted social conflict.

In reality, however, the deprivation of basic material needs *per se* does not directly give birth to conflicts. The allocation of exchange of the means to satisfy such needs is a function of *access* to the superstructure of society; *i.e.*, social institutions such as political authority or the market. Therefore, access to social institutions (that is, effective participation in society) is a crucial determinant for satisfying physical needs. Effective participation may thus also be considered a developmental need, rather than merely an *interest* which can be negotiated or denied. As is the case with scarce material values, however, a fair and just allocation of access or participation is rare in a stratified human society. Unequal distribution tends to be more pronounced in a multicommunal society where social goods involving access needs (*e.g.*, positional values) are in limited supply, in comparison to the heterogeneous and diverse demand for them.

The lack of means to satisfy basic physical needs in Third World countries is often attributed to the nature of the economic development strategy adopted (see Burton: 1984a; Maslow: 1954; Sites: 1973). Typically, an unbalanced, rapid-growth development strategy has distorted the traditional allocation of resources, leading to sectoral and regional imbalances. Certain groups of individuals, especially minority communal groups, tend to be marginalized by such rapid development strategies (see Brown: 1985; De Janvry: 1981).

In such situations, the marginalized groups create a menu of responses designed to redress their grievances. Correcting and restructuring responses are usually a function of the level of access to economic decision-making. Participation in economic decision-making is in turn determined by the overall distribution of political power. It is in this nexus that the deprivation of physical needs soon leads to discord over the just and fair distribution of political and economic power.

Access to political and economic power is by and large influenced by the level of acceptance of each community. If the ruling political elites were to recognize and politically accommodate alienated communities, then discords over the distribution of political and economic power could be managed satisfactorily. In many cases, however, deprivation of physical needs and denial of access are rooted in the refusal to recognize or accept the communal *identity* of other groups. Formation and acceptance of identity thus also may be understood as a basic developmental need, with collective identity manifest in terms of cultural values, images, customs, language, religion, and racial heritage.

Consider the example of South Africa. Blacks are denied access to social institutions precisely on the basis of their racial identity. A claim of superior identity (*i.e.*, white supremacy), rather than objective conditions (*e.g.*, economic or political motives), largely determines the nature and scope of the denial of security and identity needs of blacks.

Such denial fosters greater cohesion within victimized communal groups, and may work to promote collective violence and protract the conflict if no other means of satisfaction is available.

As another example, the perpetuation of violence in Lebanon can be ascribed more to conflict over acceptance and security of communal identity than to the acquisition of needed physical resources or power. The satisfaction of needs for communal security, fair governance by the ruling elites, and acceptance and recognition of cultural diversity, are all basic to nation-state building in that country. The deprivation of security cannot be understood without reference to equitable access to the institutions of government, cultural tolerance and acceptance of diversity. The deprivation of one form of developmental need usually leads to problems in other areas. Therefore, to elucidate the complex relationship among these needs is an important step toward understanding the causes of any protracted social conflict.

3. Governance and the state's role

Deprivation or satisfaction of human needs for physical security, access to political and social institutions, and acceptance of communal identity (*i.e.*, political pluralism) is largely a result of social, political and economic interactions. In the modern world, the regulation of such interactions, and thus the satisfaction of these basic needs, is undertaken by the political authority called *the state*. The state is endowed with authority to govern and to use force where necessary to regulate society, to protect citizens, and to provide collective goods. Therefore, the level of satisfaction or deprivation of basic needs is generally influenced by the intervening or mediating role of the state. Indeed, an ideal state characterized by a fair and just mode of governance should be able to satisfy human needs regardless of communal or identity cleavages, and promote communal harmony and social stability. In actuality however, this is rare. Most states which experience protracted social conflict tend to be characterized by incompetent, parochial, fragile, and authoritarian governments that fail to satisfy basic human needs.

Most states in protracted social conflict-laden countries are hardly neutral. In democratic societies, the state is an aggregate of individuals entrusted to govern effectively and to act as an impartial arbiter of conflicts among the constituent parts. Empirically, however, the world behaves differently. Political authority tends to be monopolized by a dominant identity group or a coalition of hegemonic groups. These groups tend to use the state as an instrument for maximizing their interests at the expense of others. In the protracted social conflict context, these groups have manifested in communal terms. The monopoly of political authority by one or more groups denies the state a capacity for fair and successful governance. As a result, the means to satisfy basic needs are unevenly shared and the potential for protracted social conflict increases. In this regard, the communal content of the state becomes basic to our study of protracted social conflict.

Further, the domination of the state apparatus by one or few communal groups is achieved through the distortion of modes of governance. To sustain their monopoly of power, these dominant groups limit access to social institutions by other identity groups and thus often precipitate crises of *legitimacy*. Such crises exacerbate already existing competitive or conflictive situations, diminish the state's ability to meet basic needs, and lead to further developmental crises. Thus, regime type and the level of legitimacy are important linkage variables between needs and protracted social conflict.

Protracted social conflicts seem to be concentrated in the developing countries, although they are not limited to the developing world. These countries are typically characterized by rapid population growth and a limited resource base. Poor resource environments amid population expansion will constrain policy options. Accordingly, the availability of resources becomes an important indicator of a state's ability to satisfy needs and prevent conflict.

Equally important is the nature of the *policy capacity* of the state, in which framework basic needs are evaluated and policies are formulated and implemented. Policy capacity is about governance and the effectiveness of the state. It is largely determined by the nature of the authority structure and the resulting pattern of decision-making. In most protracted social conflict-laden countries, policy capacity is limited by a rigid or fragile authority structure which prevents the state from responding to, and meeting, the needs of various constituents. This happens because the state is often unable to insulate the decision-making machinery from the political pressures of the dominant identity groups. Thus, the relative strength and autonomy of the state is directly linked to the level of satisfying basic needs.

4. International linkages

The role of the state in engendering or preventing protracted social conflicts by depriving or satisfying basic needs is not determined solely by endogenous factors, such as the political power configuration underlying the authority structure and regime type. Formation of domestic social and political institutions and their impact on the role of the state are greatly influenced by the patterns of linkage with the international system. Two models of international linkage can be conceived.

The first of these models focuses on economic *dependency* within the international economic system. Such a dependent relationship not only limits the autonomy of the state, but also distorts the pattern of economic development, impeding the satisfaction of security needs. Moreover, dependency often exacerbates denial of the access needs of communal groups, distorting domestic political and economic systems through the realignment of subtle coalitions of international capital, domestic capital, and the state.

The second of these international linkage models focuses on political and military *client* relationships with strong states. In a client relationship, the patron provides protection for the client state in return for the latter's loyalty. Client loyalty and obedience involves some sacrifice of autonomy and independence, which induces the client state to pursue both domestic and foreign policies disjoined from, or contradictory to, the needs of its own public. The behavior of Lebanese governments over the last four decades is an open data base for illustrating this point. The support for the Baghdad Pact in 1955 (encouraging US anti-communist actions in the region following Nasser's rise to power) and the government's acceptance of the 1969 Cairo Accords (giving the PLO the right to use southern Lebanon as a base for its war against Israel) are but two examples of how loss of autonomy and increased dependency can lead governments to trap themselves in situations which constrain satisfaction of the national need for intercommunal trust and harmony.

In brief, protracted social conflicts occur when communities are deprived of satisfaction of their basic needs on the basis of their communal identity. However, the deprivation is the result of a complex causal chain involving the role of the state and the pattern of international linkages. Furthermore, initial conditions (colonial legacy, domestic historical setting, and the multicommunal nature of the society) play important roles in shaping the genesis of protracted social conflict.

B. Process dynamics

The previous discussion identifies preconditions for the rise of a protracted social conflict. In reality, however, the existence or even recognition of these conditions by communal groups may not lead to an overt or manifest conflict. Our model of the process dynamics of protracted social conflicts attempts to elucidate factors which are responsible for the *activation* of overt conflicts. We identify as key determinants the interactive effects of three clusters of variables: communal actions and strategies, state actions and strategies, and built-in properties of conflict. (Please see diagram 1.2 below.)

1. Communal actions and strategies

Like other forms of conflict, a protracted social conflict remains latent until some effective triggers begin to operate. When organizational and communication systems break down within an environment of mutual distrust between groups, protracted social conflict can begin to escalate. Initially a trigger may, but need not be, a trivial event (*e.g.*, an insult to an individual with strong communal ties). But the trivial event tends to become a turning point at which the individual victimization is *collectively* recognized. Collective

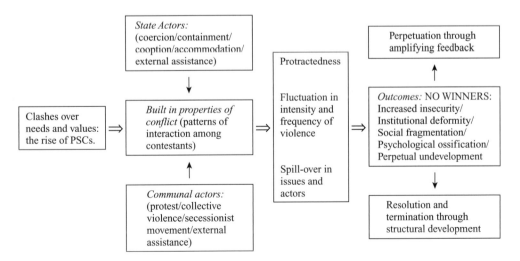

Diagram 1.2 *Process-level Dynamics and Outcomes of Protracted Social Conflict*

recognition of individual grievances (or incompatible goals) naturally leads to collective protest. Collective protest is usually met by some degree of repression or suppression. As tension increases, the victimized communal groups begin to draw the attention of their constituents not only to the event itself, but also to a broad range of issues involving communal security, access, and acceptance needs (*e.g.*, selective poverty and political inequality). The spill-over of the event into multiple issues increases the momentum for organizing and mobilizing resources. As the level of communal organization and mobilization becomes greater, communal groups attempt to formulate more diverse strategies and tactics, which may involve civil disobedience, guerrilla warfare or secessionist movements.

Demands for greater autonomy and independence may invite coercive responses, rather than accommodation and concessions, from the ruling elites or their constituents. Since the balance of power is generally in favor of the state, the communal groups tend to seek external military and economic assistance. Because national boundaries of protracted social conflict-laden countries were often defined without adequately taking into account the distribution of communal groups, appeals for assistance tend to gain neighboring actors' support. Often this external support is associated with hegemonic designs, which lead to attempts at co-option and destabilization. By manipulating communal tensions, a neighboring nation can enlist the support of disenfranchised groups to subvert their nation's ruling regime. Assistance is given as a means of furthering the regional power-play that many (especially Third World) nations are engaged in. At this stage, the internal and external demarcations of conflicts become blurred as domestic communal conflicts become regional.

In sum, the type of initial conditions, the organization and mobilization of communal groups, the emergence of effective leadership, the strategies and tactics of this leadership, and the scope and nature of external ties, become important determinants of the dynamics of protracted social conflicts. But these variables themselves are influenced by the responses of political authorities. In this context, state strategies and tactics are another crucial determinant of the behavioral properties of protracted social conflicts.

2. State actions and strategies

A protracted social conflict can be resolved or at least kept latent if the state *accommodates* communal grievances and improves the satisfaction of communal needs in the initial stage. But accommodation strategies are seldom employed. It is not only because of the political and economic costs involved, but also because of the norm of 'winner-take-all' which still prevails in multicommunal societies. Any authentic accommodation or concession may be perceived as a sign of defeat. Therefore, the state usually avoids such a strategy and employs *coercive repression* or *instrumental co-option*.

In many cases, a militant, harsh response constitutes the core of state strategy in coping with communal dissent. Such a hard-line strategy invites equally militant responses from the repressed groups. Co-option could serve to mitigate communal grievances, but it is usually perceived as being a tactical maneuver to fragment the opposition and divert its attention. Failure of the co-option strategy further justifies coercive, repressive options, leading to an upward spiral of violent clashes. Under these circumstances, states try to *contain* a conflict situation within a national boundary by attempting to sever links between domestic communal actors and external support groups. When such containment strategies do not work, the state (or dominant communal actor that monopolizes state authority) seeks its own *external assistance*. The existing dependency and client ties facilitate direct or indirect intervention of external powers, which not only amplifies the scope of the conflict, but also makes it more protracted.

3. Built-in mechanisms of conflict

Apart from the strategies and organizational capabilities of state and communal actors, the history of experience in the conflict and the nature of communication among hostile contestants are also responsible for the shaping of the behavioral properties of protracted conflict.

Conflicts associated with communal identity and fear of marginalization or loss of communal integrity, tend to involve an enduring antagonistic set of perceptions and interactions between and among communal groups and the state. The perceptions and motivations behind the behavior of the state and communal actors are conditioned by the experiences, fears and belief system of each communal group. In a situation of limited or proscribed interactions, the worst motivations tend to be attributed to the other side. There is little possibility of falsification, and the consequence is reciprocal negative images which perpetuate communal antagonisms and solidify protracted social conflict.

Parties subject to the continual stresses of protracted conflict tend to become closed-minded. In these cases, proposals for political solutions become rare, and tend to be perceived by all sides as mechanisms for gaining relative power and control. At this stage, hostility begets hostility and the process becomes institutionalized (Gurr: 1970). This mechanism of a conflict spiral, set in motion by communal fear and hostility, gains velocity with the deepening of the deprivation of basic needs. Therefore, it becomes important to analyze the perceptions and cognitive processes generated through experience of conflictual interactions, such as premature closure, misattribution of motives, stereotyping, tunnel vision, bolstering and polarization (Mitchell: 1981).

C. Outcome analysis

Most conflicts, as classically understood, involve zero-sum outcomes in which winners and losers can be differentiated. But protracted social conflicts result in negative-sum outcomes because of their innate behavioral properties: *protractedness, fluctuation,* and *actor and issue spill-over*. There are no winners: rather, all the parties to these conflicts tend to be victimized in the process. Protracted conflicts, unlike other forms of conflict, do not have clear termination points. Outcomes (military victories, negotiated agreements, *etc.*), insofar as they do not satisfy basic needs, contain latent conflicts which cause further cycles of manifest conflict, often involving a shift or spill-over in issues and actors. The perpetuation of social conflict in the Third World has thus proved to be devastating in terms of physical, psychological, political and economic costs.

In protracted conflict situations, development programs cease to function effectively, and economic retrenchment takes place. An acute trade-off in state expenditure between the maintenance of internal security and provision of welfare occurs and greatly undermines the satisfaction of basic needs. Even worse is the psychological damage and disorientation of individuals entrapped in a protracted conflict situation. They become vulnerable to absorption in a violent war culture, further separating them from normal civil life.

The process of protracted conflict deforms and retards the effective operation of political institutions. It reinforces and strengthens pessimism throughout the society, demoralizes leaders and immobilizes the search for peaceful solutions. We have observed that societies undergoing protracted social conflict find it difficult to initiate the search for answers to their problems and grievances. As the protracted conflict becomes part of the culture of the ravaged nation, it builds a sense of paralysis which afflicts the collective consciousness of the population. An environment of hopelessness permeates all strata of society, and a siege mentality develops which inhibits constructive negotiation for any resolution of the conflict.

The one element that polarizes the parties most is fear. Protracted social conflicts are rooted in fear of marginalization. Affected communities' paranoia regarding each other often leads to alliances of convenience with external actors. This state of affairs encourages dependency on external parties rather than reliance on one's own abilities and resources. Inviting outside actors to become involved simply promotes the entrenchment of a cycle of dependency, violent conflict and despair.

In short, protracted social conflicts generate (and are further reinforced by) the following conditions:

1. Deterioration of physical security

This is the most obvious consequence, exacerbating initial conditions of insecurity through further loss of life and means of support. Apart from physical destruction, protracted social conflict institutionalizes underdevelopment through the destruction of physical and social infrastructures. Efforts to pursue systematic development planning are halted and discarded as excessive military expenditure absorbs scarce resources. A vicious cycle of underdevelopment and conflict deprives not only the victimized communities, but also the dominant groups, of the economic resources for satisfying basic needs.

2. Institutional deformity

Degeneration of socio-economic and political institutions, which makes the satisfaction of communities' access needs virtually impossible, occurs in two distinctive ways. One is *de facto* paralysis of political institutions. Central governments become weak and consequently cease to effectively perform their functions of regulation, extraction, allocation and arbitration. The other form of degeneration is further fragmentation of the broader social fabric. At the onset of conflict, social and economic institutions mediating communal interrelationships may still be functional, and communal boundaries permeable. As conflict protracts, however, communal cleavages become petrified, and the prospects for cooperative interaction and nation-building become poor.

3. Psychological ossification

Protracted social conflict entails a vicious cycle of fear and hostile interactions among the communal contestants. With the continued stress of such conflict, attitudes, cognitive processes and perceptions become set and ossified. War culture and cynicism dominate. Meaningful communication between or among conflicting parties dries up, and the ability to satisfy communal acceptance needs is severely diminished.

4. Increased dependency and cliency

As conflict protracts, communal actors rely more and more on support and aid from others and thus external actors are systematically drawn into the conflict. Decision-making power is increasingly exercised by external actors, so that communities suffer further loss of access and control over their lives.

These entrenched conflicts provide the most severe challenge to those concerned with peace-building. Their apparent intractibility suggests that conventional approaches have been too narrowly conceived, failing to address the underlying dynamics which drive protracted conflicts.

References

Alcock, N. (1972), *The War Disease*, Oakville, Ontario: C.P.R.I. Press.

Azar, E.E. (1986), 'Management of Protracted Social Conflict in the Third World,' Ethnic Studies Report, 4, no.2.

Azar, E.E., *et al.*, (1978), 'Protracted Social Conflict: Theory and Practice in the Middle East,' *Journal of Palestine Studies*, 8, 1.

Azar, E.E. and S.P. Cohen (1981), 'The Transition from War to Peace between Israel and Egypt,' *Journal of Conflict Resolution*, 25, no.1, pp. 87–114.

Boulding, K. (1956), *The Image*, Ann Arbor: University of Michigan Press.

Brown, L. (1985), *The State of the World, 1985*, Washington, D.C.: The Worldwatch Institute.

Burton, J.W. (1984a), *Global Conflict: The Domestic Sources of International Crisis*, Brighton, England: Wheatsheaf.

Choucri, N. and R. North (1975), *Nations in Conflict: National Growth and International Violence*, San Francisco: W.H. Freeman.

Coser, L. (1956), *The Functions of Social Conflict*, New York: The Free Press.

De Janvry, A. (1981), *The Agrarian Question and Reformism in Latin America*, Baltimore: Johns Hopkins University Press.

Eisenstadt, S.N. and R. Rokkan (1973), *Building States and Nations*, Vol. I and II, Beverly Hills, CA: Sage Publications.

Gurr, T. (1970), *Why Men Rebel*, Princeton: Princeton University Press.

Janowitz, M. (1964), *The Military in the Political Development of New Nations*, Chicago: University of Chicago Press.

Kissinger, H. (1969), *American Foreign Policy: Three Essays*, New York: Norton.

Kreisberg, L. (1982), *Social Conflicts*, Englewood Cliffs, NJ: Prentice-Hall.

Maslow, A.H. (1954), *Motivation and Personality*, New York: Harper and Row.

Mitchell, C.R. (1981), *The Structure of International Conflict*, London: Macmillan.

Osgood, R.E. (1979), *Limited War Revisited*, Boulder, CO: Westview Press.

Paige, G. (1968), *The Korean Decision, June 24–30, 1950*, New York: Free Press.

Pirages, D. (1976), *Managing Political Conflict*, New York: Praeger.

Pruitt, D.G. and J.Z. Rubin (1986), *Social Conflict: Escalation, Stalemate, and Settlement*, New York: Random House.

Rosenau, J.N. (ed.) (1966), *Contending Approaches to International Politics*, Princeton: Princeton University Press.

Rummel, R.J. (1973), *The Dimensions of Nations*, Beverly Hills, CA: Sage Publications.

Rummel, R.J. (1963), 'Dimensions of Conflict Behavior within and between Nations,' in *General Systems Yearbook*, no. 8, pp. 1–50.

Simmel, G. (1955) *'Conflict' and 'The Web of Group-affiliations'*, New York: The Free Press.

Sites, P. (1973), *Control, the Basis of Social Order*, London: Dunellen Publishers.

Skocpol, T. (1979), *States and Social Revolutions: A Comparative Analysis of France, Russia and China*, Cambridge: Cambridge University Press.

Waltz, K. (1959), *Man, the State and War*, New York: Columbia University Press.

Wilkenfeld, J. (1973), *Conflict Behavior & Linkage Politics*, New York: D. McKay Co.

Wright, Q. (1942), *A Study of War*, Chicago: University of Chicago Press.

Yaniv, A. and E. Katz (1980), 'M.A.D., Detente and Peace: A Hypothesis on the Evolution of International Conflicts and Its Mathematico-Deductive Extension,' *International Interactions*, 7 (3), pp. 223–40.

10

The Functions of Social Conflict

Lewis Coser

The sociologist Lewis Coser once said that he did not want to be known as 'Coser – the conflict man', but his clear reanalysis of the ideas of his early twentieth-century predecessor, Georg Simmel, about the potentially beneficial effects of social conflict inevitably gives him a place in the pantheon of early conflict resolution theorists. This extract from his short but influential book deals with the manner in which being in a conflict with outsiders often produces increased levels of within-group loyalty and suppresses internal conflict and criticism.

*   *   *   *

Proposition I: Group-Binding Functions of Conflict

"A certain amount of discord, inner divergence and outer controversy, is organically tied up with the very elements that ultimately hold the group together ... the positive and integrating role of antagonism is shown in structures which stand out by the sharpness and carefully preserved purity of their social divisions and gradations. Thus, the Hindu social system rests not only on the hierarchy, but also directly on the mutual repulsion, of the castes. Hostilities not only prevent boundaries within the group from gradually disappearing ... often they provide classes and individuals with reciprocal positions which they would not find ... if the causes of hostility were not accompanied by the feeling and the expression of hostility."[1]

A CLARIFICATION IS NECESSARY HERE. Simmel shifts between sociological and psychological statements, as when he passes from discussion of personal autonomy to group autonomy, thus obscuring the fact that although the personality and the social system may be partly homologous and although they interpenetrate, they are by no means identical.[2] Genetic psychology[3] and psychoanalysis have gathered much evidence to suggest that conflict is a most important agent for the establishment of full ego identity and autonomy, i.e., for full differentiation of the personality from the outside world. However, this problem will not be the concern of the present study which intends to deal primarily with the behavior of individuals in groups. For this reason, "feelings of hostility and repulsion" will be discussed only where they are part of a social *pattern*, i.e., where their regular occurrence can be observed. Individual behavior which is merely idiosyncratic has no place in the analysis of structured social systems.

Turning to the sociological content of the proposition, we note that Simmel deals with two related yet distinct phenomena. He holds first that conflict sets boundaries between groups within a social system by strengthening group consciousness and awareness of separateness, thus establishing the identity of groups within the system. And second, he says that reciprocal "repulsions" maintain a total social system by creating a balance between its various groups. For example, conflicts between Indian castes may establish the separateness and distinctiveness of the various castes, but may also insure the stability of the total Indian social structure by bringing about a balance of claims by rival castes. Elsewhere Simmel has stressed even more strongly the group-binding character of conflict.[4]

This insight is, of course, not new. We could quote similar statements from social theorists since antiquity. Writing at the same time as Simmel, William Graham Sumner, in his discussion of in-group and out-group relations, expressed essentially the same idea.[5]

Familiar as this insight is, it is not necessarily incorporated in all contemporary sociological theory. Thus Parsons in his recent work,[6] while stressing that social systems are of the "boundary-maintaining" type, i.e., that they must maintain delimitations between themselves and the environment if they are to keep constancies of pattern, fails to mention conflict in this connection.

This function of conflict in establishing and maintaining group identities has been accorded a certain place in the work of theorists such as Georg Sorel and Karl Marx. Sorel's advocacy of "violence" is to be understood entirely in terms of his awareness of the close relations between conflict and group cohesion.[7] He felt that only if the working class is constantly engaged in warfare with the middle class can it preserve its distinctive character. Only through and in action can its members become conscious and aware of their class identity. Underlying his insistence that socialists, with whom he identified himself, must oppose humanitarian moves on the part of the governing classes, is the sociological dictum that such measures would lead to a decrease in class conflict and hence to a weakening of class identity. For Marx also, classes constitute themselves only through conflict. Individuals may have objective common positions in society, but they become aware of the community of their interests only in and through conflict. "The separate individuals form a class only in so far as they have to carry on a common battle against another class; otherwise they are on hostile terms with each other as competitors."[8]

It seems to be generally accepted by sociologists that the distinction between "ourselves, the we-group, or in-group, and everybody else, or the others-groups, out-groups"[9] is established in and through conflict. This is not confined to conflict between classes, although class conflicts have appeared as the most convenient illustrations to many observers. Nationality and ethnic conflicts, political conflicts, or conflicts between various strata in bureaucratic structures afford equally relevant examples.

Simmel goes on to say that enmities and reciprocal antagonisms also maintain the total system by establishing a balance between its component parts. This takes place, according to Simmel, because members of the same stratum or caste are drawn together in a solidarity resulting from their common enmity to and rejection of members of other strata or castes. In this way, a hierarchy of positions is maintained because of the aversion that the various members of the subgroups within the total society have for each other.

This view requires qualification. As has been pointed out,[10] out-groups, far from necessarily constituting targets of hostility, can also, under certain conditions, become positive references to the in-group. The out-group may be emulated as well as resented. Emulation is minimized only under certain conditions, for example, in a strict caste system such as the Indian in which there is no emphasis on social mobility and in which caste position is legitimized by relegous beliefs.[11] Although lower castes will look upon higher castes as their hierarchical superiors, they will not be likely to desire to move out of their own lower caste situation or to emulate the behavior of the higher caste.

The situation is fundamentally different in a class system that provides a substantial degree of social mobility. It remains true that status groups within the American system often regard each other with invidious or hostile feelings. It is also true that the structure of the system is maintained partly by these reciprocal antagonisms which preserve gradations of status. Nevertheless, members of the lower strata often emulate the higher, and aspire to membership in higher strata. Thus, voluntary associations in Yankee City[12] helped to organize the antagonisms of various "classes" to each other, but at the same time they functioned to "organize and regulate upward mobility." In societies in which upward social mobility is institutionalized, in which achieved rather than ascribed status dominates, hostility between various strata is mingled with a strong positive attraction to those higher in the social hierarchy, who provide some models of behavior. If there were no antagonisms, status groups would dissolve since boundaries between them and the outside would disappear; but these boundaries are kept fluid by the very fact that upward social mobility is the cultural ideal of such societies.

It is for this reason that feelings of interclass hostility typical in an open class system, as distinct from a caste system, are often likely to turn into *ressentiment*.[13] They do not indicate genuine rejection of the values or groups against which these negative feelings are directed, but rather a "sour-grapes" attitude: that which is condemned is secretly craved.

It should be noted that Simmel does not explicitly distinguish between feelings of hostility and the actual acting out of these feelings. There is an evident difference between the Indian caste system in which feelings of antagonism do not lead to open conflict and the American class system in which conflict (e.g., between management and labor) is a frequent and expected occurrence. Unequal distribution of privileges and rights may lead to sentiments of hostility, but they do not necessarily lead to conflict. A distinction between conflict and hostile sentiments is essential. Conflict, as distinct from hostile attitudes or sentiments, always takes place in interaction between two or more persons. Hostile attitudes are predispositions to engage in conflict behavior; conflict, on the contrary, is always a *trans*-action.

Whether feelings of hostility lead to conflict behavior depends in part on whether or not the unequal distribution of rights is considered legitimate. In the classical Indian caste system, intercaste conflict was rare because lower and higher castes alike accepted the caste distinctions. *Legitimacy* is a crucial intervening variable without which it is impossible to predict whether feelings of hostility arising out of an unequal distribution of privileges and rights will actually lead to conflict.

Before a social conflict between negatively and positively privileged groups can take place, before hostile attitudes are turned into social action, the negatively privileged group must first develop the awareness that it is, indeed, negatively privileged. It must come to believe that it is being denied rights to which it is entitled. It must reject any justification for the existing distribution of rights and privileges. Shifts in the degree of acceptance of a given distribution of power, wealth or status are closely connected with shifts in the selection of reference groups in varying social situations. In the Indian case discussed above, it would seem that changes in economic institutions (for example, from agriculture to industry, and concomitant opening of opportunities for mobility) have been instrumental in inducing the negatively privileged groups to change their definitions of self and others.

For our purposes, it need only be noted that when a social structure is no longer considered legitimate, individuals with similar objective positions will come, through conflict, to constitute themselves into self-conscious groups with common interests. This process of group formation will concern us further in the discussion of later propositions.

Social structures differ as to the degree of conflict which they tolerate. As will be seen in the next proposition, Simmel implies that where the structure inhibits the expression and acting out of hostile feelings, substitute mechanisms for the venting of such feelings can be expected to exist.

We can now rephrase Simmel's proposition:

Conflict serves to establish and maintain the identity and boundary lines of societies and groups.

Conflict with other groups contributes to the establishment and reaffirmation of the identity of the group and maintains its boundaries against the surrounding social world.

Patterned enmities and reciprocal antagonisms conserve social divisions and systems of stratification. Such patterned antagonisms prevent the gradual disappearance of boundaries between the subgroups of a social system and they assign position to the various subsystems within a total system.

In social structures providing a substantial amount of mobility, attraction of the lower strata by the higher, as well as mutual hostility between the strata, is likely to occur. Hostile feelings of the lower strata in this case frequently take the form of *ressentiment* in which hostility is mingled with attraction. Such structures will tend to provide many occasions for conflict since, as will be discussed later, frequency of occasions for conflict varies positively with the closeness of relations.

A distinction has to be made between conflict and hostile or antagonistic attitudes. Social conflict always denotes social interaction, whereas attitudes or sentiments are predispositions to engage in action. Such predispositions do not necessarily eventuate in conflict; the degree and kind of legitimation of power and status systems are crucial intervening variables affecting the occurrence of conflict.

Notes

1 Georg Simmel, *Conflict and the Web of Group Affiliations*, edited by Kurt Wolff (Glencoe, IL: The Free Press, 1955), pp. 17–18.

2 See in this respect Talcott Parsons and Edward A. Shils, "Values, Motives and Systems of Action," in *Toward a General Theory of Action* (Cambridge: Harvard University Press, 1952), esp. p. 109.

3 Especially the work of Jean Piaget.

4 *Soziologie* (Leipzig: Duncker and Humblot, 1908), pp. 610–11.

5 William Graham Sumner, *Folkways: A Study of the Sociological Importance of Usages, Manners, Customs, Mores, and Morals* (Boston, MA: Ginn and Co.), pp. 11–13.

6 Talcott Parsons, *The Social System, op. cit.*, p. 482. Cf. also Talcott Parsons and Edward A. Shils in *Toward a General Theory of Action* (*op. cit.*, p. 108), stressing the crucial significance of boundary-maintaining mechanisms for the maintenance of equilibrium of social as well as biological systems, but failing to mention conflict as one such mechanism.

7 Georg Sorel, *Reflections on Violence* (Glencoe, Illinois: The Free Press, 1950).

8 Karl Marx and Friedrich Engels, *The German Ideology* (New York: International Publishers, 1936), pp. 48–49.

9 Sumner, *Folkways, op. cit.*, p. 12.

10 Robert K. Merton and Alice S. Kitt, "Contributions to the Theory of Reference Group Behavior," in *Studies in the Scope and Method of "The American Soldier,"* Merton and Lazarsfeld (eds.), (Glencoe, Illinois: The Free Press, 1950), pp. 101–2.

11 For evidence for the fact that even the Indian caste system actually is not as immobile as often has been claimed, see Kingsley Davis, *Human Society* (New York: The Macmillan Co., 1949), pp. 378–85. For a more extended discussion, see the same author's *The Population of India and Pakistan* (Princeton: Princeton University Press, 1951).

12 Lloyd Warner and Paul S. Lunt, *The Social Life of a Modern Community* (New Haven: Yale University Press, 1941), esp. pp. 114–16.

13 Cf. Max Scheler, "Das Ressentiment im Aufbau der Moralen," in *Vom Umsturz der Werte*, Vol. I (Leipzig: Der Neue Geist Verlag, 1923), for the author's detailed discussion of this concept originally derived from Nietzsche. Cf. also Merton's comments in *Social Theory and Social Structure, op. cit.*, p. 145, and Svend Ranulf, *Moral Indignation and Middle Class Psychology* (Copenhagen: Munksgaard, 1938), *passim*.

11

The Strategy of Conflict

Tom Schelling

The recipient of a Nobel Prize for Economics in 2005, Tom Schelling's award talked about his achievements in using game theory to help understand conflict and cooperation, and it is true that the tradition in the field of using mathematical modelling and game theory owes much to pioneers such as Schelling. However, it owes much more in terms of applying rational thinking to realistic problems, as this extract demonstrates, as do his elegant writings on preventing nuclear war, problems of arms control, rational bargaining and the nature of genuine security.

*   *   *   *

Tacit Coordination (Common Interests)

When a man loses his wife in a department store without any prior understanding on where to meet if they get separated, the chances are good that they will find each other. It is likely that each will think of some obvious place to meet, so obvious that each will be sure that the other is sure that it is "obvious" to both of them. One does not simply predict where the other will go, since the other will go where he predicts the first to go, which is wherever the first predicts the second to predict the first to go, and so ad infinitum. Not "What would I do if I were she?" but "What would I do if I were she wondering what she would do if she were I wondering what I would do if I were she…?" What is necessary is to coordinate predictions, to read the same message in the common situation, to identify the one course of action that their expectations of each other can converge on. They must "mutually recognize" some unique signal that coordinates their expectations of each other. We cannot be sure they will meet, nor would all couples read the same signal; but the chances are certainly a great deal better than if they pursued a random course of search.

The reader may try the problem himself with the adjoining map (Fig. 1). Two people parachute unexpectedly into the area shown, each with a map and knowing the other has one, but neither knowing where the other has dropped nor able to communicate directly. They must get together quickly to be rescued. Can they study their maps and "coordinate" their behavior? Does the map suggest some particular meeting place so unambiguously that each will be confident that the other reads the same suggestion with confidence?

The writer has tried this and other analogous problems on an unscientific sample of respondents; and the conclusion is that people often can coordinate. The following

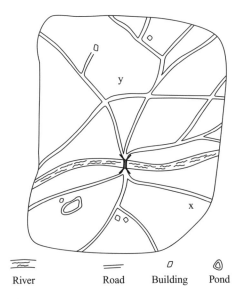

River   Road   Building   Pond

Figure 1

abstract puzzles are typical of those that can be "solved" by a substantial proportion of those who try. The solutions are, of course, arbitrary to this extent: any solution is "correct" if enough people think so. The reader may wish to confirm his ability to concert in the following problems with those whose scores are given in a footnote.[1]

1. Name "heads" or "tails." If you and your partner name the same, you both win a prize.
2. Circle one of the numbers listed in the line below. You win if you all succeed in circling the same number.

   7   100   13   261   99   555

3. Put a check mark in one of the sixteen squares. You win if you all succeed in checking the same square.

   ☐ ☐ ☐ ☐

   ☐ ☐ ☐ ☐

   ☐ ☐ ☐ ☐

   ☐ ☐ ☐ ☐

4. You are to meet somebody in New York City. You have not been instructed where to meet; you have no prior understanding with the person on where to meet; and you cannot communicate with each other. You are simply told that you will have to guess where to meet and that he is being told the same thing and that you will just have to try to make your guesses coincide.

5. You were told the date but not the hour of the meeting in No. 4; the two of you must guess the exact minute of the day for meeting. At what time will you appear at the meeting place that you elected in No. 4?

6. Write some positive number. If you all write the same number, you win.

7. Name an amount of money. If you all name the same amount, you can have as much as you named.

8. You are to divide $100 into two piles, labeled A and B.

Your partner is to divide another $100 into two piles labeled A and B. If you allot the same amounts to A and B, respectively, that your partner does, each of you gets $100; if your amounts differ from his, neither of you gets anything.

…

These problems are artificial, but they illustrate the point. People *can* often concert their intentions or expectations with others if each knows that the other is trying to do the same. Most situations – perhaps every situation for people who are practiced at this kind of game – provide some clue for coordinating behavior, some focal point for each person's expectation of what the other expects him to expect to be expected to do. Finding the key, or rather finding *a* key – any key that is mutually recognized as the key becomes *the* key – may depend on imagination more than on logic; it may depend on analogy, precedent, accidental arrangement, symmetry, aesthetic or geometric configuration, casuistic reasoning, and who the parties are and what they know about each other. Whimsy may send the man and his wife to the "lost and found"; or logic may lead each to reflect and to expect the other to reflect on where they would have agreed to meet if they had had a prior agreement to cover the contingency. It is not being asserted that they will always find an obvious answer to the question; but the chances of their doing so are ever so much greater than the bare logic of abstract random probabilities would ever suggest.

A prime characteristic of most of these "solutions" to the problems, that is, of the clues or coordinators or focal points, is some kind of prominence or conspicuousness. But it is a prominence that depends on time and place and who the people are.

…

Tacit Bargaining (Divergent Interests)

A conflict of interest enters our problem if the parachutists dislike walking. With communication, which is not allowed in our problem, they would have argued or bargained over where to meet, each favoring a spot close to himself or a resting place particularly to his liking. In the absence of communication, their overriding interest is to concert ideas; and if a particular spot commands attention as the "obvious" place to meet, the winner of the bargain is simply the one who happens to be closer to it. Even if the one who is farthest from the focal point knows that he is, he cannot withhold his acquiescence and argue for a fairer division of the walking; the "proposal" for the bargain that is provided by the map itself – if, in fact, it provides one – is the only extant offer; and without communication, there is no counterproposal that can be made. The conflict gets reconciled – or perhaps we should say ignored – as a by-product of the dominant need for coordination.

"Win" and "lose" may not be quite accurate, since both may lose by comparison with what they could have agreed on through communication. If the two are actually close together and far from the lone house on the map, they might have eliminated the long walk to the house if they could have identified their locations and concerted explicitly on a place to meet between them. Or it may be that one "wins" while the other loses more than the first wins: if both are on the same side of the house and walk to it, they walk together a greater distance than they needed to, but the closer one may still have come off better than if he had had to argue it out with the other.

Note

1 In the writer's sample, 36 persons concerted on "heads" in problem 1, and only 6 chose "tails." In problem 2, the first three numbers were given 37 votes out of a total of 41; the number 7 led 100 by a slight margin, with 13 in third place. The upper left corner in problem 3 received 24 votes out of a total of 41, and all but 3 of the remainder were distributed in the same diagonal line. Problem 4, which may reflect the location of the sample in New Haven, Connecticut, showed an absolute majority managing to get together at Grand Central Station (information booth), and virtually all of them succeeded in meeting at 12 noon. Problem 6 showed a variety of answers, but two-fifths of all persons succeeded in concerting on the number 1; and in problem 7, out of 41 people, 12 got together on $1,000,000, and only 3 entries consisted of numbers that were not a power of 10; of those 3, were $64 and, in the more up-to-date version, $64,000! Problem 8 caused no difficulty to 36 out of 41, who split the total fifty-fifty. Problem 9 secured a majority of 20 out of 22 for Robinson. An alternative formulation of it, in which Jones and Robinson were tied on the first ballot at 28 votes each, was intended by the author to demonstrate the difficulty of concerting in case of tie; but the respondents surmounted the difficulty and gave Jones 16 out of 18 votes (apparently on the basis of Jones's earlier position on the list), proving the main point but overwhelming the subsidiary point in the process. In the map most nearly like the one reproduced here (Fig. 1), 7 out of 8 respondents managed to meet at the bridge.

12

Building a Global Civic Culture: Education for an Interdependent World

Elise Boulding

Elise Boulding was a Norwegian sociologist who formed part of the pioneering group of conflict researchers in Ann Arbor at the University of Michigan. She was married to Kenneth Boulding and, as an inseparable couple, they became known simply as 'the Bouldings', although Elise separately carved out a distinguished career and reputation for herself, especially in working to invigorate the International Peace Research Association. Her main interests were in gender issues and education, and how people were socialized into roles in ways that produced social hierarchies and inequalities that could always be altered, given will and organization. The extract offered here arises from another of her interests – how to develop a civilizing culture on a global basis.

*   *   *   *

The 200 Year Present

...

Expanding our time perspective is a useful way of understanding all kinds of events, not just quarrels. It becomes particularly useful when we are trying to understand something as complex as what is going on in the world at large.

...

It is ironic that a sense of history was much greater among the ancients than it is among ourselves. The people of India could think in terms of kalpas, which consisted of four thousand million years of human reckoning. The Babylonian tradition, later adapted by the Greeks and by medieval Christendom, included the concept of the Great Year, generally used to refer to a 36,000-year cycle, after which history was thought to repeat itself.

...

Between these extremes there lies a medium range of time which is neither too long nor too short for immediate comprehension. ... This medium range is the 200-year present. That present begins 100 years ago today, on the day of birth of those among us who are centenarians. Its other boundary is the hundredth birthday of the babies born today. This present is a continuously moving moment, always reaching out 100 years in either direction from the day we are in. We are linked with both boundaries of this moment by the people among us whose life began or will end at one of those boundaries, five generations each way in time. It is our space, one that we can move around in directly in our own lives and indirectly by touching the lives of the young and old around us.

If we use this approach to thinking about the transition we are in between centuries, and between the old and the new international order, we will have a better grasp of events that cannot be properly understood in terms of what is going on this year. And we will understand better why the countries of the South want to make their own independent contribution to the world civic culture. What was going on in the 1880s? It was the heyday of colonial-style internationalism in the West. On the one hand, Belgium, France, Germany, Italy, and the United Kingdom were rapidly expanding their domains in Africa and Asia. On the other hand, Europeans were beginning to talk among themselves about eliminating war as an instrument of national policy and replacing it with diplomacy and arbitration. The Hague Peace Conference, called by Tsar Nicholas II and intended to outlaw war, lay just ahead....

A new breed of world citizen was in the making, and the new century ahead promised to distil the utopian visions of past ages into social reality. From the perspective of Africa and Asia it was a different story. Traditional societies suddenly found themselves under alien rulers. In order to make colonies profitable for their new masters, European administrators removed land right out from under whole populations of settled villages "in the name of the crown." Resettled natives were then taxed for the right to build new homes. Highly evolved indigenous systems of government and laws, land tenure, and agriculture practices were brushed aside without ever being noticed....

Where are we now, at the midpoint in our 200 year present? Western-style internationalism is on the defensive. The 26 nations that participated in the first Hague Peace Conference became the founders (either as victors or as vanquished) of the League of Nations in 1919. Augmented to 50 nations, they became the founders of the United Nations in 1946. By then the west understood that colonialism and internationalism were antithetical....

What happened to the outlawing of war? On the one hand, steady progress has been made in developing the skills of negotiation and mediation. A whole new profession has developed around conflict resolution at all levels, from local to international, and several countries have now founded governmental peace institutes. The United States Institute of Peace was established in 1984, following on the establishment of the Canadian Peace Institute the year before. Sweden, Australia, and the Netherlands also have national peace institutes (see Smith, 1985). The phenomenon of international non-governmental organizations, which scarcely existed in the 1880s has now become a major reality....

Side by side with these developments, however, we find the rise of the world military system, with an annual budget of $800 billion, organised into a bipolar alliance system which has divided the 50 founders of the United Nations....War has not only not been outlawed, the arms race has reached proportions undreamed of in the 1880s.

What does the next half of our 200 year present hold? The basis for a world civic culture and peaceful problem solving among nations is present. So is the possibility of Armageddon....

...

Is humankind up to the challenges it faces? There are two bases for answering yes to this question. The first is our own daily experience of peaceable behaviour – the constant negotiation that goes on in home, work-place, school, and community to get the ordinary business of life done without major confrontation or struggle. Here is a core experience of human peaceableness that ought to be expandable into larger public domains. The second basis for answering yes is the study of the "other side of history," which shows us that all warrior societies from Antiquity on had images of a peaceable civic culture, images that were never extinguished by the experience of the battle. It seems that there is a special human capacity for envisioning peaceableness, for conceiving utopia, which has stayed alive through the centuries....

Reference

Smith, D. C. (ed.), (1985), *The Hundred Percent Challenge: Building a National Institute of Peace*. Washington, DC: Seven Locks.

13

A Brief History of Social Psychological Theorizing about Conflict

Morton Deutsch

No one could be better qualified to write about the early history of the impact of ideas from the field of psychology on the study of peace and conflict than Morton Deutsch. From his pioneering book *The Resolution of Conflict*, published in 1973, to the first edition of the comprehensive *Handbook of Conflict Resolution*, edited with Peter Coleman in 2000, Deutsch has been a leader in maintaining the early stream of work by psychologists that first set off the academic study of conflict in the 1950s and today forms a central core of thinking – and doing something – about intractable real world conflicts. His writing throws light on central topics in the field such as cooperation, the building of trust, equity and equality, productive conflict, the nature of justice and injustice, bargaining, and mediation. This brief extract from his *Handbook* discusses the early impact of three seminal figures – Marx, Darwin and Freud – on the early development of social psychology, and gives a flavour of his own extensive writing.

* * * *

This section of the Introduction is an overview of the progress made during the past one hundred years or so in psychological study of conflict. The writings of three intellectual giants – Darwin, Marx, and Freud – dominated the intellectual atmosphere during social psychology's infancy. These three theorists significantly influenced the writings of the early social psychologists on conflict as well as in many other areas. All three appeared, on a superficial reading, to emphasize the competitive, destructive aspects of conflict.

Darwin stressed "the competitive struggle for existence" and "the survival of the fittest." He wrote that "all nature is at war, one organism with another, or with external nature. Seeing the contented face of nature, this may at first be well doubted; but reflection will inevitably prove it is too true" (quoted in Hyman, 1966, p. 29).

Marx emphasized class struggle, and as the struggle proceeds, "the whole society breaks up more and more into two great hostile camps, two great, directly antagonistic classes: bourgeoisie and proletariat." He and Engels end their *Communist Manifesto* with a ringing call to class struggle: "The proletarians have nothing to lose but their chains. They have a world to win. Working men of all countries, unite."

Freud's view of psychosexual development was largely that of constant struggle between the biologically rooted infantile id and the socially determined, internalized parental surrogate, the superego. As Schachtel (1959) has noted, "The concepts and language used by Freud to describe the great metamorphosis from life in the womb to life in the world abound with images of war, coercion, reluctant compromise, unwelcome necessity, imposed sacrifices, uneasy truce under pressure, enforced detours and roundabout ways to return to the original peaceful state of absence of consciousness and stimulation" (p. 10).

Thus the intellectual atmosphere prevalent during the period when social psychology began to emerge contributed to viewing conflict from the perspective of "competitive struggle." Social conditions too – the intense competition among businesses and among nations, the devastation of World War I, the economic depression of the 1920s and 1930s, the rise of Nazism and other totalitarian systems – reinforced this perspective.

The vulgarization of Darwin's ideas in the form of "social Darwinism" provided an intellectual rationale for racism, sexism, class superiority, and war. Such ideas as "survival of the fittest," "hereditary determinism," and "stages of evolution" were eagerly misapplied to the relations between human social groups – classes and nations, as well as social races – to rationalize imperialist policies. The influence of pseudoevolutionary thinking was so strong that, as a critic suggested, it gave rise to a new imperialist beatitude: "Blessed are the strong, for they shall prey upon the weak" (Banton, 1967, p. 48). The rich and powerful were biologically superior; they had achieved their positions as a result of natural selection. It would be against nature to interfere with the inequality and suffering of the poor and weak.

Social Darwinism and the mode of explaining behavior in terms of innate, evolutionary, derived instincts were in retreat by the mid-1920s. The prestige of the empirical methods in the physical sciences, the point of view of social determinism advanced by Karl Marx and various sociological theorists, and the findings of cultural anthropologists all contributed to their decline. With the waning of the instinctual mode of explaining such conflict phenomena as war, intergroup hostility, and human exploitation, two others have become dominant: the psychological and the social-political-economic.

The psychological mode attempts to explain such phenomena in terms of "what goes on in the minds of men" (Klineberg, 1964) or "tensions that cause war" (Cantril, 1950). In other words, it explains such phenomena in terms of the perceptions, beliefs, values, ideology, motivations, and other psychological states and characteristics that individual men and women have acquired as a result of their experiences and as these characteristics are activated by the particular situation and role in which people are situated. The social-political-economic mode, by contrast, seeks an explanation in terms of such social, economic, and political factors as levels of armament, objective conflicts between economic and political interests, and the like.

Although the two modes of explanation are not mutually exclusive, there is a tendency for partisans of the psychological mode to consider that the causal arrow points from psychological conditions to social-political-economic conditions and for partisans of the latter to believe the reverse is true. In any case, much of the social psychological writing in the 1930s, 1940s, and early 1950s on the topics of war, intergroup conflict, and industrial strife was largely non-empirical, and in one vein or the other. The psychologically trained social psychologist tended to favor the psychological mode; the Marxist-oriented or sociologically trained social psychologist more often favored the other.

The decline of social Darwinism and the instinctivist doctrines was hastened by the development and employment of empirical methods in social psychology. This early empirical orientation to social psychology focused on the socialization of the individual; in part as a reaction to the instinctivist doctrine. It led to a great variety of studies, including a number investigating cooperation and competition. These latter studies are, in my view, the precursors to the empirical, social psychological study of conflict.

References

Banton, M. 1967. *Race Relations*. New York: Basic Books.

Cantril, H. (ed.) 1950. *Tensions That Cause Wars*. Urbana: University of Illinois Press.

Hyman, S. 1966. *The Tangled Bank*. New York: Grosset & Dunlap.

Klineberg, O. 1964. *The Human Dimensions in International Relations*. Austin, TX: Holt.

Schachtel, E. 1959. *Metamorphosis: On the Development of Affect, Perception, Attention, and Memory*. New York: Basic Books.

Toolbox

A number of videotaped interviews of the first generation of conflict researchers can be viewed on the website of the School for Conflict Analysis & Resolution at George Mason University. See http://scar.gmu.edu/parents

One of the main techniques of conflict resolution developed by the first generation, especially by Burton and his collaborator, was the problem-solving workshop. This was based on the idea that conflicts can be transformed from contests to be won to problems to be solved.

Listen to Christopher Mitchell explain the uses of problem-solving workshops on YouTube at http://www.youtube.com/watch?v=kK50Np7-5x8

Many of the theoretical perspectives established by the founders of conflict resolution were later developed into a holistic methodology by Johan Galtung, called the TRANSCEND method. The TRANSCEND Manual is available online at http://www.transcend.org/pctrcluj2004/TRANSCEND_manual.pdf

Part II
Conflict Theories and Analysis

Having reviewed some of the founders of the field, we continue by introducing a range of contemporary theories of conflict and some guides to conflict analysis. Conflict resolution depends on a clear interpretation of the conflict situation, which requires a prior conceptualization of conflict. Conflict resolution therefore depends closely on conflict theory. However, a daunting range of theories exist and it is worth thinking about whether and how these can fit together and what relationship they have to the diversity of phenomena that we lump together under the general heading of conflict. Theories can be distinguished by their scope, precision and applicability to practice. Ideally, we would like a generic theory that corresponds precisely with reality and offers an accurate guide to practice. The earlier theorists, who we introduced in Part I, tended to be highly generic. Later theories became more differentiated, by domain (applying mainly to inter-state, civil, ethnic or other types of conflicts) and by academic discipline. Nevertheless the field remains highly interdisciplinary and there is much borrowing from one theoretical framework to another. Conflict theories continuously influence one another, as today's thinkers continue the conversation with the thinkers of the past in the light of the circumstances of the present.

We have selected mainly examples of theorists who work on civil wars, ethnic conflicts and contentious politics. We could have added theories at the global level (such as Cramer's work on the global sources of civil wars)[1] and the microlevel (such as Kalyvas's work on household-level factors),[2] but most contemporary studies have revolved around intermediate-level theories.

Conflicts are shaped by the contexts in which they arise, so theories depend on the domain and the context. In addition, theories use different lenses, which often make them incommensurable. For example, realism offers a universal theory of human motivation that applies mainly in the international domain. Marxism offers a competing general theory developed from a completely different perspective; it applies mainly to the domain of social development. Both theories hold that conflict is irreducible and inevitable. Nevertheless, both have influenced theorists in the conflict resolution tradition. Marxism stimulated Galtung's theory of conflict formations, which underpinned his theory of conflict transformation. Realism influenced the rational actor approach, which can be traced in the ideas of Richardson, Boulding and Rapoport and later writers. Drawing on earlier traditions, contemporary conflict theories pay attention to actors, structures, relationships, conflicts, discourse and culture, in varying combinations depending on the case and the context. There is still room for imaginative and generic theory-building, and for testing theories against evidence and in practice. In particular there is a need to bridge the space between theories that have general application and specific cases, and this often requires creative work on the part of the analyst. Applying conflict theory should never be uncritical or automatic.

Some empirically minded practitioners take the view that every conflict is unique and has to be understood in its own terms. They are sceptical that any general theory can throw light on a situation where, ultimately, individual free will determines outcomes. While it is true each conflict is unique and each decision-maker has free will, we argue nevertheless that there are general patterns and correspondences between conflicts that make the enterprise of building conflict theory worthwhile. It may be that we still have only islands of theory, which are not yet generic, precise and predictable, but they have deepened our understanding of conflicts in general and of particular cases. We need the existing theories, as well as new and better ones, for the light they throw on the drivers of conflict and the insights they offer into appropriate responses.

We follow this sampling of conflict theories with some brief guides to conflict analysis. In principle there is no limit to the length and depth of a conflict analysis. Historians and political scientists devote whole books and lifeworks to the analysis of particular conflicts. But briefer conflict assessments are possible, and analytical frameworks can help to structure them. Conflict mapping gives an overview or a snapshot of the main elements in a conflict situation. It is particularly helpful for thinking about change. Conflict mapping was developed by authors such as Wehr[3] and Fisher.[4] Development agencies have taken it up and a number of them have developed conflict assessment frameworks, such as DFID,[5] SIDA[6] and USAID.[7] We include here one guide and two applications. The guide is a summary of *Conflict Analysis Tools* by the Swiss Development Agency (Reading 26). The first application is of the SwissFAST conflict analysis framework to Angola (Reading 27). The second, by Norbert Ropers of the Berghof Foundation, applies systemic conflict analysis to the conflict in Sri Lanka (Reading 28). Readers may wish to compare and contrast these tools with the other theoretical approaches canvassed here, and to consider critiques of development aid cooperation in areas of conflict, such as that presented by Mark Duffield.[8]

Notes

1 C. Cramer, *Civil War is Not a Stupid Thing*. London: Hurst, 2006.
2 S. Kalyvas, *The Logic of Violence in Civil War*. Cambridge: Cambridge University Press, 2006.
3 P. Wehr, *Conflict Regulation*. Boulder CO: Westview Press, 1979.
4 S. Fisher, *Working with Conflict*. London: Zed Press, 2000.
5 J. Goodhand, T. Vaux and R. Walker, *Conducting Conflict Assessments*. London: Department for International Development, 2002.
6 See, for example, SIDA's *Manual for Conflict Analysis* (online), which is a shortened version of E. Melander, et al., *Conflict-Sensitive Development: How to Conduct a Conflict Analysis*. Stockholm: SIDA, 2004.
7 USAID, *Conflict Assessment Framework*. Washington, DC: US Agency for International Development, 2012.
8 M. Duffield, *Global Governance and the New Wars: The Merging of Development and Security*. London: Zed Press, 2001.

14

The Structure of International Conflict

Chris Mitchell

This piece makes a good bridge with the readings in Part I, because Mitchell's *Structure of International Conflict* shares the generic approach of many of the field's founders. It draws on Galtung's triangle, Boulding-style bargaining models and Burton's ideas about conflict and communication. The book is notable especially for its account, in chapters 4 and 5, of the cognitive and social psychological elements of conflict. Here we draw on extracts from Mitchell's chapter entitled 'Peacemaking', in which he discusses what situations are 'mediable' and what the functions of a mediator are.

Readers interested in how the field has developed may find it interesting to compare *The Structure of International Conflict* with Mitchell's new book *The Nature of Intractable Conflict* (2015).

Chris Mitchell was a member of John Burton's pioneering team at University College London in the 1960s, which developed the ideas of conflict resolution, track II diplomacy and problem-solving workshops. He has facilitated many such workshops around the world, and held faculty positions in the UK and USA. He is Emeritus Professor at the Institute for Conflict Analysis and Resolution at George Mason University, Virginia.

*　*　*　*

'Mediable' Situations

All intermediaries or mediating bodies confront a crucial problem of timing, of when third party initiatives are likely to be acceptable to parties involved in an intense, long-lasting conflict. When is an intermediary likely to be relevant, and when irrelevant? In many ways, the question resembles that raised about the overall process of ending a conflict. Factors relevant to leaders considering terminating a conflict bilaterally are also important when they consider accepting, or asking for, the efforts of an intermediary:

(a) The perceived distance from attaining the goals in conflict.
(b) The perceived probability of eventually attaining these desired goals.
(c) The availability of further resources to continue conflict behaviour in pursuit of the desired goal.

(d) The relative value of the goal in conflict compared with other objectives (in economic terms, the 'opportunity costs') and the perceived probability of achieving the latter.

(e) The resources already expended in pursuit of the disputed goals, which will add to the desirability of the original goals; and the extent of the existing sacrifices made during the conflict inter-action.

Many students of intermediary activity, both analysts and practitioners, have argued that these structural considerations really determine whether any intermediary activity will even begin, let alone succeed, and that intermediaries make little contribution to bringing about a compromise agreement. More often, the parties to the conflict themselves decide, either independently or tacitly, that they wish to arrange a compromise solution, and when this stage is reached, they look around for a convenient third party to act as go-between and legitimiser of their activity.

The basis of this argument is that the key factors determining whether or not a mediation initiative succeeds are the relative positions of advantage of the parties and not the personal qualities of the mediator, or even the prestige of the organisation he represents. Given that nobody really makes significant concessions from a position of strength, and nobody will readily agree to make concessions when they are in a position of relative weakness, no mediatory initiative is likely to have much success unless the two parties have decided to come to some agreement, or one party has decided it must cut its losses and abandon the conflict for a compromise. In either case, almost any mediation effort will succeed irrespective of mediator skills or acceptability.

…

If third party initiatives are likely to be unsuccessful in highly asymmetric circumstances, with the balance of advantage tilted significantly in one direction, then a third party's best opportunity might arise in conditions of uncertainty, stalemate or mutual exhaustion. Such circumstances allow us to reconcile the views of those who argue that the parties take a decision to use intermediaries and those who argue that third parties can themselves initiate effective action to help in developing a compromise, and thus genuinely contribute to a peacemaking process. In circumstances where the adversaries are uncertain about the likely future course of events, a third party offer of help may be tolerated, or even welcomed. There are always stages in conflicts when both parties are relatively certain about the future and stages when they are much less certain. In the latter case, parties will be unsure about likely future success for their activities in pursuit of the disputed goals, so that they are also uncertain about the relative payoffs of continuing the conflict, or compromising. Often, the decision to continue or compromise depends, to some extent, upon the changed attitudes and goals of the adversary. In such a situation, a third party can play at least a useful 'communication' role, and this is recognised by parties. Similar positive reactions to a third party's initiatives are likely to arise from circumstances where a long drawn-out conflict has led to mutually recognised exhaustion of resources and options, or to circumstances where neither side is yet exhausted, but where both can recognise a stalemate.

Apart from the existence of some generally recognised stalemate, or state of mutual exhaustion, parties must also perceive that conditions exist that offer both some advan-

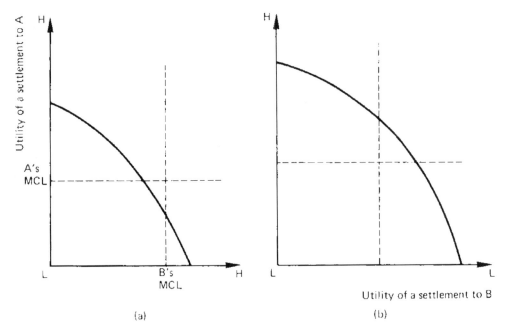

Figure 1 *Intermediary opportunities and bargaining ranges*

tages, even if they fail to achieve all desired goals. A situation similar to that encouraging bilateral negotiations also assists intermediary initiatives. If the parties' Maximum Concession Levels produce some realistic bargaining range, then the assistance of an intermediary in exploring the dimensions of this range will usually be recognised as helpful. If, on the other hand, the parties' MCLs appear to preclude any chance of a compromise, then any intermediary activity that occurs may merely be symbolic, designed to make a public case, or to demonstrate one's flexibility compared with an adversary's intransigence.

...

A model [can indicate] whether a compromise solution is possible or not, and this can also indicate the likelihood of a successful intermediary initiative, see Figure 1. In the first figure, the efforts of the intermediaries are likely to be fruitless; in the second, some opportunities for bargaining and concession exist and so, if these are perceived by the parties, a third party may have some role to play.

For any potential intermediary, the major difficulty lies in first ascertaining whether such a bargaining range exists. Much initial third party activity is devoted to exploring parties' positions separately to see whether MCLs have shifted enough to make a formal approach worthwhile. A major difficulty exists when the parties themselves are not agreed about the advisability of concessions, or how much to concede. In many cases, it is more realistic to talk about a number of factions with different MCLs, some higher than others. (Factions who would rather carry on the conflict than settle for less.) If parties contain many factions, both hard- and soft-liners, then the situation is one in

which a whole series of lines representing different MCLs exists, so that it would be more accurate to speak of a fuzzy 'concession zone' rather than a single, unambiguous MCL.
…

The main functions of an intermediary, once face-to-face discussions are underway, traditionally include:

(i) Providing ideas or possible solutions, particularly when the parties are deadlocked.
(ii) Initiating proposals which originate from one or other party, but which could not be advanced for fear of revealing weakness or uncertainty.
(iii) De-committing parties by providing some formula by which they can gracefully abandon previous positions to which public acts and statements have heavily committed them.
(iv) Acting as a substitute source of ideas or proposals for the two adversaries.
(v) Excusing the parties for making concession, both within the discussions and outside to supporters, by providing an alternative to the superior bargaining position or skill of the adversary as a rationale for concession.
(vi) Providing an 'audience' or 'spur' function through the channelling of expectations from a wider audience that the peacemaking process will continue and some compromise be reached, rather than the whole process collapsing and the conflict be renewed coercively.

In addition to these basic intermediary functions, the third party is often called upon to exercise considerable ability in managing the face-to-face discussions, which can often call for subtle skill in influencing the way in which discussions are directed, paced and timed. These skills are not peculiar to mediatory discussions alone, but apply to almost all meetings which involve a confrontation between two individuals or groups, with some third party attempting to ensure a 'productive' discussion. During both 'confrontation' and 'negotiation' stages, one of the prime tasks of the intermediary will be conducting the meeting in such a way as to maximise the productive openness of exchanges and minimise the level of expressed hostility, disruptive exchanges, accusation, emotional outbursts, and playing to the gallery that occur. Fulfilling this 'easing' function is never simple, but the intermediary can use all his skill to facilitate productive dialogue, provide emotional reassurance to participants, establish helpful rules of procedure for the exchange of views and ideas, and attempt to establish norms within the discussion group which facilitate productive, rather than disruptive, expressions of difference. A major part of this task will be fulfilled by contributing to the reliability of communication between the parties' representatives, often:

(i) By 'translating' or restating statements until sender and receiver agree on the meaning.
(ii) By procedural devices that require one side to make clear that they have truly understood what the other has said and meant.
(iii) By helping to develop a common language within the group which enables those present to deal both with highly emotional feelings or attitudes and the substantive issues which make up the conflict situation.

15

Extending the Reach of Basic Human Needs

Dennis Sandole

Dennis Sandole is a Professor of Conflict Resolution and International Relations at the School for Conflict Analysis and Resolution (S-CAR), at George Mason University, Virginia. Like Chris Mitchell, he has worked within, and developed and updated, an approach to conflict resolution based on the foundational work of John Burton. In this extract he explains the links between Burton's ideas on controlled communication, needs theory and analytical problem-solving as a core methodology of conflict resolution. The piece also explains very cogently the potential of needs as non-scarce resources to enable the achievement of win–win outcomes in conflicts. In a later study, Sandole wrote about the way in which the Organisation for Security and Co-operation in Europe (OSCE) came to institutionalize many of these problem-solving techniques in its conflict prevention policies from the 1990s (see Reading 35).[1]

Note

1 D. Sandole, *Peace and Security in the Postmodern World: The OSCE and Conflict Resolution*. London: Routledge Studies in Peace and Conflict Resolution, 2007.

*   *   *   *

Analytical Problem-Solving Facilitated Problem-Solving Processes

Burton's contributions to the development of conflict resolution processes originally took shape under the heading of "controlled communication". The objective was to have a multidisciplinary third-party panel bring representatives of conflicting parties together to facilitate clear communication, statements of purpose and definitions of the problem about which they were conflicting. Conceived initially as a technique for dealing with *subjective* "social-psychological values" that had not yet achieved *objective* "social-biological," universal status, controlled communication was similar to the casework method employed by social workers, plus the methods of conciliation and mediation used in dealing with small group and industrial conflicts. As "needs" explicitly entered Burton's thinking, controlled communication was reinvented as "analytical problem solving facilitated conflict resolution" (Burton 1990c: 328). The idea behind problem solving is that conflict may not be about territory and similar grievances, but about underlying needs for security, recognition, participation and identity. For Burton, these basic needs are *social goals*, i.e. in contrast to physical resources, they are not scarce. Hence, conflicts originally perceived as zero-sum, "win–lose" contests, often with "lose–lose" outcomes, could be reframed as positive-sum with potential "win–win" outcomes. Since this is not an option in the traditional power paradigm, "then, clearly, it is in the interests of all parties to ensure that the opposing parties achieve these social needs" (Burton 1984: 147–148). The essential objective in analytical problem-solving facilitated conflict resolution, therefore, is to encourage the parties to bring to the surface their "underlying motivations" (e.g. their basic needs for identity, recognition, participation and security). Accordingly, Burton argues that there is a need for a "paradigm shift" in thinking and behavior, from a power approach emphasizing coercion to a problem-solving or human needs perspective focusing on analysis, and a new vocabulary. Like controlled communication, problem-solving is an analytical approach that clears up misperceptions in a workshop format facilitated by trained, experienced third-party practitioners. Unlike controlled communication, however, problem-solving also deals with "objective" bases of conflict, which Burton referred to earlier as "social-biological values" and subsequently as basic human needs that are commonly held by humans and other organisms. Consequently, basic needs are universal and must be fulfilled, lest the frustrated actors concerned blast their way into our consciousness via terrorism and other forms of violence (see Burton 1979; 1984: Ch. 16; Sandole 2010: Ch. 4).

References

Burton, J. W. (1990c) "Unfinished Business in conflict resolution," in J. W. Burton and F. Dukes (eds.), *Conflict: Readings in Management and Resolution*. London: Macmillan; New York: St Martin's Press.

Burton, J. W. (1984) *Global Conflict: The Domestic Sources of International Crisis*. Brighton, UK: Wheatsheaf Books.

Burton, J. W. (1979) *Deviance, Terrorism and War: The Process of Solving Unsolved Social and Political Problems*. New York: St Martin's Press; Oxford, UK: Martin Robertson.

Sandole, D. J. D. (2010) *Peacebuilding: Preventing Violent Conflict in a Complex World*, Cambridge, UK: Polity.

16
Ethnic Groups in Conflict

Donald Horowitz

Donald Horowitz is a leading scholar of ethnic politics and James B. Duke Professor of Law and Political Science at Duke University, North Carolina. His study *Ethnic Groups in Conflict* is a classic work that helped to establish comparative ethnic conflict studies. After outlining the nature and dimensions of ethnic conflict, he proceeds to discuss the application of conflict theory to ethnic conflicts, drawing on Coser's work. The first extract comes from a chapter on Group Comparison and the Sources of Conflict. Using an example from the Sinhalese and the Tamils, it argues that inter-group comparisons are a fundamental source of ethnic competition and conflict. The second comes from his chapter on Structural Techniques to Reduce Conflict. Horowitz sees the design of constitutions, electoral systems and institutions as the fundamental means to promote accommodation between ethnic groups. Here he sets out principles for electoral systems designed to prevent or mitigate ethnic conflict.

* * * *

Group Comparison and the Sources of Conflict

In *The Village in the Jungle*, a novel about life in colonial Ceylon, Leonard Woolf describes an incident that cuts to the heart of ethnic relations in country after country. To appreciate the implications of the story is to have a very good start on the sources of ethnic conflict.

The episode involves a Hindu god, Kandeswami, whom the Buddhist Sinhalese came to venerate. One day, as Kandeswami sat in his abode overlooking a river,

> the wish came to him to go down and live in the plain beyond the river. Even in those days he was a Tamil god, so he called to a band of Tamils who were passing, and asked them to carry him down across the river. The Tamils answered, "Lord, we are poor men, and have travelled far on our way to collect salt in the lagoons by the seashore. If we stop now, the rain may come and destroy the salt, and our journey will have been for nothing. We will go on, therefore, and on our way back we will carry you down, and place you on the other side of the river, as you desire." The Tamils went on their way, and the god was angry at the slight put upon him. Shortly afterwards a band of Sinhalese came by: they also were on their way to collect salt in the lagoons. Then the god called to the Sinhalese, and asked them to carry him down across the river. The Sinhalese climbed the hill, and carried the god down, and bore him across the river, and placed him upon its banks under the shadow of the trees, where now stands his great temple. Then the god swore that he would no longer be served by Tamils in his temple, and that he would only have Sinhalese to perform his ceremonies; and that is why to this day, though the god is a Tamil god, and the temple a Hindu temple, the kapuralas [temple custodians] are all Buddhists and Sinhalese.[1]

The tale is told from the Sinhalese viewpoint. It is biased accordingly. Sinhalese devotion to a Tamil god is not explained in terms of cultural transfer but in terms of moral evaluations of Tamil and Sinhalese behavior. The Tamils, by this account, are no doubt hardworking. Indeed, they are altogether too single-minded about work, leaving them no time to perform meritorious service, even for their own god. The Sinhalese, on the other hand, understand the nature of religious service, and their sincerity is demonstrated by their unselfish conduct. They will even put important work aside to serve a Hindu god not their own, thereby making good the deficiency of the Tamils in fulfilling their obligations. The generosity of the Sinhalese stands in marked contrast to the narrow calculativeness of the Tamils. Plainly, as Kandeswami himself concluded, the Sinhalese are morally worthy people.

That the Sinhalese version of the episode has a more general meaning for ethnic relations is apparent from the congruence of the story with studies of stereotypes conducted in Ceylon.[2] Sinhalese respondents considered themselves to be kind, good, and religious, albeit twice as lazy as the Tamils, whom they viewed as cruel and arrogant as well as diligent and thrifty.

How such views come to be held is a subject to which I shall soon return, but I want now to examine the more general moral of Kandeswami's tale, which is to be found in the domain of group comparisons. The version we are given demonstrates that groups are felt to have different mixes of attributes. Group attributes are evoked in behavior and subject to evaluation. The groups are in implicit competition for a favorable evaluation of their moral worth. The competition derives from the juxtaposition of ethnic groups in the same environment, here represented by ethnically differentiated but otherwise indistinguishable bands of salt collectors. Responding to an identical request, they reveal markedly different qualities. Their responses lead immediately to judgments of merit, for the request to which they respond has a morally imperative character that leaves no room for cultural relativism, with its exasperating inconclusiveness. The judgments of merit are entirely comparative. The Sinhalese response is contrasted with the earlier Tamil response. The responses are rendered separately, so there is no question of interaction between the groups. Competition results as much from being in the same environment as from being in relationships with each other.

The evaluation that ensues has a clear moral dimension: the Tamil response actually offends the god. Kandeswami then renders a conclusive judgment of relative group worth. Who, after all, can quarrel with the judgment of a god, especially a Tamil god pronouncing judgment against Tamils? The episode shows that, for two groups in the same environment, the question of relative group worth was salient, the answer uncertain and in need of authoritative determination by the standards of a superior third party.

Kandeswami's parable is in a wider sense the tale of unranked ethnic groups in general – of Malays and Chinese, Hausa and Ibo, Maronites and Druze, Creoles and East Indians. When two or more such groups are placed in the same environment, no two groups are seen to possess the same distribution of behavioral qualities. Stereotypes crystallize, and intergroup comparisons emerge. Since each group has a distinctive inventory of imputed traits, appeals are made to alternative criteria of merit: as the Sinhalese reward was based on unselfish religious service, so a Tamil appeal might be predicated on diligence and industry. The apportionment of merit is an ongoing process, the interim outcomes of which have important consequences for ethnic relations.

Of course, one could delve further into the symbolism of Kandeswami as a father pronouncing judgment on brothers. The motif is familiar, and it is significant for ethnic relations. But more pertinent for the moment is the character of the story as wish fulfillment. Kandeswami's decision to reward the Sinhalese for their meritorious service was pleasingly permanent. In the real world of ethnic relations, there is no Kandeswami to pronounce final judgments of group worth. Group worth remains enduringly uncertain. And group worth is important, for self-esteem is in large measure a function of the esteem accorded to groups of which one is a member – the more so for memberships central to personal identity, as ethnic membership tends to be in Asia and Africa. The assessment of collective merit, we shall see presently, proceeds by comparison. In the modern state, lacking a Kandeswami, the sources of ethnic conflict reside, above all, in the struggle for relative group worth.

…

Electoral Systems and Conflict Reduction

Electoral systems have a role in fostering or retarding ethnic conflict. The delimitation of constituencies, the electoral principle (such as proportional representation or first-past-the-post), the number of members per constituency, and the structure of the ballot all have a potential impact on ethnic alignments, ethnic electoral appeals, multiethnic coalitions, the growth of extremist parties, and policy outcomes.

Unfortunately, the development of this fertile field has been arrested by two fortuitous circumstances. First, in Asia and Africa, concern for minority electoral protection initially took the form of imposition of a separate electoral roll for Muslims in India and later for certain minorities elsewhere. This began a long and sterile debate over whether the so-called communal roll widens or narrows existing gaps between ethnic groups.[3] Second, scholarly studies of electoral systems have had a completely different focus: whether proportional representation is more conducive to the proliferation of parties than is the first-past-the-post system of election.[4] Although this debate has some relevance to the impact of electoral formulae on ethnicity, it has scarcely touched explicitly on ethnic variables at all.[5]

Politicians have been more acutely aware of the ethnic impact of electoral provisions. Various forms of electoral manipulation and gerrymandering have been practiced in many countries to favor one group or another. More recently, electoral innovation has been used by a small but growing number of severely divided societies in Asia and Africa as a vehicle for ethnic accommodation.

There are several possible goals of such innovations, and there has not always been great clarity about them. All of the goals stem from the growth of ethnically based parties in severely divided societies.

Suppose, once again, that two groups, *A* and *B*, support their respective parties, *A* and *B*. Suppose further that Group *A* comprises 60 percent of the population and a majority of voters in 60 percent of the single-member electoral constituencies, with members elected on a first-past-the-post formula; Group B comprises a 40 percent minority overall and a majority in 40 percent of the constituencies. Clearly, as the election returns come in, Group A and its ethnic party appear to have gained power for the indefinite future. This, as we have seen, is a simplified version of the situation that prevailed in many Asian and African countries under free elections after independence. Ethnic parties developed, majorities took power, and minorities took shelter. It was a fearful situation, in which the prospect of minority exclusion from government, underpinned by ethnic voting, was potentially permanent. Variants of this situation were responsible for much of the instability in the postcolonial world in the first ten years of independence. Civil violence, military coups, and the advent of single-party regimes can all be traced to this problem of inclusion-exclusion. Now the question is whether anything can be done about it while free elections prevail.

In principle, there are three solutions to the pure form of the problem depicted by the 60–40 split. The first is an alternation scheme, such as the rotating presidency that was attempted unsuccessfully among three groups in Benin in the 1960s and somewhat more successfully after civil war in Colombia. Where ethnic divisions are deep, it is unlikely that such an arrangement will prove enduring. The second possibility is an all-embracing "national government." This is what many single-party regimes said they were creating when they dissolved the opposition, but what they were actually doing was something quite different. In the absence of an external emergency of the sort that produced the wartime national government in Britain, such a contrivance is no solution for ethnically divided Asian and African countries. The third solution is to use the electoral system to encourage party fragmentation with a view to producing one of two outcomes: (1) a split in Party A, resulting in two parties for Group A, neither of them with a majority of seats – hence the need for an interethnic coalition; (2) splits in both Party A and Party B, resulting in much more fluidity and, depending on how seats are apportioned, perhaps as many as four possible interethnic coalitions. It should be noted, however, that both of these solutions depend on the capacity of the electoral system to induce splits in at least one of the parties (A). Party A, however, has the most to lose if it does split, and it is thus most likely to try to avoid splitting.

There are, however, more complex versions of the ascriptive majority-minority problem. For all of them, let us assume, as before, that ethnic voting prevails; that each group has a majority in a number of parliamentary constituencies that is proportionate to ethnic shares of the population; and that the electoral formula is first-past-the-post in single-member constituencies.

Suppose Group A is 80 percent of the population, and Group B is 20 percent, but Group A is divided into two parties competing for the A vote. This is a dangerous situation, in which ethnic outbidding can occur, but it is not necessarily solved by splitting the support of Group A, which is already split. More useful would be incentives for the parties of Group A to behave moderately toward Group B or – and the two may go together – a device that would make the votes of Group B essential for the formation of a government. An even balance between the two parties of Group A may be preferable for this purpose to a system that splits Group A's support further, perhaps enabling the strongest of the

A parties to win a majority of seats by recurrent pluralities in three- or four-way contests.

Another variant of the ascriptive majority-minority problem, a common one in fact, entails a situation in which several ethnic groups, none a majority, are potential contenders for power. There are, however, affinities among Groups *A*, *B*, and *C*, on the one hand, and *D*, *E*, and *F*, on the other. Given the exigencies of forming governments under the parliamentary system, it is possible that the two clusters will form two ethnically based parties, thus producing a situation as polarized as the 60–40 situation. Two courses of prevention suggest themselves. One is to create incentives for multiethnic support that will cross the chasm between the two clusters, making consolidation into two parties less likely. The other is to make it less exigent for the existing groups to congeal into a majority. Perhaps there is an electoral formula that can help preserve a more fluid multigroup-multiparty system.

So far, for simplicity, I have hypothesized situations in which ethnic group percentages get translated into the same fractional shares of votes for the party or parties of each ethnic group, which then get translated into the same fractional shares of seats. Thus, a group with 60 percent of the population was hypothesized, first, to cast 60 percent of the total vote for its party, and that party was assumed, second, to win 60 percent of the seats. In point of fact, there is distortion at both interchanges. Demographic and behavioral differences account for the first distortion; the electoral system typically introduces the second.

Even in conditions of acute ethnic conflict, with ethnic parties, ethnic group percentages of a population do not convert perfectly into percentages of a vote. Three variables intervene: (1) relative shares of eligible voters, which, holding registration rates constant, is essentially a function of the age structure of each ethnic group (groups with the largest percentage of members under the age of eligibility obviously have a smaller share of voters than of population); (2) relative rates of voter turnout, which vary with party organization, urban or rural concentration, and certain cultural features (in some groups, for instance, it is more difficult to induce women to vote); and (3) relative rates of voting for ethnic parties (even in high-conflict cases, the incidence of ethnic voting varies marginally from group to group). There is not much an electoral system can do about these variables, which are typically not decisive in polarizing elections in any case, and I shall not consider them further. For the sake of the discussion, I shall simply assume no difference between shares of a population and shares of a vote.

The translation of votes into seats is a wholly different matter, and it gives rise to yet another majority-minority problem. Quite commonly, a party with a mere plurality of votes obtains a solid majority of seats.[6] Suppose, then, in a 60–40 situation, the support of Group *A* is divided equally between two parties, while Group *B*'s support is given solidly to one party. In three-sided contests in single-member constituencies, under a first-past-the-post formula, Group *B*'s party, with 40 percent of the vote, may end up with as much as 60 percent of the seats. So a cohesive minority group can govern a less cohesive majority group, or a group with a plurality of the vote can gain a majority of seats if the balance of the vote is at all fragmented. Both of these outcomes are generally perceived as instances of illegitimate minority-group rule. Where they occur, they tend to create explosive situations. Several very serious ethnic riots are traceable to electoral results of this kind. The question is whether the electoral system can be modified so that shares of votes are translated more faithfully into shares of seats.

These hypothetical examples give rise to essentially five possible aims for an electoral system that is to be harnessed to the goal of ethnic accommodation. An attempt can be made to utilize the electoral system to:

1. Fragment the support of one or more ethnic groups, especially a majority group, to prevent it from achieving permanent domination.
2. Induce an ethnic group, especially a majority, to behave moderately toward another group and engage in interethnic bargaining.
3. Encourage the formation of multiethnic coalitions.
4. Preserve a measure of fluidity or multipolar balance among several groups to prevent bifurcation and the permanent exclusion of the resulting minority.
5. Reduce the disparity between votes won and seats won, so as to reduce the possibility that a minority or plurality ethnic group can, by itself, gain a majority of seats.

The available evidence indicates that many of these aims can probably be achieved. That the aims are vitally important cannot be gainsaid. The alternative frequently is for ethnic party systems of the exclusionary 60–40 sort to produce violent reactions and narrowly based military or single-party regimes.

Notes

1 Woolf, *The Village in the Jungle* (London: Edward Arnold, 1913), 105–06.
2 W. Howard Wriggins, *Ceylon: Dilemmas of a New Nation* (Princeton: Princeton Univ. Press, 1960), 232–33.
3 The debate was sterile because it was abstruse and acontextual. A splendid example of the debate is W. J. M. Mackenzie, "Representation in Plural Societies," *Political Studies* 2 (Feb. 1954): 54–69.
4 See Maurice Duverger, *L'Influence des systèmes électoraux sur la vie politique* (Paris: Armand Colin, 1954); Maurice Duverger, *Political Parties*, trans. Barbara North and Robert North (New York: John Wiley, 1954); Douglas W. Rae, *The Political Consequences of Electoral Laws*, rev. ed. (New Haven: Yale Univ. Press, 1971).
5 An outstanding exception is J. A. Laponce, "The Protection of Minorities by the Electoral System," *Western Political Quarterly* 10 (June 1957): 318–39. See also J. A. Laponce, *The Protection of Minorities* (Berkeley and Los Angeles: Univ. of California Press, 1960).
6 Rae, *The Political Consequences of Electoral Laws*, 75–76.

17

New and Old Wars: Organized Violence in a Global Era

Mary Kaldor

Mary Kaldor has been an active voice in global civil society, and was the founder of European Nuclear Disarmament and the Helsinki Citizens Assembly. She is Professor of Global Governance at the London School of Economics and Political Science, and is on the governing board of the Stockholm International Peace Research Institute. She is well known for her theory of 'new and old wars', which she summarizes in this extract from the preface of the second edition (2006) of her book. She argues that the main response to the new wars must come from the development of global civil society, cosmopolitan politics and political legitimacy.

*   *   *   *

I was in London on 7 July 2005. I live and work near Tavistock Square, where the bus was blown up, and Russell Square, the scene of what was probably the worst of the underground bombs. The streets were bizarrely quiet; there was no traffic except for the emergency services. Telephones were not working and I could not reach my family and friends. But even before I had discovered what had happened, e-mail messages of concern were pouring in from India, the United States, even Baghdad and Jerusalem.

In a way, this was typical of our current security dilemmas. Time and space are distorted in 'new wars'. We are more aware than ever before of violence taking place in different parts of the world and often we know more about what is happening far away than is taking place in our immediate vicinity. These perceptions of violence shaped by television and the Internet affect our responses as much as the everyday experience of the situation on the ground.

Since I wrote the first edition of this book, there has actually been a decline in the number of wars in the world and a decline in the number of people killed in wars.[1] In Africa, some of the most terrible wars have ended, at least for the moment – in the Democratic Republic of the Congo, where some 4 million people died, in Southern Sudan, where the war lasted over twenty years causing untold devastation and human tragedy, or in Angola, Sierra Leone and Liberia – even though many wars are continuing, such as in Darfur. Wars in other places, such as the Balkans, Sri Lanka or Aceh, have also been halted. We are very conscious of the continuing wars in Iraq, Palestine and

Afghanistan, but so far the death toll has not reached the heights of the wars in the early 1990s in Bosnia or Rwanda. Indeed, the first five years of the twenty-first century are probably one of the most peaceful half decades in history.

Yet, paradoxically, the atmosphere of fear and our sense of insecurity has greatly increased since 11 September 2001. How do we explain this paradox? First of all, terrorist incidents have greatly increased, as has the number of people killed in terrorist incidents.[2] Although far fewer people die in terrorist attacks than in wars, and although most terrorist incidents take place in the Middle East or Asia, the attacks in New York, Madrid or London draw attention to the pervasiveness and apparent arbitrariness of contemporary violence. Those of us living in the wealthy parts of the world are painfully learning that violence can no longer be contained by national borders. Moreover, the idea of a 'War on Terror', and especially the invasion of Iraq, implicates us once again in a narrative of global conflict.

Secondly, the changes in patterns of violence described in this book have been accentuated by terrorism and by contemporary conflicts. Civilians continue to be the main victims, because violence is deliberately inflicted on civilians, because civilians do not have the same protection as military forces, and because it is difficult to distinguish between combatants and non-combatants. Casualties in war and terrorist incidents (both deaths and wounded) are mainly civilian. Uprooting of people (refugees and displaced persons) remains a continuing feature of contemporary conflicts as a result either of deliberate ethnic cleansing or of material and physical insecurity. Detention, torture and rape, both as a weapon of war and as a side effect of war, as well as the destruction of historic buildings and symbols are widespread in contemporary conflicts. Contemporary conflicts are also characterized by a rise in crime, so that often it is difficult to distinguish between criminal and political violence. Hostage-taking, kidnapping, smuggling, loot and pillage are all ways in which political violence is financed, and, at the same time, political causes provide a cover for purely criminal acts.

Thirdly, identity politics seems even more prevalent than it was in the mid-1990s. The growth of exclusive and/or fundamentalist religious and nationalist movements has not abated.[3] The main outcome of the 'new wars' is political mobilization around exclusivist causes; what often starts as top-down instrumentalist nationalism or religious fundamentalism is transformed into passionate grass-roots sentiments as a result of the experience of war and complicity in war crimes. Moreover, the rise of the Christian right in the United States or anti-immigrationism in Western Europe has apparently been fuelled by the insecurity associated with 9/11, the Madrid and London bombings, or race riots in Britain and France. As I show in the new chapter of this book, what began in Iraq as resistance to Western occupation has been transformed into sectarian conflict between Sunnis on the one side, and Shi'ites and Kurds on the other.

In other words, political violence at the beginning of the twenty-first century is more omnipresent, more directed at civilians, involves a blurring of the distinctions between war and crime, and is based on and serves to foment divisive identity politics – these are the characteristics of 'new wars'. Terrorism has to be understood as one variant of 'new wars' – the logical outcome of the tactics developed in contemporary conflicts. Moreover insecurity is not just the result of political violence. Natural disasters and disease kill many more people than do war and terrorism and compound a global risk environment in which war, poverty, or climate change are all intertwined.

Looking back at the period when I first wrote this book, it was a time of optimism. It was after the end of the Cold War, the last of the great 'old wars' of the twentieth century. The 1990s witnessed the emergence of global governance – stronger and more active international institutions, more multilateralist behaviour by states, a new discourse of human rights and humanitarianism, and the rise of a global civil society pressing for treaties on land mines, climate change or the International Criminal Court. I do believe that this explains the decline in the number of wars. This has been achieved through various forms of political and economic pressure on the warring parties, through the readiness to deploy troops and humanitarian agencies and to use them in new ways, or through various mechanisms for controlling the finance of wars, the Kimberly process for the certification of diamonds, for example, or restrictions on diaspora funding in places such as Sri Lanka.

What the international community has succeeded in doing is freezing conflicts, in stabilizing the level of war-related violence. However, in most conflict-affected regions, there are still high levels of human rights violations and crime; a variety of armed actors remain at large; there is high unemployment and a large informal or illegal economy; and very little has been done to confront identity politics. Big weaknesses in all international interventions are the provision of public security (policing and the rule of law) and reconstruction (infrastructure, public works, public services), even though there are ongoing efforts to redress these weaknesses. But, in my view, the biggest weakness has been the failure to promote a cosmopolitan politics. In this book I argue that the key to resolving new wars is the construction of legitimate political authority. Much of the literature, nowadays, emphasizes the need for state-building.[4] I prefer the term 'legitimate political authority', not only because this covers local and international institutions as well as states but mainly because the focus on legitimacy encompasses politics and civil society as well as institutions. International agencies tend to act in top-down ways. They talk mainly to the elites who are often the warring parties; they pay lip-service to concepts such as participation and partnerships; they are reluctant to seek local advice or to rely on local capacities. When I first wrote the chapter on Bosnia-Herzegovina, I was still hopeful that the international community could ally with local democrats and reduce the power of the nationalists. Today, as I explain in the revised chapter, the choice is between a benign imperialism, which has tried to put in place the appropriate institutions of governance and act on behalf of all ethnic groups, and local nationalists, who are as powerful as ever. The losers have been the local cosmopolitan groups and parties who were formerly a significant element in the region.

Can the efforts of the international community to stabilize 'new wars' be sustained? In the present climate of fear and division, I am doubtful. The wars in Afghanistan and Iraq may have discredited the very notion of humanitarian intervention and peacekeeping. The space for political and legal approaches to 'new wars' and terrorism has been narrowed. On the other hand, the early years of the twenty-first century have also been a moment of renewed political mobilization – the growth of social movements concerned about war, democracy, poverty or climate change. Is it possible to build on these public sentiments and regain some of the confidence of the 1990s? It is only if we are able to reverse the current atmosphere and reinstate a mood of hope and reason that we can assist those people, mainly in conflict zones, who currently lead intolerable lives.

Notes

1 Human Security Centre, *Human Security Report* (2005), http://www.humansecurityreport.info/; Nils Petter Gleditsch, Peter Wallensteen, Mikael Eriksson, Margareta Sollenberg and Håvard Strand, 'Armed conflict 1946–2001: a new dataset', *Journal of Peace Research*, 39/5 (2002), pp. 615–37; *Armed Conflict Dataset Codebook*, http://www.prio.no/cwp/armedconflict/current/Codebook_v3-2005.pdf; Project Ploughshares, http://www. ploughshares.ca/.
2 United States Department of State, *Patterns of Global Terrorism*, http://www.state.gov/s/ct/rls/pgtrpt/ [annual report].
3 Mary Kaldor and Diego Muro, 'Religious and nationalist militant groups', in Mary Kaldor, Helmut Anheier and Marlies Glasius, *Global Civil Society 2003*, Oxford: Oxford University Press, 2003.
4 See, for example, Roland Paris, *At War's End: Peace-Building after Civil Conflict*, Cambridge: Cambridge University Press, 2004; Francis Fukuyama, *State-Building: Governance and World Order in the 21st Century*, Ithaca, NY: Cornell University Press, 2004.

18

The Economic Functions of Violence in Civil Wars

David Keen

David Keen argues that although civil wars may be disastrous economically for the societies that experience them, they nevertheless have an economic rationale. People may
prosecute conflict for rational economic motives, and many people make profit from
civil wars, for example by using violence to extract resources, prey on civilians and pay
for soldiers, as in Sierra Leone, the Democratic Republic of Congo and other recent conflicts. A version of the same argument was picked up by Collier and Hoeffler in their
famous paper 'Greed and Grievance', which launched a vigorous debate.[1] The economist
Hirschleifer also pursued the argument that violence may be a means of rent-seeking
and a viable alternative to production and exchange as a form of economic activity.[2] This
argument underlined the challenges of conflict resolution, since there are losers as well
as winners in ending protracted conflicts. David Keen is Professor of Complex Emergencies at the London School of Economics and Political Science.

Notes

1 P. Collier and A. Hoeffler (2004), 'Greed and Grievance in Civil War', *Oxford Economic Papers* 56/4 (2004):
563–595.
2 J. Hirschleifer, *The Dark Side of the Force: Economic Foundations of Conflict Theory*. Cambridge: Cambridge
University Press, 2001.

* * * *

Rumours of the death of civil wars have been greatly exaggerated. There were grounds
for optimism as the Cold War ended amid talk of a 'New World Order', with a fresh
potential for international cooperation apparently exemplified by the 1991 Gulf War.
The majority of civil conflicts since the Second World War, from Afghanistan to Vietnam,
had been fuelled by superpower rivalry and injections of arms and aid. Yet, while the
old 'ideological' explanations no longer seem to apply, conflicts continue. Some have
been born precisely from the demise of communist regimes in the Soviet Union and
Yugoslavia; others have simply refused to end. Angola relapsed into civil war almost as
soon as it had tasted peace in 1992–93.[1] In some countries war, often in the guise of

'complex emergencies', has become more normal than peace – Cold War or no Cold War.[2] Myanmar has arguably been at war with itself since 1948. Even conflicts that appeared to be resolved, such as those in Cambodia, El Salvador and Mozambique, have shown signs of intractability.[3] If the persistence of civil wars has left many analysts puzzled, so has their nature. The absence of clear political programmes, the proliferation of factions, disintegrating lines of command and ferocious attacks against civilians have all produced both confusion and outrage.[4]

Under these circumstances, we need a better understanding of the forces sparking and sustaining civil wars.[5] Three broad approaches to analysing civil wars stand out. The first is an essentially Cold War model, which portrays conflict as being between two sides, usually an insurrection met by a counter-insurgency. This framework appeared suitable to describe conflicts between the 1950s and the 1980s, when anti-colonial wars often ran alongside, and sometimes gave way to, revolutionary struggles. This type of analysis focuses first on background causes to explain what the war is about and who it is 'between', then on tactics and battles won and lost by either side.

Faced with conflicts that do not fit this traditional model – in Bosnia-Herzegovina, Liberia and Rwanda, for example – some analysts have sought to explain the irrationality and unpredictability of civil wars by invoking a kind of 'chaos theory'. The end of the Cold War, so the argument goes, freed tribal, ethnic and national rivalries once kept in check by strong regimes.[6] War became evil or medieval, mindless violence propelled by a witches' brew of overpopulation, tribalism, drug-taking and environmental decline.

The third strand of analysis emphasises war's negative consequences. This apparently common-sense approach, embraced by many UN agencies and non-governmental organisations (NGOs) and emphasised in the media, portrays conflict as disrupting the economy and interrupting 'benevolent' progress. The best response is therefore a speedy transition from wartime relief to development, often urged while fighting still rages, and the setting of goals that appear self-evidently desirable. These usually begin with the prefix 're', and include rehabilitation, reconstruction, repatriation and resettlement.

None of these approaches should be too readily dismissed. It is often forgotten that 'traditional' revolutionary and political struggles, such as those for land reform in Latin America, continue, as do conflicts between government and rebel forces. Ethnic tensions are important in many countries, while the economic devastation of war has been well documented. But these analyses take us only so far:

- the old 'ideological' struggles have undergone a major change, and we need new tools to understand them;
- the ancient-hatreds thesis risks ignoring the prosaic political and economic roots of ethnic conflict; and
- explaining the negative consequences of war does not enlighten us as to its causes.

Where no clear ideological divides can be made out, how can we explain the motivation of those who allow – even cause – a disastrous conflict? How can the ancient-hatreds analysis explain why conflict should suddenly erupt between peoples who have lived peacefully together for long periods?

Analyses that focus on destruction or ethnic hatred view conflict as a collapse or failure. But the problem of war needs to be posed in more positive terms. What use is conflict? In whose interests is it waged? Who produces violence, how, and why? This paper suggests that internal conflicts have persisted not so much *despite* the intentions of rational people, as *because* of them. The apparent 'chaos' of civil war can be used to further local and short-term interests. These are frequently *economic*: to paraphrase Carl von Clausewitz, war has increasingly become the continuation of economics by other means. War is not simply a breakdown in a particular system, but a way of creating an alternative system of profit, power and even protection.

Economic interests have rarely fuelled unlimited violence. Many contemporary conflicts have been carefully contained, with only limited fighting, if not cooperation, between opposing factions. Instead, there has been a heavier emphasis on controlling production and trade, and – a related enterprise – on controlling, raiding and exploiting civilians. This cooperation is significant when considering the possibilities for peace. The distinction between war and peace may be hazy, and the two may not necessarily be opposites. War can involve cooperation between 'sides' at the expense of civilians; peace can see adversaries striking deals that institutionalise violence, corruption and exploitation. These similarities help to explain how peace can be possible, and why it has often swiftly relapsed into war.

To understand violence in civil wars, we need to understand the economics underpinning it. Conflict can create war economies, often in regions controlled by rebels or warlords and linked to international trading networks; members of armed gangs can benefit from looting; and regimes can use violence to deflect opposition, reward supporters or maintain their access to resources. Under these circumstances, ending civil wars becomes difficult. Winning may not be desirable: the point of war may be precisely the legitimacy which it confers on actions that in peacetime would be punishable as crimes. Whereas analysts have tended to assume that war is the 'end' and abuse of civilians the 'means', it is important to consider the opposite possibility: that the end is to engage in abuse or crimes that bring immediate rewards, while the means is war and its perpetuation. Rather than simply asking which groups 'support' a rebellion or counter-insurgency, it is important to ask which groups take advantage of these situations for their own purposes.

This paper distinguishes between two forms of economic violence: 'top-down', which is mobilised by political leaders and entrepreneurs; and 'bottom-up', where violence is actively embraced by 'ordinary' people, either civilians or low-ranking soldiers. Much of the violence in contemporary conflicts has been initiated not by rebels seeking to transform the state, but by élites trying to defend vested interests. Many of these élite groups gained ascendancy in post-colonial states; others enjoyed privileges under communist regimes. Both may be threatened by pressures for democracy, whether domestic or international, as well as by outright rebellion. While often amassing considerable personal wealth, these groups typically preside over states unable to fight an effective and disciplined counter-insurgency or to provide basic services to their citizens. A range of factors can contribute to top-down violence, including a weak state, an economic crisis, a strong threat to a regime and competition for valuable resources. Ordinary people, driven by fear, need or greed, may turn to violence for a solution to their economic and social problems. Bottom-up violence can be fuelled by social and economic exclusion, the absence of a strong revolutionary organisation or ideology, and the belief that violence will go unpunished.

Increasingly, civil wars that appear to have begun with political aims have mutated into conflicts in which short-term economic benefits are paramount. While ideology and identity remain important in understanding conflict, they may not tell the whole story. Portraying civil wars as simply revolutionary struggles between opposing sides obscures the emerging political economy from which the combatants can benefit. Emphasising so-called ancient ethnic hatreds offers few opportunities for policy-makers other than, perhaps, an excuse for inaction.[7] It may also disguise the role that economic and political agendas play in manipulating ethnicity. Similarly, the development approach's enthusiasm for restoring a pre-war economy fails to understand the extent to which a conflict may have been caused by precisely those pre-war conditions. To achieve more lasting solutions, we need to acknowledge that, for significant groups both at the top and at the bottom of society, violence can be an opportunity, rather than a problem. This paper suggests that taking better account of the economic agendas that can emerge in civil wars would significantly improve conflict resolution initiatives and the effectiveness of international aid.

Notes

1 Keith Somerville, 'Angola – Groping Towards Peace or Slipping Back Towards War?', in William Gutteridge and Jack Spence (eds), *Violence in Southern Africa* (London: Frank Cass, 1997), p. 27; Margaret Anstee, *Orphan of the Cold War: The Inside Story of the Collapse of the Angolan Peace Process, 1992–93* (Basingstoke, Hants: Macmillan Press, 1996); Mats Berdal, *Disarmament and Demobilisation after Civil Wars: Arms, Soldiers and the Termination of Armed Conflict*, Adelphi Paper 303 (Oxford: Oxford University Press for the IISS, 1996).

2 Mark Duffield, *Complex Political Emergencies: With Reference to Angola and Bosnia – An Exploratory Report for UNICEF* (Birmingham: University of Birmingham Press, 1994); Berdal, *Disarmament and Demobilisation after Civil Wars.*

3 *Ibid.*, pp. 20–30.

4 See, for example, Hans Magnus Enzensberger, *Civil Wars* (London: Granta, 1994).

5 While civil wars were never simply a 'theatre' for Cold War rivalries, superpower involvement and the importance of 'ideology' obscured the role of internal forces in shaping conflict. See Tim Allen, 'International Interventions in War Zones', in Tim Allen, Kate Hudson and Jean Seaton (eds), *War, Ethnicity and the Media* (London: South Bank University Press, 1996), pp. 7–22.

6 See, for example, Robert D. Kaplan, *Balkan Ghosts: A Journey Through History* (New York: Vintage Books, 1994), which is sometimes seen as influential in persuading US President Bill Clinton's administration that nothing could be done to end hostilities in the former Yugoslavia. See also Kaplan, 'The Coming Anarchy', *Atlantic Monthly*, vol. 275, no. 2, February 1994, pp. 44–76; Daniel Patrick Moynihan, *Pandaemonium: Ethnicity in International Politics* (Oxford: Oxford University Press, 1993); and Martin van Creveld, *The Transformation of War* (New York: The Free Press, 1991).

7 David Keen, 'Organised Chaos Not the New World We Ordered', *World Today*, January 1996, pp. 14–17; Charles King, *Ending Civil Wars*, Adelphi Paper 308 (Oxford: Oxford University Press for the IISS, 1997), pp. 25–28.

19

Horizontal Inequalities: A Neglected Dimension of Development

Frances Stewart

Professor Frances Stewart was Director of the Centre for Research on Inequality, Human Security and Ethnicity at the University of Oxford and was given the United Nations Development Programme's Mahbub ul Haq Award for her lifetime achievements in promoting human development. The greed and grievance literature tends to downplay the root causes of conflict in inequality and grievances. A number of studies have pointed out that individual inequality is poorly correlated with violent conflict. However, Stewart argues that group-level inequalities are significant in violent conflict, and her concept of horizontal inequalities made a major contribution to development and conflict studies. She lucidly sets out her argument in this piece, taken from the opening of a CRISE working paper. Quantitative studies such as those by Østby (2008)[1] and Cederman, Gleditsch and Buhaug (2013)[2] have subsequently given empirical support to the proposition that horizontal inequalities are associated with a higher risk of armed conflict.

Notes

1 G. Østby, 'Polarization, Horizontal Inequalities and Violent Civil Conflict', *Journal of Peace Research* 45/2 (March 2008): 143–162.
2 L.-E. Cederman, K. S. Gleditsch and H. Buhaug, *Inequality, Grievances, and Civil Wars*. Cambridge: Cambridge University Press, 2013.

* * * *

1. Introduction

Current thinking about development places individuals firmly at the centre of concern, the basic building block for analysis and policy. This is as true of the innovations led by Amartya Sen, which move us away from a focus purely on incomes to incorporate wider perspectives on well-being, as of the more traditional neo-classical welfare analysis which underpins most development policy. The present overriding concerns with reduced poverty and inequality, which stem from both types of analysis, are equally individual-focused. The Millennium Development goals, for example, are concerned with the *numbers* of individuals in poverty in the world as a whole, not with who they are, or where they live. Measures of inequality relate to the *ranking of individuals* (or households) within a country (or sometimes the globe). The issues of poverty and inequality are, of course, extremely important, but they neglect a vital dimension of human well-being and of social stability: that is the group dimension.

An intrinsic part of human life is group membership – in fact it is this that makes up the identity (or multiple identities) of individuals – their family affiliations, cultural affinities, and so on. As Gellner stated: there is a universal human need to 'belong, to identify and hence to exclude' (Gellner 1964, p. 149). Such identities are a fundamental influence on behaviour (by the individual and the group), on how they are treated by others, and on their own well-being. Most people have multiple affiliations and identities – some location based, some family based, some age or class based, and some culturally differentiated. In this lecture I shall focus particularly on 'cultural' groups: i.e. groups encompassing common cultural identities, though the argument can be extended to other forms of affiliation and group differentiation. These identities are generally based on common behaviour and values. The binding agent may be 'ethnicity' (generally associated with a common history, language, mores), or religion, or race, region, or even class. Modern societies – in rich and poor countries – generally embody large cultural differences of this sort. In fact they seem particularly important today, partly because ideological differences have lessened with the end of the Cold War bringing cultural differences to the fore, and partly because global migration has brought people of different cultures into physical proximity. At a superficial level at least, cultural differences appear to lie behind many, perhaps most, current conflicts – huge atrocities, such as occurred in Rwanda, many civil wars, much civil disturbance, and indeed, today's 'war against terrorism' which comes close to Huntington's predicted 'clash of civilisations'.

Yet while it is obvious that there are – and have been historically – numerous cultural clashes within and between countries, there are also pluralistic societies that live relatively peacefully. For example, here in Finland, the large Swedish minority has lived peacefully for many decades. In Tanzania, Uruguay, and Costa Rica too multiple cultural groups have lived together without serious tensions. It is my hypothesis that an important factor that differentiates the violent from the peaceful is *the existence of severe inequalities between culturally defined groups*, which I shall define as *horizontal inequalities* to differentiate them from the normal definition of inequality which lines individuals or households up vertically and measures inequality over the range of individuals – I define the latter type of inequality as *vertical* inequality. Horizontal inequalities are multidimensional – with political, economic and social elements (as indeed are vertical inequalities, but they are rarely measured in a multidimensional way). It is my contention that horizontal inequalities affect individual well-being and social stability in a serious way, and one that is different from the consequences of vertical inequality.

Unequal access to political/economic/ social resources by different cultural groups can reduce individual welfare of the individuals in the losing groups over and above what their individual position would merit, because their self-esteem is bound up with the progress of the group. But of greater consequence is the argument that where there are such inequalities in resource access and outcomes, *coinciding with cultural differences*, culture can become a powerful mobilising agent that can lead to a range of political disturbances. As Abner Cohen stated: 'Men may and do certainly joke about or ridicule the strange and bizarre customs of men from other ethnic groups, because these customs are different from their own. But they do not fight over such differences alone. When men *do*, on the other hand, fight across ethnic lines it is nearly always the case that they fight over some fundamental issues concerning the distribution and exercise of power, whether economic, political, or both' (Cohen 1974, p. 94). Disturbances arising from horizontal inequalities may take the form of sporadic riots, as has occurred, for example, in the towns of Yorkshire in Britain or various cities in the US; more extreme manifestations are civil wars, such as the Biafran and Eritrean attempts to gain independence; massacres, as occurred in Burundi and Rwanda; and local and international terrorism. Indeed, the events of September 11 can be seen as a manifestation of the force of horizontal inequalities, with vast economic inequalities between the US and the world's Moslem population coinciding with strong cultural differences between these groups.

We should not assume that it is only resentment by the deprived that causes political instability – although this certainly seems to be the case in many disputes (e.g. by the Southern Sudanese; the Hutus in Rwanda; or race riots in industrialised countries). But the relatively privileged can also attack the underprivileged, fearing that they may demand more resources, and, especially, political power. Moreover, where a position of relative privilege is geographically centred, the privileged area may demand independence to protect their resource position: for example, Biafra or the Basque country.

Given these extremely serious potential consequences of severe HIs, development policy ought to include policies to monitor and correct such horizontal inequalities. Yet, as noted above, this is not part of the current development agenda, which considers poverty and inequality only at the level of the individual, not as a group phenomenon. …

2. Why Assessing Group Well-being is Important as well as Assessing that of Individuals

In the introduction, I have stressed the most dramatic reason for being concerned with group well-being, i.e. for social stability, which is self-evidently important in itself, and also generally as a precondition of economic development (Stewart 2001). The impact of group inequalities on social stability will be elaborated as the lecture proceeds. But there is a strong case for being concerned with groups apart from this, even from a purely individualistic perspective.[1]

First, there are *instrumental* reasons. If group inequality persists, then individuals within the depressed group may be handicapped and therefore not make the contribution to their own and society's prosperity that they might have. For example, if one group has systematically less access to education than another, children within that group will not acquire the human resources that others of equal merit do, and not only the individuals but also society will suffer. Such inequalities may be due to the unequal distribution of public goods. In some contexts, certain public goods are exclusive to particular groups (Loury has called these 'quasi-public goods', others name them 'club' goods). This occurs, for example, where physical infrastructure is unequally distributed across areas, and communities are clustered in these areas. Overt discrimination, where certain cultural categories are barred altogether or only gain access on prejudiced terms, is another cause of unequal group access. Networking is often group based, so that every member of a relatively backward group has a networking disadvantage with economic and social implications that can only be overcome by group policies. Further self-selection for cultural reasons may lead to unequal access – for example, if cultural factors mean that children only attend certain types of (inferior) school, or there is gender discrimination, or health practices that limit access to certain resources. Policies that simply addressed deprived *individuals* may therefore fail unless accompanied by policies directed towards group inequalities.

Another type of instrumental reason is that taking action to correct group inequalities may be the most efficient way of achieving other objectives. This occurs where differential outcomes are closely identified with group characteristics. For example, the most efficient way to achieve the objective of reducing unemployment in South Africa is through policies targeted at black youths. Or, in other contexts, poverty incidence is closely correlated with a particular region, and sometimes a particular ethnic group, for example, the Indian population in some rural areas in Peru: efficient poverty targeting may involve policies directed at a particular group. The neglect of the group as a classificatory device can therefore reduce the effectiveness of policies which in themselves are not group based.

Secondly, there are *direct welfare* impacts of group inequalities. What happens to the group to which an individual belongs may affect that individual's welfare directly, i.e. individual welfare depends not just on a person's own circumstances but the prestige and well being of the group with which they identify. For this reason, Akerlof and Kranton have included a person's identity in the individual's utility function arguing that 'a person assigned a category with a higher social status may enjoy an enhanced self-image' (Akerlof and Kranton 2000, p. 719). One reason for this arises where other groups taunt members of a particular group, causing unhappiness, even if serious violence does not occur. The Catholic school girls being shouted at by Protestants in the autumn of 2001 as they traveled to school in Belfast provides a graphic example. There are negative externalities of belonging to certain groups. Membership of deprived groups can cause resentment among individuals on behalf of the group, as well as negative externalities which affect them directly. Psychologists in the US have documented effects of racial discrimination on the mental health of the Black population, finding that perceptions of discrimination are linked to psychiatric symptoms and lower levels of well-being, including depressive symptoms, and reduced self-esteem; teenagers report lower levels of satisfaction with their lives (Broman 1997; Brown, Williams et al. 1999).

Limited mobility between groups enhances each of these effects. If people can readily move between groups, then groups matter much less both instrumentally and for their direct impact on welfare, since if the effects of group membership are adverse, people can shift; and groups also become ineffective targeting devices since people can readily move into any group to which benefits are targeted thereby causing targeting errors.

This lecture is primarily concerned with *limited mobility groups* because it is these groups, whose boundaries are fairly well defined, where HIs matter.

These are substantial reasons for taking the reduction of group inequalities to be an important societal objective even before we consider the implications of horizontal inequalities for social stability – which forms the main theme of this lecture. It does not, however, follow that complete group equality should be the objective for a number of reasons. One is that – like complete individual equality – it is not a meaningful objective unless one has defined the dimension: equality of inputs (e.g. access to resources) may not result in equality of outcomes (e.g. health status) because people in different groups may not make the same use of the access provided, or because their conversion from inputs to outputs differs. A second reason is that there can be trade-offs with other societal objectives – for example, near complete group equality might only be achieved by increasing the extent of vertical inequality, or by reducing economic efficiency. A judgement has to be made on these trade-offs. Thirdly, in the short to medium term complete equality may not be achievable given the large inherited inequalities among groups.

Making group welfare and greater group equality societal objectives does not mean that the objectives of enhancing individual capabilities or achieving vertical equality should be jettisoned. The group dimension is intended to be *added* to the individual one, not to replace it. In part, indeed, improving the well-being of deprived groups is justified because it's a way of improving individual welfare, as noted above, with the promotion of group equality tending to raise output, reduce poverty and reduce vertical inequality, because it raises human capital of deprived groups and contributes to social stability. But there may be cases where enhancing group equality is at the expense of either output expansion or poverty reduction, when choices have to be made.

3. Group Formation and Mobilisation

If group differences are to provide a useful basis for policy, group boundaries must be relatively clearly defined and have some continuity over time. People can be divided into groups in many ways – geographical, behavioural, language, physical characteristics and so on. We are concerned here with those divisions which have social significance – i.e. such meaning for their members and for others in society that they influence behaviour and well-being in a significant way. Meaningful group identities are then dependent on individuals' perceptions of identity with a particular group – self-perceptions of those 'in' the group, and perceptions of those outside the group. The question then is why and when some differences are perceived as being socially significant, and others are not.

Anthropologists have differed sharply on this question. At one extreme are the so-called primordialists who argue that ethnicity is a cultural given, a 'quasi-natural state of being determined by one's descent and with, in the extreme view, socio-biological determinants' (Douglas 1988, p. 192).[2] '[B]asic group identity consists of the ready-made set of endowments and identifications which every individual shares with others from the moment of birth by chance of the family into which he is born at that given time and given place' (Isaacs 1975, p. 31, quoted in Banks 1996). For primordialists, ethnic identity is etched deep in the subconscious of individuals from birth.

The primordial view, however, doesn't explain why ethnic groups change over time – are of pre-eminent significance at some points and then boundaries and characteristics of groups change. For example Cohen has shown how some people coming to urban Nigeria became 'detribalised', while tribal identity became more important for other urbanised Nigerians; moreover cultural characteristics among the Hausa, whose consciousness of identity increased, changed quite radically (Cohen 1969). It is widely agreed that many tribal distinctions in Africa were invented by the colonial powers: 'Almost all recent studies of nineteenth century pre-colonial Africa have emphasised that far from there being a single "tribal" identity, most Africans moved in and out of multiple identities, defining themselves at one moment as subject to this chief, at another moment as a member of that cult, at another moment as part of this clan, and at yet another moment as an initiate in that professional guild' (Ranger 1983, p. 248). 'Modern Central Africa tribes are not so much survivals from a pre-colonial past but rather colonial creations by colonial officers and African intellectuals' (Wim van Binsbergen, quoted in Ranger 1983, p. 248). One example is the distinction between Hutus and Tutsis, which some historians argue was largely invented by the Colonial powers for administrative convenience (de Waal 1994; Lemarchand 1994).

Instrumentalists see ethnicity as being used by groups and their leaders in order to achieve political or economic goals. Cohen, cited above, explained the development of Hausa consciousness and customs in this way. Another pre-eminent example is the work of Glazer and Moynihan who argued that ethnicity was maintained and enhanced by migrant groups in the US in order to promote their economic interests (Glazer and Moynihan 1975). The colonial inventions, according to this view, served administrative purposes. In conflict, the use of ethnic symbols and the enhancement of ethnic identities, often by reworking historical memories, is frequently used as a powerful mechanism for the mobilisation of support. This also represents an instrumental, or partially instrumental, perspective on ethnicity. Numerous examples, presented in Alexander et al., as well as by Cohen, Turton and others, have shown how ethnicity has been used by political and intellectual elites prior to, and in the course of, wars (Alexander, McGregor et al. 2000). In international wars, this takes the shape of enhancing national consciousness, with flag waving, historical references, military parades, and so on. In civil wars, it is a matter of raising ethnic or religious consciousness. For example, the radio broadcasts by the extremist Hutus before the 1994 massacre, in which the Tutsis were repeatedly depicted as subhuman, like rats to be eliminated, echoing Nazi anti-Jewish propaganda of the 1930s. Osama Bin Laden has appealed to Moslem consciousness, arguing that the war is 'in essence a religious war' (*The Observer*, 4 Nov. 2001).

Yet even instrumentalists generally recognise that there need to be some felt differences in behaviour, customs, ideology or religion to make it possible to raise ethnic or other consciousness in an instrumental way. For example, Glazer and Moynihan themselves state that 'For there to be the possibility for an ethnic community at all, there will normally exist some visible cultural differences or "markers" which might help to divide communities into fairly well defined groupings or ethnic categories' (Glazer and

Moynihan 1975, p. 379). Some shared circumstances are needed for group construction – e.g. speaking the same language, sharing cultural traditions, living in the same place, or facing similar sources of hardship or exploitation. Past group formation, although possibly constructed for political or economic purposes at the time, also contributes to present differences. Whether the origins of a group are instrumental or not, the effect is to change perceptions and make the differences seem real to group members – this is why group identities are so powerful as sources of action. As Turton puts it: the power of ethnicity or 'its very effectiveness as a means of advancing group interests depends upon its being seen as "primordial" by those who make claims in its name' (Turton 1997, p. 82). Hence what was a dependent variable at one point in history can act as an independent variable in contributing to current perceptions.[3]

Groups which are important for their members' self-esteem and well-being and can threaten social stability invariably have some shared characteristics which may make them easy to identify; they also have some continuity. While people have some choice over their own identities, this is not unconstrained – a Kikuyu cannot decide that from tomorrow they will be part of the Luo ethnic group. Choice of identity is constrained both by characteristics of the group – its customs and symbols, norms etc. (sometimes birth itself, sometimes language, sometimes complex customs, sometimes physical characteristics) – and by other groups' willingness to admit new members. For example, assimilation to a different culture may be a choice that outsiders wish to make, but it cannot be realised unless the insiders accept it, as German Jews found. So there is some constancy about group boundaries. Yet there is also some fluidity in group boundaries, they do evolve over time in response to circumstances – for example, the Iwerri decided they were not after all Ibos in the middle of the Biafran war; the Telegu-speaking people who were an apparently homogeneous group seeking autonomy from the State of Madras, became quite sharply divided once they had gained this autonomy (Horowitz 1985, p. 66).

The hypothesis that forms the central thesis of this lecture is that horizontal inequalities matter to people in different groups. This only makes sense if the groups themselves are real to their members – which they undoubtedly are in many contexts, and it is precisely these contexts in which we would be concerned about HIs. Yet the fluidity of group boundaries can present potential problems for the approach I am advocating. If group identities can readily be chosen, the group is likely to be a much less important constraint on individual well-being and behaviour – indeed rather than a constraint, choice of group identity could constitute an extension of capabilities. For example, a child might choose to join the Girl Guides, and the possibility of doing so would add to potential welfare; not being a Girl Guide is then a chosen identity, and not a welfare-constraint, for girls (although not boys). If group boundaries were all like that – open, fluid, and changing – measurement of HIs would make little sense. It is because of the continuities, which go along with the limited choices most people have to switch identities, that inequalities among groups becomes a source of unhappiness and resentment, and a cause of social instability.

Generally speaking, it is where switching is difficult that group inequalities become relevant to social stability. In any particular case, history and social context will determine the possibilities. For example, in Europe today a change in religion is relatively easy, but this was much less so in earlier centuries when religious divisions were a major cause of conflict. Although people may find it difficult to change ethnicities, they can, in Cohen's terms become 'detribalised' in some contexts, which is a form of switching. This is more likely to be the case in urban environments or in foreign countries. From our perspective it is the conditions in which switching is difficult that are most likely to give rise to negative effects arising from HIs. Moreover, where switching is easy, group inequalities should be small, since people in the deprived group can change groups until an equilibrium is reached. Where the distinction between groups carries no political or economic baggage – i.e. does not impede opportunities – a group classification may remain but its salience becomes much less.

Notes

1 See Loury 1988.
2 This view has been associated with Smith – e.g. (Smith 1986; Smith 1991); and also with Soviet ethnobiologists – e.g. (Bromley 1974).
3 Smith has argued that 'the [past] acts as a constraint on invention. Though the past can be read in different ways, it is not any past' (Smith, 1991, pp. 357–358, quoted in Turton 1997).

References

Alexander, J., J. McGregor and T. Ranger (2000). "Ethnicity and the politics of conflict: the case of Matabeleland." In Nafziger, E. W., Stewart, F., and Vayrynen, R. *War, Hunger and Displacement: The Origins of Humanitarian Emergencies.* Oxford: Oxford University Press.

Akerlof, G. A. and R. E. Kranton (2000). "Economics and Identity." *The Quarterly Journal of Economics* cxv(3): 715–753.

Banks, M. (1996). *Ethnicity: Anthropological Constructions.* London, Routledge.

Broman, C. (1997). "Race-related factors and life satisfaction among African Americans." *Journal of Black Psychology* 23(1): 36–49.

Bromley, Y. (1974). The term 'ethos' and its definition. *Soviet Ethnology and Anthropology Today.* Y. Bromley. The Hague, Mouton.

Brown, T. N., D. R. Williams, et al. (1999). "Being black and feeling blue: mental health consequences of racial discrimination." *Race and Society* 2(2): 117–131.

Cohen, A. (1969). *Custom and Politics in Urban Africa.* Berkeley, University of California Press.

Cohen, A. (1974). *Two-dimensional Man: an Essay on the Anthropology of Power and Symbolism in Complex Society.* Berkeley, University of California Press.

de Waal, A. (1994). "The genocidal state." *Times Literary Supplement*: 3–4.

Douglas, W. A. (1988). "A critique of recent trends in the analysis of ethnonationalism." *Ethnic and Racial Studies* 11(2): 192–206.

Gellner, E. (1964). *Thought and Change.* London, Weidenfeld and Nicholson.

Glazer, N. and D. Moynihan (1975). *Ethnicity, Theory and Experience.* Cambridge, Mass., Harvard University Press.

Horowitz, D. (1985). *Ethnic Groups in Conflict.* Berkeley, University of California Press.

Lemarchand, R. (1994). "Managing transition anarchies: Rwanda, Burundi and South Africa in comparative context." *Journal of Modern African Studies* 32(4): 581–604.

Loury, G. C. (1988). "Why we should care about group equality." *Social Philosophy and Policy* 5(1): 249–271.

Ranger, T. (1983). The invention of tradition in Colonial Africa. *The Invention of Tradition*. E. Hobsbawm and T. Ranger. Cambridge, Canto: 211–262.

Smith, A. D. (1986). *The Ethnic Origin of Nations*. Oxford, Blackwell.

Smith, A. D. (1991). "The nation: invented, imagined, reconstructed?" *Millenium: Journal of International Studies* 20: 353–368.

Stewart, F., Valpy Fitzgerald and Associates (2001). *War and Underdevelopment: The Economic and Social Consequences of Conflict*. Oxford, Oxford University Press.

Turton, D. (1997). "War and ethnicity: global connections and local violence in North East Africa and Former Yugoslavia." *Oxford Development Studies* 25: 77–94.

20

Dynamics of Contention

Doug McAdam, Sidney Tarrow and Charles Tilly

This reading illustrates how theorists in the historical sociology tradition address contentious politics, emphasizing social mobilization, political opportunity structures, framing
and repertories of collective action. The authors' discussion of an episode in the American Civil Rights struggle illuminates the applications of these theories to civil conflict.
Doug McAdam is a pioneer of social movement theory, notably in relation to the American Civil Rights Movement. He is currently Professor of Sociology at Stanford University.
Sidney Tarrow is an expert on new social movements and contentious politics. He is
Emeritus Professor of Government and Sociology at Cornell University. Charles Tilly was
a historical sociologist whose work spans history, sociology and political science. He
made leading contributions to theories of state formation in relation to war and to the
study of contentious politics. He held chairs in history, sociology and social sciences at
the universities of Michigan, Toronto and Columbia.

* * * *

Montgomery, Alabama, December 1955

The Civil Rights movement's critically important phase began in this medium-size southern city. On December 1, 1955, forty-two-year-old seamstress and longtime civil rights
activist Rosa Parks was arrested for violating the city's ordinance regulating racial seating
on city buses. Her actual offense was not failing to sit in the back of the bus, but something more complicated and illustrative of the pettily degrading quality of Jim Crow
segregation. Montgomery's buses were divided into three sections: one at the front
reserved for whites; a smaller one at the back reserved for blacks; and one in the middle
that members of either race could occupy, provided that no black sat in front of any
white. On boarding the crowded bus, Parks conformed to this convention, but with the
bus now full, a second mandated requirement came into play. If a bus became full, black
riders were obliged by law to yield their seats in the middle section to any white who
boarded after them. This Parks refused to do. What followed was what history remembers
as the Montgomery bus boycott. Said Parks later:

> From the time of the arrest on Thursday night [December 1, 1955] and Friday and Saturday and
> Sunday, word had gotten around over Montgomery of my arrest. ... And people just began to decide
> that they wouldn't ride the bus on the day of the trial, which was Monday, December 5th. And Monday
> morning, when the buses were out on their regular run, they remained empty. People were walking,

getting rides in cars of people who would pick them up as best they could. On Monday night the mass meeting at the Holt Street Baptist Church had been called and there were many thousand people there. They kept coming, and some people never did get in the church, there were so many. The first day of remaining off the bus had been so successful it was organized, and that we wouldn't ride the bus until our request had been granted. [Quoted in Burns 1997: 85]

Parks later said that she simply "had been pushed as far as I could stand to be pushed … I had decided that I would have to know once and for all what rights I had as a human being and a citizen." [Quoted in Raines 1983: 44.]

Parks's arrest was hardly the first of its kind under Montgomery's bus seating ordinance. Indeed, mistreatment on city buses was so common it had "emerged as the most … acute black community problem" in Montgomery in the early 1950s (Burns 1997: 7). So why did Rosa Parks's decision provoke the broader community reaction it did in 1955? Part of the answer probably lies in Ms. Parks's strong ties to both Montgomery's civil rights and middle-class black church communities – the two organizational arenas that would form the nucleus of the subsequent boycott (Morris 1984: 51–53). But part of the reason also emerged from the dynamics of the incident itself, from how both the black and the white communities perceived it, and from how it was framed by the media and the political establishment.

Whatever the answer to the question, Montgomery's black community *did* respond to Parks's arrest in dramatic and unprecedented fashion. On the morning of December 5, an estimated 90 to 95 percent of the city's black bus patrons stayed off the buses, taking Montgomery's white establishment – and ordinary citizens – totally by surprise. Buoyed by the success of what had been planned as a one-day symbolic protest, black leaders decided to put the boycott on a more permanent footing. At a meeting held that afternoon in Dexter Avenue Baptist Church, boycott organizers formed the Montgomery Improvement Association (MIA) electing as its first President, twenty-six-year-old Martin Luther King, Jr., who was also chosen to lead the boycott. This he did for nearly thirteen tumultuous months, until the successful conclusion of the campaign and desegregation of the city's buses on December 21, 1956.

More important than the desegregation itself were the broader effects of the campaign. The boycott drew favorable attention from the national press, thereby generating much broader public awareness of the issue. The campaign then spawned similar boycotts in at least six other southern cities. More significantly, it led to the creation of the first exclusively southern civil rights organization. That organization, eventually named the Southern Christian Leadership Conference (SCLC) and also headed by King, was to serve as a key driving wedge of the mainstream movement throughout the 1950s and 1960s. The rest, as they say, is history.

But we are getting ahead of ourselves. Our real interest here is not with the subsequent movement but with the events in Montgomery. We begin with a question: What led normally accepting African-Americans both in Montgomery and throughout the South to risk their livelihoods and their lives in support of civil rights? In the "classical social movement agenda" the following factors come into play [see Figure 1]:

- *Social change processes* initiate a process of change and trigger changes in the political, cultural, and economic environments.

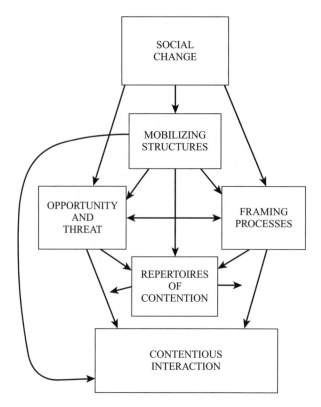

Figure 1 *The Classic Social Movement Agenda for Explaining Contentious Politics*

- *Political opportunities and constraints* confront a given challenger. Though challengers habitually face resource deficits and are excluded from routine decision making, the political environment at any time is not immutable; the political opportunities for a challenger to engage in successful collective action vary over time. These variations shape the ebb and flow of a movement's activity.
- *Forms of organization* (informal as well as formal) offer insurgents sites for initial mobilization at the time opportunities present themselves and condition their capacity to exploit their new resources. Despite some evidence to the contrary (Piven and Cloward 1977), a large body of evidence finds organizational strength correlated with challengers' ability to gain access and win concessions (Gamson 1990).
- *Framing*, a collective process of interpretation, attribution, and social construction, mediates between opportunity and action. At a minimum, people must both feel aggrieved at some aspect of their lives and optimistic that acting collectively can redress the problem (Snow, et al. 1986; Snow and Benford 1988). Movements frame specific grievances within general collective action frames which dignify claims, connect them to others, and help to produce a collective identity among claimants.
- *Repertoires of contention* offer the means by which people engage in contentious collective action. These forms are not neutral, continuous, or universally accessible; they constitute a resource that actors can use on behalf of their claims (Traugott, et al.

1995). The use of transgressive forms offers the advantages of surprise, uncertainty, and novelty, but contained forms of contention have the advantage of being accepted, familiar, and relatively easy to employ by claimants without special resources or willingness to incur costs and take great risks.

That classical agenda made three enduring contributions to the study of social movements. First, it made strong claims regarding the close connection between routine and contentious politics, helping to reframe the study of social movements as the proper province of both sociology and political science. Second, calling attention to the role of "mobilizing structures," it represented a powerful challenge to the stress on social disorganization and breakdown in the older collective behavior paradigm. Third, it produced a credible picture of mobilization into social movements that was supported by a good deal of empirical evidence correlating the factors outlined above with increases in mobilization.

We have not abandoned the central questions that motivated the formulation of that model. But it has four major defects as a tool for the analysis of contentious politics: (1) It focuses on static, rather than dynamic relationships. (2) It works best when centered on individual social movements and less well for broader episodes of contention. (3) Its genesis in the relatively open politics of the American "sixties" led to more emphasis on opportunities than on threats, more confidence in the expansion of organizational resources than on the organizational deficits that many challengers suffer. (4) It focused inordinately on the *origins* of contention rather than on its later phases (for a more detailed critique see McAdam 1999).

Perhaps no case is more closely associated with the classic social movement account of the origins of mobilization than the U.S. Civil Rights struggle (McAdam 1982; Morris 1984). The prevailing account of that movement mirrors the model sketched above, first, in holding that it developed in response to a series of cumulative societal and political changes between 1930 and 1955. Those changes, runs the argument, gradually undermined the system of racial politics that had prevailed in the United States since Reconstruction ended in 1876 (McAdam 1982, ch. 5). The key environmental mechanisms that destabilized the system were the decline in the southern cotton economy and the twin migratory flows – south to north and rural to urban – that the collapse of King Cotton set in motion.

All four of the constitutive "boxes" in the classical social movement agenda then go to work:

- By transforming the previously nonexistent "black vote" into an increasingly important electoral resource in presidential politics, the northern exodus reshaped the *political opportunities* available to African-Americans.
- At the same time as northern migration was reshaping the political landscape, the urbanization of the South was keying the development of the specific *mobilizing structures* – black churches, black colleges, and NAACP chapters – within which the mass movement of the 1950s was to develop.
- These changes loosened the cultural hold of Jim Crow, thus enabling civil rights forces to *frame grievances* in new and more contentious ways.

- It also gave them the capacity to embrace a broader *repertoire of contention* through marches, sit-ins, and other transgressions of white power.

Students of civil rights have offered plenty of evidence in support of this account. But the account was static rather than dynamic, focused on a single movement rather than on the broader episode of contention of which it was a part, underspecified the historical and cultural construction of the dispute, and featured the period of transgressive contention, leaving out many of the more contained transactions that preceded and accompanied it. Morover, it offered a structurally determined account of what must be explained: the creation of the organizational, the institutional, and the behavioral bases for mobilization. We begin our quest with a reformulation of that agenda for mobilization.

Toward a Dynamic Mobilization Model

Where the classic social movement agenda assigned central weight to social change, political opportunities, mobilizing structures, frames, and transgressive forms of action, we try to identify the dynamic mechanisms that bring these variables into relation with one another and with other significant actors. Our perspective puts each of the constituent parts of the classical agenda – opportunities, mobilizing structures, framing, and repertoires – into motion.

- Rather than look upon "opportunities and threats" as objective structural factors, we see them as subject to attribution. No opportunity, however objectively open, will invite mobilization unless it is a) visible to potential challengers and b) perceived as an opportunity. The same holds for threats, an underemphasized corollary of the model (but see Aminzade et al., 2001, ch. 2). While the threat of repression is more palpable than the opportunity to participate, numerous movements arose because their participants either failed to perceive them or refused to recognize them as a menace. Attribution of opportunity or threat is an activating mechanism responsible in part for the mobilization of previously inert populations.
- Instead of pointing to pre-existing mobilizing structures, we call attention to the active appropriation of sites for mobilization. The original resource mobilization theorists built their theory on a trend they correctly observed in the United States in the 1960s and 1970s: expansion of organizational opportunities for collective action (McCarthy and Zald 1973, 1977). But that emphasis does not ring true in much of the world, where challengers are more likely to possess organizational deficits than resources. Even in the United States, challengers, rather than creating new organizations, appropriated existing ones and turned them into vehicles of mobilization. Social appropriation is a second mechanism that permits oppressed or resource-poor populations sometimes to overcome their organizational deficits.
- Rather than limit "framing" to a strategic tool of movement leaders, we expand our view of framing to involve the interactive construction of disputes among challengers, their opponents, elements of the state, third parties, and the media. The political context in which a movement is mounted helps to frame its demands; the media and

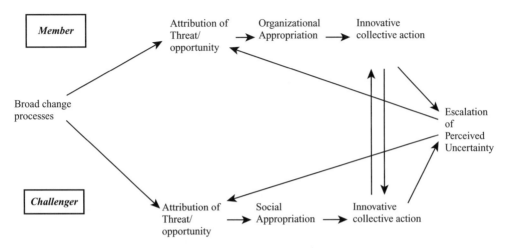

Figure 2 *A Dynamic, Interactive Framework for Analyzing Mobilization in Contentious Politics*

other sources of communication inadvertently frame a movement for its participants as well as for others; and cultural resources constrain and shape the deliberate framing efforts of movement leaders.

- Instead of limiting our purview to the action repertoires of challenging groups, we focus on innovative collective action by challengers and their member opponents.
- Finally, rather than focus on the origins of an episode of contention in which previously inert people mobilize into action, we focus on the mobilization process in general, leaving the question of the origins of contention to be specified as an empirical variant of the general process.

The transformations from a static agenda to a set of interactive mechanisms are summarized in our revised mobilization model in Figure 2.

References

Aminzade, Ronald R., Jack A. Goldstone, Doug McAdam, Elizabeth J. Perry, William H. Sewell, Jr., Sidney Tarrow, and Charles Tilly, eds. (2001): *Silence and Voice in the Study of Contentious Politics*. Cambridge: Cambridge University Press.

Burns, Stewart, ed. (1997): *Daybreak of Freedom*. Durham: University of North Carolina Press.

Gamson, William A. (1989): *Power and Discontent*. Homeward: Dorsey. Rev. edn. (1990) *The Strategy of Social Protest*. Belmont, CA: Wadsworth. 2d edn. (1992): *Talking Politics*. Cambridge: Cambridge University Press.

McAdam, Doug (1982): *Political Process and the Development of Black Insurgency 1930–1970*. Chicago: University of Chicago Press.

McAdam, Doug (1999): *Political Process and the Development of Black Insurgency, 1930–1970*, rev. edn. Chicago: University of Chicago Press.

McCarthy, John, and Mayer N. Zald (1973): *The Trend of Social Movements in America: Professionalization and Resource Mobilization*. Morristown, NJ: General Learning Corporation.

McCarthy, John, and Mayer N. Zald (1977): "Resource Mobilization and Social Movements: A Partial Theory," *American Journal of Sociology* 82: 1212–1241.

Morris, Aldon (1984): *The Origins of the Civil Rights Movement: Black Communities Organizing for Change*. New York: Freedom Press.

Piven, Frances Fox, and Richard Cloward (1977): *Poor People's Movements: Why They Succeed, How They Fail*. New York: Vintage Books.

Raines, Howell (1983): *My Soul is Rested: Movement Days in the Deep South Remembered*. New York: Penguin Books.

Snow, David A., E. Burke Rochford, Jr., Stephen K. Worden, and Robert D. Benford (1986): "Frame Alignment Processes, Micromobilization and Movement Participation," *American Sociological Review* 51: 464–481.

Snow, David, and Robert Benford (1988): "Ideology, Frame Resonance and Participant Mobilization," in Bert Klandermans, Hanspeter Kriesi, and Sidney Tarrow, eds., *From Structure to Action: Social Movement Participation Across Cultures*. Greenwich, CT: JAI.

Traugott, Mark, ed. (1995): *Repertoires and Cycles of Collective Action*. Durham, NC: Duke University Press.

21

A Nested Theory of Conflicts

Marie Dugan

Marie Dugan has taught peace studies at the Centre for Peaceful Change and Conflict Resolution at Columbia College and at the Institute for Conflict Analysis and Resolution at George Mason University. She is a mediator and the founder and director of Race Relations 2020. This piece encapsulates the key idea that local conflicts are often embedded in larger conflicts, but that it may be possible to address larger conflicts by dealing with their manifestations at the local level. Dugan proposes a nested model of conflict and describes how she developed it through working with a particular conflict in a school which involved much wider social fault lines. She also highlights the role that women can play in mediation and peacebuilding. The nested model of conflict was taken up by John Paul Lederach, and Gandhi's nonviolent campaigns in India were based on a similar insight.

* * * *

Conflict, as most conflict theorists and resolvers agree, is neither good nor bad but simply an integral part of life, necessary for growth and change (and for deterioration and regression). As such, it is organic and dynamic. Most of our models seem inherently limited in that they tend toward the mechanistic and static. Additionally, the models that have developed in the field offer little by way of connection between theory and analysis on the one hand and choices about ways of handling conflict on the other.

The Case

I was confronted in a very direct way by these limitations as I attempted to figure out what to suggest by way of intervention in an all-too-real (and, unfortunately, all-too-typical) case.

The newspapers in Northern Virginia had carried front-page news of a racial confrontation at a local school for several days when the topic was brought up at the ICAR weekly faculty meeting. We made two decisions: first, that we did want to make ICAR services and expertise available to the school; second, that I had the best, albeit tenuous, connection to the principal and that I, therefore, should make the initial contact. As I prepared to make a telephone call to the school's principal, I gave serious thought to what we could offer. What should we suggest? What was an appropriate intervention?

The incident entailed a fight on school grounds between two like-sized groups of white and black teenage male students. The precipitation of the eruption occurred when the white boys had arrived on campus with jackets emblazoned with the Confederate flag. Fortunately, the fight had not resulted in any serious physical injury, but it was clear from the articles that deep emotional wounds had been inflicted and that this injury was not limited to the boys who had been involved in the fight. Beyond this, it seemed that the racial equilibrium of the school and surrounding community had been shattered.

In analyzing what to recommend by way of intervention, I began by asking myself how other conflict resolvers would handle the situation. As I mulled this over, I conjectured that most professionals in the field would want to gather all of the boys involved in the fight and would wish to facilitate a conversation among them. A conflict resolver would consider approaches on the negotiation end of the scale mentioned above inappropriate in that, having been recently hurt by each other, the boys were unlikely, by themselves, to be able to engage in the "exchange of promises" which is the core of negotiation. On the other extreme, arbitration would not be seen as an optimal approach, because the value content of the dispute suggested by the symbolism of a flag suggests the need for the boys to be able to understand and appreciate each other's values, a situation unlikely to result from any impositional mechanism. So, the conflict resolver would likely suggest an approach near the middle of the continuum, some form of mediation or facilitated conversation.

The aim of such a conversation would be to help the boys in reaching understanding and agreement on the concerns that prompted the fight and the ways in which such disagreements could be better handled in the future. A mediator/facilitator would wish to create an environment in which the boys could speak and listen to each other openly and fully about what the Confederate flag meant to each of them, why the white boys would wish to wear it, why the black boys felt affronted by it. As the boys became more aware of each other's perspectives, the mediator would help them identify where they shared common ground and help them build agreement upon that ground. Maybe together they would be able to identify other symbols of the aspects of the tradition of the American South that the white boys held dear and the black boys would not find racist or insulting.

A mediator in this situation would hope that the boys could leave the room shaking hands and, at the least, not feeling belligerent and resentful toward each other. In all probability the mediator would hope for more than this, that some of them, having discovered and learned about each other, might actually become friendly, or even friends. In the most optimal situation, the mediation might serve as a watershed event in the lives of the boys, one or more might even dedicate himself to improving race relations in his community.

These are all noble, even exemplary, goals. Yet, I thought, this is not enough. It is not sufficient to seek to enable these boys to resolve the differences among them, not even if they achieve an agreement and transform themselves in the process. Not even if all of them do this. As I write this, I imagine you reading it, thinking "Why not? Why shouldn't these goals be enough? They are good goals; should we not applaud, support and reward those who seek them?" The simple answer is that these goals, while noble, will not in themselves bring about a resolution of the conflict, and that should become the bottom-line goal of the conflict resolver.

To explain why a conversation among the boys is insufficient to resolve the conflict – regardless of whether the mediator is helping them seek an agreement on fighting or wearing the Confederate flag, improved relationships among them, and/or personal transformation – I must supply some additional parts of the story. I did not leave them out earlier to be cute, but rather I am trying to follow my own line of reasoning as these events and their interpretation became clear to me.

There is already a clue to the rest of the story in the information I have given thus far – the object of the brawl, the Confederate flag. While this symbol had some potency to both the white boys and the black boys, sufficient to fight over, it was not of their creation. Its existence as a symbol precedes their own births or the births of anyone in their social or familial circles. It is the symbol the South chose as its banner when it seceded from the Union, proclaiming their right as states to a high degree of self-determination, including the right to maintain the institution of slavery of African Americans. It is a symbol that seems to have become all the more revered after the Civil War, at least possibly due to the humiliation and suffering visited upon the vanquished by the victors over the next decades.

Nor was the flag the only indicator that the dispute went beyond the boys; additional symbols abounded. Up until a few years preceding the incident the school's mascot had been Johnny Reb. The school sits on a street still called Rebel Run, and the Confederate flag earlier had been part of the school's official emblem. Unfortunately, the indicators of the conflict's extending beyond the particular boys in the fight were not limited to symbols. The painful fact was that this was not an aberrant event in the life of this school. Racial conflicts of different size and seriousness had plagued the school for many years.

As I mused on the broad and deep roots of the incident, it occurred to me that my wisdom and insight would be less than well received if I were to call the principal and say, "What we have here is not just about these boys; what we have here is a manifestation of societal racism." I suspect he would have hung up the phone, thinking, "Well, now, there's an academic for you, taking up my time to supply me with a perspective that, while it may be true, is totally useless. What am I supposed to do with that little tidbit of information?" And, it is from asking myself this question over and over again before making that call – what can anyone do with the insight that a particular dispute between individuals may be the manifestation of an older, longer, and deeper social conflict? – that my nested model of conflict emerged.

The Model

I began to think of conflicts as being one of four different types that may be interrelated as shown in Figure 1.

The first type of conflict, that represented by the innermost circle of the diagram, is an issues-specific conflict. Issues-specific conflicts are analytically the simplest and most frequent types of conflict (which does not mean that they are always easy to resolve, nor even that they are always resolvable) and can occur between or among individuals or groups of any size. As its name suggests, the source of an issues-specific conflict is one

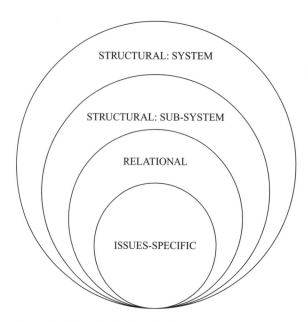

Figure 1 *A Nested Model of Conflict*

or more issues. The disagreement may occur over information, differing interpretations of agreed-upon information, or divergent interests over the item(s) of concern.

In a workplace, two employees may be competing for the same advancement which, by company policy, will be made available to only one of them. The two may otherwise be respectful colleagues, but each may feel that she is more qualified for the position and that to decide in the other's favor is to show unfair favoritism. In a living situation, two housemates may have very different musical tastes and may find the playing of the other's music irritating. Two neighbors may have very different schedules and have their sleep disturbed by noise associated with the other's recreation or household mainte-nance activities. Some citizens may see welfare as the moral imperative of a rich society making sure that the basic needs of all members are met. Others may see it as an all-too-minimal attempt to achieve justice by redistributing some of the wealth, while still others may see it as a wasteful reward for laziness. One nation may take the position that a given territory is its historical and cultural heritage, while another nation sees itself as the rightful possessor. While the issues may be complex and may be further complicated by their interconnections to other issues, so long as only issues are involved, the conflict is still issues-specific.

Sometimes, however, the issues themselves are not the real source of the conflict. A relational conflict is one which emerges from problems having to do with the interaction patterns of the parties and their feelings toward each other. Two brothers battling over the estate left by their parents may be their playing out the pain of long-ago inflicted wounds from their parents' failure to make each of them feel loved as children. Children fighting over the use of playground equipment may be prompted by derogatory insults made by one group at a previous specific time toward the other, or by remarks made over time. Two sports teams may be unable to agree upon a shared stadium because of personal animus between their owners. A nation may refuse to sign an apparently mutually beneficial trade agreement with another because of slights made by the staff of the other's head of state during a previous state visit. Each of these conflicts involves issues – distribution of an estate, use of playground equipment, building of a sports arena, finalizing a trade agreement – but the issues themselves are not the source of the conflict; the relational problems are. Further, if not dealt with directly to the satisfaction of the parties, the relationship issues are likely to "become the one hurdle no handshake, promise, or carefully written clause could wipe away" (Hyde, 1996, p. 1A).

Sometimes, the source of the conflict is beyond the relationship of the particular disputing parties and may be institutionalized in a structured way within the social system. I find it helpful to separate out structural conflict at the broad system level and structural conflict which has its source in the subsystem level. I will speak to the former first.

System-level structural conflict emerges from inequities that are built into the social system. I wish to note here that I am not speaking of naturally occurring differences such as the fact that women are not physically able to compete with men in throwing forward lateral passes. Rather, I am speaking of inequities that occur as the result of human constructs. To stay with the example of differences in the capacity to pass a football for a moment, it is not that this difference exists that is an example of structural conflict, but that the game of football, and, in fact, most sports played in the United States on the school or professional level, are built on, "structured" around, skills that boys and men possess in greater measure than girls and women. It is this sort of sexism, structured into the social system, not simply in sports, but in almost all arenas of human endeavor, that takes gender conflict to the level of system-level structural conflict.

This does not mean that each dispute between a man and a woman emanates from a systemic structural source; any of the sorts of conflicts described above under issues-specific and relational conflicts may occur between a man and a woman as well as between exclusively male or female parties and still be limited to issues-specific or relational sources. It does, however, suggest that if a conflict exists between two or more parties who are members of groups between or among which structural conflict has existed that we should be extra mindful to look to see whether the particular conflict is rooted on the system level. It also means that the parties may be impacted by this broader conflict as they try to work their way out of a conflict that analytically appears to be either issues-specific or relational.

The import of the systemic level notwithstanding, most of us do not live on a day-to-day basis in the somewhat ethereal world of the system structure. We spend most of our lives in our neighborhoods with our families, circles of friends, and colleagues going to our jobs in specific businesses or nonprofit organizations or to learn at particular schools or training centers, or to recreate at a defined beach, sports establishment, concert hall, bar, or street corner. It is not that the system does not affect us; it certainly does in deep, pervasive, and all-embracing (or suffocating) ways. But it is often difficult to be in touch with how we are connected to the larger system, much less how to impact it. Thus, the importance of identifying the layer of subsystemic structural conflict, which refers to those conflicts which have their source in rules, procedures, and traditions of particular social organizations which are, or are perceived to be, inequitable, antiquated, or ineffectual.

...

Subsystem level conflicts often mirror conflicts of the broader system, bringing inequities such as racism, sexism, classism, and homophobia to the offices and factories in which we work, the houses of worship in which we pray, the courts and beaches on which we play, the streets on which we greet neighbors, even the houses in which we live. System level problems may also exist on their own produced by broader societal realities.

...

It seems to me that conflicts such as this offer us the opportunity to spark larger beacons of light than an exclusive focus on the boys or the issues would allow.

This can be done by focusing on the structural nature of the conflict, not at the broad societal level but at the subsystem level of the school as a social institution. Neither the school nor anyone at it has created social racism, nor does anyone at the school or the school itself have the power base to do away with racism in our society. But, each and every person associated with the school has some access points for removing racism at the school.

...

To undertake defining what should be done, let alone undertaking the doing of it, requires more than meeting with the boys who were fighting, because the problem and its possible solutions go well beyond them. For different reasons, it is also important not to limit the search for solutions to the people at the top.

...

Dealing with a subsystem structural conflict should involve all the parties who contribute to its existence and who can contribute to its solution.

...

In the case of the school, this probably means engaging not only the boys, but in fact the student body as a whole. Beyond this, the resolution process should also include teachers, administrators, and parents.

The question that remains is what kind of a process could a conflict resolver use which would enable the various members of the school community to engage with each other in grappling with the school's racist heritage? How would the conflict resolver help the various parties at the school identify racist policies within the school (or any other institution) and design a plan to create a more egalitarian organization? An answer can be found in one of the many contributions of women peacemakers referred to at the beginning of this article: we can utilize Elise Boulding's work on futures invention. It offers us a potent tool for envisioning a desirable future for an organization, a society, or even the global system. Boulding describes a futures invention workshop as beginning

> with each participant making a list of things he or she wants to find in a future world based on hopes, not fears. Next he or she enters a world three decades hence, in fantasy, to explore as a time traveler what it is like to live in such a world. After the individual "fantasying", participants form groups to construct composite worlds from individual images and then in the analytic mode conceptualize the

institutional infrastructure, values, and behavior patterns that would make the fantasied world a sustainable, continually evolving one. Next an imagined history is constructed, working back from the future to the present, and finally strategies are examined for action in the present to bring about a desired future. (Boulding, 1996, p. 413)

Futures invention enables participants both to develop a shared design of a future in which all members of the school community would be valued and treated with respect and to develop strategies for moving together to that desired state. The conflict resolver trained in futures invention could facilitate this process, probably with representatives of the various institutional constituencies.

Additionally, the conflict resolver would need to engage directly the other conflicts nested within the structural one, utilizing mediation to work with the boys who had been in the fight, working both to heal their damaged relationships and to help them come to agreement on more constructive ways of responding to future conflicts in which they are involved.

Conclusion

Dealing with structural conflicts as described above generates the opportunity of creating not just beacons of light to warm us in the darkness of racism but, in fact, models of what we intend our society to become.

...

Women leaders have a particular role in this effort.

...

When structural conflicts are thus approached as opportunities, however painful, for growth and development, we have the opportunity for building minimodels of what a better world might look like.

22

Building Peace: Sustainable Reconciliation in Divided Societies

John Paul Lederach

John Paul Lederach is one of the foremost teachers and practitioners in conflict transformation active today. He has supported conflict transformation efforts in Colombia, the Philippines, Nepal, Kenya and many other countries. He is Professor of International Peacebuilding at the Kroc Institute for International Peace Studies, University of Notre Dame, Indiana, and concurrently Distinguished Scholar at the Eastern Mennonite University, Virginia. At first Lederach's idea of conflict theory may seem disorienting to those who expect theory to describe reality. He is interested in constructing theories of change, so he thinks about how to envision the future. He distinguishes between conflict resolution that aims to end an unwanted situation and conflict transformation that aims to create a desired situation. He shifts attention from the conflict to its context, aiming to transform the conflict by working on the relationships, systems and structures in which it is embedded. This led him to conceptualize conflict transformation in two dimensions, as shown here: one linking the presenting issue to its wider context, the other connecting present realities to a desired future. He developed these ideas, showing how they can generate a novel approach to conflict mapping, in his *Little Book of Conflict Transformation*[1] and in later works.

Note

1 J. P. Lederach, *Little Book of Conflict Transformation*. Intercourse, PA: Good Books, 2003.

*   *   *   *

An Integrated Framework

We see here the natural and crucial overlap between the structural and procedural lenses, as elements of a broad peacebuilding paradigm. "Structure" suggests the need to think *comprehensively* about the affected population and *systemically* about the issues. "Process" underscores the necessity of thinking creatively about the *progression* of conflict and the *sustainability* of its transformation by *linking* roles, functions, and activities in an integrated manner. Together, the two sets of lenses suggest an integrated approach to

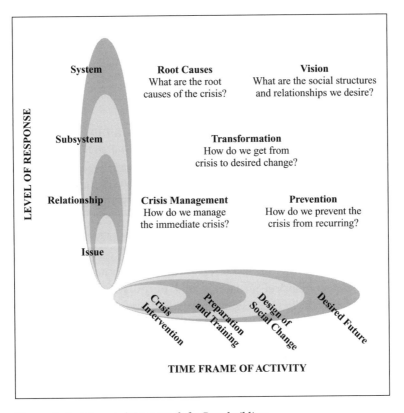

Figure 1 *An Integrated Framework for Peacebuilding*

peacebuilding, visualized in figure 1 by linking the two nested models into an overall matrix. The vertical axis is taken from the Dugan nested paradigm that allows us to link the foci and levels of intervention in the conflict. The horizontal axis is the time frame model that links short-term crisis with longer-term perspective for change in the society. The two dimensions intersect at five points, each of which represents a distinct – and all too often discrete – community of thought and action in the broader field of peace-building. Let us look at each in more detail.

Root causes

Those who are concerned with systemic perspectives underlying the crisis tend to pursue a structural analysis of the root causes of the conflict. They often reflect back on the long history of the current crisis to analyze and explain the broader systemic factors that must be taken into account.

Crisis management

People who have the tasks of responding to the immediate issues and ameliorating humanitarian suffering, who seek a respite in the fighting, are most concerned about how to manage the crisis and achieve some agreement between the parties on immediate issues. They rarely have time to review all the information generated by the "root cause" community and are driven by pragmatism and common sense. They want to know what needs to be done and to get it done as soon as possible.

Prevention

At the level of the immediate issues but looking toward the future, another set of people concentrate on how to learn the lessons of the crisis in order to anticipate and prevent its recurrence. Their work involves identifying the factors that precipitated the violence, helping the affected society prepare to better handle such situations in the future and disseminating to other societies the lessons of what went wrong and what went right.

Vision

With a generational perspective on system-level subjects, another group of people focus on desirable social and political structures and future relationships between those groups currently in conflict. The visions they articulate center on the well-being of coming generations.

Transformation

Where a focus on the subsystem intersects with a concern to think in terms of decades and to design social change, people pose the strategic question, How to move from this crisis to the desired change? Here, transformation is posited at a middle range, which requires input from the other four communities.

The basic proposal put forward in this book is the need for an integrated approach to peacebuilding. Integration begins with a recognition that the middle range holds special potential for transformation, but that change will be needed at every level of human experience and endeavor. Specifically, the middle-range perspective suggests that we need to achieve integration in at least three strategic ways.

- We must develop the capacity to think about the design of social change in time-units of decades, in order to link crisis management and long-term, future-oriented time frames.
- We must understand crisis issues as connected to systemic roots and develop approaches that explicitly anchor issues within a set of relationships and subsystems.
- We must recognize the integrative potential of middle-range leaders, who by their locus within the affected population may be able to cultivate relationships and pursue the design of social change at a subsystem level, thus helping to make the vertical and horizontal connections necessary to sustain a process of desired change.

Here, we can begin to define an understanding of *conflict transformation* that goes beyond the resolution of issues. In essence, conflict transformation refers to change that can be understood in two fundamental ways – descriptively and prescriptively – across four dimensions – personal, relational, structural, and cultural.

Descriptively speaking, transformation refers to the empirical impact of conflict – in other words, to the effects that social conflict produces. In this case, we use the word "transformation" to describe the general changes social conflict creates and the patterns it typically follows. At a *prescriptive* level, transformation implies deliberate intervention to effect change. In this instance, transformation refers to the goals we have as intervenors as we work with conflict.

At both descriptive and prescriptive levels, transformation is operative across four interdependent dimensions. The *personal* dimension refers to the changes effected in, and desired for, the individual. This involves emotional, perceptual, and spiritual aspects of conflict. From a descriptive perspective, transformation suggests that individuals are affected by conflict both negatively and positively – for example, in terms of their physical well-being, self-esteem, emotional stability, capacity to perceive accurately, and spiritual integrity. Prescriptively, transformation represents deliberate intervention to minimize the destructive effects of social conflict and maximize its potentialities for personal growth at physical, emotional, and spiritual levels.

The *relational* dimension depicts the changes effected in, and desired for, the relationship. Here we take into consideration the areas of relational affectivity and interdependence, and the expressive, communicative, and interactive aspects of conflict. Descriptively, transformation refers to the effects of conflict on relational patterns of communication and interaction. It looks beyond the tension around visible issues to the underlying changes produced by conflict in the patterns of how people perceive themselves, one another, and the conflict itself, and in their hopes for their future relationship: how close or distant, how interdependent, how reactive or proactive a role to play, what the other party will want. Prescriptively, transformation represents intentional intervention that minimizes poorly functioning communication and maximizes mutual understanding, and that brings to the surface the relational fears, hopes, and goals of the people involved in terms of affectivity and interdependence.

The *structural* dimension highlights the underlying causes of conflict and the patterns and changes it brings about in social structures. At times understood as the "content" or "substance" of a conflict, the structural dimension may encompass issues such as basic human needs, access to resources, and institutional patterns of decision making. Transformation at the descriptive level refers to the analysis of social conditions that give rise to conflict and the way that conflict effects change in existing decision-making structures and patterns. At a prescriptive level, transformation represents deliberate invention to provide insight into underlying causes and social conditions that create and foster violent expressions of conflict, and to openly promote nonviolent mechanisms that reduce adversariness, minimize and ultimately eliminate violence, and foster structures that meet basic human needs (substantive justice) and maximize participation of people in decisions that affect them (procedural justice).

The *cultural* dimension refers to the changes produced by conflict in the cultural patterns of a group, and to the ways that culture affects the development and handling of conflict. At a descriptive level, transformation is interested in how conflict affects and changes the cultural patterns of a group, and how those accumulated and shared patterns affect the way people in that setting understand and respond to conflict. Prescriptively, transformation seeks to understand the cultural patterns that contribute to the rise of violent expressions of conflict, and to identify, promote, and build on the resources and mechanisms within a cultural setting for constructively responding to and handling conflict.

In summary, conflict transformation represents a comprehensive set of lenses for describing how conflict emerges from, evolves within, and brings about changes in the personal, relational, structural, and cultural dimensions, and for developing creative responses that promote peaceful change within those dimensions through nonviolent mechanisms. As such, the integrated framework provides a platform for understanding and responding to conflict and developing peacebuilding initiatives. The overall process of conflict transformation is related to our broader theme of reconciliation inasmuch as it is oriented toward changing the nature of relationships at every level of human interaction and experience.

23

Conflict Resolution and the Structural Sources of Conflict

Richard Rubinstein

Richard Rubinstein has been a lawyer, an academic and an activist. He is University Professor of Conflict Resolution and Public Affairs at George Mason University, Virginia. This piece discusses how to resolve conflicts which are structural, in the sense that their resolution requires restructuring relationships and the system in which they are embedded. The first extract suggests that third-party attempts may bring conflict parties to agreement without ameliorating the conflict's underlying causes and conditions. The second extract discusses whether conflict resolution can assist parties in serious social conflicts to make revolutionary social changes without intense mass violence.

* * * *

Conflict Resolution and the Problem of 'the System'

A social system, to employ the broadest definition, is any patterned arrangement of social relationships, and a social structure is an assemblage of interdependent systems (Galtung, 1969, p. 81; Kourvetaris, 1997, p. 40). When we say that a conflict has structural causes or conditions, then, this means that it is *not* generated by a misunderstanding or communications failure, incompatible goals of the parties, competing interests, or clashing values alone, although some or all of these conditions may also be present. Structural conflict is the product of patterned social relationships that fail to satisfy the basic needs or secure the vital interests of one or both parties.

An example provided by Barrington Moore is the historic conflict between lord and peasant generated when the lord proved unable to carry out his obligation to protect the peasant against military depredations by outsiders and other dangers (Moore, 1966). Another is the 'structural violence' generated during the past several decades by the effects of deindustrialisation on minority and working-class communities in the United States (Galtung, 1976, p. 298; Bluestone and Harrison, 1982). These examples suggest that structural conflict is often the product of alterations in patterned relationships that were once functional for both parties, but that have now broken down in crucial respects. Another implication is that resolving this type of conflict requires the *restructuring* of these relationships and of the social structures in which they may be embedded.

One may well ask why this should pose a problem for conflict resolution. Serious cases of interpersonal conflict are generally assumed to require restructuring or transformation of the system of personal relations embracing the parties. Family media-tors, for example, are accustomed to presenting the disputing parties with a wide range of restructuring alternatives, ranging from the reconfiguration of roles within a poten-tially viable family to 'secession' by spouses or children unable to satisfy their needs within the original familial context. Similarly, political conflicts involving warring ethno-nationalist groups often spring from obvious breakdowns of old intergroup arrangements and call for new or revised political constitutions. Through a process of negotiation aided at the local level by intergroup facilitations, South Africa abandoned the system of racial *apartheid* in favour of a modified majoritarian constitution (Midgely, 1998). Similarly ambitious efforts are currently underway in Cyprus, Israel/Palestine, Syria, Nepal, and elsewhere to end violent, protracted conflicts by assisting the parties to make fundamental changes in the political systems that previously defined their relations.

These examples might seem to suggest that resolving structural conflict is no more problematical in cases of large groups divided by politics or ethnicity than in the case of a dyad or family experiencing interpersonal problems. There is some truth in this assertion, since what generally makes conflicts more or less intractable is not their scope, or even the presence of structural causes, but the extent to which deeply embedded or strongly defended structures satisfy or fail to satisfy people's basic human needs or vital interests (Burton, 1990b). Nevertheless, the *structural* sources of conflict *do* pose serious problems for conflict analysts and resolvers under two circumstances: where relevant structures are hidden or ignored, and where, although recognised, these structures are considered either unchangeable or unreachable.

Consider again the examples of restructuring mentioned above in connection with family and ethno-nationalist conflicts. In neither case are the structures that require refashioning conceptually obscure or practically out of reach. However complex they may be, the marital-relations and political-constitution systems are conscious human creations. Like the contracts on which they are sometimes said to be based, they are describable, they have a determinate origin in time, and they are mutable: they can be amended or terminated at the will of the parties. Where these 'open' systems are clearly malfunctioning or defunct, the existence of protracted conflicts within their domains leads quite naturally to analyses of the causes of system breakdown and prescriptions for structural change. Few observers of the current civil conflicts in Syria, Libya, Thai-land, or Ukraine, for example, would maintain that these struggles can be resolved by returning to the *status quo ante*. The question in such cases is always how best to recon-struct a failed or failing sociopolitical system.

By contrast, in other serious conflict situations the structural sources of violent strife may be either hidden or accepted as substantially immutable 'givens'. Examples of hidden sources are legion. They frequently involve an assumption by the analyst or observer that the conflict is purely personal when it is also sociopolitical, that it is purely political when it is also socioeconomic, or that it is driven solely by ideological differ-ences when deeper psychological structures are also implicated. In general, the tendency to think about social conflict non-structurally seems related to conscious or unconscious desires to exculpate the broader system and its principal representatives from responsibility for failed social relationships. The structural sources of race rioting in the United States, for example, were minimised or ignored by most analysts prior to the U.S. Riot Commission's 1968 Report, just as the 'lone lunatic' approach to political assassinations focused attention exclusively on deranged individuals rather than dysfunctional socio-political institutions (U.S. Riot Commission, 1968; Rubenstein, 1972). Few studies of political scandals have dealt with corruption as a structural norm, nor does street crime appear to have systemic roots when looked at from the point of view 'crime control'.

More problematical still are the situations in which the structures causing or conditioning conflict are *not* hidden, but the idea of altering them seems unwise or impossible. This seems to occur particularly where social conflicts are subject to the jurisdiction of a functioning state authority, generated by an existing socioeconomic system, or features of a society's deep culture. In these situations conflict resolvers may attempt to alter an immediate, malfunctioning system of relations (for example, the relations between a company's workers and supervisors) without changing more encompassing systems (e.g., worker-management relations in the industry or the economy). As a result, unless the immediate system is substantially autonomous, what is called conflict resolution turns out in practice to be only a temporary settlement (see Burton and Dukes, 1990). When 'third party' facilitators attempt to bring the parties to agreement *without* ameliorating the conflict's underlying causes and conditions, the failure to restructure on a broader or more fundamental basis virtually guarantees a continuation of the conflict. Under these circumstances what is often called 'alternative' dispute resolution is not an alternative to military, diplomatic, or legal processes, but an adjunct or supplement to conventional power-based methods of conflict management.

Two possible reasons for these self-imposed limitations are fairly obvious. All parties may either consider the larger system beneficial and functional, or they may believe that attempts to change it are hopeless. A third reason is less evident and more structural. It is that conflict resolution as a field of knowledge/power has been called into existence by the desires of national and global elites for more acceptable and efficient means of managing, *not* resolving, serious social conflicts (see Foucault, 1972). These elites seek to maintain their hegemony both by initiating structural changes that they desire and by limiting changes proposed by others. Such limitations may be imposed forcibly, but the most efficient (i.e., immediately conflict-minimising) method of enforcing them involves permitting changes to be made at the level of local or peripheral social systems, while insulating more central structures from significant alteration. To the extent that the theory and practice of conflict resolution embody this limited mandate, the field as presently theorised and practised is rendered incapable of identifying and eliminating crucial structural sources of social conflict.

...

Resolution, Reform and Revolution

This essay began by presenting structurally based conflict as a problem for conflict resolution, in particular where the causes of conflict are rooted in more central, encompassing, or fundamental social structures. By critiquing the approaches to structural conflict taken by reformist 'technocrats' and 'politicals', it implicitly raised the question whether a more radical approach – one that aims at resolving serious conflicts by altering fundamental social structures – is conceivable. The central practical question emerging from the analysis is this: *Can conflict resolution assist the parties to serious social conflicts to make revolutionary system changes without intense mass violence?*

One's response to this inquiry will depend, in part, upon whether one considers the historical association between basic structural change and mass violence to be necessary or contingent. My own view of the matter, paralleling that of Marx, is that the relationship is essentially contingent. While history offers few examples (if any) of entirely nonviolent change in fundamental structures of class and culture, the intensity, scope, and duration of the violence accompanying such alterations depends upon many factors. For example:

1   *The size and relative power of the movement demanding change.* Marx believed that a revolution of 'the immense majority, in the interests of the immense majority' would conquer swiftly, without protracted civil violence (McLellan, 1977, p. 230). That view seemed to be borne out later by the rapid progress of the Revolution of 1917 in Russia's major cities, although the onset of civil war in the countryside revealed the divisive effects of highly uneven socioeconomic and cultural development. Today, of course, the assessment of relative power must also take into account the authorities' control of sources of public information and weapons of mass destruction. Even so, the relatively nonviolent triumph of majoritarian populist movements like that of the late Hugo Chavez in Venezuela suggests the continuing relevance of this factor.

2   *The extent of demoralisation and division within ruling or hegemonic elites.* As Brinton and other students of revolution have noted, these changes in attitude and organisation sometimes lead substantial elements of the elite to accede to processes of fundamental change (Brinton, 1956). Recent examples are the processes of division that weakened the apartheid regime in South Africa and the neo-Stalinist regimes of the Soviet Union and Eastern Europe prior to their relatively nonviolent collapse.

3   *The presence of powerful external forces supporting fundamental change.* Social revolutions are notoriously difficult to 'export' but, as the history of Eastern Europe in the periods 1945–1950 and 1980–1990 shows, a dominant external sponsor can minimise the violence of revolutionary change in dependent states. (Conversely, a powerful sponsor devoted to resisting such change can radically increase the scope and intensity of civil violence.)

4   *Loss of cohesion by older social and political structures.* The existence of this crucial factor can produce a situation in which both power and violence are effectively decentralised. Under these circumstances, mass violence may be averted, while anomie or small-group violence (crime or terrorism) accompanies incoherent but large-scale change. We see a version of this situation being played out at present in many parts of the Islamic world and in Africa, where 'failed' or 'failing' states become arenas for terrorist and anti-terrorist violence.

Ironically, perhaps, the recent event which best illustrates all four conditions is the relatively nonviolent collapse of the Communist system in the former USSR and the

Soviet bloc states, and its replacement by capitalist political and socioeconomic structures. I have argued elsewhere that this transformation is not, in the long run, conflict-resolving (Rubenstein, 1992), but there is little doubt either that the changes in question were systemic or that, in making them, both old elites and new mass movements largely avoided intense mass violence. Other factors creating situations in which conflicting parties can make significant structural alterations without plunging their societies into civil war can also be described. To the extent that conflict analysts and resolvers *assume* that such transformations are impossible without intense violence, they unwittingly disempower the parties to resolve serious structural conflicts. Conversely, those willing to recognise situations in which basic structures are open to conscious change may find their assistance to be more potent and useful than they had imagined.

What *processes* of conflict resolution will be most effective under these circumstances? Without discussing the question at length, it seems to me that a combination of confidential and public processes is required. For example, the confidential 'problem-solving workshop' techniques developed by practitioners like John Burton, Herbert Kelman, Michael Banks, and Christopher Mitchell seems well suited to assist conflicting parties to identify key social structures requiring transformation, and to envisage alternative methods of transforming them (Mitchell and Banks, 1996). Without facilitated joint analysis behind closed doors, the Oslo Accords between Israeli and Palestinian representatives would not have been concluded, nor would the recent Northern Ireland peace talks have been convened. But where 'constitutional' structural changes are contemplated, extensive and intensive public participation is also needed, both on general democratic principles and (as suggested above) to avoid mass violence. The fact that this was *not* part of the Oslo process may be responsible, in part, for the inefficacy of the Accords.

One example of a public/private process deserving further study is the complex process that led to the creation and adoption of the United States Constitution in the eighteenth century. A work on the subject by a leading scholar in conflict studies emphasises the importance of organised, intense public discussion before and after the Constitutional Convention in securing mass acceptance of the startling changes proposed by that document (Galtung, 1994). Similarly, 'constitutional' negotiations in Northern Ireland were followed by an elaborate process of consensus-building. More recently, a comparable combination of confidential negotiations and public discussions has taken place in Colombia in an attempt to end the decades-long civil war in that nation, and attempts to organise similar processes are underway in Nepal, Myanmar, and elsewhere.

One must admit that the examples cited above involve political structures primarily. None illustrates a deliberate effort to alter the system of production and the socioeconomic, political and legal structures that instantiate it. Nevertheless, there is no obstacle in theory to conceiving and implementing 'social-constitutional' processes that would help parties in conflict reorganise a community's socioeconomic system as well as its political constitution. A major practical obstacle has been the fact that such structural changes tend to be made irreversibly, greatly raising the stakes of conflict, and tempting conflicting parties to resort to violence to secure their long-term interests. It may be persuasively argued that processes of nonviolent structural change *are* practically feasible, provided that they embody the 'principle of reversibility'. In the same way that we can amend a written constitution or make significant political changes, knowing that a loss of consensual support will generate further change, the parties to conflict need to know that socioeconomic structures can also be altered and re-altered. *That* would be true 'empowerment'.

Those interested in the resolution of conflict, as opposed to its temporary settlement or management in the interests of existing elites, will understand that substantial changes in the social 'constitution' are sometimes needed to resolve deep-rooted, protracted conflicts. To the extent that such changes may be accompanied by intense mass violence, conflict resolvers are committed (as many reformists have been) to avoiding bloody cycles of revolution and counter-revolution. But what seems most important at the present historical juncture is to focus attention on conflict resolution's capacity to assist warring parties to make structural changes that are revolutionary in depth and scope, if not in method. The pressures on conflict resolvers to become instruments of United States or Western global hegemony are very intense. Especially where Great Powers are direct or indirect parties to conflict, rather than neutral 'third parties,' these pressures need to be resisted. In cases in which violent conflict is a product of the system itself, we ought not shrink from assisting the parties to arrive at methods of transforming core structures.

Where, practically speaking, might such efforts be made in the near or mid-term future? Three key conditions for the possible success of 'constitutional' conflict resolution, in my view, are:

- actual or potential recognition by the conflicting parties that fundamental structural changes of some sort are necessary;
- inability or unwillingness of outside forces, individually or in concert, to block the changes that may be agreed to by the parties; and
- willingness of the parties to participate in a process that aims at identifying relevant failing structures and proposing alternative methods of altering or replacing them.

The first condition may be close to realisation in a number of locales around the world, including several Middle Eastern, African, and Latin American nations. It is farther from realisation (but still potentially on the agenda) in Asian and Western nations experiencing evident structural difficulties: e.g., Japan, Indonesia, the nations of southern Europe, and (especially with regard to depressed urban and deindustrialized areas) the United States. The second condition exists, or may soon exist, in regions of relatively little interest to the Great Powers, or in which Great Power competition has created room for regional players to manoeuver: e.g., South Africa, Brazil, and the former Soviet republics. Only now can the third condition come into existence, because conflict resolvers have so seldom offered their services as facilitators of fundamental system change.

This is precisely the challenge that now confronts theorists and practitioners of conflict resolution: to bring the third condition – the existence of viable processes for facilitating fundamental structural change – into existence. By developing forums and techniques for social-constitutional dialogue and problem solving, the profession may yet transcend the technocratic and minimally reformist perspectives that currently limit its usefulness.

References

Bluestone, B. and Harrison, B. (1982), *The Deindustrialization of America*. Basic Books, New York.

Brinton, C. (1956), *The Anatomy of Revolution*. Beacon Press, Boston.

Burton, J. W. (ed.) (1990b), *Conflict: Human Needs Theory*. Macmillan, London.

Burton, J. W. and Dukes, F. (1990), *Conflict: Practices in Management, Settlement and Resolution*. Macmillan, London.

Foucault, M. (1972), *Archaeology of Knowledge*, trans. A. M. Sheridan Smith. Pantheon, New York.

Galtung, J. (1969), 'Violence, Peace, and Peace Research', *Journal of Peace Research*, vol. 6 no. 3, pp. 167–191.

Galtung, J. (1976), 'Three Approaches to Peace: Peacekeeping, Peacemaking and Peacebuilding', in *Peace, War and Defense*. Copenhagen: Christian Ejilers.

Galtung, J. (1994), *Human Rights in Another Key*. Polity, Cambridge.

Kourvetaris, G. (1997), *Political Sociology: Structure and Process*. Allyn & Bacon, Boston.

McLellan, D. (1977), (ed.), *Karl Marx: Selected Writings*. Oxford University Press, Oxford.

Midgely, M. (1998), *Animals and why They Matter*. University of Georgia Press, Georgia.

Mitchell, C. and Banks, M. (1996), *Handbook of Conflict Resolution: The Analytical Problem-Solving Approach*. Pinter, London.

Moore, B. (1966), *The Social Origins of Dictatorship and Democracy*. Beacon Press, Boston.

Rubenstein, R. E. (1972), 'Assassination as a Political Tradition', in William J. Crotty, ed., *Assassination and the Political Order*. Harper & Row, New York.

Rubenstein, R. E. (1992), 'Dispute Resolution on the Eastern Frontier: Questions for Modern Missionaries'. *Negotiation Journal*, vol. 8 (July), pp. 205–213.

U.S. Riot Commission (1968), *Report of the National Advisory Commission on Civil Disorders*. Bantam, New York.

24

Telling Each Other Apart: A Discursive Approach to Violent Conflict

Jolle Demmers

Jolle Demmers is Associate Professor at the University of Utrecht and co-founder of its Centre for Conflict Studies. Her book *Theories of Violent Conflict* offers an up-to-date review exploring social identity theory, structural theories of conflict, mobilization, collective action and rational actor theories. In the penultimate chapter, from which these extracts are taken, Demmers shows how discourse theories explain violent conflict. She draws on Giddens's theory of structuration, which sees agency and structure as mutually constitutive. Structures constitute agents through discourse and agents constitute structures through social practices. Relating this framework to war, the extracts use episodes from films and documentaries to illustrate how discourse legitimizes violence.

*   *   *   *

The Big Red One: War As Institutional Form

In the final scene of the movie *The Big Red One* (1980), a film about how four American privates and their legendary 'Sergeant' (Lee Marvin) try to survive WWII, we see the Sergeant sitting in a forest, at night, having just buried a small boy he had befriended after liberating a concentration camp. Out of the fog a German soldier approaches, the Sergeant turns, and stabs him. Soon after, his squad arrives on the scene informing him, excitedly, that the war has ended: 'The war has been over for four hours.' They quickly pack their things to go back to their headquarters. But as the others leave, one of the privates checks the body of the German and calls out: 'Hey, sarge, the dead Kraut, he's still warm!' When it turns out the German is still alive, the men come running back and proceed to give him First Aid treatment. The German seems to recover and opens his eyes. The Sergeant then lifts him on his shoulders, mumbling 'Live, you son of a bitch. ... You're gonna live if I have to blow your brains out.'

Some think *The Big Red One* is the ultimate film about the absurdity of war, others see it as one among many war movies on male-bonding, masculinity and glory. The point I like to emphasize here is that what the film shows, intentionally or not, is that apart from horrific and tough, war is normal. To us, the audience, the shift in the soldiers' code-of-conduct, from killing the enemy to giving him First Aid, is not in the least surprising. We all know that these are the rules of the game. Actions that are considered taboo in peacetime are glorified in times of war. And vice versa. Discourse theorists argue that it is not aggressive instinct, identity competition, or collective need deprivation, utility maximization or exploitation that makes these soldiers kill. No, it is the simple and straightforward routines of warfare that steer their actions. Underlying their routines is the idea of war as an accepted and institutionalized form of human conduct. It is against this background of 'war as institution' that discourse theorists argue we can understand violent action, not just in cases of 'regular' inter-state warfare, but also in situations of 'irregular' war and conflict. In this debate, Jabri's focus is on how deeply embedded discourses centred around concepts such as militarism, statehood, nationalism and masculinity have conditioned us, through time and across space, to see war as normality. War repeats and reproduces itself through discourses which render it acceptable and necessary, and through social institutions (armies, Ministries of Defence, war cabinets) which serve as war-making machinery. For Jabri (1996: 4):

> War and violent conflict are social phenomena emerging through, and constitutive of, social practices which have, through time and across space, rendered war an institutional form that is largely seen as an inevitable and at times acceptable form of human conduct.

The idea of war as routine and social phenomenon can help to explain why both decision-makers and audiences can shift relatively easily into what Richardson (1948) named a 'war mood'. This is the sudden and widespread support for war that takes hold of entire populations. How can audiences be mobilized so quickly? For Jabri, the war mood can arise because the language of war draws upon deeply embedded discourses of moral legitimacy and superiority. The language of war contains two classic dualisms. First, the dualism between 'self' and 'other' (or: us/them), where the self is associated with courage and civilization while the other is represented as barbaric and diabolical. The second dualism is that between 'conformity' and 'dissent'. Individuals and groups refusing to participate in the war effort are seen as traitors to their community and therefore deserving of censure, punishment or even banishment (Jabri 1996: 108). War as a social continuity hence draws upon discursive repertoires framed around exclusion and inclusion, be it at the level of the nation, the community or the group. This context, of discursive and institutional continuities, is central to Jabri's view of the role of the individual and the constitution of identity. For identity is assumed to be the link between the individual and mass mobilization for conflict. 'A central aspect of the mobilisation of support for armed conflict is identity with the group, community, or state whose representatives decide on the use of force as a means of handling conflict' (1996: 121). The categorization of 'self' and 'other' is not merely a product of cognition and the need for social identity differentiation, as for instance claimed by social identity theorists, but derives from discursive and institutional continuities which are reproduced through everyday acts of stereotyping and categorizing. Individuals are born into discursive and institutional continuities which define and bind societies. They form their identities on the basis of these continuities. As societies are containers of a plurality of discourses and discursive sites, this implies that identity is always a point of active selection and contestation. Active selection, however, is not the same as free selection: our freedom to construct our identities is limited by dominant norms, and symbolic orders. Ultimately, it is through structures of domination and control that discourses of identity emerge. For Jabri, social identity is constituted through deeply engrained institutional and discursive continuities which situate the self within bounded communities, the definition of which is based on modalities of inclusion and exclusion. Social identity, therefore, is 'a product of all that which is located in the realm of society, as context of communication, power relations, contestations, and dominant discursive and institutional practices' (1996: 134).

There is a tension between Jabri's analysis of power, identity and discourse, and her goal to advocate 'counter-discourses' of peace. Staying rather close to the abstract level of Giddens' theory of structurationism, Jabri argues that since structure and agency are mutually constitutive, actors can act to change the war structure in which they operate. Since we have agency, we can emancipate ourselves (and 'de-identify') from dominant rules of social life and create new discourses of peace, which in turn could serve to institutionalize a context of peace as social continuity. These discourses of peace, established in the public arena, reject exclusionary discourses of us/them dichotomies in favour of a tolerance of diversity and recognize difference as a formative component of subjectivity (1996: 185). Put simply, as long as enough people participate in the discourse of peace, it will become an alternative structure that can legitimize decisions for peace. In her discussion of peace discourse, however, Jabri seems determined to overlook – if only for a moment – that which she explains so eloquently in her book: that is, how discourses are produced in contexts of power asymmetry and how hegemonic groups can mobilize structures of signification to legitimate their sectional interests. This seems to imply that a 'hegemony of peace' – and again, whose peace are we talking about? – needs to be not only socially meaningful but also politically functional.

...

In a documentary named *We are All Neighbours* (1993, Granada TV), the anthropologist Tone Bringa shows how relationships between neighbours and friends change in a small village near Sarajevo in the early 1990s, in the run-up to war. The distant shelling, the constant rumours and the stories of refugees slowly begin to affect relationships within the village. People turn inwards, away from each other. They stop visiting old friends for a cup of coffee. Slowly, ethnic boundaries become salient. 'People change their faces' – as one woman describes it – 'It happened to me in a day.'

As we have seen in the introductory chapter, conflict is defined as a situation in which two or more entities or 'parties' perceive that they possess mutually incompatible goals. It is in the study of this perception that discourse analysis becomes useful.

Discourse theory aims to study the formation of discourses in and on war. It aims to give an explicit and systematic description of the ways in which people form discourse communities, and how collective narratives on the origins of war, the enemy, victims and perpetrators are formed and sustained. An important underlying principle is that discourse formation is seen as a social process. Powerful groups (elites, specialists, intellectuals, leaders) may try – for a variety of reasons – to convince their audiences that a certain incompatibility of goals is threatening them, and try to turn this into a dominant discourse. This can, however, not be established top-down. Discourse formation has a dynamics of its own, where coding, interpretation and meaning are the outcome of a complex dynamics of interaction between a wide variety of actors: the so-called 'crafters' of discourse.

Now, for the sake of clarity: what is a discourse? There are many definitions of discourse, but they all share the idea that discourses are stories about social reality. These stories are stated in relational terms, and give a representation of what is considered the 'social truth'. The shortest definition of discourse states that 'discourse is action'. Discourses are not just words or descriptions, they actually do things. These two notions of 'discourse as relational' and 'discourse as action' underlie the definition of discourses given by Jabri (1996: 94–95):

> Discourses are social relations represented in texts where the language contained within these texts is used to construct meaning and representation … The underlying assumption of discourse analysis is that social texts do not merely *reflect* or *mirror* objects, events and categories pre-existing in the social and natural world. Rather, they actively *construct* a version of those things. They do not describe things, *they do things*. And being active they have social and political implications.

What is implied here is that although classifications such as 'terrorism', 'ethnic identity' or 'race' are the product of our imagination, this does not make them imaginary. Since people perceive certain classifications as real, they act upon them as real, and therefore they have very real consequences. This is the power of discourse. In the BBC documentary *Racism: a History* (2007) by Tim Robinson, one of the commentators explains the very real everyday practice of the mythology of race through sketching a scene of a black man in New York City trying to hail a cab.

> Black man: Excuse me, cab, I know you think I am a black man, and that race exists. But I am a fiction! I am a figment of your imagination! I am a social construct! There is no biological base or empirical verification for my differential. I am simply another human being possessing a different magnitude of melanin.
> Cab: I still ain't picking you up, 'cause you're trying to go to Harlem, brother. That's race.

Another example of the social and political implication of the use of text is the case of the 'listing' of the Liberation Tigers of Tamil Eelam (LTTE) as a terrorist organization by the Council of the European Union in May 2006. As can be deduced from the Council's statement, by putting the LTTE on their terrorist list, they hoped to push the organization (back) to the negotiation table. The formal categorizing of persons, groups or entities on the list allows the EU to take specific restrictive measures such as a ban on the provision of funds, financial assets and economic resources, as well as police and judicial measures. The Council argued that the decision to list the Tigers was invoked by 'the actions of that organisation'. At the same time, the EU recognized that the LTTE could not be held solely responsible for the upsurge in violence. The Government of Sri Lanka was also urged to clamp down on all acts of violence and stop the culture of impunity. However, it was the LTTE, and not the Government of Sri Lanka that was given the terrorist label. What was striking about this case is that the EU did not accuse the LTTE of changing tactics: violence intensified, but remained largely the same. Although it is impossible to track the precise rationale behind the 'terrorist labelling' of the LTTE, it seems the EU expected that the use of this label would effectively cut off the organization's economic resources. This then would leave the Tigers powerless and hence willing to renegotiate peace. Although the EU measures certainly had an effect on the LTTE fund-raising capacity, the 'terrorist' label, however, above all offered the incoming Rajapakse Government a justification to start a full-fledge war against the LTTE. For terrorists, in the post 9/11 meaning of the term, are people 'without moral conscience', with whom you 'do not negotiate' and who 'need to be smoked out of their holes'. In the discursive context of the 'war on terror', labelling an organization as terrorist in order to push it to the negotiation table is, at best, paradoxical.

As Michael Bhatia (2005: 7) points out, the pronouncement of the 'war on terror' has forced many to 'verbally negotiate and assert who they are, who they are allied with, and who they are against':

> This is the new dominant framework in which both governments and non-state armed movements present their acts. Indeed, a transnational element has again been transplanted onto a series of pre-existing local disputes, as occurred during the Cold War. From Uzbekistan to Colombia, from the Philippines to Algeria, the conflict over 'names' and 'naming' is becoming furious.

The underlying assumption is that, in contradiction to the old childhood axiom of 'sticks and bones', in armed conflict 'names and images' do matter and are seen to 'hurt' (Bhatia 2005: 6). Or as Foucault argued, discourse can be conceived as 'a violence which we do to things' (1984: 127). Discourse is a tool for governments and organizations and a battleground and contested space in war and conflict.

In studying 'text in context' discourse theorists do not focus on words alone. Schröder and Schmidt (2001) describe how violence becomes sanctioned as the legitimate course of action through the imagining of violent scenarios. These 'violent imaginaries' include *narratives, performances* and *images*. Narratives keep violence alive in stories, either by glorifying one's own group or derogating the enemy. Performances are public rituals in which antagonistic relationships are staged and enacted, here the many formal and informal 'war ceremonies' come to mind, such as memorial days and parades. Discourses can also be inscribed in the cultural landscape as images on walls, bodies, buildings, flags and banners. Murals, graffiti, but also clothing are all important sources of discursive expression (Peteet 1996, 2005). In our highly mediatized world, an image is indeed 'worth a thousand words' and the role of visual displays of antagonisms in the (new) media is highly influential in staging a message before an audience.

Discourse analysis hence is about the 'politics of portrayal', examining how names and images are made, assigned and disputed, and how this battle at times translates into political and judicial measures and instruments (such as 'terrorist listing'). Discourse analysts are interested not only in the contested 'naming' of parties in war and the 'portrayal' of episodes of violence but also importantly aim to gain insight in the functions of discourse. Discursive representations are seen to fulfil at least two functions: (1) to recruit supporters by propagating a concrete us/them divide, and (2) to legitimize violent action.

...

The Legitimization of Violence

It is not hard to see how discourse plays an important role in the legitimization of action. The struggle over the representation of war and violence involves a struggle over the legitimacy of violent acts. In his book *The Legitimation of Violence*, David Apter succinctly argues that 'people do not commit political violence without discourse, they need to talk themselves into it' (1997: 2). Discourse analysis can thus be helpful in understanding the onset of war, and the step to violence in conflict. As we have seen above, discourses include 'representations of how things are and have been, as well as imaginaries – representations of how things might or could or should be' (Fairclough 2003: 207). For violence to start, it first has to become imaginable. A crucial stage in the run up to war is hence its 'dress-rehearsal' in the form of Klemperer's 'million repetitions' of 'single words, idioms, and sentence structures' imposed on people. Anthropologists Schröder and Schmidt argue that 'violence needs to be imagined in order to be carried out' (2001: 9). In describing the processual characteristics of violent action they propose a four-stage model leading from 'conflict' to 'war'. The first stage, 'conflict', is seen as the (socio-economic) contradiction at the base of intergroup competition. However, organized violence ('war') does not automatically result from contradiction. 'Wars are made by those individuals, groups or classes that have the power successfully to represent violence as the appropriate course of action in a given situation' (2001: 5). So, for war to break out, a second and third stage, named 'confrontation' and 'legitimation' are necessary. 'Confrontation' relates to the parties involved coming to look upon the 'contradiction' as somehow *relevant*, creating an antagonistic relationship. During the third stage ('legitimation') violence is officially sanctioned as the legitimate course of action through the imagining of violent scenarios, what Schröder and Schmidt call 'violent imaginaries'. Finally, during 'war' violence is put into practice (2001: 19). It is thus in particular the third stage of 'legitimation' in which violence becomes 'possible'. For Schröder and Schmidt 'the most important code of war is its historicity' (2001: 9):

> Wars are fought from memory, and they are often fought over memory, over the power to establish one's group view of the past as the legitimate one. From this perspective violence is not only a resource for solving conflicts over material issues, but also a resource in world making, to assert one group's claim to truth and history against rival claims, with all the social and economic consequences this entails.

But by what means is the legitimacy of violence 'impressed upon those who are to march into battle and those who are to cheer them on?' (2001: 9). Violent imaginaries, 'the emphasising of the historicity of present-day confrontations' play an important role in the creation of a 'hegemonic accord' among the larger public. Through their participation in narratives, performances and inscriptions people come to accept and support the violent course of action proposed by their leaders as legitimate and justified. Violent imaginaries, although strongly related to the strategic interests of those who disseminate them, are reproduced through a complex and multifaceted dynamics of interaction. As Schröder and Schmidt highlight, there are wide variations in the degree of people's acceptance of the hegemonic message. 'They correspond with one another on a general level, but in practice each conflict party is made up of numerous subgroups pursuing their own agendas' (2001: 10). In his documentary series *Blood and Belonging: Journeys into the New Nationalism* (1993, BBC), in the episode on the Orange marches in Belfast, Michael Ignatieff shows us how the 'Loyalist' community constructs its limits, its relationship to that what it is not or what threatens it, and the narratives, performances and inscriptions through which violence against 'the Catholics' is imagined and legitimated.

Ignatieff travels to Belfast in Northern Ireland to study the meaning of the Orange marches that take place every summer between 1 and 12 July. What he finds is a discourse community, a very diverse group of people who call themselves Loyalists and who all produce a similar answer when asked what it is they are celebrating: the victory of 'King Billy' (William of Orange) at the Battle of the Boyne in 1690, and the Battle of the Somme in 1916, when 'thousands of Ulstermen gave their lives for Britain'. But whereas the July celebrations mean adventure and fun for the little boys building and protecting the huge stacks of wood that are set on fire on the evening of 12 July, with an effigy of the Pope on top, the same celebrations are seen as a yearly display of 'victory' over 'the Catholics', with teenage males staging the message 'we won' to their 'rivals' on the other side. They paint the curb stones in the colours of the Union Jack to mark off 'their territory', and enjoy the 'buzz' of being part of one of the brass bands that lead the marches. There is also the older generation of males, who enjoy status through their participation in the dignified 'Orange Order', with its sashes and flags. And then there is the role of the Church as guardian of the community, and, ultimately, the paramilitary Ulster Defence Force, whose images are depicted on murals, and who in many ways make this a discourse community at gun point. Whereas the little boys' July bonfires speak to an audience of neighbourhood pals ('ours is higher'), and the teenagers enjoy 'pissing off' rival gangs through ethnic marking and marching in bands, the Church, Orange Order and UDF use the July celebrations to convey a political message to 'the mainland' and to their political adversaries, in both Northern Ireland and Ireland. Where the celebration of the victory of King Billy brings the message of religious superiority (of Protestants over Catholics) the ceremonies around the Battle of the Somme emphasize how Ulstermen have made great sacrifices for the British nation and how they are loyal to the Crown. Clearly, there is a very contemporary and political message contained within these celebrations of the past.

In showing the multiple meanings and functionalities of violent imaginaries the documentary is a wonderful illustration of what Schröder and Schmidt call 'the dialectic nature of violence', and the complex relation between violent imaginaries and violent practices. Violence and its many symbolic displays is not merely a strategy of bargaining for power, it is also a 'form of symbolic action that conveys cultural meanings, most importantly ideas of legitimacy' (2001: 8). Schröder and Schmidt base their understanding of legitimacy on Weber's (1972) classic definition, which states that a social order is accepted as valid either due to its historicity, its emotional value or to instrumental reasoning. The legitimization of violence through the re-enactment of narratives, performances and inscriptions can be based upon all of these three aspects: it recreates the past, it appeals to strong feelings of inclusion, based on the experience of either suffering or superiority, and it is a direct route to the assertion of power, established by the other two mechanisms (2001: 8). As the example of Belfast shows, the symbolic meaning of prior wars or violent confrontations is reinterpreted and adapted to the present, and is generating symbolic value to be employed in the future. Violence is thus communicative and expressive: it has a performative quality. 'Violence without an audience will still leave people dead, but is socially meaningless. Violent acts are efficient because of their staging of power and legitimacy, probably even more so than due to their physical results' (2001: 6).

So far, we have discussed approaches which emphasize how discourses are helpful in preparing audiences for violence and war, and hence how discourse theory helps us to understand the step to (the normalization of) actual violence. An author who would very much agree with the above quotation from Schröder and Schmidt, but who adds a slightly different tack on the role of discourses on violence, is Paul Brass (1996). Where Schröder and Schmidt (2001) and also Apter (1997) emphasize the stage *prior* to the violence, Brass has looked at the dynamics of after-the-act interpretations of violence as of key importance. He suggests focusing on the interpretative processes in the *aftermath* of violent practices. The core idea underlying this approach is to not simply identify the multiple contexts in which violence occurs 'because it can occur anywhere and can be organized or random, premeditated or spontaneous, directed at specific persons, groups, or property, or not' (1996: 2). Brass acknowledges that these aspects of violence must be identified insofar as possible. However, he claims that we also need to examine the discourses on violence, and the ways in which participants and observers seek to explain incidents of violence. In his work Brass aims to go beyond analysing the violent struggle to investigate as well the struggle to *interpret* the violence. That is, 'the attempts to govern a society or a country through gaining not a monopoly on the legitimate use of violence, but *to gain control over the interpretation of violence*' (1996: 45, my emphasis). For Brass, the contest for gaining control over the interpretation of violence is 'at least as important, and probably more important' than the outcome of specific struggles themselves (1996: 45):

> The struggle over the meaning of violence may or may not lead to a consensus or a hegemonic interpretation. It will certainly not lead to the 'truth' but at most to a 'regime of truth' which will give us a pre-established context into which we can place future acts of a similar type into the same context and for the reinterpretation of previous acts of violence in history.

This analysis of the struggle over meaning is not different from the study of violent imaginaries: both approaches focus on how and why certain acts of violence are selected from a plethora of other possibilities and how they are turned into symbolic markers of power and belonging, which, in turn, legitimize future acts of violence.

What Brass' analysis brings to the fore, is how over the past centuries the power to define and interpret local instances of violence, to place them in specific contexts of local knowledge, has been removed from the local societies in which they occur. From colonial racism, to the Cold War ideological stand-off, and the War on Terror, different systems of 'knowledge' have all produced 'authorities' who define and interpret local incidents of violence, but also, and importantly, act upon these interpretations. We have seen many examples of this throughout the book. Brass argues that the very tendency to place particular kinds of violence (e.g., hooliganism, rape, land grabbing, car burning) into a particular frame often involves misplacement, which in turn may contribute to the distribution and persistence of those events in space and time (1996: 2). The portrayal of a bar room brawl as an 'ethnic clash', car-burnings in French suburbs as a 'new intifada', and sexual violence in the Democratic Republic of the Congo as 'an instrument of war' are all examples of how violent acts are increasingly framed in terms that are removed from – but certainly feed into – the local settings in which they occur. It is this global–local dialectics of framing, in which a variety of actors fight a discursive battle over image, the justification of violence, blame and accountability, which is at the core of a discursive approach to violent conflict.

References

Apter, David E. (ed.) (1997) *The Legitimization of Violence*, New York: New York University Press.

Bhatia, Michael (2005) 'Fighting Words: Naming Terrorists, Bandits, Rebels and Other Violent Actors', *Third World Quarterly* 26, 1: 5–22.

Brass, Paul (1996) *Riots and Pogroms*, New York: New York University Press.

Fairclough, Norman (2003) *Analysing Discourse*, London and New York: Routledge.

Foucault, Michel (1984) 'The Order of Discourse', in M. J. Shapiro (ed.) *Language and Politics*, New York: New York University Press.

Jabri, Vivienne (1996) *Discourses on Violence: Conflict Analysis Reconsidered*, Manchester and New York: Manchester University Press.

Peteet, Julie (1996) 'The Writing on the Walls: The Graffiti of the Intifada', *Cultural Anthropology* 11(2): 139–59.

Peteet, Julie (2005) 'Words as Interventions: Naming in the Palestine-Israel Conflict', *Third World Quarterly* 26 (1): 153–72.

Richardson, Lewis F. (1948) 'War Moods', *Psychometrika* 13, Part I (3): 147–74.

Schröder, Ingo W. and Bettina Schmidt (2001) 'Introduction: Violent Imaginaries and Violent Practices' in B. Schmidt and I. Schröder (eds) *Anthropology of Violence and Conflict*, London and New York: Routledge.

Weber, Max (1972/1921–22) *Wirtschaft und Gesellschaft: Grundriss der verstehenden Soziologie*, Tübingen: J.C.B. Mohr.

25

Ethnicity, Insurgency, and Civil War

James D. Fearon and David D. Laitin

James Fearon and David Laitin are Professors of Political Science at Stanford University and are well known for their rationalist approach to wars and insurgencies. They see wars as bargaining failures, which arise because states or insurgents are unwilling to commit to solutions they might prefer to war because of information failures or fear that the other side may renege. Based on a quantitative analysis of civil wars globally since 1945, they argue that the key factor in precipitating war is not grievances or ethnic diversity, but the existence of opportunities that favour insurgencies – such as state weakness, rough terrain, a large population to hide in and superior knowledge of the local population to government forces. The article from which this introduction comes was a landmark study in the quantitative literature on civil wars.

* * * *

An influential conventional wisdom holds that civil wars proliferated rapidly with the end of the Cold War and that the root cause of many or most of these has been ethnic and religious antagonisms. We show that the current prevalence of internal war is mainly the result of a steady accumulation of protracted conflicts since the 1950s and 1960s rather than a sudden change associated with a new, post-Cold War international system. We also find that after controlling for per capita income, more ethnically or religiously diverse countries have been no more likely to experience significant civil violence in this period. We argue for understanding civil war in this period in terms of insurgency or rural guerrilla warfare, a particular form of military practice that can be harnessed to diverse political agendas. The factors that explain which countries have been at risk for civil war are not their ethnic or religious characteristics but rather the conditions that favor insurgency. These include poverty – which marks financially and bureaucratically weak states and also favors rebel recruitment – political instability, rough terrain, and large populations.

Between 1945 and 1999, about 3.33 million battle deaths occurred in the 25 interstate wars that killed at least 1,000 and had at least 100 dead on each side. These wars involved just 25 states that suffered casualties of at least 1,000 and had a median duration of not quite 3 months. In contrast, in the same period there were roughly 127 civil wars that killed at least 1,000, 25 of which were ongoing in 1999. A conservative estimate of the total dead as a direct result of these conflicts is 16.2 million, five times the interstate toll. These civil wars occurred in 73 states – more than a third of the United Nations system – and had a median duration of roughly six years. The civil conflicts in this period surely produced refugee flows far greater than their death toll and far greater than the refugee flows associated with interstate wars since 1945. Cases such as Afghanistan, Somalia, and Lebanon testify to the economic devastation that civil wars can produce. By these crude measures, civil war has been a far greater scourge than interstate war in this period, though it has been studied far less.

What explains the recent prevalence of violent civil conflict around the world? Is it due to the end of the Cold War and associated changes in the international system, or is it the result of longer-term trends? Why have some countries had civil wars while others have not? and Why did the wars break out when they did? We address these questions using data for the period 1945 to 1999 on the 161 countries that had a population of at least half a million in 1990.

The data cast doubt on three influential conventional wisdoms concerning political conflict before and after the Cold War. First, contrary to common opinion, the prevalence of civil war in the 1990s was *not* due to the end of the Cold War and associated changes in the international system. The current level of about one in six countries had already been reached prior to the breakup of the Soviet Union and resulted from a steady, gradual accumulation of civil conflicts that began immediately after World War II.

Second, it appears *not* to be true that a greater degree of ethnic or religious diversity – or indeed any particular cultural demography – by itself makes a country more prone to civil war. This finding runs contrary to a common view among journalists, policy makers, and academics, which holds "plural" societies to be especially conflict-prone due to ethnic or religious tensions and antagonisms.

Third, we find little evidence that one can predict where a civil war will break out by looking for where ethnic or other broad political grievances are strongest. Were this so, one would expect political democracies and states that observe civil liberties to be less civil war-prone than dictatorships. One would further anticipate that state discrimination against minority religions or languages would imply higher risks of civil war. We show that when comparing states at similar levels of per capita income, these expectations are not borne out.

The main factors determining both the secular trend and the cross-sectional variation in civil violence in this period are not ethnic or religious differences or broadly held grievances but, rather, conditions that favor *insurgency*. Insurgency is a technology of military conflict characterized by small, lightly armed bands practicing guerrilla warfare from rural base areas. As a form of warfare insurgency can be harnessed to diverse political agendas, motivations, and grievances. The concept is most closely associated with communist insurgency, but the methods have equally served Islamic fundamentalists, ethnic nationalists, or "rebels" who focus mainly on traffic in coca or diamonds.

We hypothesize that financially, organizationally, and politically weak central governments render insurgency more feasible and attractive due to weak local policing or inept and corrupt counterinsurgency practices. These often include a propensity for brutal and indiscriminate retaliation that helps drive noncombatant locals into rebel forces. Police and counterinsurgent weakness, we argue, is proxied by a low per capita income.

Shocks to counterinsurgent capabilities can arise from political instability at the center or the sudden loss of a foreign patron. On the rebel side, insurgency is favored by rough terrain, rebels with local knowledge of the population superior to the government's, and a large population. All three aid rebels in hiding from superior government forces. Foreign base camps, financial support, and training also favor insurgency.

Our data show that measures of cultural diversity and grievances fail to postdict civil war onset, while measures of conditions that favor insurgency do fairly well. Surely ethnic antagonisms, nationalist sentiments, and grievances often motivate rebels and their supporters. But such broad factors are too common to distinguish the cases where civil war breaks out. Also, because insurgency can be successfully practiced by small numbers of rebels under the right conditions, civil war may require only a small number with intense grievances to get going.

Using data on about 45 civil wars since 1960, Collier and Hoeffler (1999, 2001) find similarly that measures of "objective grievance" fare worse as predictors than economic variables, which they initially interpreted as measures of rebel "greed" (i.e., economic motivation). More recently, they argue that rebellion is better explained by "opportunity" than by grievance (cf. Eisinger 1973 and Tilly 1978) and that the main determinant of opportunity is the availability of finance and recruits for rebels. They proxy these with measures of primary commodity exports and rates of secondary-school enrollment for males. We agree that financing is one determinant of the viability of insurgency. We argue, however, that economic variables such as per capita income matter primarily because they proxy for state administrative, military, and police capabilities. We find no impact for primary commodity exports, and none for secondary schooling rates distinct from income. Our theoretical interpretation is more Hobbesian than economic. Where states are relatively weak and capricious, both fears and opportunities encourage the rise of would-be rulers who supply a rough local justice while arrogating the power to "tax" for themselves and, often, for a larger cause.

References

Collier, Paul, and Anke Hoeffler 1999 Justice Seeking and Loot-seeking in Civil War. World Bank. Typescript. http://econ.worldbank.org/programs/conflict/library (November 18, 2002).

Collier, Paul, and Anke Hoeffler. 2001. "Greed and Grievance in Civil War." World Bank. Typescript. http://econ.worldbank.org/programs/library (November 18, 2002).

Eisinger, Peter. 1973. "The Conditions of Protest Behavior in American Cities." *American Political Science Review* 67: 11–28.

Tilly, Charles. 1978. *From Mobilization to Revolution.* Reading, MA: Addison–Wesley.

26

Conflict Analysis Tools

Simon Mason and Sandra Rychard

Simon Mason and Sandra Rychard prepared this review of *Conflict Analysis Tools* for the Swiss Agency for Development and Cooperation's Conflict Prevention and Transformation Division. The full document outlines seven tools. Here we include sections about three: the Conflict Wheel, Conflict Mapping and Needs-Fears Mapping. Students and practitioners can use these tools to map their own conflicts..

* * * *

Introduction

This conflict analysis Tip Sheet summarizes seven tools that can be used to assess different characteristics of a conflict in a structured way. It focuses our attention on particular aspects of a conflict, to bring order into a confused conflict perception. Conflict analysis is not an "objective" art. It is influenced by different world-views. The Harvard Approach, the Human Needs Theory and the Conflict Transformation approach are frequently used:

1 The *Harvard Approach* emphasizes the difference between positions (what people say they want) and interests (why people want what they say they want). It argues that conflicts can be resolved when actors focus on interests instead of positions, and when they develop jointly accepted criteria to deal with these differences.
2 The *Human Needs Theory* argues that conflicts are caused by basic "universal" human needs that are not satisfied. The needs should be analyzed, communicated and satisfied for the conflict to be resolved.
3 The *Conflict Transformation* approach sees conflicts as destructive or constructive interactions, depending on how conflicts are dealt with or "transformed". Conflicts are viewed as an interaction of energies. Emphasis is given on the different perceptions, and the social and cultural context in which reality is constructed. Constructive conflict transformation seeks to empower actors and support recognition between them....

Summary of Conflict Analysis Tools

1. Conflict Wheel: Introduces six important dimensions of conflict analysis (dynamics, actors, causation, structures, issues and options/strategies). It organizes the other conflict analysis tools and is a "meta" tool.

2. Conflict Tree: The conflict tree deals with the difference between structural and dynamic factors, visualizing how conflict issues link these two aspects.
3. Conflict Mapping: The conflict mapping focuses on actors and their interrelationships. It is a good tool to start analyzing a conflict. Power asymmetry can be represented by the relative size of the actors' circles. Animosity and alliances are symbolized with lines.
4. Glasl's Escalation Model: The model aims to fit our conflict intervention strategy to the conflict parties' escalation level. The message is that it may be pointless to talk to a suicide bomber, or shoot people who are shouting at each other.
5. INMEDIO's Conflict Perspective Analysis (CPA): The Conflict Perspective Analysis (CPA) focuses on the different perspectives of the various parties. By putting them side by side, one can see where there are differences and things in common. CPA follows the phases of a mediation. It is a good preparation for a mediation, can also be used to coach one conflict party. CPA does not look explicitly at structures or context.
6. Needs-Fears Mapping: Similar to the CPA, this method focuses on actors and their issues, interests, needs, fears, means and options. It allows for a clear comparison of actors' similarities and differences in the form of a table.
7. Multi-Causal Role Model: This model focuses on causation, on the different quality of reasons, triggers, channels, catalysts, and targets. Content and actors, dynamics and structures are also considered.

Tool 1: The Conflict Wheel

Description: The conflict wheel is a "meta" conflict analysis tool, introducing the other tools. Each of the six sections of the wheel can be further analysed using tools presented below (or references to other Tip Sheets). The Wheel gives a first overview of a conflict, before analysing specific aspects. The Wheel symbolizes wholeness and movement, once the various aspects have been examined, they need to be brought together again, to get the conflict analysis "rolling".

Aim: → To organize the other conflict analysis tools
         → To serve as an overview when first approaching a conflict.

1. Actors/Relations: Actors or "parties" are people, organizations or countries involved in a conflict. If they are directly involved in the conflict they are called "conflict parties", if they become involved transforming the conflict, they are called "third parties". Stakeholders have an interest in the conflict or its outcome, but are not directly involved. Conflicts by definition refer to frictional relationships between parties.
2. Issues are the topics of the conflict; what people discuss or fight about.
3. Dynamics refer to the escalation level of the conflict, the intensity of interaction, the "temperament" and the energy of a conflict that transforms people.
4. Context/Structures: The conflict context and structural factors are often outside the conflict system one is looking at. Structural violence refers to violence that is not directly caused by people, but by the economic and political systems in place, e.g. causing poverty.

5. Causation: Conflicts are never mono-causal, but multi-causal and systemic factors interact. Instead of saying that everything is related to everything, it is helpful to differentiate between different "causes" or influence factors.
6. Options/Strategies: This point examines ways to deal with the conflict, strategies that are used or could be used, conflict party or third party efforts to de-escalate the conflict.

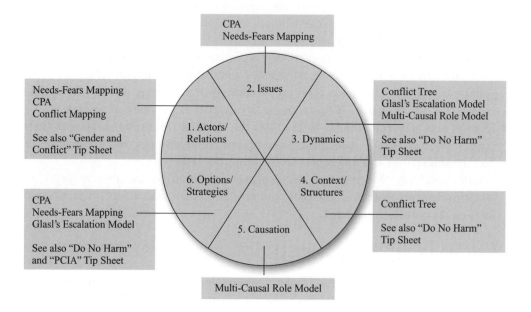

Step by step Instructions:

1. Draw a wheel, list the various aspects in the six sections of the wheel.
2. Choose further conflict analysis tools for those aspects you want to examine in more depth.

Tool 3: Conflict Map

Description: Similar to a geographic map that simplifies terrain so that it can be summarized on one page, a conflict map simplifies a conflict, and serves to visualise 1) the actors and their "power", or their influence on the conflict, 2) their relationship with each other, and 3) the conflict theme or issues. A conflict map represents a specific view point (of the person or group mapping), of a specific conflict situation (it should not not be too complex!), at a specific moment in time, similar to a photograph.

Aim: → To clarify relationships between actors
  → To visualize and reflect on the "power" of various actors
  → To represent the conflict on one sheet of paper, to give a first conflict overview

Sudan North South Conflict

Issues: 1) Security, military arrangement, 2) Sharing power, 3) Sharing wealth, 4) The capital, 5) The three areas: Blue nile, Nuba and Abyey

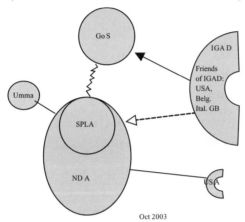

Oct 2003

Possible symbols used in conflict mapping

Circle = parties involved in the situation. The size of the circle symbolized the power of the conflict party in relation to the conflict. The name can be written in the circle.

Straight line = close relationship

Double line = Very good relationship, alliance

Dotted line = weak, informal or intermittent links

Arrow = predominant direction of influence or activity

Zig zag line = discord, conflict. Lighting bolts can be added to indicate hot events.

Crossed out line = broken connection

Half circles or quarter circle – external parties, third parties

Rectangular boxes = issues, topics or things other than people and organizations

Step by step instructions:

1. Decide on the conflict you want to analyse. Set the conflict system boundaries.
2. Form groups of two or more people. One can make a conflict map by oneself, but in a group is better. If there are people in the group that know nothing of the conflict, they can help by asking clarifying questions, by being a person the involved actor can talk to and test ideas on.
3. Take a large sheet of paper and draw the actors as circles on the paper, or on cards that can be pinned on a paper, the size of the circle representing an actors' "power". Do not forget to put yourself as an actor on the page as well, if you or your organization is involved. List third parties as semi-circles.

4. Draw lines (see symbols below) between the circles representing the relationship between the actors.
5. In square boxes, or at the top of the map, list the main themes. For more details on each actor, use the Needs-Fears mapping tool.
6. Don't forget to add title and date to the conflict map, and if not confidential, also the name or organization of the person mapping.

Tool 6: Needs-Fears Mapping

Description: The Needs-Fears Mapping is an actor oriented clarification tool. For each actor, the issues, interests/expectations/needs, fears, means and options are listed in a table. This enables comparison and quick reference. The table is comparable to the CPA tool. It can be used 1) to analyse a conflict by one actor, writing the points for the other actors hypothetically, 2) by a third party to clarify her/his perception of the actors hypothetically, 3) during mediation an abbreviated table can be used, e.g. with issues and interests. By seeing one's issues and interests written down on a flip chart or pin board, a conflict party has some assurance that his/her point has been heard, 4) it can be used as a conflict perspective change exercise, when each actor fills in the table for the other actors, and they then exchange about "self" and "foreign" images. A certain degree of trust and understanding is needed for this last version to work.

Aim: → To clarify in a comparable format the various actors' attributes
     → To leave deadlocked positions, and focus on needs and fears, and possible options to deal with these
     → To help people understand each other's perceptions
     → To stimulate discussion

The following example is about a conflict over a planned irrigation scheme:

Parties	Issues	Interest/Needs	Fears	Means	Options
Irrigation farmers	Financing of irrigation scheme	Income generation	Scheme will be stopped, they will have to leave their job	Political lobbying, shooting the cows or pastoralists	Join the dialogue process, suggest employment of pastoralists on the farms
Pastoralists	Access to water for their herds	Livelihood and survival	Their herds cannot survive, they will have to migrate	Political lobbying, pushing the herds into the irrigated area, shooting the farmers	Join the dialogue process suggest a corridor to the water
Development Cooperation agency	Implementation of project in a "Do no harm" manner	Wish to fullfill mandate, income and status at home	Project fails and the agency is blamed	Financial incentives, convening power	Bringing parties together to discuss issues
Government	Economic growth without social unrest	Re-election, popularity	Civil unrest, lack of development	Financial, political and legal means	Influence the dialogue process, compensation fund

Step by step instructions:

1. Draw a table with the following columns: Issues, interests/needs, fears, means and options.
2. a) A conflict party or third party fills the table in as a conflict analysis tool, the table is not viewed by the other conflict parties.

   b) In a moderated workshop setting, each conflict party fills in the table for their own situation. The joint table is discussed in the group. The facilitator clarifies the importance of focusing on interests (why people want something) and not positions (what people say they want). The options don't necessarily need to be realisable in the near future.

   c) In a mediated workshop setting, each conflict party fills the table in for the other parties. This helps to switch perspective. It makes the actors walk in someone else's shoes for a moment. Trust is needed, else stereotype pictures may dominate.
3. In the case of b) and c), discuss the table in the plenum. Allowing each conflict party to respond to the "self" and "foreign" image.

27

FAST Conflict Analytical Framework applied to Angola

Swisspeace

The FAST Analytical Framework, developed by Swisspeace, offers another approach to analysing conflict. It identifies root causes, proximate causes, and positive or negative intervening factors that influence the likelihood of armed conflict. This reading shows an application to the conflict in Angola. Swisspeace is a Swiss peace research institute based in Bern. FAST is its early warning division and provides monitoring of countries for development agencies and nongovernmental organizations.

* * * *

FAST Analytical Framework Angola (May 2007)

F A S T
International

swisspeace

LIKELIHOOD OF ARMED CONFLICT

IMPACT ON

POSITIVE INTERVENING FACTORS
Decreasing the likelihood of conflict

- Electoral preparations under way: voter registration (until June 2007)
- UNITA unwilling and incapable to resort to war, Government of National Unity (GURN)
- Increasing regional cooperation
- Infrastructure reconstruction and growing business opportunities in non-oil sectors
- Cabinda: Ongoing peace process since signing of Memorandum of Understanding in August 2006 opens space for development and donor support

NEGATIVE INTERVENING FACTORS
Increasing the likelihood of conflict

- Increasing politically motivated violence on local level due to electoral preparations largely unaddressed
- End of humanitarian aid phase creates assistance gap for vulnerable populations (especially former IDPs and refugees)
- Lack of impact of increasing oil revenues and reconstruction boom on poverty reduction
- Serious human security threats by spreading epidemics (cholera)
- Cabinda: Lack of tangible peace dividend for local population. Sustainability of peace process undermined by non-inclusive peace accord, ongoing low-intensity war, mismanagement of provincial resources, climate of political intimidation and crisis within local Catholic Church

PROXIMATE CAUSES (since April 2002)

Political / Governance
- Highly centralized power system and de facto one-party rule especially in the provinces
- Deficit in democratic governance: first post-war general elections delayed to 2008
- Fragmented opposition, ongoing internal divisions
- Poor state administrative capacity, weak governance and widespread corruption
- Restrictive media environment in the provinces

Security
- Over-sized Angolan Armed Forces (120-140,000) and other security forces; Slow demobilization of Civil Defense Organization; Slow disarming of civilian population
- Insufficiently attended grievances of demobilized UNITA soldiers and other war veterans (earlier peace processes)
- Ongoing high military presence in Cabinda
- Widespread landmine infestation

Social
- High humanitarian and social costs of war, extreme vulnerability and poverty of the majority of the population
- Lack of access to justice; culture of violence and impunity
- Fast spreading of HIV/AIDS and other epidemics

Economic
- "Dutch disease" hampers diversification of economy, "home-grown" economic reforms hardly sustainable (long-term)
- Dominant development vision focused on infrastructure rather than human development; reconstruction boom fails to create employment
- Real estate interests of power elite fuel land conflicts esp. in urban areas

International
- Strategy to diversify strategic partnerships (China), reducing leverage of Western donors and IMF
- Hegemonic ambitions of Angola in the region (Southern Africa, Golf of Guinea)

ROOT CAUSES

Historic
- 40 years of armed conflict, two failed peace processes (1991-92, 1994-97)
- Portuguese colonial legacy (until 1975): centralism, authoritarianism, bureaucracy, widespread analphabetism, 13 years of liberation war, hasty de-colonization with power hand-over to MPLA (excluding other liberation movements)
- Authoritarian socialist rule, MPLA one-party rule after independence (de jure until 1991); trauma of MPLA – internal cleansing after 27 May, 1978
- Peace process since 2002 resulted from military defeat of UNITA (international community and Angolan peace movement excluded from truce negotiations)

Political
- Lack of democratic tradition both within MPLA and UNITA
- Weak justice and education system
- Widespread corruption, patronage and clientelism

Social
- Civil War 1975-2002 partially linked to ethnic, regional and rural-urban cleavages rooted in the colonial era
- Culture of violence and impunity
- Over-urbanization, extremely low human development levels contrast with highly enriched power-elite

Economic
- Natural resources exploitation fuelled civil war in 1990s: offshore oil (enclave economy of MPLA) and diamond-smuggling (UNITA)
- War economy fuelled corruption ("privatization of war")
- Oil-dependent economy (90% of state income)

International
- Civil war in 1970s and 1980s fuelled by Cold War dynamics
- Intervention of Angolan Armed Forces in Congo-B and Zaire/ DRC in 1997/98: ambition of regional hegemony by Angola

28

Systemic Conflict Transformation: Reflections on the Conflict and Peace Process in Sri Lanka

Norbert Ropers

Norbert Ropers was the founder of the Berghof Research Centre for Constructive Conflict Management in Berlin, and was its director until 2005. He has focused on facilitating dialogue, mediation and peacemaking and has been active in Sri Lanka, Southeast Asia and other parts of the world. This reading includes an extended assessment of systemic conflict analysis methods of the kind pioneered by Coleman[1] and an application of them to Sri Lanka. Here we include a diagram showing Ropers's mapping of the Sri Lanka conflict and some reflections about the further development of systemic conflict analysis.

Note

1 P. Coleman, 'Conflict, Complexity and Change: A Meta-Framework for Addressing Protracted, Intractable Conflicts. III: Peace and Conflict', *Journal of Peace Psychology* 12/4 (2006): 325–348.

* * * *

A Short History of Systemic Thinking

Systemic thinking is rooted in a wide current of theories and practices which can be interpreted as a reaction to the early modern tendency of atomising, separating and de-constructing with the aim of controlling the course of events. The first contributions to systems *theory* were guided by the insight that such reductionism risked losing key features of the "whole", which was more than the sum of its parts, and inspired by the wish to overcome the ensuing fragmentation of the natural and social sciences in order to jointly serve the "human condition".

The idea of developing a general systems theory motivated a large group of scholars from the 1950s to the 1980s. So far, however, no generally accepted theoretical framework has been developed. Instead, several strands have emerged. Some focused on the complex interaction between different factors in specific areas (i.e. systemic thinking in a narrow sense). Others explored the conditions in which mental processes concerning these interactions lead to knowledge, reasoning and judging (now primarily defined as "constructivism"). In its most radical form, the two strands are merged to imply that there is no "reality" as such, but only constructs of reality (which has implications for the interaction between different "realities"). For the purposes of this article, a pragmatic approach has been chosen which accepts two basic assumptions of applied systemic thinking, namely that (1) all statements have to be seen in the social context of the persons making them, and that (2) explanations for social phenomena are most often complex and of circular character.

...

Of particular influence was the approach of "system dynamics", first developed in the 1960s by the management and engineering expert Jay W. Forrester (1968). It can be seen as a specific methodology to understand, and simulate, the behaviour of complex systems over time. It makes use of diagramming interactions within systems in the form of interconnected feedback loops and time delays, emphasising the fact that the growth of one factor in a system rarely develops in a linear way *ad infinitum*. More often, this growth is "balanced" or "controlled" by other factors. In the following, this is illustrated with an ideal-typical example of two extremely simplified factors influencing the sustainability of peace processes (see *Diagram 1*).

At the centre of the diagram is the level of support for a pro-active peace policy by the involved leaderships of two conflict parties. This support level is influenced by two loops, one reinforcing and one counteracting (or "balancing"), which makes it highly unlikely that it will grow in any unilinear way. In other words, peace processes under the influence of these two loops tend to be highly fragile or are in permanent danger of eventually breaking down.

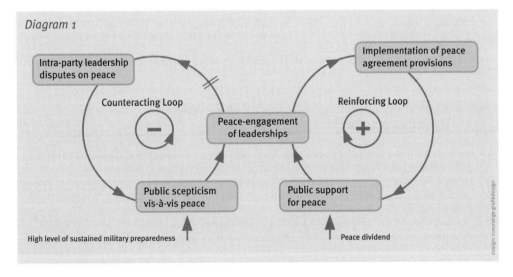

Diagram 1

The positive reinforcement loop on the right indicates that the stronger this support, the more likely it is that peace agreement provisions will be implemented, and that this will then enhance public support for the future peace process. This effect can additionally be nurtured if a peace dividend is generated for the constituencies of both parties.

The negative reinforcement loop on the left (also called counteracting or balancing) indicates factors which work against a sustained pro-active peace engagement of the leaderships. The first of these factors is the fact that in most protracted conflicts there are differences *within* the parties about the policies to be pursued vis-à-vis "the enemy". The implication of a serious peace effort is that opponents of this policy will be tempted to work against it as part of their strategy in the internal power struggle (in Sri Lanka often described as "ethnic outbidding"). In the diagram, the double stroke indicates that it might take some time before this strategy is pursued because it might not be opportune for the affected parties to express their opposition at a time of peace euphoria. But when it is expressed with whatever arguments (e.g. an imbalanced peace dividend for the parties), it can reduce public support for a sustained peace engagement.

In most cases peace processes will be influenced by many more factors, but this basic diagram illustrates that also in most cases it is too simple to envision peace efforts as linear processes in which "more of the same", i.e. consecutive and courageous initiatives of two determined conflict parties, will lead to sustained de-escalation. This is one of the most substantive arguments of system dynamics: Because of the complexity of causal interactions, of time delays and various in-built resistances, systems do not function in the way a linear expectation of "the more the better" would assume.

This simple model can be complemented with other variables, whose weight and causal interactions can also be qualified and then exposed to simulation exercises. Obviously, the results of such simulations depend on the variables used, the model structure and the causal assumptions. This is why critics of system dynamics have argued that the models might produce exactly the results one wants to see. This can be the case, but it is not an argument against the method as such because it is always possible to compare the assumptions of alternative models, and elaborate various more accurate and fine-tuned models (see *Box 1*).

Box 1 Basic steps of conflict analysis using a system dynamics approach

- Defining the *boundaries* of the system. It is important to reflect on the main variables which have an impact on the particular area under study, e.g. the peace process in a crisis region. The world outside this area is framed as *environment* which influences the system through certain parameters.
- Identifying *key issues*, the *"flows"* and *time delays* between them and the way in which they affect the "stock levels" of issues. In a next step, information on these factors is collected to determine their reliability and validity.
- Conceptualising the main *feedback loops* (patterns of interaction with a strong dynamism of their own) and other causal loops in a comprehensive "architecture" – and drawing an adequate diagram or simulating it in a computer model.
- Discussing and reflecting the *composite causal interaction* as a starting point for identifying entry points for intervention.

Diagram 2

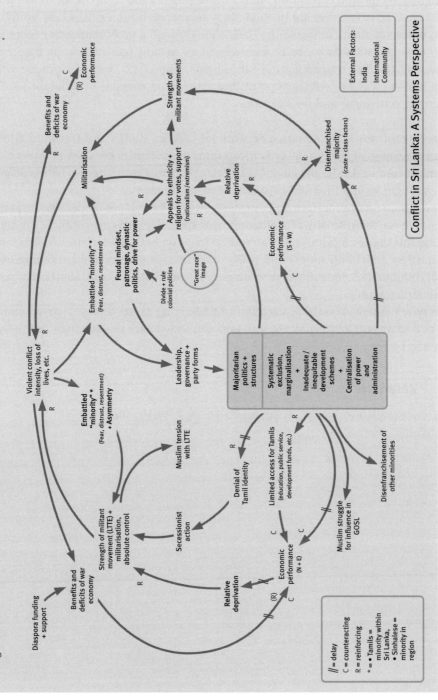

Conflict in Sri Lanka: A Systems Perspective

Diagram 2

As outlined above, one of the main benefits of this approach is that it offers a practical tool to understand and explain non-linear developments and complex social and political change. The advantages are twofold: such an approach can explain how protracted conflicts develop their "intractability" over time through a set of reinforcing loops, and it can help explain why peace processes have an in-built tendency to be fragile and ambivalent. Conflict transformation can, in this context, be seen as a process which rarely leads to a stable reference point, but rather to a corridor of different kinds of mitigation, settlement and re-escalation.

…

Inspired by this work, the Resource Network for Conflict Studies and Transformation in Sri Lanka team used the system dynamics approach to identify key driving forces of the Sri Lankan conflict. Under the guidance of Peter Woodrow they came up with a diagram which is slightly simplified and expanded here (*see Diagram 2*).

The diagram uses reinforcing and counteracting feedback loops to identify the pattern responsible for the intensity of violence in this specific protracted conflict. The centre box contains the key driving factors of several loops on both sides of the divide between the Sinhalese and Tamil society and polity: majoritarian politics and structures, exclusion of communities, inequitable development schemes and the centralisation of power and administration …

The systemic reflection drew attention to underlying causes and resistances and the need to find ways of addressing the mindsets connected with the dominant attitudes in polity and society.

Reference

Forrester, Jay W. (1968). *Principles of Systems*. Cambridge: Wright-Allen.

Toolbox

The development of conflict resolution theory has proceeded in tandem with the gathering of data about conflicts, including location, intensity/severity, duration and type. It was argued by the early theorists that gathering such data was an essential prerequisite for analysis. The field of conflict research has matured and many datasets and databases are now available. Most of these are concerned to gather conflict data. Some, more recently, are concerned to identify factors that sustain peace. Three of these resources are identified here, the first being the well-established Uppsala Conflict Data Programme, available at http://www.pcr.uu.se/research/UCDP/. The second resource, the Global Peace Index, concentrates on indicators associated with stable peaceful societies; it is available at http://www.visionofhumanity.org/#/page/indexes/global-peace-index. The third resource is the Minorities at Risk (MAR) Project developed at the University of Maryland, which monitors and analyses the status and conflicts of politically active communal groups in all countries with a current population of at least 500,000. http://www.cidcm.umd.edu/mar/.

Part III
Praxis (1) Conflict Prevention and Nonviolence

From the inception of the field of conflict resolution, pioneers have based their work on the idea that the rigorous development of multidisciplinary research would result in both theory-building and the collection of empirical data to explain conflict causation, escalation and de-escalation. In Parts I and II we have presented readings which illustrate the progress made in these areas. The guiding principle was not only to improve the academic science of conflict research, but also to find ways of applying it in order to reduce or eliminate the devastation, human and material, caused by war. This reflexive relationship between theory and practice, expressed in the ancient Greek word *praxis*, is a fundamental characteristic of conflict resolution. In Parts III–V we explore how this relationship has developed, beginning in Part III with the idea that conflicts could be prevented by developing tools, techniques and institutions to manage conflict constructively and nonviolently.

Readings from ten sources are presented here: four *reflective pieces* on the role of theory in guiding practice (Kriesberg and Dayton, Leatherman et al., Varshney and Dudouet); two *guides to practice*, taken from the report of the Carnegie Commission on Preventing Deadly Conflict and Gene Sharp's influential guide to nonviolent resistance; and four *case studies* covering applied conflict prevention by the OSCE in Estonia, the prevention of conflict between the Arctic states, Solidarity's struggle with the Communist Party authorities in Poland in the 1980s, and one of Gandhi's nonviolent campaigns in India.

The extracts reproduced here allow readers to deepen their understanding of themes which occur throughout *Contemporary Conflict Resolution*, but especially in the chapter 'Preventing Violent Conflict' and the parts of the Introduction which deal with the relationship between nonviolence and conflict resolution and the role of game theory and its Prisoner's Dilemma variant in modelling conflict dynamics.

Work on conflict prevention was pursued for much of the decade following the publication of the Carnegie Commission Report on the Prevention of Deadly Conflict in 1997 (see Reading 33 below), and although prevention remains an important objective of conflict resolution, in recent years the focus has concentrated on a discourse around the Responsibility to Protect (R2P). The R2P norm is based on the insistence that state sovereignty and the non-intervention principle should not be unquestioned in situations where states failed to protect their populations from mass atrocities, genocide and crimes against humanity. In this way the cutting edge of debates about conflict prevention currently is about whether and how to operationalize the R2P norm, as called for by the Report of the International Commission on Intervention and State Sovereignty (Responsibility to Protect, December 2001).[1]

Nonviolent resistance and pacifist values have been associated with academic conflict resolution since its inception, and many of the founders of the field (the Bouldings, Adam Curle, Gene Sharp, Johan Galtung), and indeed many of those now at the forefront of conflict resolution, both as academics and practitioners (John Paul Lederach, Diana Francis), have been and are committed pacifists, whether from religious conviction and/ or political or moral choice. However, for a number of years there has been something of a separation between, on the one hand, pacifist nonviolent activists and movements and, on the other, the conflict resolution academy. On balance, the academics have been preoccupied with theory-building, the development of models and concepts of conflict dynamics, and the scientific testing of hypotheses, while pacifists and nonviolent activists have been more concerned with engagement in the politics of nonviolent struggle. This division, however, is beginning to break down and there is an increasing cross-fertilization of knowledge, ideas and strategies. Nonviolent and pacifist values are becoming integrated with conflict resolution concepts and methods, especially in situations where seemingly rational positions are confronted by rigid and dictatorial power structures and dictatorships that prefer to use threat power and are unwilling to negotiate or accommodate. Thomas Weber convincingly makes the argument that Gandhian values and ideas (especially *satyagraha*) should be part of conflict resolution discourse.[2] The readings in Part III illustrate the potential for cross-fertilization between the two fields.

Notes

1 Report of the International Commission on Intervention and State Sovereignty (2001), International Development Research Centre, Ottawa, ON, Canada, at http://www.idrc.ca.
2 Thomas Weber, 'Gandhian Philosophy, Conflict Resolution Theory and Practical Approaches to Negotiation', *Journal of Peace Research* 38/4 (July 2001): 493–513.

29

Constructive Conflict: From Escalation to Resolution

Louis Kriesberg and Bruce W. Dayton

Louis Kriesberg was the Director of the Program on the Analysis and Resolution of Conflicts at Syracuse University. Bruce Dayton is a Research Assistant Professor in Political Science and Associate Director of the Moynihan Institute of Global Affairs at Syracuse University. Their book was an important step forward in synthesizing and developing conflict theory and applying it to real world cases, building on the thinking of the pioneers of the field. The purpose of theory development was to understand the complexity of conflict in order to guide conflict parties to resolve their differences in noncoercive ways. In the extract selected here, Kriesberg and Dayton show how a better understanding of goal definition (what the parties want) has an important bearing on improving the prospect of evolving alternative noncoercive and constructive strategies to prevent violent conflict – including nonviolent action and problem-solving. The parties themselves can influence whether conflict takes a constructive or destructive course in the way that they formulate their goals.

* * * *

Forming Contentious Goals

For a conflict to emerge, the cause of the grievance must be attributed to the conduct of other persons. The members of an aggrieved party must formulate a goal directed at those others that if achieved they believe would reduce their grievance. The aggrieved may seek more money, control over land, more autonomy, or other matters from another party.

Contentious goals are infinitely various. Nevertheless, it is useful to consider two major dimensions of goals. One is the direction of the change sought: toward greater integration or toward greater separation. The other dimension pertains to the magnitude of the changes being sought in the relationship between the adversaries, ranging from small reforms to fundamental restructuring.

Along the dimension of integration-separation, goals to achieve greater integration include attaining equal opportunities for educational and occupational positions, becoming assimilated, or converting the other side. At the opposite extreme, goals to achieve greater separation include autonomy, independence, or the expulsion or destruction of the adversary. In between are goals that seek not to alter the existing state of integration, but seek rather to modify the adversary relationship.

The magnitude of the changes sought range greatly. At one extreme, the goals aspire to only small changes, such as modifications in allocating the resources to be shared or modifications in the policies being implemented by the adversary. These goals are often of an aggregate rather than a collective character. That is, the goals pertain to opportunities for members of the quasi group as individuals, rather than as a unitary group.

At the other extreme, a revolutionary change in who has the authority to make allocations may be the objective. These goals often have a relatively collective character, as when a transformation is sought so that new groups or classes dominate. In between the extremes, are goals to reform relationships, alter policies, or oust leaders. Leaders of an ethnic minority, for example, may seek increased representation by its members in policy making. Even a coup by a military junta taking over the highest government offices from another junta, regarded as a palace revolution, often does not entail a radical change in the society.

In a sense, the magnitude of the change sought is a function of the discrepancy between the goals of the adversary camps. The greater the difference between their goals, the more radical each side's goals will be regarded by their opponent....[G]reater discrepancy also tends to result in using relatively destructive means of struggle.

Finally, we note a frequently used designation of variations in goals: the left-right dimension. This designation is used by many partisans, often contesting its meanings. Therefore, we should consider this dimension, even if the more general variations previously discussed better meet our analytic needs. Seeking to restructure the relationship or change the policy between social strata is generally considered "left" insofar as the objective is to increase equality in class, status, or power differences. Another characterization of this dimension stresses who is making claims on whom. Thus, when the disadvantaged make claims against those who have relative advantage, their objectives are considered leftist. When members of the dominant group seek to maintain or enhance their position, their objectives are regarded as rightist or even reactionary.

Certainly, the nature of the goals being pursued has implications for the course of a conflict. For example, conflicts about the allocation of resources are relatively amenable to compromise, since the resources are generally divisible. This is typically the case in consensual disputes. Some consensual conflicts, however, involve radical restructuring of the adversary relationship and are not easily settled. This is the case when a revolutionary group seeks to end private ownership of large agricultural estates; such goals are unitary and not easily divisible.

Dissensual conflicts are often about issues that are viewed as involving significant changes in the adversary and are relatively difficult to settle via compromise. This is typically the case when one party tries to convert the other to its way of believing. However, a group's goal, for example, to attain greater autonomy for its members to practice their religion, is often amenable to negotiation.

Goals incorporate mental constructs of future desired conditions and usually are embedded in a set of ideas about the partisans' plight and what can be done about it. These goals and ideas may be more or less shared and deeply held by group members. They also are varyingly well articulated, they may only be implicit and inferred from indirect verbal expressions and from conduct.

...

Adversary Relations

Similar to the formation of identity, adversaries help shape each other's contentious goals. A potential conflict group may formulate objectives that in some ways mimic those of its opponent or develop ones that magnify the differences. An illustration of the former process may be seen in the formation of Zionist goals in response to the intensified persecution of Jews in Russia toward the end of the nineteenth century. Zionists aimed to establish a national home and have a social and economic life like the Russians and others among whom they lived, emphasizing doing productive labor, especially on the land. This was one kind of response to persecution and the denial of the right to own land and to farm it. If they could not be accepted as Russians or Germans because they were Jews, then as Jews they would have their own country. Palestinian nationalism, in turn, was strongly affected by Palestinians' experience with Zionism and the establishment of Israel.

...

The analysis indicates the significance of three components in addition to feeling aggrieved. A sense of identity for each party in the conflict is necessary, although sometimes taken for granted by analysts. Furthermore, formulating a goal to bring about a change in a particular other person or group in order to redress the grievance is a critical element in the emergence of a conflict. Finally, the belief among members of the aggrieved party that by their efforts they can attain what they want, even against the wishes of the other side, is necessary.

It is important to recognize the significance of a party considering its ability to gain what it seeks in deciding to engage in a conflict. But that does not mean that a conflict results simply from a rational calculation by each party to get as much as it thinks it can get. An overwhelming sense of grievance may also engender a conflict as an aggrieved party acts from desperation.

Three sets of sources for each component have been mapped out. One set is internal to each potential conflict party. These internal sources may result in beliefs among members of a potential conflict party about who is responsible for their troubles, and that may target scapegoats so that the resulting conflict is regarded by observers and analysts as unrealistic.

The internal features and the social context of potential adversaries affect each of the components necessary for the emergence of a conflict. In this analysis, however, the ways adversaries affect each other's conduct is emphasized. This is important because it means that no one party is totally in charge of a struggle's outbreak or course. It also means that each party can influence how its possible adversary behaves in the emergence and development of a conflict.

This analysis has wide-ranging implications for conflict prevention and resolution. It suggests several strategies for preventing the eruption of social conflicts: inhibiting the development of salient oppositional identities, ameliorating the grounds for a sense of grievance, diverting the formulation of goals attributing responsibility for the grievance to others, or inhibiting the development of the belief that those feeling a sense of grievance can redress it by acting against another person or group. Merely listing such possibilities should suggest that often we do not want to prevent a conflict from emerging. We may think that justice would be served if a conflict were waged, constructively if possible.

30

Breaking Cycles of Violence: Conflict Prevention in Intrastate Conflicts

Janie Leatherman, William DeMars, Patrick Gaffney and Raimo Väyrynen

Janie Leatherman is Professor of Politics and International Studies at Fairfield University, Connecticut; William DeMars is Chair of the Department of Government at Wofford College, South Carolina; Patrick Gaffney is Associate Professor of Anthropology at the University of Notre Dame; Raimo Väyrynen has been Professor of Government and International Relations at the University of Notre Dame and Director of its Joan B. Kroc Institute for International Peace Studies. *Breaking Cycles of Violence* looks at how the international community can more effectively mobilize resources to help societies at risk of experiencing violent conflict. In the extract selected here, the focus is on early warning indicators, set within a theory of the causes of violent conflict. Early warning requires not only networks for acquiring information about conflicts, but sophisticated models for analysing them in order to guide appropriate intervention that does not fall into the error of unintentional escalation. Partnerships between local and international actors are important in this.

* * * *

Prerequisites of Early Warning

For early warning systems to be effective, the initial information gathering phase of early warning should cast a fairly wide net to gain as complete a picture as possible, and keep it up-to-date. It has to gauge social reality in a valid manner that is *also* usable in everyday political practice. This means that: (1) the instruments of early warning systems have to be streamlined and contextualized according to relevant criteria; (2) the information produced by them must be user-friendly and tailored to specific decision needs; and (3) the main early warning messages must be continuous and consistent (Spencer 1994). We also argue for replacing the mechanical view of early warning with a more realistic understanding of the multiple and complex political consequences of such action. This presupposes the consequences are well understood and their adverse effects are minimized.

Departing from a structurationist perspective, we also call for "engaged sensing." This point of departure is informed by the methodological assumptions we see underpinning early warning and conflict prevention. Whereas the objectivist perspective assumes that structures largely constrain actors, the structurationist approach contends agents and structures interact and affect each other as 'codetermined' or 'mutually constituted entities' (Wendt 1987, 339). Early warning and conflict prevention are dynamic processes. The interaction of early warning systems and parties to a conflict influences the way the conflict develops, including changes in the latters' goals, demands and behaviors, and perception of the issues at stake. Policymakers need to be aware of these developments, and understand their implications for the effectiveness of early warning and conflict prevention.

For these reasons, early warning systems have to be capable of producing nuanced interpretations of the behavior and stakes of the parties to conflict. This generally requires personnel involved in early warning on the ground (which also means that the engaged actor has negotiated either explicitly or implicitly its access to the conflict zone) or contact with local actors in the conflict area. It also means that local monitors need to be culturally sensitive – though not culturally indoctrinated. The question is not only of *cultural*, but also of *political* sensitivity: policymakers and practitioners have to know how to navigate between different expectations and requirements. Hence, cultural awareness and a capacity for making context specific evaluations of the conflict and its political components are essential. There is also a need to put the deeper understanding of local and national developments into a broader perspective, including how they relate to the regional setting. In any event, early warning and prevention can never be "objective" actions in which the accuracy of information and the effectiveness of actions alone are decisive. They form a morass in which the understanding of, for example, socioeconomic structures and cultural values by a scholar or decision maker is important, but not sufficient. He/she must also be aware of the objectives and operations of the parties to the conflict to be able to provide a valid judgment of the situation.

Another prerequisite for preventive action is an early warning system which gathers information in an anticipatory fashion and carries out analyses of the potential for conflicts to develop. In contrast to traditional approaches by which NGOs and the news media typically monitor and report on human rights violations and atrocities ex post facto, preventive action is, by definition, a pre-emptive enterprise. This imposes special requirements for the gathering and use of information for early warning.

When scholars are involved in the process, in contrast to the related activities of intelligence agencies and business enterprises, it also should be an open and accountable endeavor. However, this can lead to other problems. First, the actors collecting "time-urgent" early warning information must recognize that, through their network of contacts, they become involved in quite a variety of political developments in which they cannot always stay neutral. As a result, their preventive activities may be perceived as serving the cause of one party over the other. Any incidents or problematic developments mentioned in reports can be magnified in importance through the manipulation of media, or public pronouncements by one party as a propaganda tool against the other. Such problems are not insignificant, since they undermine governments' support for preventive diplomacy. As Boutros-Ghali reports in the 1995 Supplement to the *Agenda for Peace*, states collectively support preventive diplomacy, but are often reluctant to contribute to it, especially if they are one of the antagonists.

Another important consideration is whether early warning notification should be conveyed through public or private diplomacy. This concerns both the "who" and "how" of early warning. "Going public" with an early warning can itself exacerbate the conflict; this may be the case whether governments, intergovernmental bodies, or NGOs issue an early warning. Some disputants may be encouraged to exploit a conflict situation for enhanced status and attention to their cause, or other gains, which they expect from the added media exposure. Early warning then leads to the outcomes it aims to avert. Early warnings of ethnic cleansing, for example, may well lead the targeted communities to decide to leave. At the very least, this will result in the massive displacement of peoples, and possibly create refugee flows. Worse yet, instead of forestalling adverse developments, such warnings can fulfill the very aims of the perpetrators of such policies. Issuing a public early warning could also disrupt other efforts of quiet diplomacy carried out within international organizations, or by other third parties.

As observed earlier, monitoring and reporting on conflicts can have unintended consequences, affecting how the parties perceive their stake in the conflict, and its resolution. Consequently, early warning requires considerable diplomatic finesse, and sensitivity to the implications of such action given the political context. Because of the politicized nature of such activity, NGOs whose primary activity is service related will probably be constrained from issuing early warning statements, whether publicly or privately. Confidentiality must be weighed, however, against the necessity of mobilizing the political will of other governments or non-governmental actors to take action and commit the necessary resources to avert violence. Thus, early warning faces some of the same requirements as impartial mediation in conflicts in which violence has already broken out – unless the purpose of early warning is to help one party win the conflict.

We draw on a structurationist perspective to inform not only the methods of early warning, but also the approach we bring to the analysis of early warning information. In our opinion, a successful early warning system should combine the use of generalizable models and in-depth case studies involving local engagement. Early warning requires models specifying the key criteria by which the present and future degree of stability in a society and its breaking points, can be assessed. Case studies help to approximate the timing, mode and consequences of social and political explosion. In this study, we are interested in the particularities of conflict, but the testing of similar parameters relating to the background factors and escalatory processes of conflicts across different cases allows us to retain an element of comparability. Indeed, we need comparisons to show how the background conditions, conflict processes, and outcomes differ from one case to another and how these differences shape the success or failure of early warning and preventive action.

For both analytical and practical reasons, the early warning of conflict needs a wide network of on-going information gathering. It should cover both the historical evolution and present circumstances of the targeted societies. The collection and selection of necessary information requires core analytical and institutional competencies by which the incoming information can be assessed and utilized. Early warning is necessarily a decentralized form of transnational action because of the multitude of actors, issues, methods, and targets involved. To be effective, an early warning network requires nodes which crystallize the information and convert it into warning signals, or "red flags." Early warning is ultimately an evaluative process that leads to a political judgement about whether or not to take action. The main *actors* involved are academic scholars and policy analysts, non-governmental organizations, news media, intelligence agencies, and governmental policymakers. They all have their strengths and weaknesses in gathering and assessing information for early warning.

Roughly it may be said that there are three critical issues in the collection of early warning information; access to information, its validity and reliability, and the degree of openness in the utilization of information.

...

Both background conditions and dynamics of violence differ between structural, material, institutional, and identity conflicts. In *structural conflicts* tensions stem from such conditions as social hierarchies and cleavages, or territorial divisions. Structural conflicts result in the marginalization of some groups and the privileging of others, along class, ethnic or gender lines, for example. In *material conflicts*, the scarcity and allocation of resources and demographic and environmental pressures lead to adverse social effects that shape politics and potentially lead to violence (see, for example, Homer-Dixon 1994). In *institutional conflicts*, the political struggle mobilizes the ideological values and material interests of the people to fight for the control of the state, the resources it commands and, in that way, hegemony and autonomy within society (see, for example, Esman 1994). In cultural or *identity conflicts*, violence is embedded in the socio-economic and cultural cleavages of society, but reproduced in the perception of threats to the individual and group core values and belief system (that is, myths and memories) leading to the resort to force to defend or augment them. By examining the dynamics of identity conflicts, we also see how the different *levels of conflict* (from the individual to group, national and international levels) are activated, and various actors are mobilized.

The distinction between background factors and escalation dynamics also has a practical side: it is associated with the difference between long-term and short-term conflict management strategies. The amelioration of background causes of violence requires *long-term strategies* focusing on equitable and sustainable economic development, the establishment of strong and legitimate political institutions, the relaxation of cultural tensions, and the strengthening of social practices to resolve peacefully deadly disagreements. Engaged monitors, particularly individuals who are culturally sensitive, politically aware, and know well the needs of the society, can provide valuable early warning information that prioritizes and targets resources where they are most needed and have the greatest chance of amplifying peace. For example, given the role that the media played in exacerbating inter-ethnic fears and tensions in the former Yugoslavia, the training of journalists in the cultural sensitivity and multi-culturalism were wisely given a high priority in the preventive measures introduced in Macedonia.

Short-term strategies are needed when the outbreak of violence is imminent and there is not enough time to wait for the long-term strategies to have an impact. Here, engaged monitors need to be able to judge how conflict is intensifying, that is, whether it is spreading horizontally to mobilize more actors, or to achieve more extreme goals, or whether it will intensify vertically, as the parties become more polarized and they turn to increasingly violent means. Whether early warning notifications should be issued publicly at such junctures is a critical question. Again, it is important to ensure that such action does not inadvertently precipitate what the perpetrators themselves seek. Short-term solutions almost always are political by their nature and require that the leaders of the opposed groups cooperate to thwart off violence, for example, by sharing power, accepting an external mediator, or peacekeeping troops. Thus, short-term strategies usually favor a "top down" approach, or preventive action with muscle. Meanwhile, long-term strategies can also operate "from below," strengthening social, economic, and political structures of peace through impartial preventive action. "Bottom up" solutions tend to be more effective and durable as they change the society and do not just temporarily paper over the differences between the leaders of contending communities. However, both bottom up and top down approaches can have a socializing effect, for example, by reinforcing democracy and civil rather than ethnic conceptions of citizenship.

In short, the multidimensionality and multiple levels of conflict make for phases and escalatory dynamics that are seldom neatly ordered; rather they overlap and are contingent on each other. The matters are further complicated by the fact that types of conflict issues can vary with actors' interests and ideologies and their disagreements on how to accomplish even a shared goal (Druckman 1993, 26–29). Therefore, in designing conflict early warning indicators and preventive measures, there must be attention to the constant interaction across levels, issues, and dimensions. To simplify the analytical tasks, the *phases* of conflict can be divided between pre-conflict, intra-conflict, and post-conflict stages in which the first and third phase are predominantly non-violent. Each of these three phases can be explored in terms of the distinction between *background factors* versus *process*. While in the pre-conflict phase background factors tend to shape processes, the outbreak of violence is such a fundamental trigger that it also transforms the social context of the conflict.

Preventive action has to be tailored to different phases, with their characteristic structures and processes, types and levels of violent conflicts. In terms of phases, preventive action has three basic objectives: (1) to prevent latent disputes from developing into hostilities, and to find means to resolve them non-violently when they do; (2) to hinder the further escalation of violence; and (3) to avert a breakdown and relapse into violence during the post-conflict peace building phase. Different preventive policies and tools apply to each of these objectives. The task of early warning is to detect the development of potentially violent conflicts and provide adequate time to find out preferably non-coercive means by which the acute escalation of a crisis can be avoided and the conflict channeled constructively.

Preventive strategies can be divided into *external* versus *internal* ones, depending on who has the main responsibility for action, and *muscular* versus *impartial* ones, depending especially on the means used in preventive action. Internal prevention happens among the parties to a given conflict, while in external prevention third parties become involved.

In the pre-conflict phase preventive strategies are primarily internal and non-coercive, relying on bargaining between the main parties to the dispute. Ideally, this means that the parties institutionalize a process or create mechanisms that permit a mutual dialogue to address their long-term relationship and transform the root causes of the conflict. In the intra-conflict phase, the opportunities for an internal settlement diminish and the need of external involvement increases. External involvement in most cases has been non-coercive, comprising efforts at mediation and reconciliation between the parties with the objective to prevent escalation and, ultimately, to stop war. Here early warning should pinpoint the likelihood that its perpetrators aim to escalate the war by crossing salient qualitative or quantitative limits. Such notification should give time for the international community to try to prevent the escalation. In the post-conflict phase, the reconstruction and reintegration of a war-torn society cannot succeed without the internal commitment of the main parties to accomplish these goals. At the same time external, non-coercive economic and political assistance is vital for success. The post-conflict early warning should alert policymakers to any breakdown in the peace building process that could relapse into violent confrontation. The objective is to create stable conditions for the long-term peaceful management of society (cf. Conflict Management Group 1994, 6).

The bottom line of the above argument is that early warning and prevention are both strategic actions. Therefore, in addition to means, which the traditional cyclical models of conflict stress, we have to pay attention also to causes and goals of action. The reliance on means in model building can lead to circular reasoning. It can be avoided if the strategies of early warning and prevention are designed to reflect the underlying structural material identity and institutional sources of conflict (that is socio-economic, territorial and cultural conditions) on the one hand, and the dynamics of the conflict processes, on the other. In looking at conflict dynamics, both the issues over which the conflict is waged and the stakes that actors hold in them are particularly important as they provide a measure of the seriousness of the conflict and the lengths to which the parties are ready to go to reach their goals.

Both the early warning and prevention of conflicts may be short-term activities, while conflict resolution and peace-building usually demand more time. Thus, the time span and urgency of these two phases of conflict are different. This also means that the nature of politics – that is, issues and stakes – are different in these phases. In early warning and prevention the stakes are associated primarily with tactical advantages and public images, while in conflict resolution and peace-building they concern more the long-term allocation of political power and material values. This conclusion is not surprising as it simply states that with the exacerbation of conflict, it casts a longer shadow and its impact on the parties becomes more pervasive and long-lasting.

Alert messages and preventive measures must be both materially capable, politically feasible, and focus on malleable factors ("independent variables") whose transformation can prevent the escalation of conflict. As a rule, socio-economic, territorial, and cultural background conditions of conflicts may merit attention in early warning, but their transformation requires too much time and effort to provide a feasible approach in the political environment in which risks are high and expectations of action are immediate.

Therefore, preventive strategies must primarily focus on the dynamics of conflicts, while early warning should probably utilize both sets of factors.

Conclusion

There are many obstacles to making early warning and conflict prevention a regular practice in the management of international peace and security. States have to make a commitment to manage the causes, not just consequences of violence and repression. Identifying and acting early on them to prevent conflicts needs to become a priority. Nevertheless, emerging conflicts are overshadowed by the great number of full-blown intrastate crises crowding the international agenda during the 1990s.

With the shift toward multi-polarity, there is an expanding political space for preventive action. A more diverse group of actors is also becoming involved in the collection of early warning information, but there are still problems with access to information, its validity and reliability, and the degree of openness in as much as there will also always be trade-offs between the need for timely evaluations and systematic analyses drawing from a deep knowledge of local conditions. The latter will translate more readily into concrete policy initiatives, but are of little use for preventive action if they are not forthcoming in a timely fashion. The international community also has to overcome the challenge of integrating systematically the monitoring and reporting capabilities of NGOs and the media with other international and national means of intelligence gathering, reporting, and analysis.

The interface between early warning, including its monitoring and reporting functions, and preventive action is especially critical. However, numerous obstacles stand in the way of translating information about potential crises into collective action, including the problems of factual and political validity of the assessment, building a consensus on it, and then organizing an appropriate response. While the barriers to NGO–governmental cooperation have been lowered in recent years, in acute crises governments still have the main responsibility for organizing preventive action.

Early warning and conflict prevention have a role to play in the pre-, as well as intra- and post-conflict phases. In the intra-conflict phase, the first priority is to contain the proximate causes of violence, and to deal with its immediate consequences including preventing its spill over into neighboring regions and providing humanitarian assistance to victims. There are, however, many impediments for mobilizing preventive action with muscle. More readily available are the kinds of actors and resources which can be deployed to target background or antecedent causes of conflict. Such efforts should be introduced not only in the pre- and post-conflict phases, but also, to the extent possible, in the intra-conflict phase in order to lay the groundwork for a durable peace. Conflict transformation depends on containing escalatory processes over the short term, while altering the underlying structural conditions over the long term, including the material, cultural, and institutional dimensions of conflict. Of course, short term strategies are needed when the outbreak of violence or its spread is imminent and time is too short to wait for the long term strategies targeted on background conditions to take effect.

Ultimately, there needs to be more of a preventive developmental approach taken to targeting international resources on vulnerable and poor societies. In practice, vast resources are spent instead on rescue missions which do little to bring durable social and economic justice and political stability. Those conflicts on which the international community targets preventive action with muscle are more often the exception than the rule.

References

Conflict Management Group. 1994. *Methods and Strategies in Conflict Prevention*. Report of an Expert Consultation on the Activities of the CSCE High Commissioner on National Minorities, Cambridge, MA.

Druckman, Daniel. 1993. An Analytical Research Agenda for Conflict and Conflict Resolution. In *Conflict Resolution and Practice. Integration and Application*, ed. Dennis J. D. Sandole and Hugo van der Merwe, 25–42. New York: Manchester University Press.

Esman, Milton J. 1994. *Ethnic Politics*. Ithaca, NY: Cornell University Press.

Homer-Dixon, Thomas F. 1994. Environmental Scarcities and Violent Conflict. Evidence from Cases. *International Security* 19(1): 5–40.

Spencer, William J. 1994. Implications for Policy Use: Policy Uses of Early Warning Models and Data for Monitoring and Responding to Humanitarian Crises. *Journal of Ethno Development* 4(1): 111–115.

Wendt, Alexander E. 1987. The Agent-Structure Problem in International Relations Theory. *International Organization* 41(3): 335–370.

31

Ethnic Conflict and Civic Life; Hindus and Muslims in India

Ashutosh Varshney

Ashutosh Varshney is a political scientist and a specialist in ethnic conflict and South Asian Studies, based at Brown University, Rhode Island. In *Ethnic Conflict and Civic Life*, he provides a comparative study of violent and nonviolent development in Indian cities and emphasizes the role of intraethnic associations in preventing violence. In an analysis that reflects the work of Azar and Horowitz, he shows that violence between the Hindu and Muslim communities in Indian cities is less likely where there are strong existing cross-community linkages. This echoes Robert Putnam's ideas about bridging and bonding social capital.

* * * *

Sooner or later, scholars of ethnic conflict are struck by a puzzling empirical regularity in their field. Despite ethnic diversity, some places – regions, nations, towns, or villages – manage to remain peaceful, whereas others experience enduring patterns of violence. Similarly, some societies, after maintaining a veritable record of ethnic peace, explode in ways that surprise the observer and very often the scholar as well. Variations across time and space constitute an unresolved puzzle in the field of ethnicity and nationalism.

How does one account for such variations? With isolated exceptions,[1] uncovering commonalities across the many cases of violence has been the standard research strategy. This strategy will continue to enlighten us, but it can only give us the building blocks of a theory, not a theory of ethnic conflict. The logic underlying this proposition is simple, often misunderstood, and worth restating.[2] Suppose that on the basis of commonalities we find that interethnic economic rivalry (a), polarized party politics (b), and segregated neighborhoods (c) explain ethnic violence (X). Can we, however, be sure that our judgments are right? What if (a), (b), and (c) also exist in peaceful cases (Y)? In that case, either violence is caused by the intensity of (a), (b), and (c) in (X); or, there is an underlying and deeper context that makes (a), (b), and (c) conflictual in one case but not in the other; or, there is yet another factor (d), which differentiates peace from violence. It will, however, be a factor that we did not discover precisely because peaceful cases were not studied with the conflictual ones.

In short, until we study ethnic peace, we will not be able to have a good theory of ethnic conflict. Placing variance at the heart of new research is likely to provide by far the biggest advances in our understanding of ethnicity and ethnic conflict. Despite rising violence, many communities in the world still manage their interethnic tensions without taking violent steps.

The argument about the necessity of studying variance leads to another important methodological question: At what level must variance itself be studied? What should our unit of analysis be – nations, states, regions, towns, or villages? What methodologists call a large-n analysis can help us identify the spatial trends and allow us to choose the level at which variance is to be analyzed. The project, therefore, went through all reported Hindu-Muslim riots in the country between 1950 and 1995.[3]...For purposes of identifying larger trends, two results were crucial.

First, the share of villages in communal rioting turned out to be remarkably small. Between 1950 and 1995, rural India, where two-thirds of Indians still live, accounted for less than 4 percent of the deaths in communal violence. Hindu-Muslim violence is primarily an urban phenomenon. Second, within urban India, too, Hindu-Muslim riots are highly locally concentrated. Eight cities – Ahmedabad, Bombay, Aligarh, Hyderabad, Meerut, Baroda, Calcutta, and Delhi – account for a hugely disproportionate share of communal violence in the country: a little more than 49 percent of all urban deaths (and 45.5 percent of all deaths) in Hindu-Muslim violence. As a group, however, these eight cities represent a mere 18 percent of India's urban population (and about 5 percent of the country's total population, both urban and rural). Eighty-two percent of the urban population (95 percent of the total population) has not been "riot-prone."

Consider another way of understanding the role of local concentrations. Two cities alone in the state of Gujarat – Ahmedabad and Vadodara – account for nearly 80 percent of the total deaths in the state; 88 percent of all deaths in Maharashtra took place in the six worst towns of the state, leaving many more towns untouched; and 80 percent of all deaths in the state of Andhra Pradesh occurred in the city of Hyderabad. All these states had many more cities that were peaceful than were violent, and state-level aggregate data on deaths were simply artifacts of riots in a handful of cities. Given such high local concentrations in urban India, the large-n analysis clearly establishes the "town or city" as the unit of analysis. India's Hindu-Muslim violence is city-specific. State (and national) politics provides the context within which the local mechanisms linked with violence are activated. In order to understand the causes of communal violence, we must investigate these local mechanisms.

Following this reasoning, the project selected six cities – three from the list of eight riot-prone cities and three peaceful – and arranged them in three pairs. Thus, each pair had a city where communal violence is endemic and a city where it is rare or entirely absent. To ensure that we did not compare "apples and oranges," roughly similar Hindu-Muslim percentages in the city populations constituted the minimum control in each pair. The first pair – Aligarh and Calicut – was based on population percentages only. The second pair – Hyderabad and Lucknow – added two controls to population percentages: previous Muslim rule and reasonable cultural similarities. The third pair – Ahmedabad and Surat – was the most tightly controlled. The first two pairs came from the north and the south. The third came from the same state, Gujarat, sharing history, language, and culture but not endemic communal violence. All of these cities, at this point, have a population of more than 500,000, and the biggest, Hyderabad, is a metropolis of more than 4.2 million people.

Why was similarity in demographic proportions chosen as the minimum control in each pair? Both in India's popular political discourse and in theories about Muslim political behavior, the size of the community is considered to be highly significant. Many politicians, especially those belonging to the Hindu nationalist Bharatiya Janata Party (BJP), have argued that the demographic distribution of Muslims makes them critical to electoral outcomes in India. Muslims constitute more than 20 percent of the electorate in 197 of 545 parliamentary constituencies in the country. In a first-past-the-post system, wherein 30–35 percent of the vote is often enough to win a seat in multicornered contests, these percentages make the Muslims electorally highly significant.[4] The higher the numbers of Muslims in a given constituency, argue politicians of the BJP, the greater the inclination of centrist political parties to pander to their sectional-communal demands, and the lower the incentive, therefore, for Muslims to build bridges with the Hindus. Thus, according to this argument, "Muslim appeasement," based on the significance of numbers in a democracy, is the cause of communal conflicts in India.[5]

That Muslim demography has political consequences is, however, not an argument confined to the Hindu nationalist BJP. Leading Muslim politicians also make a demographic claim, though they reverse the causation in the argument. The higher the numbers of Muslims in a town, they argue, the greater the political threat felt by the leaders of the Hindu community, who react with hostility to legitimate Muslim anxieties about politics and identity. An unjustified, even self-serving, opposition on the part of Hindu leaders, they argue, is the source of communal hostilities. Thus, both extremes of the political spectrum heavily rely on demography for their explanations.

These popular arguments are, to some extent, shared by social scientists as well. Rudolph and Rudolph, for example, argue that when a town or constituency has a Muslim majority or plurality, Muslims typically favor confessional parties, not the centrist, intercommunal parties.[6] Muslims support centrist parties when their share of the population or electorate is small in a town or constituency. Smaller numbers make it rational to seek the security of a large, powerful mainstream party.

Can one find cases – cities or constituencies – where similar demographic distributions lead to very different forms of political behavior? Selecting from a larger sample of such cases, this study seeks to do precisely that. As described above, it compares three pairs of cities where a rough similarity in demographic proportions coexists with variance in political outcomes: peace or violence.

The Argument

What accounts for the difference between communal peace and violence? Though not anticipated when the project began, the pre-existing local networks of civic engagement between the two communities stand out as the single most important *proximate* cause. Where such networks of engagement exist, tensions and conflicts were regulated and managed; where they are missing, communal identities led to endemic and ghastly violence. As already stated, these networks can be broken down into two parts: *associational* forms of engagement and *everyday* forms of engagement. The former ties are formed in organizational settings; the latter require no organization. Both forms of engagement, if intercommunal, promote peace, but the capacity of the associational forms to withstand national-level "exogenous shocks" – such as India's partition in 1947 or the demolition of the Baburi mosque in December 1992 in full public gaze by Hindu militants – is substantially higher.

The mechanisms

What are the mechanisms that link civic networks and ethnic conflict? And why is associational engagement a sturdier bulwark of peace than everyday engagement?

One can identify two mechanisms that connect civil society and ethnic conflict. First, by promoting communication between members of different religious communities, civic networks often make neighborhood-level peace possible. Routine engagement allows people to come together and form temporary organizations in times of tension. Such organizations, though short-run, turned out to be highly significant. Called peace committees and consisting of members of both communities, these organizations policed neighborhoods, killed rumors, provided information to the local administration, and facilitated communication between communities in times of tension. Such neighborhood organizations were difficult to form in cities where everyday interaction did not cross religious lines or where Hindus and Muslims lived in highly segregated neighborhoods. Sustained prior interaction or cordiality allowed appropriate crisis-managing organizations to emerge.

The second mechanism allows us also to sort out why associational forms of engagement are sturdier than everyday forms in dealing with ethnic tensions. If vibrant organizations serving the economic, cultural, and social needs of the two communities exist, the support for communal peace not only tends to be strong but it can also be more solidly expressed. Everyday forms of engagement may make associational forms possible, but associations can often serve interests that are not the object of quotidian interactions. Intercommunal business organizations survive by tying together the business interests of many Hindus and Muslims, not because neighborhood warmth exists between Hindu and Muslim families. Though valuable in itself, the latter does not necessarily constitute the bedrock for strong civic organizations.

That this is so is, at one level, a profound paradox. After all, we know that at the village level in India, face-to-face, everyday engagement is the norm, and formal associations are few and far between.[7] Yet rural India, which had more than 80 percent of India's population in the early 1950s and still contains more than two-thirds of the country's people, has not been the primary site of communal violence. In contrast, even though associational life flourishes in cities, urban India, containing about one-third of India's population today and less than 20 percent in the early 1950s, accounts for an overwhelming proportion of deaths in communal violence between 1950 and 1995.

Why should this be so? … Informal engagement may often work in villages in keeping peace, but it does not in cities, which tend to be less interconnected and more anonymous. Size, it can be shown, reduces the effectiveness of quotidian interaction. Associations are critical when village-like intimacy is impossible.

Organized civic networks, when intercommunal, not only withstand the exogenous communal shocks – partitions, civil wars, desecration of holy places – but they also constrain local politicians in their strategic behavior. If politicians insist on polarizing Hindus and Muslims for the sake of electoral advantage, they can tear the fabric of everyday engagement apart through the organized might of criminals and gangs. In all violent cities in the project, a nexus of politicians and criminals was in evidence. Organized gangs could easily disturb neighborhood peace, often causing migration from communally heterogeneous to communally homogenous neighborhoods. People moved for the sake of physical safety. Without the involvement of organized gangs, large-scale rioting and tens and hundreds of killings are most unlikely, and without the protection afforded by politicians, such criminals cannot escape the clutches of the law. Brass has rightly called this arrangement an institutionalized riot system.[8]

In peaceful cities, however, an institutionalized peace system exists. When organizations such as trade unions, associations of businessmen, traders, teachers, doctors, lawyers, and at least some cadre-based political parties (different from the ones that have an interest in communal polarization) are communally integrated, countervailing forces are created. Associations that would suffer losses from a communal split fight for their turf, making not only their members aware of the dangers of communal violence but also the public at large. Local administrations are far more effective in such circumstances. Civic organizations, for all practical purposes, become the ears and arms of the administration. A synergy emerges between the local wings of the state and local civic organizations, making it easier to police the emerging situation and prevent it from degenerating into riots and killings. Unlike violent cities where rumors and skirmishes, often strategically planted and spread, are quickly transformed into riots, such relationships of synergy in peaceful cities nip rumors, small clashes, and tensions in the bud. In the end, polarizing politicians either don't succeed or eventually stop trying to divide communities by provoking and fomenting communal violence.

This argument, it should be noted, is probabilistic, not law-like. It indicates the odds, but it should not be taken to mean that no exceptions to the generalization would exist. Indeed, pending further empirical investigation, law-like generalizations on ethnic violence may not be possible at all. For example, a state bent on ethnic pogroms and deploying the might of its army may indeed institute veritable ethnic hells. My argument, therefore, would be more applicable to *riots* than to *pogroms* or *civil wars*. A theory of civil wars or pogroms would have to be analytically distinguished from one that deals with the more common form of ethnic violence: riots.

Indeed, perhaps the best way to understand the relationship between civic life and political shocks is to use a meteorological analogy. If the civic edifice is *interethnic and associational*, there is a good chance it can take ethnic earthquakes that rank quite high on the Richter scale (a partition, a desecration of a holy place, perhaps a civil war); if it is *interethnic and quotidian*, earthquakes of smaller intensity can bring the edifice down (defeat of an ethnic political party in elections, police brutality in a particular city); but if engagement is only *intraethnic*, not interethnic, small tremors (unconfirmed rumors, victories and defeats in sports) can unleash torrents of violence. A multiethnic society with few interconnections across ethnic boundaries is very vulnerable to ethnic disorders and violence.

Notes

1 Among the exceptions are James Fearon and David Laitin, "Explaining Ethnic Cooperation," *American Political Science Review* (December 1996): 715–35; Horowitz, *Ethnic Groups in Conflict*; Myron Weiner, *Sons of the Soil: Migration and Ethnic Conflict in India* (Princeton: Princeton University Press, 1978); Crawford Young, *The Politics of Cultural Pluralism* (Madison: University of Wisconsin Press, 1976).

2 The need for variance in social science research has been emphasized by Gary King, Robert Keohane, and Sydney Verba, *Designing Social Inquiry* (Princeton: Princeton University Press, 1993).

3 The data set was put together in collaboration with Steven Wilkinson, whose own work, based on the statistics thus collected, formed the basis of his Ph.D. dissertation, "The Electoral Incentives for Ethnic Violence: Hindu-Muslim Riots in India" (Political Science Department, MIT, 1998). The preliminary results of our collaboration were reported in Ashutosh Varshney and Steven I. Wilkinson, "*Hindu-Muslim Riots (1960–93): New Evidence, Possible Remedies*," Special Paper Series (Delhi: Rajiv Gandhi Foundation, June 1995).

4 Lloyd Rudolph and Susanne Rudolph, *In Pursuit of Lakshmi* (Chicago: University of Chicago Press, 1987), p. 196.

5 L. K. Advani, a leader of the BJP, interviewed in *Sunday* (Calcutta), July 22, 1990.

6 Rudolph and Rudolph, *In Pursuit of Lakshmi*, p. 195.

7 M. N. Srinivas, *Remembered Village* (Berkeley: University of California Press, 1979).

8 Paul Brass, *Theft of an Idol* (Princeton: Princeton University Press, 1997).

32

Nonviolent Resistance and Conflict Transformation in Power Asymmetries

Veronique Dudouet

In this reading, Veronique Dudouet, a researcher at the Berghof Research Centre for Constructive Conflict Management in Berlin, distinguishes between principled and pragmatic (or 'Gandhian' and 'Sharpian') theories of nonviolence. She shows how four types of nonviolent action can function as a form of third-party nonviolent intervention in asymmetric conflicts.

* * * *

3 Theoretical and Empirical Developments since 1945

The theory and practice of nonviolent resistance have developed in parallel, and this section presents both the main research themes in the literature as well as the increase in NVR (Non Violent Resistance) campaigns since 1945, which has been accompanied by a similar growth in organisations providing training for nonviolent activists or engaging in cross-border conflict intervention in the spirit of nonviolence.

3.1 Conceptual developments: principled and pragmatic nonviolence

The overall field of nonviolent theory is generally divided between two tendencies or sub-schools. The label "principled nonviolence" refers to the approach which advocates the recourse to NVR for religious, moral or philosophical reasons or, in other words, by conviction rather than by expediency. Violence is condemned because it causes unnecessary suffering, dehumanises and brutalises both the victim and the executioner, and only brings short-term solutions (Boserup/Mack 1974, 13). Furthermore, the refusal to harm one's opponent does not come from the absence of alternative options, and would still be advocated even if violent means were available.

The key elements of principled nonviolence were most clearly formulated by Gandhi, and further in his interpreters' work (Bondurant 1958; Naess 1958; Gregg 1960; Lanza del Vasto 1971). He coined the word "satyagraha" to describe the theory of conflict intervention which could best accommodate his moral philosophy (Gandhi 1928). It is made up of an amalgamation of two Gujarati words, *Satya* (truth) and *Agraha* (firmness), and has most commonly been translated into English as 'truth-force'. Although the term satyagraha now tends to be employed in reference to all forms of social or political opposition without violence, its original meaning encompassed much more than a simple technique of action against social and political injustice.

Gandhi believed in the unity of means and ends, and upheld nonviolence as a goal in itself, as the only way to live in truth. Therefore, the success of any particular satyagraha campaign should not be solely measured by objective criteria such as the degree of social and political freedom achieved by activists, but rather focus on spiritual, even existential elements such as the search for truth and self-realisation (Naess 1958). Contemporary approaches to principled nonviolence (e.g. Burrowes 1996; Weber 2001, 2003) have clarified the linkages between Gandhian theory and the integrative goals of conflict transformation, arguing that satyagraha provides a technique for conflict prosecution that simultaneously fights injustice, resolves disagreements and brings about mutually satisfactory solutions.

Among the proponents of principled nonviolence, one also finds religious and spiritual organisations such as the International Fellowship of Reconciliation, Pax Christi and the North American peace churches (e.g. Quakers and Mennonites). In fact, churches and religious leaders (among them Martin Luther King Jr., Desmond Tutu, Dom Helder Camara) have played an important catalytic and mobilizing role in numerous nonviolent campaigns such as the US civil rights movement, the South African anti-apartheid campaign, the 1986 "People Power" movement in the Philippines, the Eastern European revolutions in 1989–91 and Latin American social movements.

If Gandhi is the philosopher of nonviolence, Gene Sharp embodies the pragmatic, strategic, or technique-oriented approach to NVR, which is why he is often nicknamed the Clausewitz of nonviolent struggle. He justifies the recourse to civil resistance on strategic grounds, as "one response to the problem of how to act effectively in politics, especially how to wield power effectively" (Sharp 1973, 64). According to the pragmatic school of nonviolent action, empirical evidence shows that in most registered cases of NVR in recent history, the protagonists were not motivated by a principled commitment to the avoidance of bloodshed. Instead, they selected this strategy in order to defeat a particular opponent with the most effective and least costly means at hand (Ackerman/Kruegler 1994, 17), or for the lack of better alternatives, because a viable military option was not available (Sémelin 1993, 30).

This approach in fact shares more similarities with the academic field of strategic studies than with the conflict transformation school, and it has variously been described as "a war by other means" or a "functional equivalent to asymmetric [e.g. guerrilla] warfare", the only difference lying in the absence of physical violence on the part of the unarmed activists (Curle 1971, 184). It involves the waging of "battles", requires wise strategy and tactics, employs numerous "weapons", and demands courage, discipline and sacrifice of its "soldiers" (Weber 2003, 258). There is no room for problem-solving in pragmatic nonviolent action, which integrates the realist principle of incompatibility of interests, and defines conflict as a win-lose struggle for ascendancy of one group over another (Boserup/Mack 1974, 13).

The approach originally stems from the writings of young scholars during the inter-war and early post-WWII period (e.g. Clarence Case, Adam Roberts), and became strongly influenced by the work of Sharp and his colleagues, who founded a Program on Nonviolent Sanctions at Harvard University as well as the Albert Einstein Institution in Boston. These institutions have sought to establish contact with the political, strategic and military communities, and in fact one of its leading trainers, Robert Helvey (2004), is a former US Army Colonel.

Spreading since the 1990s, a new pragmatic research agenda now focuses on improving the marginal utility of nonviolent struggles by using prior knowledge and careful planning of strategy and tactics. The literature offers a wide range of comparative analyses of past campaigns (e.g. Sémelin 1993; Ackerman/Kruegler 1994; Zunes et al. 1999; Ackerman/Duvall 2000; Sharp 2005; Schock 2005) or statistical studies (e.g. Bond 1994; Karatnycky/Ackerman 2005; Stephan/Chenoweth 2008), which have drawn out a certain number of conditions facilitating the success of unarmed rebellions, as well as factors of vulnerability.

Schock (2005, xviii) notes the general tendency for strategic nonviolent scholars to overstress the role of agency in promoting political change. In other words, they put primary emphasis on internal, organisational factors of effectiveness as opposed to the external conditions in which the activists operate. The most frequently cited variables include the level of mobilization, social cohesion and unity of the movement, the degree of legitimacy and popular support which it receives, the range of tactics and types of methods selected, the presence of effective leadership, and the degree of nonviolent discipline. In particular, most studies argue that when nonviolent techniques are mixed with violent tactics, the power and effectiveness of resistance are undermined.

The role of external factors affecting the outcome of nonviolent campaigns has recently been reasserted by scholars who integrate social movements theory into the study of NVR (McAdam/Tarrow 2000; Schock 2005), as well as by the organisers of the Oxford conference on "civil resistance and power politics" in March 2007 (Roberts 2007). Such variables include the means of control and repression by the regime, the level of active support from outside powers, the degree of media coverage of the campaign, the social distance between the adversary parties, the degree of loyalty within the state bureaucracy and security forces, or the broader geopolitical context.

Despite the dissimilarities and tensions between the 'Gandhian' and 'Sharpian' theories described above, it seems that the principled and pragmatic arguments do not exclude each other, but should rather be treated as complementary. For example, key methods such as non-cooperation and civil disobedience are advocated by both schools, and in the end, in practice, "the pragmatics and the believers unite in most situations" (Fisher et al. 2000, 97). Gandhi and King used both types of arguments in their civil disobedience campaigns, which were regarded as leading both to an increased level of truth and an efficient reversal of power balance. The term nonviolent resistance must therefore be understood in this article as a combination of the two strands, which complement each other by providing a framework to guide the efforts of people who wish to resist structural violence effectively, but also do this in a way which is the most likely to lead to a satisfactory resolution of the underlying conflict.

...

(c) Third-party Nonviolent Intervention

Nonviolent action has also been increasingly used as a technique of cross-border intervention by third parties (most often transnational grassroots networks or NGOs) in order to prevent or halt violence, or bring about constructive social change, in acute conflict situations. This empirical trend has been accompanied by a scholarly recognition of the specificities of this mode of intervention (Moser-Puangsuwan/Weber 2000; Hunter/Lakey 2003: Schirch 2006; Müller 2006; Clark 2009).

A crucial distinction should be made here between third-party roles in the conflict transformation and nonviolent traditions, according to their ethical stance vis-à-vis the conflict parties. Whereas the former always emphasises the need for impartiality (or "multipartiality") on the part of external actors, most nonviolent advocacy interveners deliberately work on the sides of the victims or the low-power group, to assist them towards empowerment and the reduction of imbalance in the conflict, even if some nonviolent organisations (e.g. Peace Brigades International) insist on non-interventionist and non-partisan approaches.

Cross-border nonviolent advocates also place an important emphasis on the concept of "local ownership" in effecting social and political change. This is highly compatible with the conflict transformation stance of "elicitive" action, according to which indigenous protagonists should be the primary drivers of social change (Lederach 1995). Whereas external third-party opinion and action can act as a powerful supporting force, the primacy of action should belong to internal civil society activists (Sharp 2005, 412). For this reason, most authors reject the terminology of "assistance" (which might have connotations of victimisation of local populations), referring instead to crossborder support or accompaniment (Muller 2005, 187). An ideal-typical set of roles for internal and external actors is visualised in Figure 1.

The main types of third-party nonviolent advocacy can be described as the following:

- *Off-site nonviolent campaigns* consist of taking nonviolent initiatives in support of a struggle in another country. The goal can be either to try to halt violence or injustice directly by launching nonviolent sanctions against repressive regimes (e.g. an economic or cultural boycott), or, indirectly, to exert pressure on Western governments to reverse policies which support these regimes. Between the 1950s and 1990s, many groups and individuals across the world attempted to put pressure on the South African government to end apartheid, by organising consumer boycotts of South African exports, and campaigns to persuade foreign governments and corporations to stop supplying

	Multipartiality	Pro-justice stance
Internal action	Bridge-builder	(Nonviolent) Activist
External intervention	Mediator	(Nonviolent) Advocate

Figure 1 *Complementary Roles in Conflict Transformation (adapted from Dudouet 2005)*

finance, oil and weapons to the apartheid regime. Transnational protest or "public shaming" activities are also carried out by organisations such as Amnesty International, Human Rights Watch or the recent online petition resource Avaaz.

- *Mobilization actions* are primarily geared towards exerting cross-border pressure for change by drawing international attention to acts of violence and injustice. Diasporas often play a crucial leading role in organising such campaigns, as well as transnational solidarity networks (e.g. Guatemala Solidarity Network, Free Burma Coalition, etc.).
- *Nonviolent accompaniment* refers to on-site activities carried out in conflict areas in order to create a safe, localised political space where activists can engage in nonviolent activities. Organisations such as Peace Brigades International (in Guatemala, Sri Lanka, Colombia, Mexico, Aceh), Christian Peacemakers Team (in Haiti, Palestine, Colombia, Iraq), the Balkan Peace Team (in former Yugoslavia), and Nonviolent Peaceforce (in Sri Lanka and the Philippines) accompany threatened local human rights activists in their daily work, acting as unarmed bodyguards. Their effectiveness stems from the reluctance of armed forces or paramilitary groups to risk upsetting Western governments by attacking foreign volunteers during their protection missions. Protective accompaniment also encourages civil society activism, by allowing threatened organisations more space and confidence to operate in repressive situations (Mahony/Eguren 1997).
- *Nonviolent interposition*, finally, is performed by unarmed activists placing themselves as a 'buffer' force between conflicting parties (or between a military force and its civilian target), to help prevent or halt war. The Christian organisation Witness for Peace claims that its interposition activities in Nicaragua during the 1980s, sending 4,000 US activists to live in war zones across the country, significantly reduced the number of attacks on the Nicaraguan people by the US-sponsored Contras (Burrowes 2000, 64).

References

Ackerman, Peter and Christopher Kruegler 1994. *Strategic Nonviolent Conflict: The Dynamics of People Power in the Twentieth Century.* Westport: Praeger.

Ackerman, Peter and Jack DuVall 2000. *A Force More Powerful: A Century of Nonviolent Conflict.* New York: Palgrave.

Bond, Doug 1994. Nonviolent Direct Action and the Diffusion of Power, in: Paul Wehr, Heidi Burgess and Guy Burgess (eds.), *Justice without Violence.* Boulder: Lynne Rienner, 59–79.

Bondurant, Joan V. 1958. *Conquest of Violence: The Gandhian Philosophy of Conflict.* Princeton: Princeton University Press.

Boserup, Anders and Andrew Mack 1974. *War Without Weapons.* London: Frances Pinter.

Burrowes, Robert J. 1996. *The Strategy of Nonviolent Defense: A Gandhian Approach.* Albany: State University of New York Press.

Burrowes, Robert J. 2000. Cross-Border Nonviolent Intervention: A Typology, in: Yeshua Moser-Puangsuwan and Thomas Weber (eds.), *Nonviolent Intervention Across Borders: A Recurrent Vision.* Hawaii: University of Hawaii Press, 45–69.

Clark, Howard (ed.) 2009. *People Power. Unarmed Resistance and Global Solidarity.* London: Pluto Press.

Curle, Adam 1971. *Making Peace.* London: Tavistock.

Dudouet, Véronique 2005. Peacemaking and Nonviolent Resistance. A Study of the Complementarity between Conflict Resolution Processes and Nonviolent Intervention, with Special

Reference to the Case of Israel-Palestine. Bradford: Department of Peace Studies, University of Bradford. [PhD Thesis.]

Fisher, Simon, Dekha Ibrahim Abdi, Jawed Ludin, Steve Williams, Richard Smith and Sue Williams 2000. *Working with Conflict: Skills and Strategies for Action.* London: Zed Books.

Gandhi, Mohandas K. 1928. *Satyagraha in South Africa.* Ahmedabad: Navajivan Publishing House.

Gregg, Richard B. 1960. *The Power of Nonviolence.* Exeter: Wheaton and Co.

Helvey, Robert 2004. *On Strategic Nonviolent Conflict: Thinking about the Fundamentals.* Boston: Albert Einstein Institution.

Hunter, Daniel and George Lakey 2003. *Opening Space for Democracy: Training Manual for Third-Party Nonviolent Intervention.* Philadelphia: Training for Change.

Karatnycky, Adrian and Peter Ackerman 2005. How Freedom Is Won. From Civic Resistance to Durable Democracy, in: *International Journal of Not-for-Profit Law* 7(3). Available at http://www.icnl.org/research/journal/vol7iss3/special_3.htm.

Lanza del Vasto, Giuseppe 1971. *Technique de la Non-Violence.* Paris: Denoël.

Lederach, John Paul 1995. *Preparing for Peace: Conflict Transformation Across Cultures.* New York: Syacuse University Press.

Mahony, Liam and Enrique Eguren 1997. *Unarmed Bodyguards: International Accompaniment for the Protection of Human Rights.* West Hartford: Kumarian Press.

McAdam, Doug and Sidney Tarrow 2000. Nonviolence As Contentious Interaction, in: *Political Science and Politics* 33(2), 149–154.

Moser-Puangsuwan, Yeshua and Thomas Weber 2000. *Nonviolent Intervention across Borders: A Recurrent Vision.* Hawaii: University of Hawaii Press.

Müller, Barbara 2006. *The Balkan Peace Team 1994–2001: Non-Violent Intervention in Crisis Areas with the Deployment of Volunteer Teams.* Stuttgart: Ibidem-Verlag.

Muller, Jean-Marie 2005. *Dictionnaire de la Non-Violence.* Paris: Editions du Relié.

Naess, Arne 1958. A Systematization of Gandhian Ethics of Conflict Resolution, in: *Conflict Resolution* 2(2), 140–155.

Roberts, Adam 2007. Introduction, in: Adam Roberts and Timothy Garton Ash (eds.), *Civil Resistance and Power Politics.* Oxford: Oxford University Press, 1–24.

Schirch, Lisa 2006. *Civilian Peacekeeping: Preventing Violence and Making Space for Democracy.* Uppsala: Life and Peace Institute.

Schock, Kurt 2005. *Unarmed Insurrections: People Power Movements in Nondemocracies.* Minneapolis: University of Minnesota Press.

Sémelin, Jacques 1993. *Unarmed Against Hitler: Civilian Resistance in Europe, 1939–1943.* Westport: Praeger.

Sharp, Gene 1973. *The Politics of Nonviolent Action.* Boston: Porter Sargent.

Sharp, Gene 2005. *Waging Nonviolent Struggles. Twentieth Century Practice and Twenty-First Century Potential.* Boston: Porter Sargent.

Stephan, Maria and Erica Chenoweth 2008. Why Civil Resistance Works: The Strategic Logic of Nonviolent Conflict, in: *International Security* 33(1), 7–44.

Weber, Thomas 2001. Gandhian Philosophy, Conflict Resolution Theory and Practical Approaches to Negotiation, in: *Journal of Peace Research* 38(4), 493–513.

Weber, Thomas 2003. Nonviolence Is Who? Gene Sharp and Gandhi, in: *Peace and Change* 28(2), 250–270.

Zunes, Stephen, Lester Kurtz and Sarah Beth Ashler 1999. *Nonviolent Social Movements: A Geographical Perspective.* Oxford: Blackwell.

33

Report of the Carnegie Commission on Preventing Deadly Conflict

This Commission was set up in May 1994 to examine new ways of responding to violent conflict with the specific intention of developing the ability of the international community to use a variety of conflict prevention tools and strategies to intervene early in conflicts that were likely to escalate to high levels of deadly violence. The resulting report was an early response to the shock that reverberated throughout the world when up to 800,000 Rwandans were massacred in a genocide that occurred in April 1994, more deaths in three months than had happened in the Balkan Wars in the four years between 1991 and 1995. The Commission reported in 1997, and its recommendations, to develop a comprehensive culture and strategy for prevention, were instrumental in persuading a wide range of regional security organizations and national foreign and defence ministries to develop their own conflict prevention and early warning policies and capacities. The report marked a decisive shift in moving from academic research on conflict prevention to operationalization of capacity, and can be seen as emphatic evidence of the impact of academic theory-building in conflict resolution on real world policymaking. This debate continues to this day, using the terminology of Responsibility to Protect (R2), as noted in the introduction to this part.

The first part of the extract summarizes the findings of the report, which in total runs to more than 250 pages, with extensive analyses and practical activities that NGOs, governments and international agencies can engage in to improve preventive action. The second part of the extract specifies nine practical roles that NGOs can play to support conflict prevention.

* * * *

Three inescapable observations form the foundation of this report. First, deadly conflict is not inevitable. Violence on the scale of what we have seen in Bosnia, Rwanda, Somalia, and elsewhere does not emerge inexorably from human interaction. Second, the need to prevent deadly conflict is increasingly urgent. The rapid compression of the world through breathtaking population growth, technological advancement, and economic interdependence, combined with the readily available supply of deadly weapons and easily transmitted contagion of hatred and incitement to violence, make it essential and urgent to find ways to prevent disputes from turning massively violent. Third, preventing deadly conflict is possible. The problem is not that we do not know about incipient and large-scale violence; it is that we often do not act. Examples from "hot spots" around the world illustrate that the potential for violence can be defused through the early, skillful, and integrated application of political, diplomatic, economic, and military measures.

The Carnegie Commission on Preventing Deadly Conflict does not believe in the unavoidable clash of civilizations or in an inevitably violent future. War and mass violence usually result from deliberate political decisions, and the Commission believes that these decisions can be affected so that mass violence does not result.

To undertake effective preventive action, the Commission believes that we must develop an international commitment to the concept of prevention, a habit of preventive investment, more effective regimes for controlling destructive weaponry, and a working portfolio of legal standards that rest on a normative consensus regarding the responsibilities of governments to each other and to their peoples. Responsible leaders, key intergovernmental and nongovernmental institutions, and civil society can do far better in preventing deadly conflict than the record of this century and the current epidemic of violence suggest.

The Nature of the Problem

Violent conflict has often resulted from the traditional preoccupation of states to defend, maintain, or extend interests and power. A number of dangerous situations today can be understood in these terms. Yet, one of the most remarkable aspects of the post–Cold War world is that wars within states vastly outnumber wars between states. These internal conflicts commonly are fought with conventional weapons and rely on strategies of ethnic expulsion and annihilation. More civilians are killed than soldiers (by one estimate at the rate of about nine to one), and belligerents use strategies and tactics that deliberately target women, children, the poor, and the weak.

Many factors and conditions make societies prone to warfare: weak, corrupt, or collapsed states; illegitimate or repressive regimes; acute discrimination against ethnic or other social groups; poorly managed religious, cultural, or ethnic differences; politically active religious communities that promote hostile and divisive messages; political and economic legacies of colonialism or the Cold War; sudden economic and political shifts; widespread illiteracy, disease, and disability; lack of resources such as water and arable land; large stores of weapons and ammunition; and threatening regional relationships. When long-standing grievances are exploited by political demagogues, the scene is set for violence.

The Commission's work has identified three broad aims of preventive action:

- *First, prevent the emergence of violent conflict.* This is done by creating capable states with representative governance based on the rule of law, with widely available economic opportunity, social safety nets, protection of fundamental human rights, and robust civil societies. The aim is to prevent dangerous circumstances from developing and coalescing through efforts to establish these more desirable circumstances. A network of interlocking international regimes underwritten by the rule of law provides a supporting environment for this purpose. This approach is comparable to primary prevention in public health – and has been the Commission's main emphasis.

- *Second, prevent ongoing conflicts from spreading.* This is done by creating political, economic, and, if necessary, military barriers to limit the spread of conflict within and between states. Firebreaks may be created through well-designed assertive efforts to deny belligerents the ability to resupply arms, ammunition, and hard currency, combined with humanitarian operations that provide relief for innocent victims.
- *Third, prevent the reemergence of violence.* This is done through the creation of a safe and secure environment in the aftermath of conflict and the achievement of a peace settlement. This environment can be established through the rapid introduction of security forces to separate enemies, oversee disarmament plans, and provide a stabilizing presence. Simultaneous, immediate steps will also be necessary to restore legitimate political authority, to install functioning police, judicial, and penal systems, and to integrate external and internal efforts to restore essential services and restart normal economic activity.

Effective preventive strategies rest on three principles: early reaction to signs of trouble; a comprehensive, balanced approach to alleviate the pressures, or risk factors, that trigger violent conflict; and an extended effort to resolve the underlying root causes of violence.

- *Early reaction to signs of trouble.* Early action requires early detection and skilled analysis of developing trends. In addition, leaders and governments will need to formulate clear statements of interest, develop measured, pragmatic courses of action to respond to the warning signs, and provide support for locally sustainable solutions. Normally, early reaction will also require broad political consultations to gain the confidence of the parties to the dispute and to establish a common framework for preventive engagement. And this demands that governments develop a flexible repertoire of political, economic, and military measures – and options for their use – to stop dangerous trends.
- *A comprehensive, balanced approach to alleviate the pressures that trigger violent conflict.* Large-scale crises strain the capacity of any single government or international organization. This strain becomes particularly unbearable when, as is often the case in intrastate disputes, a government is itself party to a worsening conflict. Outside help is often necessary to deal with building crises within and between states. An effective response usually requires a range of political, economic, social, and military measures and the deliberate coordination of those measures.
- *An extended effort to resolve the underlying root causes of violence.* Discrimination and deprivation combine in deadly fashion, particularly when deliberately and systematically imposed. To address the root causes of violence, leaders and governments must ensure fundamental security, well-being, and justice for all citizens. Such a structural approach to prevention not only makes people better off, it inhibits the tendency to use violence to settle differences.

Strategies for prevention fall into two broad categories: operational prevention (measures applicable in the face of immediate crisis) and structural prevention (measures to ensure that crises do not arise in the first place or, if they do, that they do not recur). The report develops these approaches and suggests how governments, international organizations, and the various institutions of civil society might implement them.
...
Many NGOs have deep knowledge of regional and local issues, cultures, and relationships, and an ability to function in adverse circumstances even, or perhaps especially, where governments cannot. Moreover, nongovernmental relief organizations often have legitimacy and operational access that do not raise concerns about sovereignty, as government activities sometimes do. Some NGOs have an explicit focus on conflict prevention and resolution. They may:

- Monitor conflicts and provide early warning and insight into a particular conflict
- Convene the adversarial parties (providing a neutral forum)
- Pave the way for mediation and undertake mediation
- Carry out education and training for conflict resolution, building an indigenous capacity for coping with ongoing conflicts
- Help to strengthen institutions for conflict resolution
- Foster development of the rule of law
- Help to establish a free press with responsible reporting on conflict
- Assist in planning and implementing elections
- Provide technical assistance on democratic arrangements that reduce the likelihood of violence in divided societies

34

From Dictatorship to Democracy

Gene Sharp

Gene Sharp founded the Albert Einstein Institution in 1983 to advance the understanding of the theory and practice of nonviolent action in conflicts worldwide. He has published widely on the philosophy and practice of nonviolence, and Einstein wrote the foreword to Sharp's first book on Gandhi, *Gandhi Wields the Weapon of Moral Power*, in 1953. Sharp has been called 'the Machiavelli of nonviolence', and his book *From Dictatorship to Democracy*, published in Thailand in 1993 to guide Burmese dissidents, has since been published in more than 30 languages. Sharp's writings, and this book in particular, are said to have influenced many recent nonviolent uprisings against dictatorships, including those now known as the Arab Spring. This reading outlines four tasks for those who seek to enable an oppressed population to overthrow a dictatorship nonviolently. It explores means of undermining the dictatorship's power and sets out four conditions of successful nonviolent change.

*   *   *   *

Facing the Hard Truth

The conclusion is a hard one. When one wants to bring down a dictatorship most effectively and with the least cost then one has four immediate tasks:

- One must strengthen the oppressed population themselves in their determination, self-confidence, and resistance skills;
- One must strengthen the independent social groups and institutions of the oppressed people;
- One must create a powerful internal resistance force; and
- One must develop a wise grand strategic plan for liberation and implement it skillfully.

A liberation struggle is a time for self-reliance and internal strengthening of the struggle group. As Charles Stewart Parnell called out during the Irish rent strike campaign in 1879 and 1880:

> It is no use relying on the Government....You must only rely upon your own determination....[H]elp yourselves by standing together...strengthen those amongst yourselves who are weak..., band yourselves together, organize yourselves...and you must win...
> When you have made this question ripe for settlement, then and not till then will it be settled.[1]

Against a strong self-reliant force, given wise strategy, disciplined and courageous action, and genuine strength, the dictatorship will eventually crumble. Minimally, however, the above four requirements must be fulfilled.

As the above discussion indicates, liberation from dictatorships ultimately depends on the people's ability to liberate themselves. The cases of successful political defiance – or nonviolent struggle for political ends – cited above indicate that the means do exist for populations to free themselves, but that option has remained undeveloped.

...

The Workings of Nonviolent Struggle

Like military capabilities, political defiance can be employed for a variety of purposes, ranging from efforts to influence the opponents to take different actions, to create conditions for a peaceful resolution of conflict, or to disintegrate the opponents' regime. However, political defiance operates in quite different ways from violence. Although both techniques are means to wage struggle, they do so with very different means and with different consequences. The ways and results of violent conflict are well known. Physical weapons are used to intimidate, injure, kill, and destroy.

Nonviolent struggle is a much more complex and varied means of struggle than is violence. Instead, the struggle is fought by psychological, social, economic, and political weapons applied by the population and the institutions of the society. These have been known under various names of protests, strikes, noncooperation, boycotts, disaffection, and people power. As noted earlier, all governments can rule only as long as they receive replenishment of the needed sources of their power from the cooperation, submission, and obedience of the population and the institutions of the society. Political defiance, unlike violence, is uniquely suited to severing those sources of power.

Nonviolent Weapons and Discipline

The common error of past improvised political defiance campaigns is the reliance on only one or two methods, such as strikes and mass demonstrations. In fact, a multitude of methods exist that allow resistance strategists to concentrate and disperse resistance as required.

About two hundred specific methods of nonviolent action have been identified, and there are certainly scores more. These methods are classified under three broad categories: protest and persuasion, noncooperation, and intervention. Methods of nonviolent protest and persuasion are largely symbolic demonstrations, including parades, marches, and vigils (54 methods). Noncooperation is divided into three sub-categories: (a) social noncooperation (16 methods), (b) economic noncooperation, including boycotts (26 methods) and strikes (23 methods), and (c) political noncooperation (38 methods). Nonviolent intervention, by psychological, physical, social, economic, or political means, such as the fast, nonviolent occupation, and parallel government (41 methods), is the final group. A list of 198 of these methods is included as the Appendix to this publication.

The use of a considerable number of these methods – carefully chosen, applied persistently and on a large scale, wielded in the context of a wise strategy and appropriate tactics, by trained civilians – is likely to cause any illegitimate regime severe problems. This applies to all dictatorships.

In contrast to military means, the methods of nonviolent struggle can be focused directly on the issues at stake. For example, since the issue of dictatorship is primarily political, then political forms of nonviolent struggle would be crucial. These would include denial of legitimacy to the dictators and noncooperation with their regime. Noncooperation would also be applied against specific policies. At times stalling and procrastination may be quietly and even secretly practiced, while at other times open disobedience and defiant public demonstrations and strikes may be visible to all.

On the other hand, if the dictatorship is vulnerable to economic pressures or if many of the popular grievances against it are economic, then economic action, such as boycotts or strikes, may be appropriate resistance methods. The dictators' efforts to exploit the economic system might be met with limited general strikes, slowdowns, and refusal of assistance by (or disappearance of) indispensable experts. Selective use of various types of strikes may be conducted at key points in manufacturing, in transport, in the supply of raw materials, and in the distribution of products.

Some methods of nonviolent struggle require people to perform acts unrelated to their normal lives, such as distributing leaflets, operating an underground press, going on hunger strike, or sitting down in the streets. These methods may be difficult for some people to undertake except in very extreme situations.

Other methods of nonviolent struggle instead require people to continue approximately their normal lives, though in somewhat different ways. For example, people may report for work, instead of striking, but then deliberately work more slowly or inefficiently than usual. "Mistakes" may be consciously made more frequently. One may become "sick" and "unable" to work at certain times. Or, one may simply refuse to work. One might go to religious services when the act expresses not only religious but also political convictions. One may act to protect children from the attackers' propaganda by education at home or in illegal classes. One might refuse to join certain "recommended" or required organizations that one would not have joined freely in earlier times. The similarity of such types of action to people's usual activities and the limited degree of departure from their normal lives may make participation in the national liberation struggle much easier for many people.

Since nonviolent struggle and violence operate in fundamentally different ways, even limited resistance violence during a political defiance campaign will be counterproductive, for it will shift the struggle to one in which the dictators have an overwhelming advantage (military warfare). Nonviolent discipline is a key to success and must be maintained despite provocations and brutalities by the dictators and their agents.

The maintenance of nonviolent discipline against violent opponents facilitates the workings of the four mechanisms of change in nonviolent struggle (discussed below). Nonviolent discipline is also extremely important in the process of political jiu-jitsu. In this process the stark brutality of the regime against the clearly nonviolent actionists politically rebounds against the dictators' position, causing dissension in their own ranks as well as fomenting support for the resisters among the general population, the regime's usual supporters, and third parties.

In some cases, however, limited violence against the dictatorship may be inevitable. Frustration and hatred of the regime may explode into violence. Or, certain groups may be unwilling to abandon violent means even though they recognize the important role of nonviolent struggle. In these cases, political defiance does not need to be abandoned. However, it will be necessary to separate the violent action as far as possible from the nonviolent action. This should be done in terms of geography, population groups, timing, and issues. Otherwise the violence could have a disastrous effect on the potentially much more powerful and successful use of political defiance.

The historical record indicates that while casualties in dead and wounded must be expected in political defiance, they will be far fewer than the casualties in military warfare. Furthermore, this type of struggle does not contribute to the endless cycle of killing and brutality.

Nonviolent struggle both requires and tends to produce a loss (or greater control) of fear of the government and its violent repression. That abandonment or control of fear is a key element in destroying the power of the dictators over the general population.

Openness, Secrecy, and High Standards

Secrecy, deception, and underground conspiracy pose very difficult problems for a movement using nonviolent action. It is often impossible to keep the political police and intelligence agents from learning about intentions and plans. From the perspective of the movement, secrecy is not only rooted in fear but contributes to fear, which dampens the spirit of resistance and reduces the number of people who can participate in a given action. It also can contribute to suspicions and accusations, often unjustified, within the movement, concerning who is an informer or agent for the opponents. Secrecy may also affect the ability of a movement to remain nonviolent. In contrast, openness regarding intentions and plans will not only have the opposite effects, but will contribute to an image that the resistance movement is in fact extremely powerful. The problem is of course more complex than this suggests, and there are significant aspects of resistance activities that may require secrecy. A well-informed assessment will be required by those knowledgeable about both the dynamics of nonviolent struggle and also the dictatorship's means of surveillance in the specific situation.

The editing, printing, and distribution of underground publications, the use of illegal radio broadcasts from within the country, and the gathering of intelligence about the operations of the dictatorship are among the special limited types of activities where a high degree of secrecy will be required.

The maintenance of high standards of behavior in nonviolent action is necessary at all stages of the conflict. Such factors as fearlessness and maintaining nonviolent discipline are always required. It is important to remember that large numbers of people may frequently be necessary to effect particular changes. However, such numbers can be obtained as reliable participants only by maintaining the high standards of the movement.

Shifting Power Relationships

Strategists need to remember that the conflict in which political defiance is applied is a constantly changing field of struggle with continuing interplay of moves and counter-moves. Nothing is static. Power relationships, both absolute and relative, are subject to constant and rapid changes. This is made possible by the resisters continuing their non-violent persistence despite repression.

The variations in the respective power of the contending sides in this type of conflict situation are likely to be more extreme than in violent conflicts, to take place more quickly, and to have more diverse and politically significant consequences. Due to these variations, specific actions by the resisters are likely to have consequences far beyond the particular time and place in which they occur. These effects will rebound to strengthen or weaken one group or another.

In addition, the nonviolent group may, by its actions exert influence over the increase or decrease in the relative strength of *the opponent group* to a great extent. For example, disciplined courageous nonviolent resistance in face of the dictators' brutalities may induce unease, disaffection, unreliability, and in extreme situations even mutiny among the dictators' own soldiers and population. This resistance may also result in increased international condemnation of the dictatorship. In addition, skillful, disciplined, and persistent use of political defiance may result in more and more participation in the resistance by people who normally would give their tacit support to the dictators or generally remain neutral in the conflict.

Four Mechanisms of Change

Nonviolent struggle produces change in four ways. The first mechanism is the least likely, though it has occurred. When members of the opponent group are emotionally moved by the suffering of repression imposed on courageous nonviolent resisters or are rationally persuaded that the resisters' cause is just, they may come to accept the resisters' aims. This mechanism is called conversion. Though cases of *conversion* in nonviolent action do sometimes happen, they are rare, and in most conflicts this does not occur at all or at least not on a significant scale.

Far more often, nonviolent struggle operates by changing the conflict situation and the society so that the opponents simply cannot do as they like. It is this change that produces the other three mechanisms: accommodation, nonviolent coercion, and disintegration. Which of these occurs depends on the degree to which the relative and absolute power relations are shifted in favor of the democrats.

If the issues are not fundamental ones, the demands of the opposition in a limited campaign are not considered threatening, and the contest of forces has altered the power relationships to some degree, the immediate conflict may be ended by reaching an agreement, a splitting of differences or compromise. This mechanism is called *accommodation*. Many strikes are settled in this manner, for example, with both sides attaining some of their objectives but neither achieving all it wanted. A government may perceive such a settlement to have some positive benefits, such as defusing tension, creating an impression of "fairness," or polishing the international image of the regime. It is important, therefore, that great care be exercised in selecting the issues on which a settlement by accommodation is acceptable. A struggle to bring down a dictatorship is not one of these.

Nonviolent struggle can be much more powerful than indicated by the mechanisms of conversion or accommodation. Mass noncooperation and defiance can so change social and political situations, especially power relationships, that the dictators' ability to control the economic, social, and political processes of government and the society is in fact taken away. The opponents' military forces may become so unreliable that they no longer simply obey orders to repress resisters. Although the opponents' leaders remain in their positions, and adhere to their original goals, their ability to act effectively has been taken away from them. That is called *nonviolent coercion*.

In some extreme situations, the conditions producing nonviolent coercion are carried still further. The opponents' leadership in fact loses all ability to act and their own structure of power collapses. The resisters' self-direction, noncooperation, and defiance become so complete that the opponents now lack even a semblance of control over them. The opponents' bureaucracy refuses to obey its own leadership. The opponents' troops and police mutiny. The opponents' usual supporters or population repudiate their former leadership, denying that they have any right to rule at all. Hence, their former assistance and obedience falls away. The fourth mechanism of change, *disintegration* of the opponents' system, is so complete that they do not even have sufficient power to surrender. The regime simply falls to pieces.

In planning liberation strategies, these four mechanisms should be kept in mind. They sometimes operate essentially by chance. However, the selection of one or more of these as the intended mechanism of change in a conflict will make it possible to formulate specific and mutually reinforcing strategies. Which mechanism (or mechanisms) to select will depend on numerous factors, including the absolute and relative power of the contending groups and the attitudes and objectives of the nonviolent struggle group.

Note

1 Patrick Sarsfield O'Hegarty, *A History of Ireland Under the Union, 1880–1922* (London: Methuen, 1952), pp. 490–491.

Case Studies

35

Conflict Prevention in the Baltic States: The OSCE High Commissioner on National Minorities in Estonia, Latvia and Lithuania

The Organisation for Security and Cooperation in Europe emerged as one of the leading institutions for the operationalization of conflict prevention. Its Conflict Prevention Centre was established in Vienna in March 1991 to coordinate and develop the preventive policies of the OSCE. At its Istanbul Summit in 1999 the OSCE presented its Charter for European Security, in which it declared its commitment to preventing the outbreak of violent conflict as a cornerstone of European security policy.

One of the specialist offices of the OSCE is that of the High Commissioner on National Minorities (HCNM) and the extract selected here provides an insight into the work of this office, credited with being an effective positive influence in ensuring that the dissolution of the Soviet Empire and the emergence of independent states in the former Soviet bloc was managed in large part nonviolently. The extract, edited by Rob Zaagman, is an example of a diplomatic intervention which contributed to conflict prevention. The letters and statements from High Commissioner Max van der Stoel to President Meri of Estonia illustrate the use of diplomatic language and conventions in communications between an international high representative and a head of state, and show how the dialogue about minority rights in Estonia served to defuse the tensions and protect the rights of Russian minority populations in an independent Estonia. Indeed, one study by Dennis Sandole[1] showed the OSCE, measured across all its offices and activities, to be at the forefront of a new security paradigm driven by a culture of conflict prevention and resolution which was correlated with a distinct decline in major armed conflict (a 40 per cent reduction) over the period 1992–2003, precisely the period over which the findings of academic research into conflict dynamics was fed into operationally effective new security institutions such as the OSCE.

Note

1 D. J. Sandole, *Peace and Security in the Post Modern World: The OSCE and Conflict Resolution*. London: Routledge Studies in Peace and Conflict Resolution, 2007.

* * * *

Statement of the High Commissioner on National Minorities, Mr Max van der Stoel (Tallinn, 12 July 1993)

On July 10–12, 1993, I visited Estonia again. I had meetings with President Meri and Prime Minister Laar. I also met with the chairmen of the City Councils of Narva and Sillamaee, Mr Chuikin and Mr Maksimenko, and with Mr Yugantsov and Mr Semjonov of the Representative Assembly. Main subject of discussion was the development of the situation now that the Riigikogu has adopted a revised version of the Law on Aliens and the President has decided not to promulgate the law on education, but to send it back to Parliament for further consideration. In conversations with the Prime Minister, I received the following assurances:

1) The Estonian Government is determined to develop a relationship of friendship and cooperation with the Russian community in Estonia, expecting loyalty towards the Republic of Estonia in return.

2) To promote such a relationship, the Government of Estonia is determined to have an intensive and continuous dialogue with representatives of the Russian community, during which they will be free to raise any question about which they feel concerned.

3) The fact that non-Estonian residents who entered the country before 1 July 1990 must apply for residence permits under the new law on aliens, must not be interpreted as an obligation for the residents concerned to accept that in future there will be no other possibility for them than to remain non-citizens. In principle, any non-citizen residing in Estonia for more than two years can apply for citizenship of Estonia if he or she wishes to do so.

4) As far as the requirements for citizenship are concerned, the Government intends to take concrete steps in the near future to ensure that the recommendations made on this subject by the High Commissioner on National Minorities last April will be put into effect. Directives will be issued to ensure that the language requirements will not exceed the ability to conduct a simple conversation in Estonian and that the requirements will be even lower for persons over 60 and invalids.

5) The Government of Estonia wants to restate categorically that it does not intend to start a policy of expulsion from Estonia of Russian residents. This also applies to persons who are unemployed. As far as former members of the Soviet armed forces and their families are concerned, humanitarian considerations will determine the attitude of the Estonian Government. Those who received some kind of military training during their university studies but have not actively served in the Soviet armed forces will not be considered as belonging to the category of former members of the Soviet armed forces.

6) The Government of Estonia will implement article 8:4 of the law on aliens, concerning aliens' passports in such a way that no complicated procedures are needed in order to get an alien's passport.

7) The Government of Estonia will examine the possibilities of facilitating the naturalisation of resident non-citizens who will be presented as candidates in the forthcoming local elections.

8) The Government of Estonia intends to make a special effort to improve the economic situation in Northeastern Estonia.

9) The Government of Estonia, even though considering the referenda planned in Narva and Sillamaee as illegal, will not use force to prevent them from being held.

10) The statement of the Committee of Senior Officials of the CSCE of June 30 supporting the continuous involvement of the High Commissioner on National Minorities in Estonia is welcomed by the Government of Estonia.

In conversations with the representatives of the Russian community in Estonia I received the following assurances:

1) The representatives of the Russian community on their part will play an active and constructive role in the dialogue with the Government.

2) They will fully respect the Constitution and the territorial integrity of Estonia.

3) Moreover, the presidents of the City Councils of Narva and Sillamaee assured me that if the question of the legality of the referenda planned in Narva and Sillamaee is submitted to the National Court, they will abide by its ruling.

I am aware that in the dialogue between the Government and the Russian community many difficult questions still have to be solved. However, I am also convinced that the assurances I have received provide a solid basis for a fruitful dialogue.

HCNM Letter of 19 December 1998 to President Lennart Meri

Excellency,

I have the honor to address you with regard to the adoption by the Riigikogu on 15 December 1998 of an amendment to the Estonian Laws on Parliamentary Elections, Local Elections and the State Language according to which "knowledge of written and spoken Estonian" would be required in order to be a member of the Riigikogu or a local governmental council.

As you know, I issued a statement recently confirming my intention not to come forward with new proposals regarding the Law on Citizenship after adoption by the Riigikogu of the recent amendments to that Law in relation to otherwise stateless children. I wish to reiterate that this is still my intention. However, the issue at hand relates to the use of language, about which I have made a number of recommendations in the past. It is against this background that I should like to submit to you the following considerations.

In my view, the amendment to the Estonian Laws on Parliamentary Elections, Local Elections and the State Language is in accord neither with the Estonian Constitution nor with Estonia's international obligations and commitments. Moreover, I believe that promulgation of the law amending the Laws on Parliamentary Elections, Local Elections and the State Language would not constitute a constructive contribution to the national integration process.

With regard to the law applicable in Estonia, the amendment in question is in my view not compatible with specific requirements of the Constitution which, *inter alia*, stipulates no linguistic requirements as a condition to vote or to stand for office. Moreover, the Constitution stipulates the supremacy of international treaties binding on Estonia over Estonian laws which contradict such obligations. This leads me to draw your attention to the requirements of Article 3 of Protocol 1 of the European Convention on Human Rights and Article 25 of the International Covenant on Civil and Political Rights which stipulate that the will of the People (i.e. the citizenry) is to be the basis of government. It is to be noted that Article 3 of Protocol 1 of the European Convention on Human Rights is to be read in conjunction with Article 14 of the same Convention which forbids discrimination on the basis of language. Article 25 of the International Covenant on Civil and Political Rights is even more explicit in providing as follows:

> "Every citizen shall have the right and the opportunity, without any of the distinctions mentioned in article 2 and without unreasonable restrictions:
>
> "(a) to take part in the conduct of public affairs, directly or through freely chosen representatives;
>
> "(b) to vote and to be elected at genuine periodic elections which shall be by universal and equal suffrage and shall be held by secret ballot, guaranteeing the free expression of the will of the electors;
>
> "(c) to have access, on general terms of equality, to public service in his country."
>
> The destinations mentioned in Article 2, referred to above, are as follows:
>
> "1. Each State Party to the present Covenant undertakes to respect and to ensure to all individuals within its territory and subject to its jurisdiction the rights recognized in the present Covenant, without distinction of any kind, such as race, color, sex, language, religion, political or other opinion, national or social origin, property, birth or other status." (emphasis added)

It is clear from the above that there is to be absolutely no distinction regarding the language of a candidate for election nor any "unreasonable restriction"; in relation to this last point, it is further to be noted that only prescription of a minimum age, legal competence, nonincarceration and non-judicial service are generally accepted as the very few reasonable restrictions.

The rationale for the above-noted absolute entitlement to stand for office to be enjoyed by citizens (without unreasonable restriction) is rooted in the essence of the democratic process, i.e. they should be essentially free to decide among themselves who they would wish to elect, and each citizen should be equally free to present themselves for elections. Linguistic or other proficiency is fundamentally irrelevant to this process or objective. Should the electorate so choose, they should be free to elect persons who may enjoy their confidence but who may not in the opinion of others possess relevant or desirable skills or abilities, much less purported "proficiencies". The critical matter is that the elected person is deemed by the electorate (through the secret ballot) to represent them. There is no other matter of relevance. To require anything more would be to interfere with the basic democratic process and undermine the will of the people as the basis of government.

Permit me to note that the above arguments are not merely academic. By way of citing more extreme examples, the current Minister of Education in the United Kingdom, Mr. David Blunkett, is blind; as such, he is unable to read or write in the English language.

As another example, a current Member of Parliament in Canada is deaf, as such, he is unable to read or write in either of the official languages, nor is his spoken "proficiency" necessarily at the highest level (he is provided with a signer to assist him in his work as Member of Parliament).

In neither of two aforementioned cases may it be said that the elected persons do not serve their electorate, the citizenry at large or the State: in each case they have been specifically elected by their immediate constituents according to the constituency system. Indeed, in the British case, the person has been included within the Government and accorded Ministerial responsibilities. By reference to these extreme cases, it is evident *a fortiori* that "proficiency" in the State language cannot be a requirement for public service as an elected representative and that to require such could interfere with the will of the people being the basis of government.

Allow me, Mr. President, also to draw your attention to the requirements of the Council of Europe's Framework Convention for the Protection of National Minorities which provides in Article 4 that State Parties are "to adopt, where necessary, adequate measures in order to promote, in all areas of economic, social, political and cultural life, full and effective equality between persons belonging to a national minority and those belonging to the majority. In this respect, they shall take due account of the specific conditions of the persons belonging to national minorities." In addition, Article 15 of the same Convention provides that "The Parties shall create the conditions necessary for the effective participation of persons belonging to national minorities in cultural, social and economic life and in public affairs, in particular those affecting them." In my view, excluding such persons without "proficiency" in the Estonian language would in effect exclude them from the possibility to participate in the most fundamental aspects of political life and public affairs, i.e. to stand for elected office.

Finally, as High Commissioner on National Minorities of the Organization for Security and Cooperation in Europe, permit me to draw your attention also to the requirements of (among other relevant OSCE documents) the 1990 Copenhagen Document through which Estonia has committed itself to the principle of fully democratic elections and to ensure the effective participation of persons belonging to national minorities in public decision-making processes.

In my view, to exclude persons without "proficiency" in the Estonian language from holding elected office would be in contradiction with Estonia's OSCE commitments. As a consequence of the above arguments, I appeal to you not to promulgate the amendments in question as adopted by the Riigikogu. In so doing, I wish to stress that maintaining the fully open and democratic nature of the Estonian representative political institutions in no way undermines the preservation and protection of the Estonian language. I am confident that the Republic of Estonia possesses, within the wide scope of its sovereignty the means to protect, promote and develop the use of the Estonian language – including through prescription of the Estonian language as the language of Parliament and public administration in general. I am fully committed to supporting the Republic of Estonia in this objective.

Yours respectfully,

(Max van der Stoel)

36

Chill Out: Why Cooperation is Balancing Conflict among Major States in the New Arctic

Andrew Hart, Bruce Jones and David Steven

As global warming melts the ice caps, the potential scramble over oil, gas and mineral resources in the Arctic is a potential source of international conflict. This reading shows that institutional structures are being developed that have a potential to sustain cooperation. In the Arctic, the Ilulissat Declaration of 2008 by the five coastal states of the Arctic Ocean (United States, Russia, Canada, Norway and Denmark) set a precedent for states to apply the provisions of the Law of the Sea. These Arctic states have managed to resolve disputes through negotiation in a region which pessimists feared would ignite conflict because of the competition for energy resources made more accessible for commercial exploitation as a result of the melting of Arctic ice and the advance of extraction and marine transportation technologies. The authors argue that this case study might have relevance for other regions where energy and resource competition intensified by climate change threatens to escalate conflict. We return to the issue of new conflicts driven by climate change in Reading 67.

* * * *

Introduction

As the Cold War receded, so too did the strategic significance of the Arctic, once a zone of U.S.-Soviet contestation. In recent years, tensions have once again been rising. From the infamous planting of the Russian flag on the floor of the Arctic Ocean in 2007 to Secretary Clinton's appearance at the May 2011 Arctic Council ministerial, states have turned their attention to the North. The drivers of this shift are rapidly melting ice and the consequent prospects for the development of energy resources; its facilitators have been innovating in extraction technologies and marine transportation systems to move cargoes of hydrocarbons and hard minerals along previously inaccessible sea routes. Rising oil prices in 2004–2008 generated investment resources. These changes have created a complex and, to some, worrying political picture. Many fear the Arctic will see an intensifying battle for sovereign control and commercial advantage. While such a view may be "more alarmist than alarming," insecurity in the far North has increased risks of political and military conflict and highlighted the need for a stable maritime security system to manage disputes and other security concerns.

The bleakest forecasts have overlooked positive developments in the region. Despite the Arctic's dangerous mix of great power competition, unresolved territorial disputes, and increasingly accessible oil and gas reserves, there has to date been little actual discord. Unlike in the South China Seas, which faces a similar mix of uncharted energy resources and contested boundaries, Arctic states have pledged to solve disputes in an orderly process, managed the peaceful resolution of a major territorial conflict, and concluded a binding agreement to cooperate on search and rescue. This is not to say there is no reason for worry. The most contentious issues are yet to be resolved. There is scope for strategic miscalculation, a loss of faith in multilateral processes that deliver unwelcome findings, or an environmental disaster triggering a spiral of mistrust.

The Arctic therefore emerges as a rich case study of current and potential areas of international cooperation and tension, with implications for energy security, global trade, global power politics, sustainable development, and climate change. In this paper, we first address the Arctic's growing strategic relevance and its potential conflict dynamic. Second, we offer background on the existing institutions and legal regimes, assessing their strength and effectiveness, and then reviewing recent negotiations. Finally, we examine ongoing risks in the region, assessing their likely scale and evolution.

We conclude that – for now – the prospects for continued cooperation outstrip the potential for conflict among Arctic states, and that the Arctic offers lessons, and even elements of a model, for tackling evolving challenges in other regions.

…

Conclusion

Over the coming decades, risk in the Arctic will continue to intensify, although there could be a pause if the region experiences a run of cold summers, if resources prove hard to extract at a reasonable cost, or if global economic malaise drives down the oil price to a level where the Arctic's resources have no hope of being competitive. Recent years, however, have already heightened states' sensitivity to the challenges a changing Arctic poses. Sufficient momentum has been created that the impetus to explore routes for cooperation, or to unleash unilateral and coercive responses when cooperation fails, is likely to remain strong in the short to medium term.

So far, the Arctic has defied the predictions of pessimists who expected the region to become a focus for unchecked commercial and strategic competition. Given this success, can it offer some lessons for deconfliction, the management of tensions, and perhaps even cooperation in other regions where energy or resource competition has the potential to create geopolitical friction? Hardest will inevitably be the South China Seas.

At one level, that terrain has a similar mix of uncharted energy resources, ill-defined boundaries, and great power security tensions. In the Arctic, the Ilulissat Agreement has set a precedent for states to apply the provisions of the Law of the Sea, despite the US not ratifying that agreement. Such an approach will not easily be followed in the South China Seas, given the intensity of boundary disputes and long running tensions over

Taiwan. However, some of the second-order mechanisms that have emerged in the Arctic could provide lessons towards the reduction of conflict and crisis containment in that more volatile region.

In the Arctic, states are recognizing the need for new types of cooperation to address fast-changing challenges. The United States and Russia are, of course, playing a central role, but middle powers have demonstrated their potential as conveners and pioneers of new approaches. Perhaps most importantly, the assumption of inevitable conflict in the region has been successfully challenged. In an unstable world, and one where many global arrangements are straining to adapt to changing power dynamics, we could do worse than learn lessons from what the Arctic states are trying to achieve.

37
Negotiation Games
Steven Brams

Solidarity's struggle with the Polish communist authorities in the early 1980s is a good example of what Kriesberg calls 'constructive conflict' – pursuing a conflict but limiting the means. In this reading, Steven Brams, a Professor of Politics at New York University, applies two-person game theory to explore the strategic elements of this conflict.

In standard two-person game theory, players choose strategies at the same time in ignorance of each other's choices. When each chooses their best response to the worst the other can do, it is called a Nash equilibrium. In Prisoner's Dilemma, for example, Both Defect is a Nash equilibrium because whatever one player does, the payoff for the other of defecting is higher than the payoff for cooperating; defection dominates cooperation. Brams calls this a myopic equilibrium, because there may be other outcomes (like Both Cooperate in Prisoner's Dilemma) which are better for each player.

In his book, Brams develops a 'theory of moves' which avoids Prisoner's Dilemma-like traps by allowing the players to move sequentially. In this theory a player may move away from the myopic equilibrium, even if the move makes her worse off, so long as the other player then has an incentive to move to an outcome which is better for the first mover than the myopic equilibrium. The players are assumed to carry out an analysis of the game tree of possible successive moves and to be able to determine the best outcome where no further moves are improvements. An outcome is a nonmyopic equilibrium when the first mover cannot make a move without the second mover being able to force a response that leaves the first mover worse off.

This reading offers an interesting application of game theory and an analysis of a largely nonviolent conflict that played a crucial role in the ending of the Cold War. Readers may care to think about the interplay between conflict regulation norms and strategic calculations in this and other nonviolent conflicts.

*   *   *   *

The Use of Threat Power in Poland, 1980–81

The conflict between the leadership of the independent trade union, Solidarity, and the leadership of the Polish Communist party/government/state (assumed to be the same for present purposes) in 1980–81 was rife with threats and counterthreats. I shall model this conflict as a game pitting Solidarity against the party and stress the use of threats by both sides.

Although the threat of Soviet intervention was certainly a factor in the Polish game, I will not introduce the Soviet Union as a separate player. It is not clear to what extent Polish Communist party preferences differed from Soviet ones – that is, to what extent the party's preferences would have been changed if the Soviet influence, whether real or perceived, had been absent. If it is true that Soviet preferences essentially paralleled those of the Polish Communist party, then the Soviets are modeled not as a separate player but instead as a force on the side of the party that affected the balance of power in the game and, hence, the eventual outcome.

Each of the two sets of leaders may be treated as if it were a single decision maker. Of course, internal divisions within Solidarity and the party led to certain intra-organizational games; however, these subgames generally concerned not strategic choices on broad policy issues but rather tactical choices on narrow operational questions. Focusing on the main game has the advantage of highlighting the most significant political-military choices each side considered, the relationship of these choices to outcomes in the game, and the dependence of these outcomes on threats and threat power.

The two players faced the following choices:

1. *Party.* Reject or accept the limited autonomy of plural social forces set loose by Solidarity. Rejection would, if successful, restore the monolithic structure underlying social organizations and interests; acceptance would allow political institutions other than the party to participate in some meaningful way in the formulation and execution of public policy.
2. *Solidarity.* Reject or accept the monolithic structure of the state. Rejection would put pressure on the government to limit severely the extent of the state's authority in political matters; acceptance would significantly proscribe the activities of independent institutions, and Solidarity in particular, to narrower nonpolitical matters, with only minor oversight over certain state actitivities.

Designate these strategies of both sides as "rejection" and "acceptance," and label them *R* and *A*, respectively. These strategies might also be designated "confrontation" and "compromise," but I prefer the former, more neutral labels because the disagreements were generally over specific proposals rather than general postures that the two sides struck.

The two strategies available to each side give rise to four possible outcomes:

1. A-A. Compromise that allows plural institutions but restricts their activities to nonpolitical matters, with negotiations commencing on the sharing of political power.
2. R-R. Possibly violent conflict involving the entire society, opening the door to outside (mainly Soviet) intervention.
3. A (Solidarity)-R (Party). Status quo ante, with tight restrictions on all activities of Solidarity and its recognition of the supremacy of party/state interests.
4. R (Solidarity)-A (Party). Authorization of independent political activity, and a corresponding gradual reduction of the party/state role in implementing public policy decisions made collectively.

These four outcomes represent what may be considered the four major scenarios pertinent to the Polish situation. Each of these scenarios can accommodate differences in

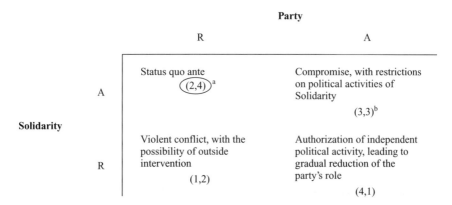

Party

		R	A
Solidarity	A	Status quo ante (2,4)ᵃ	Compromise, with restrictions on political activities of Solidarity (3,3)ᵇ
	R	Violent conflict, with the possibility of outside intervention (1,2)	Authorization of independent political activity, leading to gradual reduction of the party's role (4,1)

Key: (x,y) = Solidarity, party); 4 = best; 3 = next best; 2 = next worst; 1 = worst; A = acceptance; R = rejection.
ᵃParty's compellent threat outcome.
ᵇSolidarity's deterrent threat outcome.
Circled outcome is a Nash and nonmyopic equilibrium.

Figure 1 *Payoff matrix of Polish game, 1980–81*

details, but these differences seem more tactical than strategic. The four outcomes, and the rankings I assign them, are shown in the payoff matrix of Figure 1.

The party leadership repeatedly emphasized the unacceptability of any solution that would constrain its political power, which implies that its two worst outcomes are those associated with Solidarity's choice of R. Commenting on the Polish events, Bialer (1981, 530) wrote, "Some [Party] leaders are more conservative and some more reformist; none, to our knowledge, questions the need to preserve the Party's monopoly." The Eleventh Plenary Meeting of the Central Committee of the Polish United Workers Party (PUWP) was explicit on this point:

> The Central Committee of PUWP unequivocally rejects ... concepts of abandoning the leading role of the Party, of reducing this role to the ideological sphere and dispossessing the Party of the instruments of political power. This is the main danger. (*Nowy Dziennik*, June 17, 1981, p. 2)

In fact, the available evidence indicates that the party preferred an all-out confrontation (*R-R*) to relinquishing its supremacy [R (Solidarity)-A (Party)]. Speaking at the Ninth Congress of PUWP, Deputy Prime Minister Mieczyslaw Rakowski announced: "To the enemies of socialism we can offer nothing but a fight, and not merely verbal at that" (*Nowy Dziennik*, July 21, 1981, p. 2). A later declaration of the Politburo reiterated that challenge: "We shall defend socialism as one defends Poland's independence. In this defense the state shall use all the means it deems necessary" (*Nowy Dziennik*, September 22, 1981, p. 2). Finally, between its two best outcomes associated with Solidarity's choice of A, the party clearly preferred the status quo [A (Solidarity)-R (Party)] to compromise (A-A).

As for Solidarity, there is considerable evidence that it preferred the party's capitulation [R (Solidarity)-A (Party)] most, and violent conflict (R-R) least. In between, it preferred a compromise solution (A-A) to its own capitulation [A (Solidarity)-R (Party)]. Solidarity statements echoed this sentiment. Its chairman, Lech Walesa, said: "We don't want to change the socialist ownership of the means of production, but we want to be real masters of the factories. We were promised that many times before" (*Time*, September 8, 1980, p. 34). Jacek Kuron, one of Solidarity's advisers, further clarified where the line on party activities should be drawn: "The Party's leading role means the monopoly of power over the police forces, the army and foreign policy. All other matters must be open to negotiations with society" (*Time*, December 29, 1980, p. 29). In short, Solidarity preferred not to try to rob the party of its most significant functions, hoping to gain the party's acquiescence and thereby at least Solidarity's next-best outcome (*A-A*).

The reason for Solidarity's preference is evident. Solidarity was aware of the unacceptability of its best outcome [R (Solidarity)-*A* (Party)] to its adversary:

> From the start, the Polish workers understood [that] to think of overthrowing the Party in Poland was madness, for it would inevitably lead to Soviet invasion and the destruction of all liberties gained in the past ten or even twenty-five years. (Ascherson 1982, 18–19)

Addressing Solidarity members, Walesa said: "Our country needs internal peace. I call on you to be prudent and reasonable" (*Time*, December 29, 1980, p. 20). On another occasion he said, "[There are] fighters who want to fight at every opportunity; but we must understand that both the society and the union have had enough of confrontation . . . we ought not to go to the brink" (*Solidarność*, April 10, 1981, p. 1). Kuron concurred: "The goals of the government and of the democratic movement are completely opposite. But the struggle between the two tendencies, the totalitarian and the democratic one, are to be fought exclusively by peaceful means." Thus, Solidarity preferred *R* only if the party chose *A*; if the party chose *R*, it preferred *A*.

Viewed statically (i.e., as a nonsequential game, in which players make simultaneous strategy choices ... the party has a dominant strategy of *R*, better for it whatever Solidarity chooses. Anticipating this strategy choice of the party, Solidarity would prefer *A* to *R*, leading to (2, 4), the unique Nash equilibrium in this game.

... (2, 4) is also a nonmyopic equilibrium in the sequential game, indicating that this outcome is stable in the long as well as the short run. Given that neither side enjoys any power advantage over the other, (2, 4) is therefore the apparent solution of this game in the sense that neither player can, by unilaterally departing from this outcome, ensure a better outcome for itself, whether this departure results in subsequent (rational) moves or not. Because this solution is the best outcome for the party, and only next worst for Solidarity, the game seems to be inherently unfair to Solidarity.

Solidarity, however, can undermine the nonmyopic equilibrium in this game if it possesses threat power. In fact, it can induce (3, 3) by a deterrent threat: choosing *A*, it can threaten *R*, and the party's two worst outcomes, unless the party accepts Solidarity's threat outcome, (3, 3). Solidarity's breakdown outcome, (1, 2), however, is also the breakdown outcome for the party if it is the player with threat power. The party's threat is compellent and is implemented by its choosing, and staying at, *R*, forcing Solidarity to choose *A* and the party's threat outcome, (2, 4).

Thus, with confrontation (*R-R*) being the common breakdown outcome, the game turns on who (if either player) holds the balance of power. If Solidarity is the more powerful of the two players, or is at least perceived as such, it can implement (3, 3). Otherwise, (2,

4), as the Nash and nonmyopic equilibrium, would presumably obtain – and be reinforced should the party possess threat power. Note that Solidarity can implement its threat outcome, (3, 3), by choosing its "soft" strategy *A*, relegating its "hard" strategy *R* to a (deterrent) threat. This, of course, is the proverbial "speak softly and carry a big stick" policy, with the big stick being used only if necessary.

In contrast to Solidarity, the party always does at least as well as Solidarity [(3, 3), if it does not have threat power], and sometimes better [(2, 4) if it does, or neither player does], at least in terms of the comparative rankings of the two players. Thus, a power asymmetry unfavorable to itself is not as serious for the party as for Solidarity, based on a comparative ranking of the two threat outcomes. Moreover, because the party's threat is compellent, it can implement its best outcome simply by choosing and then maintaining its hard strategy R, whereas Solidarity must first take a soft position and then threaten escalation to its hard position, putting the onus for breakdown and subsequent disruption on itself.

This game-theoretic analysis based on threat power offers meaningful insights into the actual unfolding of events in Poland in 1980–81. Clearly, the party was stunned by the quick pace of developments and the widespread support for Solidarity after the August 1980 Lenin shipyard strike in Gdansk, which are events that I take as the starting point of the analysis and do not attempt to explain. Whatever set off the crisis, the party did in fact consider Solidarity to be more powerful during the last part of 1980 and into the beginning of 1981. Reluctantly, it followed its acceptance strategy, *A*; Solidarity, for its part, repeatedly emphasized the nonpolitical character of its demands (*A*) while threatening R, for the union's very existence was "based on adversary relations, not on a partnership" (Szafar 1981,79). As the economic situation worsened, however, the instability of the (3, 3) compromise outcome became evident, setting the stage for a test of strength between Solidarity and the party.

In March 1981, for the first time, the government used force against Solidarity. Although the force was limited in scope, its use can be interpreted as an attempt to switch to the party rejection strategy R. Yet Solidarity chose to avoid confrontation, and the game remained at (3, 3).

Although "the game was to leave the authorities with a semblance of power but to take its substance away" (Watt 1982, 11), the events of March 1981 began to split Solidarity, strengthening proponents of the rejection strategy. But the moderate leadership of Solidarity, and Walesa in particular, kept pointing to society's unwillingness to support the rejection strategy. In doing so, the leadership cast doubt upon the viability of Solidarity's breakdown strategy, thereby undermining the union's power.

In December 1981 the party, apparently believing that the balance of power had shifted, switched decisively to *its* rejection strategy R, moving the game to its threat outcome, (2, 4), by imposing martial law and jailing many Solidarity leaders in a massive crackdown. The relative stability of this outcome until 1989 seemed to validate the party's assessment that the balance of power favored it in Poland – or at least demonstrated that Solidarity's power was not greater than its own.

Although Solidarity showed no appetite to switch to R, by 1989 the catastrophic economic situation led the party to take a much more accommodationist position. (I have not tried to model how this situation evolved.) In eight-week roundtable talks in March and April 1989 between the party and Solidarity, an agreement was reached to hold elections in June, in which Solidarity was allowed to compete for 35 percent of the seats in the lower house, and all the seats in the upper house, of parliament. In an embarrassing turn of events, Solidarity not only won virtually all the contested seats, but many party members failed to win majority support even in uncontested elections.

The negotiated compromise and election results can perhaps be viewed as a return to the (3, 3) outcome. It was not so much provoked by threats of violent conflict but rather a recognition by both sides that the (4, 2) outcome after the December 1981 crackdown had, because of severe economic problems, degenerated to something probably approaching (1, 2). Faced with a disastrous economy, both sides saw benefit in trying to reach a modus vivendi.

The Polish game, at least in the 1980–81 period, illustrates when threat power is effective: it makes a difference – depending on whether Solidarity or the party possesses it – on what outcome is implemented. When one player can, by using its power, implement for itself an outcome superior to that which an adversary can achieve using its power, then there will be good reason for the players to vie for influence.

References

Ascherson, Neal. 1982. *The Polish August: The Self-Limiting Revolution*. New York: Viking.

Bialer, Seweryn. 1981. "Poland and the Soviet Imperium." *Foreign Affairs* 59, no. 3 (Fall): 522–39.

Szafar, Tadeusz. 1981. "Brinkmanship in Poland." *Problems of Communism* 30, no. 3 (May/June): 75–81.

Watt, Richard M. 1982. "Polish Possibilities." New York Times Book Review, April 25, pp. 11, 19.

38

Nonviolence in Peace and War

Mohandas K. Gandhi

This reading reveals Gandhi's distinctive approach to conflict, involving an extremely high degree of personal risk and commitment. After his successful campaign of nonviolence had helped to free India from British colonial rule, a violent conflict erupted between the Hindu and Muslim populations of India. Gandhi threw himself into efforts to respond to this conflict nonviolently, intervening personally with his companions to protect minorities. This passage describes his response to the violent conflict in Bengal in 1946. The approach he developed here, involving nonviolent protection of minorities and returning refugees, is still a prominent method of nonviolent action in conflicts today.

*   *   *   *

Early in the morning on Wednesday last Gandhiji announced to his party an important decision. He had decided to disperse his party detailing each member, including the ladies, to settle down in one affected village and make himself or herself hostage of the safety and security of the Hindu minority of that village. They must be pledged to protect with their lives, if necessary, the Hindu population of that village. His decision was not binding on any one of his party, he said. Those who wanted to, were free to go away and take up any of his other constructive activities. "Those who have ill-will against the Mussulmans or Islam in their hearts or cannot curb their indignation at what has happened should stay away. They will only misrepresent me by working under this plan."

So far as he was concerned, he added that his decision was final and irrevocable and left no room for discussion. He was going to bury himself in East Bengal until such time that the Hindus and Mussalmans learnt to live together in harmony and peace. He would deprive himself of the services of all his companions and fend for himself with whatever assistance he could command locally.

…

To Sevagram Ashram people he wrote:

"I am afraid you must give up all hope of my early returning or returning at all to the Ashram. The same applies to my companions. It is a Herculean task that faces me. I am being tested. Is the Satyagraha of my conception a weapon of the weak or really that of the strong? I must either realise the latter or lay down my life in the attempt to attain it. That is my quest. In pursuit of it I have come to bury myself in this devastated village. His will be done."

On the 24th Gandhiji broke up his camp at Kazirkhil, Columbus-like, to face the dark unknown, accompanied only by his stenotypist, Shri Parsuram and Prof Nirmal Kumar Bose, his Bengali interpreter. Before embarking the little group around him held a short prayer when his favourite hymn, "Vaishnava jana to tene kahiye" was sung. Many voices were husky, many eyes dim with tears as the tiny country boat bearing him disappeared beyond the bridge, in the direction of Shrirampur.

Following upon his departure the members of his party dispersed themselves one by one in various appointed places.

Toolbox

The development and institutionalization of capacity for conflict prevention has led to a number of resources which provide practical guides to engage in preventive activities. One of the best guides to the range of tools and information available for practical conflict prevention is the Beyond Intractability website, at http://www.beyondintractability .org/resources/violence-prevention

The Nonviolent and Violent Campaigns and Outcomes (NAVCO) Data Project at the University of Denver compares the effectiveness of violent with nonviolent campaigns, at http://www.du.edu/korbel/sie/research/chenow_navco_data.html.

Part IV

Praxis (2) Mediation, Negotiation and Reconciliation

Mediation, negotiation and reconciliation are at the heart of conflict resolution. Negotiation is the main approach used by parties to discuss their differences and seek mutually acceptable outcomes. Mediation involves third parties who step in to help the primary parties to explore the scope for a possible agreement. Reconciliation aims to repair broken relationships and make them whole again. Since dealing with protracted conflicts involves grappling with knots of issues that are difficult to untie, as well as breakdowns in communications and in relationships, in Part IV we deal with all three together.

You are a negotiator, as Fisher and Ury point out in Reading 46. You are also a mediator and a reconciler. These roles are part of the basic human repertoire of responding to conflict. Even primates engage in reconciliatory behaviour.[1] We can find records of negotiated agreements in the cuneiform tablets in ancient Egypt,[2] in Confucius's journeys in the states of ancient China,[3] and in the Viking Sagas.[4] Mediation, negotiation and reconciliation appear in every human society and culture.

However, cultural and social contexts influence what forms these practices take and there are vigorous debates over what approaches are appropriate in different types of conflict. The reflective pieces, guides to practice and case studies in this part illustrate the contrasts between approaches that attempt to *settle, resolve* and *transform* conflicts. Settlement is the prevalent approach in official efforts to manage international and civil conflicts. Coercion frequently accompanies bargaining, and negotiations reflect the balance of power. In such settings, as Touval and Zartman point out (Reading 41), international mediators have their own interests to pursue. The US mediation in Bosnia which led to the Dayton Treaty (Reading 55) was an example of this. In contrast, non-official, facilitative approaches aimed to resolve conflicts which developed out of industrial, social and community settings. Burton (Reading 5) was an early champion of applying a problem-solving approach to international and civil conflicts. Others, such as Dugan, Lederach, Rubinstein and Curle, argue that when disputes are embedded in unbalanced relationships or wider conflicts, a transformative approach is required (Readings 21, 22, 23 and 40).

The *reflective pieces* in this part start with an introductory extract by Wallensteen (Reading 39), which offers a definition of conflict resolution and seven ways in which conflicts can be resolved in general. It continues with a piece by Curle (Reading 40), which stresses the personal and transformative dimensions of peace-making. Pruitt (Reading 42) outlines a new theory of when parties are ready to settle. Hampson (Reading 43) advocates the nurturing of peace processes by international organizations and great powers, while Beardsley's piece (Reading 44), based on the quantitative research literature, cautions that short-term mediation successes may fail to resolve the key issues. Assefa (Reading 45) places reconciliation in the spectrum of other methods of handling conflict.

As *guides to practice*, we include an extract from Fisher and Ury's *Getting to Yes* on principled negotiation, an outline of Rothman's ARIA framework, Fitzduff's typology of community relations work from Northern Ireland, Curle's guide to mediation practice and an explanation of active listening with some exercises in impartial language for mediators. These can be read in conjunction with readings in other parts, on conflict mapping (Readings 26–28) and Codes of Conduct for NGOs (Reading 63).

As *case studies*, we include an anthropologist's account of negotiations over disputed land in east Africa (Reading 53), and a political scientist's view of what made Jerusalem negotiable in 2000 (Reading 54). These can be read in conjunction with the account of women's peacemaking in Wajgir, Kenya (Reading 64) and the efforts to find constitutional and institutional formulas for Kirkuk in Iraq (Reading 65). We also include documents to illustrate two peace settlements.

Research and practice are continuously developing in this area, and new theoretical conceptualizations and new approaches to praxis are appearing all the time. The field as a whole is engaged in a version of Kolb's reflective learning cycle (see the opening section, 'Debating Conflict Resolution: Texts, Voices and Narratives'). By engaging with these readings and pursuing the trails that they suggest, we hope our readers will find themselves able to contribute to this dynamic field.

Notes

1 F. de Waal, *Peacemaking among Primates*. Cambridge, MA: Harvard University Press, 1989.
2 R. Cohen and R. Westbrook, eds, *Armana Diplomacy; The Beginnings of International Relations*. Baltimore, MD: Johns Hopkins University Press, 2000.
3 M. McArthur, *Confucius*. London: Quercus, 2010.
4 See, for example, Njal's Saga, which describes the development of an Icelandic parliament as a means of resolving the feuds among Viking dynasties.

39

Understanding Conflict Resolution

Peter Wallensteen

Peter Wallensteen is the founding Professor of Peace and Conflict Research at Uppsala University and a pioneer of the Uppsala Conflict Data Program, which is one of the most authoritative sources of statistics on global conflicts and peace settlements. This reading includes a definition of conflict resolution as a process in which conflict parties agree to live with or transform the incompatibilities that divide them. Wallensteen distils seven distinct ways to do this.

*   *   *   *

[Wallensteen offers] the following definition of conflict resolution:

> a social situation where the armed conflicting parties in a (voluntary) agreement resolve to peacefully live with – and/or dissolve – their basic incompatibilities and henceforth cease to use arms against one another.

This means that the conflict is transformed from violent to non-violent behaviour by the parties *themselves*, not by somebody else, such as an outsider or third party. The first test of conflict resolution is that arms are no longer used. This means that a cease-fire and a process of demilitarization are initiated according to agreed plans. To the general public this is *the* sign that the situation has actually changed. Then comes the implementation of the agreement's basic issues, which should follow soon. A second test is that the parties do not resort to violence or to the threat of violence in this phase.

    The definition stipulates that the parties enter into agreement. This means that the primary parties take responsibility for the accords and commit themselves to their implementation and legitimation.

…

    How can parties with such incompatible positions ever be able to arrive at the stipulation in the definition: 'live with – and/or dissolve – the incompatibility'?

…

    In theory, there are seven distinct ways in which the parties can live with or dissolve their incompatibility. These are mechanisms, procedures or forms of transcendence.

First, a party may change its goals – that is, *shift its priorities*. It is rare that a party will completely change its basic positions, but it can display a shift in what it gives highest priority to. This may open ways in which the other side can reciprocate. Leadership changes are particularly pertinent in this respect. With such changes, new possibilities are created. It means that conflict resolution does not have to wait for a revolution, for example. Leadership is often recruited from a limited segment of the population and continuity remains important. Still, new leaders think differently and, thus, new leadership matters. There are also other changes that can take place. Changes in the surrounding world may be important, leading to shifts in strategic priorities. Among major powers, the rise of a new power or the fall of an old one may be such a condition. For less powerful actors, changes in major power relations have many implications. Shifts between *détente* and confrontation can be important for conflict resolution, as was clearly seen at the end of the Cold War. Economic crises can change priorities. The costs of pursuing a war may drain important resources and, thus, the chances of a peace dividend may seem more attractive. However, the possibility for such changes should not be over-estimated and it would be outright dangerous for a party to hinge a negotiation policy on expectations of change in a particular direction. New leaders may be weaker, major power relations may change for the worse, economic crises may induce less interest in compromise and so on, so it is important for the parties continuously to probe the other side, to find out if there are shifts in priority.

The second way is a classical one: the parties stick to their goals but find a point at which resources can be *divided*. It is sometimes seen as the essence of compromise, but it is only one form of compromise. It may mean that both sides change their priorities. However, it needs to be done in such a way that the change by side A is coupled to a change by side B. To meet halfway, at some point that has a symbolic value, is easier for the parties than one side giving in to the other. Then, it is also possible for them to defend the deal to other decision-makers and the general public. It may appear reasonable and be in accordance with values in the society. If the incompatibility concerns territory, this may mean drawing a border approximately half the distance between the two demands. It makes sense, but only so long as the areas are not inhabited by people who will have their own interests or contain resources that should also be part of the deal.

Compromise is most readily made with monetary resources. Negotiations between employers and employees have a long history of finding optimal points at which to draw the dividing line between the two sides. In many such situations, it is important for the parties to get some resources rather than nothing. With power positions this may be more difficult, but even so there are ways in which power can be divided – along the lines of central–regional divisions or functions (president, prime minister, speaker, supreme court, important committees and so on) for example. As mentioned, there are examples of two prime ministers in the same cabinet (Cambodia). Rotation of the office of prime minister has been used in Israel, each party getting an equal number of years – an interesting timesharing arrangement. This is institutionalized in Switzerland, with its annual shifting of presidency.

A third way is *horse-trading*, which is when one side has all of its demands met on one issue, while the other has all of its goals met on another issue. It means using two separate incompatibility diagrams, one for each issue, and each party getting 100 per cent. This can also be described as a compromise, but works in a different way from the division we just described. In horse-trading over territory, the idea would be that A takes area 1 and B takes area 2, although both of them have had demands on areas 1 and 2. Instead of making a complicated division, an entire piece of territory is taken over by one or the other. As we noted before, this assumes that there are no particular features to the territory or that such features somehow are equal for both (for instance, oil in both). In a contest over political power positions, A may support B in some matters and receive corresponding support from B in others, meaning A and B abandon previous views and together form what is sometimes referred to as 'national pacts' or 'historical compromises'.

A fourth way is *shared control*. In this case, the parties decide to rule together over the disputed resource. A territory can be shared by being ruled as a condominium, where decisions require the consent of both parties. An economic resource can be operated by a joint company and a formula devised for investment and profitsharing. A country can be run by a coalition government – a frequent phenomenon in most parliamentary democracies. Shared control may require some degree of trust; it may also be a temporary arrangement for a transition period. Powersharing arrangements also exemplify this. This is where all parties are represented in government according to a formula agreed on beforehand (for each 5 per cent of the national vote, a party gets a seat in the cabinet, for instance). Even if agreed to for only a predetermined period, it can mean that a conflict is successfully transcended and, at the end of the period, the conflict situation is very different from what it was at the beginning. This can also be applied to international regimes setting up rules for using water in shared rivers. In international affairs, such arrangements may mean the beginning of regional integration; in internal affairs, they can be contributions to the integration of a fragmented society.

A fifth way is to *leave control to somebody else*, which means externalizing control so that the warring parties agree not to rule the resources themselves. The primary parties agree, or accept, that a third actor takes control. Such solutions have gained prominence in the discussions on international conflicts during the 1990s. The notion of protectorates has returned to serious discussions. There are recent examples of independent countries having had their sovereignty strongly circumscribed. Bosnia-Herzegovina is one case with its complex constitution. In 1999, one part of a sovereign country was placed under international protection – Kosovo, in the south of the Federal Republic of Yugoslavia. In the case of Kosovo, it has meant that neither the Yugoslav authorities nor the Kosovo Albanian representatives run the area, but, instead, authority resides with a UN Commissioner, for the time being. In these cases, the parties accepted the outcome, but only after considerable warfare (the Bosnian War and NATO's actions in 1995, the Kosovo wars and the aerial bombardments of Yugoslavia in 1999). Similarly, East Timor was under UN administration 1999–2002, neither a part of Indonesia nor an independent country. It was more a trusteeship than a protectorate.

Obviously, there are other, less dramatic, ways to hand control to third parties. Economic resources can be given as concessions to private companies. The cabinet can be taken over by parliamentary minorities or experts, in order to detach the official administration from major political divides in the country. The latter can be important, particularly at times of elections. Bangladesh now has such a stipulation in its constitution.

Sixth, there is the possibility of resorting to *conflict resolution mechanisms*, notably arbitration or other legal procedures that the parties can accept. It means finding a procedure that can resolve the conflict according to some of the previously mentioned five ways, with the added quality that it is done through a process outside the parties' immediate control. The legal mechanism builds on the idea of neutrality, distance and resort to precedents and history. Among conflict resolution mechanisms we would also include holding new elections and arranging a referendum, which means leaving the issue to a concerned but still non-predetermined audience. For this to be a legitimate way of ending a conflict, the conflicting parties should have a fair chance to present their views. Studies show that if parties believe that they have been given a fair chance, they are more likely to accept defeat than if they think the process has been unfair in some way. A number of border disputes have been resolved with the use of arbitration. A remarkable case is the drawing of the border between Iraq and Kuwait after the Gulf War, settled according to an exchange of documents between the two parties, but under the authorization of the UN Security Council. The democratic system solves some disputes by resorting to new elections or referenda. Territorial issues can also be resolved this way, by giving a voice to the population itself. That was part of the agreement ending the Ethiopian–Eritrean war in 1991, through a referendum in 1993.

Seventh, issues can be *left to later* or even to oblivion. By appointing a commission, parties can gain time and, when the commission reports, political conditions and popular attitudes may have changed. Some issues may gain from being delayed, as their significance may pale or their symbolic character may be reduced. This is an argument for not solving all questions at the same time, but it requires that there be a second chance to bring them up. In fact, the second chance is important for a loser to accept defeat or enter into a compromise. If there is a credible way in which one can return to the issue later or run in a new election, then the agreement is more acceptable. The party does not argue that the issue is given less priority, only that its time is not yet ripe. In the case of the first mechanism, in contrast, there is a significant change of position and the party does not return to its previous view.

40
Making Peace
Adam Curle

Adam Curle was a leading Quaker mediator and the first Professor of Peace Studies at Bradford University. In his 1971 book, *Making Peace*, he argues that peacemaking must be concerned with positive peaceful relationships. In cases of asymmetric conflict, this suggests a transformative approach to unbalanced power relations. In this extract he anticipates the idea of conflict transformation.

*   *   *   *

Peaceful Relations

Peaceful relations can be defined negatively in terms of absence of conflict. Absence of conflict may, however, mean little more than absence of association: there are many people with whom one does not quarrel because one does not know them well and is never placed in a position where a clash of interests or personalities could arise. But I would term this negative peace. Another form of negative peace characterizes those relationships in which violence has been avoided or reduced, without the removal of the conflict of interest, or in which the conflict has been mystified, that is to say, concealed or disguised. The latter, as I have noted, is a not uncommon outcome of industrial disputes. The workers may have a genuine grievance which, if it were to be redressed, would be very costly to the employers; the employers therefore avoid both expense and disturbance by expressing sympathy with the workers, meeting with them cordially, and making some minor but ostentatious concession to them by which they hope the workers will be dazzled. In my terms, these forms of negative peace constitute unpeaceful relationships.

I prefer to define peace positively. By contrast with the absence of overt strife, a peaceful relationship would, on a personal scale, mean friendship and understanding sufficiently strong to overcome any differences that might occur. On a larger scale, peaceful relationships would imply active association, planned cooperation, an intelligent effort to forestall or resolve potential conflicts. This aspect of peace contains a large quotient of what I term development.

If development is to occur, that is to say, if a relationship is to grow in harmony and productiveness, it is axiomatic that there must be equality and reciprocity in large measure. The mutuality of a peaceful relationship differentiates it from an unpeaceful one: mutuality in which one partner assists the other to achieve his ends and so serves his own. In peaceful relationships there is neither domination nor imposition. Instead there is mutual assistance, mutual understanding, mutual concern, and collaboration founded on this mutuality. As I define it, the process of peacemaking consists in making changes in relationships so that they may be brought to a point where development can occur. As we shall see, some of these changes may not accord with other definitions of peace. Revolutionary upheavals may be necessary if, for example, the slave seeks equality with his master. But if he achieves it – and who can say what price should be paid or danger incurred for this end – the relationship changes into one of man to man. If two men can find common ground and live together without destroying each other (and this is the next task in the quest for peace), they may then begin to learn to work with and for each other; this is the quality of development that typifies positive peace.

Peaceful relationships may be balanced or unbalanced. Examples of unbalanced peaceful relationships would be those between parent and child, family and community, provincial and federal government, small state and large state, and so on. The essence of these relationships is that the smaller or weaker partner is helped to develop his potentialities and that, in the process, he contributes to the development of the stronger. It is equally easy to think of examples where such relationships have engendered an element of conflict: many Americans, for instance, are keenly aware of conflict between the rights of individual states and the demands of the federal administration; the relationship between parent and child may be agonizingly conflicted. In these cases the potential of the smaller or weaker partner is prevented from being realized.

I would emphasize these points relating to development and to the positive definition of peace because they dominate the arguments that follow. The kind of peace we want determines our approach to peacemaking and the methods we employ.

These types of peaceful and unpeaceful relationships – except alienation, which is in a somewhat different category – are set out in Figure 1. Note that no example is given of an unpeaceful relationship in a balanced/lower-awareness-of-conflict situation, since this combination is probably never as clear cut as the others, though there is an element of ambiguity in many. The nearest to it is a pseudo-balanced relationship coupled with a low awareness of conflict, as shown in Figure 2.

	UNPEACEFUL RELATIONS		PEACEFUL RELATIONS
	Lower awareness of conflict	*Higher awareness of conflict*	*No conflict*
Balanced		Approximately evenly matched conflict; e.g. India/Pakistan.	Development; e.g. the European Common Market and other peaceful and constructive associations.
Unbalanced	Ignorantly passive groups; negative peace; e.g. the Faqir Mishkin.	Revolution of the underdog; confrontation, violent or non-violent; the essential effort is to achieve a more equal relationship; e.g. the Black Americans.	Development; harmonious relationship of unequal partners; e.g. parent/child, state/federal government, France/Monaco.

Figure 1 *Peaceful and unpeaceful relationships*

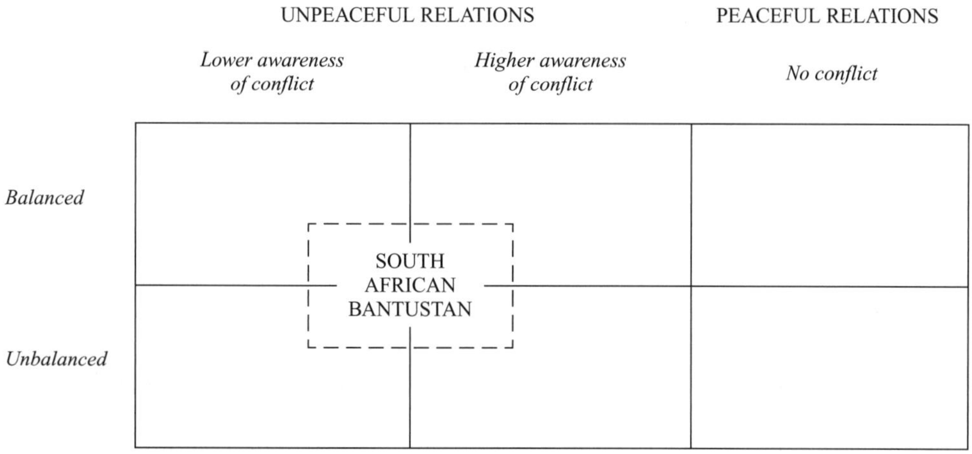

	UNPEACEFUL RELATIONS		PEACEFUL RELATIONS
	Lower awareness of conflict	*Higher awareness of conflict*	*No conflict*
Balanced			
Unbalanced		SOUTH AFRICAN BANTUSTAN	

Note: No one could assert that all South African blacks have a low perception of conflict in their society, but in many of them awareness is low and this has prevented the development of an effective resistance movement. The creation of Bantustans gives some impression of a balanced relationship and serves to maintain in many their low perception of conflict. In effect, of course, the conflict persists.

Figure 2 *A pseudo-balanced relationship*

41

International Mediation in Theory and Practice

Saadia Touval and William Zartman

Saadia Touval was an Israeli who taught on the conflict management program at the Paul Nitze School of Advanced International Studies at Johns Hopkins University. He is well known for his view that biased mediators are the most effective in international disputes. William Zartman is Emeritus Professor at the Paul Nitze School and a prolific author on international negotiations. Here, Touval and Zartman argue that mediators always have interests in conflicts and that they are inevitably engaged in a bargaining relationship with the parties.

*   *   *   *

The Motives of Mediators and Parties

Mediators aim at reducing or resolving conflict between adversaries. This peacemaking goal legitimates their intervention and may not appear to require much elaboration. However, peacemaking is often intertwined with less generous motives inspired by self-interest. These can best be described within the context of power politics.

It would be rare for governments to engage in mediation for humanitarian reasons only. In fact, in view of the considerable investment of political, moral, and material resources that mediation requires, and the risks to which mediators expose themselves, it is reasonable to assume that mediators are no less motivated by self-interest than by humanitarian impulses. To some extent, then, the mediator is a player in the plot of relations surrounding a conflict, and has some interest in the outcome (or else it would not mediate). A parallel statement can be made about the parties to the conflict. It is unlikely that they invite or accept mediation because they are interested only in peace; they probably expect the mediator's intervention to work in their favor.

From the mediator's point of view, there appear to be two kinds of interest that can be promoted through mediation. One, essentially defensive, occurs when a conflict between two actors threatens the mediator's interests. Resolving a conflict in such a case may be important to the mediator because of the conflict's effects on its relations with the parties. For example, conflict between two of the mediator's allies may weaken the alliance. Or a conflict between two states may upset a regional balance or provide opportunities for a rival power to increase its influence by intervening in the conflict. In such situations, third parties often seek to limit damage to themselves by promoting a settlement. If they see risks in direct mediation, they may appeal to an international organization or another party. Leaving the mediation to others is not without risks, however. One may lose the ability to influence developments or control events. Or, the mediation may be ineffective, particularly if carried out by an international organization. Even worse, mediation by an international organization may provide an opportunity for, or legitimate the involvement of, one's rivals. Such considerations often appear to justify direct mediation of the conflict. The interests invoked above are essentially defensive ones; mediation is used in such cases to protect the mediator's interests.

A second, self-interested motive for mediation may be the desire to extend and increase one's influence. Solution of the conflict may have no direct importance to the mediator, but is only a vehicle for an interest in developing closer relations with the parties. A third party may hope to win the gratitude of one party by helping it reach somewhat better terms than it could obtain otherwise. To be sure, the mediator cannot throw its full weight behind one party without compromising its status as a mediator; the other side would withdraw its acceptance of the mediator's diplomatic intervention and cease to cooperate. Within limits, however, a mediating party may succeed in increasing its influence with one side in a conflict, particularly if its relations with the other side are closer at the outset of the mediation. The mediator may further increase its influence by making its involvement essential for any negotiations between the two adversaries, rendering each dependent upon the mediator whenever something is desired from the other. Mediators can also increase their influence by becoming guarantors for whatever agreement is reached.

It follows from the foregoing that a mediator will seldom be indifferent to the terms being negotiated. The mediator sometimes seeks peace in the abstract, but usually seeks to promote terms that are in accord with its own interests. Yet these interests usually allow for a wider range of acceptable outcomes than do the interests of the antagonists. The mediator may also have greater flexibility in bargaining through having incurred fewer commitments and invested less in the conflict than did the parties. Mediators are likely to seek terms that will increase the prospects of stability and deny their rivals opportunities for intervention. They may also wish to ensure that the terms of a settlement will enable them to continue "to have a say" in relations between the adversaries.

The political interests that may lead parties in conflict to seek or accept mediation are several. The most obvious is the expectation that a certain mediator will help one party gain a more favorable settlement than would otherwise be possible. Although the other party may have a similar assessment of consequences of the mediator's intervention, it may still agree to mediation if rejection would cause even greater harm, for example, by damaging relations with the would-be mediator. The parties may accept mediation in the hope that negotiation through an intermediary will help them reduce some of the risks that compromises entail, by protecting their image and reputation when making concessions. They may also believe that a mediator's involvement will constitute a guarantee for the eventual agreement, thus reducing the risk of violation by the adversary.

Invitation or acceptance of mediation may be related to additional power-political considerations. One or both parties may wish to gain time, or to be relieved of the dilemma of choosing between escalation and concessions. Or, one side may wish to engage the third party and enlist its support in the expectation that the negotiations will fail to produce an agreement. Another possibility (as in the case of Egypt's view of American mediation in the conflict with Israel) is that mediation will provide the occasion for improving relations with the mediator, while souring relations between the mediator and the adversary. Such power-related side effects may be an important motive for inviting or accepting mediation.

Within this context, the relationship between the mediator and the antagonistic parties is never devoid of tension. It is a relationship of continuous bargaining, and the mediator's conduct and its consequences are subject to constant scrutiny by both parties. The parties' acceptance of the mediator is not unconditional, but rather is qualified by tacitly understood conditions. These limit the respective bargaining power of the mediator and the parties.

42

Readiness Theory and the Northern Ireland Conflict

Dean Pruitt

Dean Pruitt taught psychology at New York State University at Buffalo and is well known for his experiments in integrative agreements and escalation. Now at the Institute for Conflict Analysis and Resolution at George Mason University, he developed 'readiness theory' as an alternative to Zartman's 'ripeness theory'. Zartman argued elsewhere that a conflict is ripe for settlement when the parties mutually accept that the costs of continuing outweighs the benefits of a negotiated agreement.[1] Here, Pruitt argues that negotiation to end a conflict does not have to be a last-ditch option that parties resort to only when other means of prosecuting the conflict have failed. He contends that conflicts become ready for negotiation when sufficient parties are motivated to negotiate and are optimistic about the prospects of agreement. These arguments are illustrated in the extract with reference to the Northern Ireland peace process.

Note

1 I. W. Zartman, *Ripe for Resolution: Conflict resolution in Africa* (2nd ed.). New York: Oxford University Press, 1989.

* * * *

Readiness Theory

Readiness theory is a revision and elaboration of ripeness theory (Zartman, 1989, 2000). It differs from ripeness theory in that it uses the language of variables rather than necessary states and focuses on the thinking within a single party rather than on the joint thinking of both parties to a conflict. These changes allow the development of some new theoretical ideas that are presented in this article and elsewhere (Pruitt, 2005a, 2005b).

Readiness is a characteristic of an organization (a "party") reflecting the thinking of its top leaders with regard to a conflict with another organization (the "adversary"). Readiness fosters conciliatory behavior. At moderate strengths, it encourages mild gestures of conciliation. If it increases in strength, the party's behavior becomes increasingly conciliatory and may eventually take the form of a cease-fire and entry into negotiation. Additional levels of readiness are needed for the party to stay in negotiation and to make concessions. Some readiness is needed on both sides of a conflict for negotiation to start and agreement to be reached.

Readiness has two components, which combine multiplicatively:

Motivation (that is, a goal) to end the conflict, which is fed by (a) a sense that the conflict is unwinnable or poses unacceptable costs or risks and/or (b) pressure from powerful third parties such as allies.
Optimism about the outcome of conciliation and negotiation.

Motivation and optimism are compensatory, in the sense that more of one can substitute for less of the other. However, both must be present, in some degree, for any conciliatory behavior to be enacted.

Motivation to end the conflict

The origins of the motivation to end a military conflict like that in Northern Ireland can best be understood in the context of four tactical choices open to leaders:

Continue current hostilities
Escalate
Seek allies
Explore or enter negotiation

In Zartman's (1989) terminology, the first three items in this list are "unilateral" tactics that seek to defeat the adversary in one way or another. The fourth item is a "bilateral" tactic, because negotiation requires cooperation from the adversary. Combinations of all of these tactics are possible, though the first two tactics (continue hostilities and escalate) are more compatible with exploration of negotiation than with actual entry into negotiation, because adversaries will seldom agree to negotiate with a gun at their head.

There is usually an order of preference among these tactics corresponding to the order in which they are listed above. Thus escalation is attempted if current tactics seem unworkable (unlikely to succeed, too costly, or too risky); allies are sought if current tactics and escalation seem unworkable; and negotiation is a last-ditch tactic, adopted if all three unilateral tactics seem unworkable. In addition, seeking allies may be a prelude to negotiation if the sought or obtained allies put pressure on the party to end hostilities and start negotiation. That is likely to happen if the available allies are more moderate than the actor recruiting them.

This discussion of tactical alternatives allows us to elaborate a point made earlier about the origins of motivation to end conflict. Motivation to end conflict (and hence openness to negotiation) develops to the extent that all unilateral tactics seem unworkable and to the extent that allies or potential allies press for an end to hostilities and a start on negotiation.

Readiness theory is especially applicable to intractable conflicts because these conflicts involve severely fractured relationships between the disputants. Research (Mikolic, Parker, & Pruitt, 1997; Sarat, 1976) suggests that in more moderate conflicts, negotiation (talking with the other side) is a preferred rather than a last-ditch tactic, presumably because of a desire to avoid antagonizing the adversary and because the adversary is viewed as a part of one's moral community.

…

Optimism about negotiation

Being motivated to end a conflict and start negotiation is not enough to get one into negotiation. One must also have some optimism about the outcome of the negotiation – some faith that the final agreement will satisfy one's goals and aspirations without too much cost. Optimism results from three states of mind:

Lowered aspirations: parties with less ambitious goals can be more optimistic about achieving them in negotiation.

Working trust: this is a belief that the other party also wants to escape the conflict and has reasonable or flexible aspirations.

Perceived light at the end of the tunnel: the perception that an acceptable agreement is shaping up, that the other party is ready to make the concessions one needs. This produces more optimism than working trust and must eventually develop for a peace process to be successful.

Motivation and optimism are intimately related in that motivation to end a conflict often encourages the development of optimism. This is especially likely to occur if the adversary is also motivated to end the conflict. However, it is not an inevitable development. Many conflicts fester despite strong motivation to escape them on both sides, because the parties' aspirations are too rigid to make concessions or their basic mistrust is too deep for working trust to develop.

There are four ways in which the motivation to end a conflict (and its logical accompaniment, openness to negotiation) can encourage optimism (Pruitt, 2005b):

Discouragement about achieving one's goals. If it looks as though a conflict cannot be won at acceptable cost or risk, leaders are likely to become discouraged about achieving their goals and scale down these goals. When goals are scaled down, agreement is easier to reach. Of course, there are always limits to a party's willingness to reduce its aspirations; for example, the IRA was unwilling to commit to any disarmament to get the negotiations going.

Information gathering. The thought of abandoning a conflict and starting negotiation may produce a desire to size up the adversary – to examine the adversary's motives and assess the adversary's flexibility. Previously unquestioned diabolical enemy images may come under scrutiny. If the adversary is also motivated to end the conflict, the information gathered should encourage working trust.

Testing the waters. Information gathering may extend to sending conciliatory signals or making secret contacts with the other side. Such initiatives are often small and ambiguous at first – a spoken hint or roundabout contact – so that their conciliatory intent can be denied if the other side does not respond in a conciliatory fashion (Mitchell, 2000; Pruitt & Kim, 2004). But if people on the other side are also so motivated and seeking new information, they are likely to notice the initiative, take it seriously, and reciprocate, enhancing the first party's optimism enough to allow it to send a stronger conciliatory signal. A conciliatory spiral then ensues and optimism flourishes.

Third-party mobilization. Changes in a disputant's outlook on a conflict will often be noted by third parties. If they are also motivated to end the conflict, this should encourage them to take initiatives to bring the parties together. For example, they may coordinate a series of conciliatory gestures, facilitate an exchange of messages between the disputants, or help the disputants sketch out a possible agreement that produces a glimmer of light at the end of the tunnel. All of these actions should encourage optimism by the disputants.

...

Central coalition theory is a generalization of readiness theory to the multiparty case. It assumes that the parties who enter and stay in a negotiation all share a readiness for negotiation and, hence, that they are motivated to end the conflict and optimistic about what can be achieved from negotiation. It does not assume that they see eye to eye on the issues, as do most other coalition theories, but only that they are willing to engage in a common task of seeking agreement.

The political spectrum

To understand coalitions of the kind that put together the Good Friday Agreement, it is useful to think of a political spectrum running from hawks on one side of the conflict through moderates and doves on that side, and onward to doves, moderates, and hawks on the other side of the conflict, as shown in Figure 1. All of the politically active groups occupy regions along this spectrum – the larger the group, the broader the region occupied. There may also be neutrals at the midpoint between the two sides.

Hawks are assumed to differ from moderates and especially from doves in many ways. They have more extreme goals and are less flexible about the concessions they are willing to make. They are also more alienated from the other side and more willing to take risks to achieve their goals. Hawks are often well organized and may be well armed, making them more powerful on their side than their numbers would otherwise allow.

There is a profound social distance between the hawks on either side of a conflict. They have sharply contrasting values and narratives and often are unwilling to meet each other. By contrast, doves on either side share some perspectives and may be in contact with each other in an effort to understand the nature of the conflict and to move it in a peaceful direction.

A readiness analysis needs to be done separately for each segment of the political spectrum. Readiness for negotiation is always smallest for the hawks and greatest for

Figure 1 *Political Spectrum Running From Party I's Hawks to Party II's Hawks*

the doves. This is partly because hawks tend to feel the issues more deeply and hence to have a singularity of purpose that makes them more immune to costs and risks. Loss of home, family support, and even their own lives may be less important than the success of their cause. Furthermore, hawks are likely to be less optimistic about the success of negotiation because of the extremity of their demands and their lack of trust in the other side. Hence they usually oppose negotiation and often act as spoilers to destroy a negotiated agreement if one is reached (see Stedman, 2000).

Nevertheless, hawks do at times develop a readiness for negotiation and become involved in talks that create an agreement to which they adhere. They are like everybody else in their response to perceived infeasibility or a clearly looming catastrophe.
...

Central coalitions

Negotiations designed to construct peace agreements usually involve neutrals and doves, and often they reach further into adjacent regions along the political spectrum. Hence, the participants in such negotiations can be called a "central coalition." Central coalitions vary in size from very broad, including neutrals, doves, moderates, and most hawks, to very narrow, including only neutrals and doves.
...

Central coalition theory (Pruitt, 2005a, 2005b) includes a proposition about the size and shape of the kind of central coalition that is necessary to settle a conflict: The better armed the hawks on either side of the conflict are, the broader must be the central coalition on that side, so as to include the bulk of the extremists and isolate the others politically. Otherwise armed attacks by spoilers and the retaliation they provoke are likely to destroy the peace process or the settlement that emerges from it.
...

Conclusions

Readiness theory, a derivative of Zartman's ripeness theory, concerns movement to and through a negotiation in an intractable conflict. The theory has two parts. One is a basic two-party version of the theory, which traces readiness for negotiation to two psychological states: motivation to end an intractable conflict and optimism about the outcome of negotiation. The other is central coalition theory, an extension of readiness theory to the multiparty case. This theory conceptualizes the groups that participate in a peace negotiation as an alliance of doves on either side of the controversy plus whatever adjacent groups join them. All members of the coalition must be above threshold in readiness. This part of the theory holds that (a) a peace process will be more successful the broader the central coalition is (that is, the more groups are above the readiness threshold) and (b) the central coalition must include the bulk of the armed groups. Point b implies that it is often essential to negotiate with terrorists (Pruitt, 2006).

References

Mikolic, J. M., Parker, J. C., & Pruitt, D. G. (1997). Escalation in response to persistent annoyance: Groups vs. individuals and gender effects. *Journal of Personality and Social Psychology*, 72, 151–163.

Mitchell, C. (2000). *Gestures of conciliation: Factors contributing to successful olive branches*. London: Macmillan.

Pruitt, D. G. (2005a). Ripeness theory: Past, present and future. In G. F. Faure & NEGOCIA, *La négociation: Regards sur sa diversité*. Paris: Publibook.

Pruitt, D. G. (2005b). *Whither ripeness theory?* Working Paper #25, Institute for Conflict Analysis and Resolution, George Mason University, Fairfax, VA. Available online at www.gmu.edu/departments/ICAR/wp_25_pruitt.pdf

Pruitt, D. G. (2006). Negotiation with terrorists. *International Negotiation*, 11, 371–394.

Pruitt, D. G., & Kim, S. H. (2004). *Social conflict: Escalation, stalemate and settlement* (3rd ed.). New York: McGraw-Hill.

Sarat, A. (1976). Alternatives in dispute processing: Litigation in a small claims court. *Law and Society*, 10, 339–375.

Stedman, S. J. (2000). Spoiler problems in peace processes. In P. C. Stern & D. Druckman (Eds.). *Conflict resolution after the Cold War* (pp. 178–224). Washington, DC: National Academy Press.

Zartman, I. W. (1989). *Ripe for resolution: Conflict resolution in Africa* (2nd ed.). New York: Oxford.

Zartman, I. W. (2000). Ripeness: The hurting stalemate and beyond. In P. C. Stern & D. Druckman (Eds.). *Conflict resolution after the Cold War* (pp. 225–250). Washington, DC: National Academy Press.

43

Why Orphaned Peace Settlements are More Prone to Failure

Fen Hampson

Fen Hampson was director of the Norman Paterson School of International Affairs at Carleton University, Ontario, and is a leading Canadian commentator on international conflict and international relations. Arguing against those who say that international mediation can only work in a hurting stalemate, Hampson suggests that international championing of peace processes is vital to their success. Third parties have to create the conditions of ripeness (or readiness) by their mediation, conciliation and arbitration efforts.

* * * *

The failure of humanitarian interventions and various international mediation efforts in Rwanda, Somalia, and, until quite recently, Bosnia-Herzegovina have tarnished the reputation of the United Nations and jeopardized public support for peacekeeping, and third-party involvement in the settlement intrastate disputes. If there is 'new' conventional wisdom in some circles, it is that outside third parties have little to contribute to the peaceful settlement and resolution of such disputes, and that intervention is only desirable when a conflict has reached a "hurting stalemate" and the parties themselves are exhausted and sufficiently wearied by war to begin searching for alternatives to the use of force. Consider the following admonition by *New York Times* columnist Thomas L. Friedman: "There is no such thing as a peacekeeper or neutral force in an ethnic conflict. The very meaning of an ethnic conflict is that a society has been torn asunder, every community has grabbed a slice and there is no neutral ground left." Friedman says that "to try to extinguish one of these ethnic conflicts when it is raging at full force is futile ... No amount of rational argument can tone it down, and if you try to smother it with your own body or army it will burn a hole right through you."[1]

The same pessimistic outlook is echoed by historian and foreign policy analyst Benjamin Schwarz in the pages of the *Atlantic Monthly*. Schwarz writes that "stability in divided societies is normally based on some form of domination, and once internal differences become violent, usually only the logic of force can lay them to rest." He believes that the United States has only two real options in dealing with ethnic, nationalistic and separatist conflicts. Adopting a passive role once violence has erupted in a failed state, Washington can await the time when mutual exhaustion or the triumph of one group over another will create an opening for intervention in a purely peacekeeping capacity. Alternatively, the United States, can effectively intervene, not only by building civil societies or pacifying such conflicts but by helping one side impose its will on the other, as Turkey did in Cyprus.[2] This refrain, which has become all too familiar, construes the options and potential role of outside third parties in the peaceful settlement of civil disputes too narrowly. There are other options beyond "doing nothing" or, "at the other extreme, intervening with large-scale military force." Not all civil conflicts have to end with a victor and a vanquished. It is possible to construct power-sharing arrangements between dissatisfied minorities and intransigent majorities through third-party assisted negotiations. By sustaining a process of mediation, negotiation, and assistance with the subsequent implementation of the peace settlement in question, third parties can help bring an end to military conflict and lay the basis for a durable settlement that advances the process of national reconciliation in divided societies. The challenge is to cultivate the right conditions that will bring warring parties to the negotiating table and sustain the peace process once a settlement is in place.

This chapter argues that third parties have a critical role to play in nurturing peace and helping implement peace settlements. Who are these third parties? Typically they include international organizations like the United Nations and its associated relief and development agencies, non-governmental organizations (NGOs), regional organizations, great powers, regional powers, and even groupings of states. By acting independently or in unison, these third parties can help sustain the commitment and cooperation of the disputing parties in the overall peacemaking and peace-building process. This chapter discusses the potential contribution of these third parties to the peace process, not only in "cultivating ripeness" but also in helping establish the conditions that can move the peace process forward.

...

Given that negotiated settlements are difficult to achieve, and obviously somewhat of a rarity, the question of what determines success in bringing about a restoration of domestic order and an end to civil violence is a critical one. The recent history of international relations is marked by some notable successes and some conspicuous failures in post-conflict peace building efforts directed at ending civil conflict. While some peace settlements have proven durable and have succeeded in bringing an end to military hostilities and violence, others have failed to prevent a relapse into armed confrontation and violence or, to transform a cease-fire into a genuine political settlement.

Outside interventions are typically more effective when third parties entrench and institutionalize their role in the peacemaking and peace-building process, that is, when they cultivate ripeness. A successful peace process depends upon a lot of outside help and assistance, not only with the negotiation of a peace agreement, but also with its implementation. By being involved in the implementation phase of a peace settlement, third parties can help restore confidence, build trust, and change the perceptions and behavior of disputing parties. Their involvement can include technical activities ranging from peacekeeping and monitoring cease-fires, which help reduce the likelihood of armed confrontation and "accidental" encounters, to assisting with the establishment of participatory political institutions (for example, externally supervised and monitored elections) that channel the frustrations and aspirations of the politically mobilized elements of society thus reducing the prospects of armed violence. As Brian Mandell notes, confidence-building measures are especially crucial in the early stages of a peace settlement because they can forestall a resort to the use of force by the disputants, generate additional confidence-building measures beyond those initially implemented, heighten the cost of returning to the status quo, and create additional incentives for collaboration.[3] Mediation, conciliation, and arbitration by third parties can also help resolve outstanding or unanticipated issues that emerge during the postconflict peace-building phase and threaten to derail the peace process. This means that third parties must have enough resources and resolve to remain fully engaged in the negotiations leading up to the settlement and through the subsequent peace-building process. Settlements that fail have generally been "orphaned," because third parties either failed to remain fully engaged in implementing the settlement or were unable to muster the requisite level of resources, both economic and political, to build the foundations for a secure settlement.

Notes

1 Thomas L. Friedman, "Lift, lift, Contain," *New York Times*, June 4, 1995.

2 Benjamin Schwarz, "The Diversity Myth: America's Leading Export," *Atlantic Monthly*, May 1995, pp, 66, 67.

3 Brian S. Mandell, "Anatomy of a Confidence Building Regime: Egyptian-Israeli Security Cooperation," *International Journal* 45, No, 2 (Spring 1990), pp. 202–223.

44

The Mediation Dilemma

Kyle Beardsley

Kyle Beardsley is an Associate Professor at Duke University, North Carolina, and a leading researcher in the quantitative study of international mediation. Based on his research, Beardsley argues that official international mediation tends to encourage short-term settlements that fail to resolve the longer-term incompatibilities that underlie conflicts. This leads to a dilemma: international mediation may be inimical to long-term peace, but failure to mediate may mean continuing short-term war and destruction.

*　*　*　*

Careful consideration of the potential effects of mediation suggests an important, dilemma. Most starkly, reliance on mediation risks the relapse of conflict after a brief interlude of peace, whereas avoidance of mediation risks imminent brutality as the scourge of war runs its course. If mediation occurs, the international community can play an active and often necessary role in pushing for the cessation of hostilities, but this itself frequently exacerbates long-term instability. Third-party conflict management, especially when the mediator employs substantial leverage, can be inimical to enduring peace. The alternative to mediation, however, is not strictly a better way to reach peace. Outside actors can remain aloof in hopes the combatants will be able to reach a sustainable accord on their own; meanwhile, people perish and resources are destroyed. Agreements that are reached without assistance will be more likely to be self-enforcing – when the interests of the principal disputants alone are enough to sustain a commitment to the terms – but the physical, political, and economic costs of getting there can be enormous.

Third-party involvement through mediation can shape the prospects for peaceful bargains for the better in the short run and for the worse in the long run. In the short run, mediators can provide incentives that expand the set of mutually acceptable alternatives, pledge post-conflict security guarantees, help the combatants to recognize appropriate offers, and give leaders political cover for concessions. But in the long run, the involvement of an intermediary can introduce artificial incentives for peace that do not persist, interfere with the ability for the actors to fully understand the bargaining environment, and enable the belligerents to stall in hopes of gaining an advantage during the peace process. The inclusion of an external peacemaker is thus often a necessary ingredient for short-term progress, but intermediaries can also make future renegotiation more likely and more difficult. So, although disputants typically seek mediation as a means of reducing their immediate barriers to successful bargaining, they do so at the risk of decreasing the durability of any peaceful arrangements that are reached.

The dilemma is not simply a matter of whether mediation should be employed at all but also a matter of how much involvement third parties should have when they do mediate. Third-party leverage exaggerates the trade-off because such intrusive involvement is best able to shape the short-term incentives for peace and least able to facilitate durable self-enforcing settlements. In the midst of substantial leverage, especially when the leverage creates a false sense of security or is used to level the playing field and create an artificial stalemate, the disputants' degree of satisfaction with their terms of peace will be even more prone to falter as third parties disengage themselves from the peace processes over time. In addition, heavy-handed third parties are more likely to interrupt the ability for the actors to learn from the dispute environment and to learn how best to engage one another directly. As one example, Shibley Telhami describes the trade-off that Henry Kissinger contributed to in his manipulation of the bargaining environment in the wake of the 1973 October (Egyptian-Israeli) War: "But while Kissinger's shuttle diplomacy succeeded in separating the forces in a fashion that reduced the risk of a new surprise war, it also contributed to the eventual stalemate of the negotiations. By defusing the crisis situation through a partial and technical agreement, a historical moment of opportunity for a more lasting settlement may have been lost" (1990, 68).

Reference

Telhami, Shibley (1990) *Power and Leadership in International Bargaining: The Path to the Camp David Accords*. New York: Colombia University Press.

45

The Meaning of Reconciliation

Hizkias Assefa

Reconciliation is the 'holy grail' of conflict resolution, often seen as desirable but beyond reach. Here, Hizkias Assefa describes reconciliation as just one of a range of approaches to conflict. Compared to negotiation and mediation, it is the approach requiring the highest active participation of the parties and the most proactive engagement. Assefa is an Ethiopian mediator, founder and coordinator of the African Peacebuilding and Reconciliation Network in Nairobi, Professor of Conflict Studies at Eastern Mennonite University, Virginia, and associate member of the Institute for Conflict Analysis and Resolution at George Mason University, Virginia.

*   *   *   *

Compared to conflict handling mechanisms such as negotiation, mediation, adjudication, and arbitration, the approach called 'reconciliation' is perhaps the least well understood. Its meaning, processes, and application have not been clearly articulated or developed. A place to start understanding what it entails might be by trying to distinguish it from the other approaches used in peacemaking and peacebuilding.

If we were to look at the degree of mutual participation by the conflict parties in the search for solutions to the problems underlying their conflict we could place these approaches in a spectrum as follows. (See Figure 1)

At the left end of the spectrum, we find approaches where mutual participation is minimal. The use of force by one of the parties to impose a solution would be an example of a mechanism that would be placed at this end of the spectrum. Further to the right of the spectrum, we could place mechanisms such as adjudication. Here a third party, instead of an adversary imposes a solution to the conflict. However, the mutual participation of the parties in the choice of the solution is comparatively higher here than in the first. In the adjudication process, at least the parties have an opportunity to present their cases, to be heard, and submit their arguments for why their preferred solution should be the basis upon which the decision is made. Nonetheless, the choice of the solution is made by a third party, and the decision is backed by force (enforced) which ensures that the losing party complies.

Arbitration is placed further to the right of 'adjudication'. Here, the participation of the parties is even higher since both adversaries can choose who is going to decide the issues under dispute, whereas in adjudication the decision maker is already appointed by the state. The parties in conflict can sometimes identify the basis upon which their

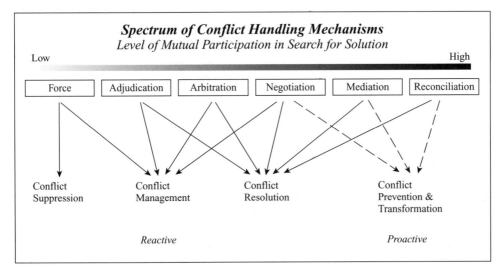

Spectrum of Conflict Handling Mechanisms
Level of Mutual Participation in Search for Solution

Low   High

| Force | Adjudication | Arbitration | Negotiation | Mediation | Reconciliation |

Conflict
Suppression

Conflict
Management

Conflict
Resolution

Conflict
Prevention &
Transformation

Reactive   *Proactive*

Figure 1 *The place of reconciliation in conflict handling*

case will be decided and whether the outcome will be binding or not. Although the mutual involvement of the parties in the decision making process is much higher than adjudication, the solution is still decided by an outsider and, depending on the type of arbitration, the outcome could be imposed by the power of the law.

Further to the right on the spectrum we find negotiation. Here the participation of all the involved parties in the search for solution is very high. It is the parties themselves who have to formulate the issues, and find a resolution that is satisfactory to all of them. In this situation, however, particularly in bargaining type negotiations (as opposed to problem-solving type of negotiations)[1], the final choice of the solution might depend on the relative power position of the adversaries rather than on what might be the most satisfactory solution to everyone involved. The party with the higher bargaining leverage might end up getting the most out of the negotiations.

Mediation is a special type of negotiation where the parties' search for mutually satisfactory solutions are assisted by a third party. The third party's role is to minimize obstacles to the negotiation process including those that emanate from power imbalance. Unlike adjudication, however, in the final analysis it is the decision and agreement of the conflict parties that determines how the conflict will be resolved.

Towards the far right of the spectrum we find reconciliation. This approach not only tries to find solutions to the issues underlying the conflict but also works to alter the adversaries' relationships from that of resentment and hostility to friendship and harmony. Of course, for this to happen, both parties must be equally invested and participate intensively in the resolution process.[2]

Before we move on to examine the insights that emerge from this spectrum, it will clarify our thinking if we quickly glance at one more issue of definitions and distinctions.

The conflict handling mechanisms illustrated in the spectrum can be categorized into three groups which we will call conflict management, conflict resolution, and conflict prevention approaches. Conflict management approaches generally tend to focus more on mitigating or controlling the destructive consequences that emanate from a given conflict than on finding solutions to the underlying issues causing it. On the other hand, conflict resolution approaches aim at going beyond mitigation of consequences and attempt to resolve the substantive and relational root-causes so that the conflict comes to an end. While conflict management and resolution are reactive, they come into motion once conflict has surfaced, conflict prevention tries to anticipate the destructive aspects of the conflict before they arise and attempts to take positive measures to prevent them from occurring.

Most of the mechanisms identified on the left hand of the spectrum are conflict management approaches. The use of military force for deterrence or in peace-keeping (separating the conflict parties from each other so that they do not keep inflicting harm on each other) are typical conflict management strategies. To the extent that adjudication, arbitration, and bargaining negotiations do not become avenues to solve the underlying issues of the conflict, and in most instances they do not, they become mere stop-gap conflict management measures. But if they provide an opportunity to work out not only differences on substantive issues but also negative relationships, they can become conflict resolution mechanisms.

Observations

We notice that as we move from the left to the right on the spectrum, i.e., as the participation of all the parties in the search for solution increases, the likelihood of achieving a mutually satisfactory and durable solution also increases. We know that solutions imposed by force will only last until the vanquished is able to muster sufficient force to reverse the situation. Solutions imposed by adjudication and arbitration, unless somehow the loser gives up, can always be frustrated by the latter's endless appeals or lack of cooperation in the implementation process. If, however, the parties are engaged earnestly in the search for the solutions and are able to find resolutions that could satisfy the needs and interests of all involved, there could be no better guarantee for the durability of the settlements. It would be in the interest of every one to see to it that they are fully enforced. This is what we believe problem-solving negotiations, mediation, and reconciliation can do.

What is noteworthy however is that as we move from the left to the right end of the spectrum, although the likelihood of effectiveness and durability of the solutions increases, our knowledge and understanding of the approaches to be utilized become sketchy, less developed and unsystematic. Our knowledge and methodology of conflict management approaches (the mechanisms on the left hand side of the spectrum) such as the use of force, adjudication, or arbitration are quite advanced. They are highly developed disciplines within institutions that command high respect and resources devoted to training and practice. Military and police science, jurisprudence and legal studies, as well as the entire military and police academies, law schools, ministries of defence and justice, police departments, courts, prison systems, are examples of these disciplines and institutions that advance the practice of these approaches. In contrast, conflict resolution approaches such as problem solving negotiation and mediation are less developed and institutions and resources devoted to their training, advancement and practice are meager. Whatever is in place is voluntary and ad-hoc. Then, when we come to reconciliation, let alone establish procedures and institutions charged with the application of the concept, there is not even much understanding of what it means, especially, among social scientists. Religious people and theologians are a bit better equipped to discuss the concept. But even there, there is a great gap between articulation and translation of the ideas into practice.

Healing and Reconciliation

Despite the lack of knowledge about how to operationalize reconciliation, there is however no question about the tremendous need for it. In fact, it could be said that the need in today's world is much greater than at any other time in the past.

One reason is that conflict management strategies are not adequate to deal with the kinds of contemporary conflicts raging in many parts of the world. Especially since the end of the Cold War, civil wars have replaced interstate wars as the most predominant large scale social conflicts. To a certain extent, in interstate conflicts strategies aimed merely at separating the conflicting parties might suffice. Even if the underlying issues of the conflict are not resolved, the separation could help avoid the recurrence of the conflict. Because states tend to isolate themselves from each other by their national boundaries, the task of separating them by peace-keeping forces is relatively easier.

However, in civil war situations the relationships between the protagonists is much more intimate and complex. In most cases, the parties share the same geographic area and even community, there might be strong economic interdependence between them, they usually have all sorts of social ties among each other including intermarriages. In these instances it is quite difficult to separate the protagonists since the boundaries between them are very difficult to draw. Even if it is possible to do it for a short while, it is not feasible to think of conflicts management strategies such as separation as long term solutions. For that matter even decisions imposed by adjudication on other such processes will not be solutions since the winning party cannot expect to enjoy, its victory without facing the consequences of the loser's wrath. Therefore in civil war situations conflict management strategies are not adequate. One has to move towards conflict resolution and reconciliation processes where not only the underlying issues in the conflicts are resolved to everyone's satisfaction but also the antagonistic attitudes and relationships between the adversaries are transformed from negative to positive.

Moreover, even in interstate relations we are increasingly realizing that the components of the modern international system are no more the nineteenth century autarchic states. The globe is shrinking and the fates of peoples of the world are becoming more and more inextricably intertwined. Thus, it would be increasingly difficult to expect unilateral approaches to handling conflicts, such as imposition of solutions by force, as viable approaches. In an interdependent and closely interconnected world even those that are supposedly weak can have their own way of subverting or undermining the imposed order. Therefore those groups must somehow be enabled to participate in the search for solutions in their conflicts even with the most powerful actors. In fact, the democratic values that the current international order is trying to promote as a universal value in all societies of the world necessitates movement more and more towards integrative negotiation, mediation and reconciliation as the predominant ways of dealing with conflict instead of unilateral measures that entail the use of coercion.

What Does Reconciliation Entail?

Reconciliation as a conflict handling mechanism entails the following core elements:

a) Honest acknowledgment of the harm/injury each party has inflicted on the other;
b) Sincere regrets and remorse for the injury done;
c) Readiness to apologize for one's role in inflicting the injury;
d) Readiness of the conflicting parties to 'let go' of the anger and bitterness caused by the conflict and the injury;
e) Commitment by the offender not to repeat the injury;
f) Sincere effort to redress past grievances that caused the conflict and compensate the damage caused to the extent possible;
g) Entering into a new mutually enriching relationship.

Reconciliation then refers to this new relationship that emerges as a consequence of these processes. What most people refer to as 'healing' is the mending of deep emotional wounds (generated by the conflict) that follow the reconciliation process.

A very important aspect of the process of reconciliation and one that distinguishes it from all the other conflict handling mechanisms is its methodology. In most of the conflict handling mechanisms such as adjudication, arbitration, and for that matter even negotiation and mediation the method used for establishing responsibility for the conflict or its consequences is adversarial. In these processes, the parties present their grievances and make a case for the adversary's fault or responsibility, thereby demanding that it should be the latter that should make amends. Each party begins by defending its own behaviour and denying its own guilt or responsibility until the opponent proves it to his or her satisfaction or to the satisfaction of outside observers, be they judges or mediators. In such a process, one's behaviour is always explained as a reaction to the behaviour of the adversary. The typical pattern of the interaction is: 'I did this to you because you did such and such a thing to me!' The aim is to get the adversary to change his or her future conduct by proving the person's guilt. Of course, the expectation is that both parties will change each other in this way and will eventually transform their relationship from negative to positive.

On the other hand, the essence of reconciliation is the voluntary initiative of the conflict parties to acknowledge their responsibility and guilt. The interactions that transpire between the parties are not only meant to communicate one's grievances against the actions of the adversary, but also to engage in self-reflection about one's own role and behaviour in the dynamic of the conflict. In other words, in this kind of dialogue, as much as one attributes guilt and responsibility to the adversary for the damage generated by the conflict, one has to also be self-critical and acknowledge responsibility for his or her own role in the creation or perpetuation of the conflict and hurtful interaction. The aim of such interaction is that, in the final analysis, each of the parties acknowledges and accepts his or her responsibility and out of such recognition seeks ways to redress the injury that has been inflicted on the adversary, to refrain from further damage, and to construct new positive relationships.

It is true that in both reconciliation and other conflict resolution mechanisms the process of dialogue is expected to generate change and transformation. In reconciliation, however, the forces for change are primarily internal and voluntary; while in the other approaches they are external and to a certain extent coerced. In the situation where the source is external it is possible that it might be the adversary's skill in marshaling and presenting its arguments; its strong will and intransigence; or its capacity to manipulate, exert pressure, or administer punishment that might intimidate the other party into accepting responsibility and settlement. Under such circumstances, therefore, it is questionable to what extent reluctant acceptance of guilt can serve as a force for significantly altering the future conduct and relationship between the adversaries.

This is not to imply that it is not possible to induce change in behaviour and relationships by forces outside the person, nor that every person changes his or her behaviour and relationships wilfully or voluntarily. The point here is that unless the need for change is internalized, the change is likely to be only temporary. The relationship would not have been significantly altered, and the conflict would not have found enduring solutions. It would emerge again as soon as circumstances change. More enduring transformation is likely to emerge when motivated by an internal need to change, especially when it emanates from self-reflection and criticism.

Reconciliation and Justice

Here it would be important to clarify the often misunderstood relationship between reconciliation and justice. Especially in horrendous conflict situations like Rwanda, Yugoslavia, Cambodia and others, many have argued that reconciliation is not appropriate because it is too soft on criminal conduct of offenders, and might even encourage it. They feel that justice (usually meaning the punishment of the offenders) precedes reconciliation. However, this argument presents a false dichotomy. An attempt at reconciliation without addressing the injustice in the situation is indeed a mockery and belittling the suffering of the victim. There cannot be reconciliation without justice. Justice and equity are at the core of reconciliation. The central question in reconciliation is not whether justice is done, but rather how one goes about doing it in ways that can also promote future harmonious and positive relationship between parties that have to live with each other whether they like it or not. Justice is a necessary but not sufficient condition for reconciliation. Reconciliation takes the concern for justice a step further and is preoccupied with how to rebuild a more livable, and psychologically healthy environment between former enemies where the vicious cycle of hate, deep suspicion, resentment, and revenge does not continue to fester.

For this reason, the methodology used to arrive at justice in the reconciliation process is different from that used to arrive at justice in the conventional (juridical) approach. The aim of the latter processes (particularly of the criminal justice process) is primarily to identify guilt and administer the punishment that the law requires with little attention to healing the bitterness and resentment that exist between the parties in the conflict. Identifying ways in which offenders are assisted to redress the material and emotional damage they have inflicted through self-reflection, acknowledgment of responsibility, remorse, and compensation would be an important step towards establishing an environment of reconciliation. The approach known as 'restorative justice' as opposed to 'retributive justice' brings us closer to the point where justice can be done but at the same time the possibilities for reconciliation are enhanced.[3]

Applying this concept in some of the catastrophic situations like Rwanda, Yugoslavia, Cambodia or Chile, reconciliation does not mean that the offenders are just pardoned. It means creating a process and an environment where the offenders take the responsibility to acknowledge their offense and get motivated to change the situation and relationship in a positive and durable manner instead of keep denying their guilt until it is proven to them by the juridical process.

The important thing to note is that to the extent the offenders keep denying their guilt, even if their responsibility is proved juridically and they are punished, the internal change that needs to take place to change the relationship from destructive to constructive, from hate to cooperation and harmony may not happen. Particularly in group conflicts, the punishment of the offenders alone does not prevent them or their followers and (at times, even their descendants) from continuing to hate and desiring to retaliate against those that punished them or their forefathers. Reconciliation has a much better chance of stopping the cycle of violence and hatred that sometimes transcends generations than any other conflict handling mechanism. Although flawed in many ways, this is what the experiments with Truth and Reconciliation Commission in conflict-ravaged societies are trying to do. In a number of instances, these commissions have been able to go as far as obtaining voluntarily acknowledgment of guilt by offenders. But they have not gone far enough to get them to demonstrate sincere remorse, or take active steps to compensate and repair the relationship vis a vis their victims.[4]

Notes

1 See Roger Fisher and William Ury, Getting to Yes, for the distinction between the bargaining type (distributive) and problem-solving type (integrative) negotiation approaches.

2 Of course these categories are neither exhaustive nor water tight. There are many more mechanisms that mix the various types and fall somewhere in between. One example is a mechanism that has come to be known as med/arb, where the process starts as mediation with the voluntary and full participation of the parties, but if that fails in resolving the problem, the solution is determined by a third party, an arbitrator. There are also other non-formal processes such as advocacy by interest groups, political mobilization at the grass-roots level in order to put pressure on leaders, etc. that can be placed at various points on the spectrum. 'Advocacy' operates in the adjudication framework although the body to whom the appeal is done might be the courts of national or international public opinion instead of the regular courts of law. 'Political mobilization' could be seen as a tactic in the negotiation

process in which the adversaries are marshaling their forces to improve their bargaining leverage or capacity to be heard and be taken seriously.

3 See Howard Zehr. *Changing Lenses* (Scottdale, Pennsylvania: Herald Press), 1990.

4 For a critique of Truth and Reconciliation Commissions and more detailed elaboration of concepts, approaches, and methodologies, and examples see Hizkias Assefa. Process of Expanding and Deepening Engagement. Reconciliation Methodology in Large Scale Social Conflicts (forthcoming).

46

Getting to Yes: Negotiating Agreement Without Giving In

Roger Fisher and William Ury

In this extract from their classic book *Getting to Yes*, Fisher and Ury set out a four-stage model of effective negotiations. Roger Fisher was a Professor at the Harvard Law School and director of the Harvard Negotiation Project. His colleague William Ury is an experienced mediator and set up the International Negotiation Network with former US President Jimmy Carter.

* * * *

Like it or not, you are a negotiator. Negotiation is a fact of life.

Although negotiation takes place every day, it is not easy to do well. Standard strategies for negotiation often leave people dissatisfied, worn out, or alienated – and frequently all three.

People find themselves in a dilemma. They see two ways to negotiate: soft or hard. The soft negotiator wants to avoid personal conflict and so makes concessions readily to reach agreement. He or she wants an amicable resolution; yet often ends up exploited and feeling bitter. The hard negotiator sees any situation as a contest of wills in which the side that takes the more extreme positions and holds out longer fares better. He or she wants to win; yet often ends up producing an equally hard response that exhausts the negotiator and his or her resources and harms the relationship with the other side.

There is a third way to negotiate, a way neither hard nor soft, but rather both hard *and* soft. The method of *principled negotiation* developed at the Harvard Negotiation Project is to decide issues on their merits rather than through a haggling process focused on what each side says it will and won't do. It suggests that you look for mutual gains whenever possible, and that where your interests conflict, you should insist that the result be based on some fair standards independent of the will of either side. The method of principled negotiation is hard on the merits, soft on the people. It employs no tricks and no posturing. Principled negotiation shows you how to obtain what you are entitled to and still be decent. It enables you to be fair while protecting you against those who would take advantage of your fairness.

There Is an Alternative

If you do not like the choice between hard and soft positional bargaining, you can change the game.

The game of negotiation takes place at two levels. At one level, negotiation addresses the substance; at another, it focuses – usually implicitly – on the procedure for dealing with the substance. The first negotiation may concern your salary, the terms of a lease, or a price to be paid. The second negotiation concerns how you will negotiate the substantive question: by soft positional bargaining, by hard positional bargaining, or by some other method. This second negotiation is a game about a game – a "meta-game." Each move you make within a negotiation is not only a move that deals with rent, salary, or other substantive questions; it also helps structure the rules of the game you are playing. Your move may serve to keep the negotiations within an ongoing mode, or it may constitute a game-changing move.

This second negotiation by and large escapes notice because it seems to occur without conscious decision. Only when dealing with someone from another country, particularly someone with a markedly different cultural background, are you likely to see the necessity of establishing some accepted process for the substantive negotiations. But whether consciously or not, you are negotiating procedural rules with every move you make, even if those moves appear exclusively concerned with substance.

The answer to the question of whether to use soft positional bargaining or hard is "neither." Change the game. At the Harvard Negotiation Project we have been developing an alternative to positional bargaining: a method of negotiation explicitly designed to produce wise outcomes efficiently and amicably. This method, called *principled negotiation* or *negotiation on the merits*, can be boiled down to four basic points.

These four points define a straightforward method of negotiation that can be used under almost any circumstance. Each point deals with a basic element of negotiation, and suggests what you should do about it.

People: Separate the people from the problem.
Interests: Focus on interests, not positions.
Options: Invent multiple options looking for mutual gains before deciding what to do.
Criteria: Insist that the result be based on some objective standard.

The method of principled negotiation is contrasted with hard and soft positional bargaining in the table below, which shows the four basic points of the method in bold-face type.

The first point responds to the fact that human beings are not computers. We are creatures of strong emotions who often have radically different perceptions and have difficulty communicating clearly. Emotions typically become entangled with the objective merits of the problem. Taking positions just makes this worse because people's egos become identified with their positions. Making concessions "for the relationship" is equally problematic, because it can actually encourage and reward stubbornness, which can lead to resentment that ends up damaging the relationship. Hence, even before working on the substantive problem, the "people problem" should be disentangled from it and addressed on its own. Figuratively if not literally, the participants should come to see themselves as working side by side, attacking the problem, not each other. Hence the first proposition: *Separate the people from the problem.*

The second point is designed to overcome the drawback of focusing on people's stated positions when the object of a negotiation is to satisfy their underlying interests. A negotiating position often obscures what you really want. Compromising between positions is not likely to produce an agreement that will effectively take care of the human needs that led people to adopt those positions. The second basic element of the method is: *Focus on interests, not positions.*

The third point responds to the difficulty of designing optimal solutions while under pressure. Trying to decide in the presence of an adversary narrows your vision. Having a lot at stake inhibits creativity. So does searching for the one right solution. You can offset these constraints by setting aside a designated time within which to think up a wide range of possible solutions that advance shared interests and creatively reconcile differing interests. Hence the third basic point: Before trying to reach agreement, *invent options for mutual gain.*

Where interests are directly opposed, a negotiator may be able to obtain a favorable result simply by being stubborn. That method tends to reward intransigence and produce arbitrary results. However, you can counter such a negotiator by insisting that his single say-so is not enough and that the agreement must reflect some fair standard independent of the naked will of either side. This does not mean insisting that the terms be based on the standard you select, but only that some fair standard such as market value, expert opinion, custom, or law determine the outcome. By discussing such criteria rather than what the parties are willing or unwilling to do, neither party need give in to the other; both can defer to a fair solution. Hence the fourth basic point: *Insist on using objective criteria.*

The four propositions of principled negotiation are relevant from the time you begin to think about negotiating until the time either an agreement is reached or you decide to break off the effort. That period can be divided into three stages: analysis, planning, and discussion.

During the *analysis* stage you are simply trying to diagnose the situation – to gather information, organize it, and think about it. You will want to consider the people problems of partisan perceptions, hostile emotions, and unclear communication, as well as to identify your interests and those of the other side. You will want to note options already on the table and identify any criteria already suggested as a basis for agreement.

During the *planning* stage you deal with the same four elements a second time, both generating ideas and deciding what to do. How do you propose to handle the people problems? Of your interests, which are most important? And what are some realistic objectives? You will want to generate additional options and additional criteria for deciding among them.

Again during the *discussion* stage, when the parties communicate back and forth, looking toward agreement, the same four elements are the best subjects to discuss. Differences in perception, feelings of frustration and anger, and difficulties in communication can be acknowledged and addressed. Each side should come to understand the interests of the other. Both can then jointly generate options that are mutually advantageous and seek agreement on objective standards for resolving opposed interests.

To sum up, in contrast to positional bargaining, the principled negotiation method of focusing on basic interests, mutually satisfying options, and fair standards typically results in a *wise* agreement. The method permits you to reach a gradual consensus on a joint decision *efficiently* without all the transactional costs of digging in to positions only to have to dig yourself out of them. And separating the people from the problem allows you to deal directly and empathetically with the other negotiator as a human being regardless of any substantive differences, thus making possible an *amicable* outcome.

Problem		Solution
Positional Bargaining: Which Game Should You Play?		Change the Game – Negotiate on the Merits
Soft	**Hard**	**Principled**
Participants are friends.	Participants are adversaries.	Participants are problem-solvers.
The goal is agreement.	The goal is victory.	The goal is a wise outcome reached efficiently and amicably.
Make concessions to cultivate the relationship.	Demand concessions as a condition of the relationship.	**Separate the people from the problem.**
Be soft on the people and the problem.	Be hard on the problem and the people.	Be soft on the people, hard on the problem.
Trust others.	Distrust others.	Proceed independent of trust.
Change your position easily.	Dig in to your position.	**Focus on interests, not positions.**
Make offers.	Make threats.	Explore interests.
Disclose your bottom line.	Mislead as to your bottom line.	Avoid having a bottom line.
Accept one-sided losses to reach agreement.	Demand one-sided gains as the price of agreement.	**Invent options for mutual gain.**
Search for the single answer: the one *they* will accept.	Search for the single answer: the one *you* will accept.	Develop multiple options to choose from; decide later.
Insist on agreement.	Insist on your position.	**Insist on using objective criteria.**
Try to avoid a contest of will.	Try to win a contest of will.	Try to reach a result based on standards independent of will.
Yield to pressure.	Apply pressure.	Reason and be open to reason; yield to principle, not pressure.

47

From Identity-Based Conflict to Identity-Based Cooperation

Jay Rothman

Jay Rothman is an Associate Professor in the International Conflict Resolution and Management Program at Bar-llan University in Israel. He is best known in the conflict resolution field for the development of the ARIA approach to the transformation of identity-based conflicts. The approach begins by acknowledging the antagonism between the conflict parties, but then moves on, via 'reflexive reframing' that leads to 'resonance', to the opening of space for the formulation of inventive options and for subsequent action. Rothman emphasizes that careful analysis which distinguishes types and levels of conflict must precede a 'contingency approach' which can then fit appropriate responses.

* * * *

Putting It All Together: The ARIA Conflict Contingency Approach

While the focus of ARIA was originally on creatively engaging identity-based conflicts with the idea that the deeper the conflict the more need and potential for creativity, ARIA has evolved into a more comprehensive approach that builds upon and synthesizes other approaches, with the type of intervention dependent upon the analysis of the nature and depth of the conflict.

Step one: conflict analysis

ARIA begins with a detailed process of conflict analysis asking disputants to determine separately and interactively: What is this conflict about? Why does it matter to you? How deep does it run? What is functional about it? What is destructive about it? For whom, when and why? What might be done to mine its creative potential and reduce its destructiveness? Diagnosis is a form of creative conflict engagement in itself that sometimes requires nothing additional afterward since clarity and insight can themselves often heal wounds derived from misunderstanding and misperception. Often, however, analysis leads to concrete plans and strategies for intervention of one form or another (e.g. from mediation to dialogue and many methods in between).

Picture conflict as an iceberg, with identity conflicts at the murky bottom. Goal conflicts rise above identity-based conflicts and reside just beneath the water's surface. Resource conflicts are above the water and are in plain sight, the most empirical and tangible of the three.

Another way of differentiating these conflict levels is by the simple questions "What?" "What for?" and "Why?" At the top of the iceberg are the tangible "Whats" of a conflict. For example, "I want that house. I understand you do too." Going down one level are the slightly less tangible "What fors" of a conflict. "I want that house because it fits my family perfectly. How about you?" Finally, the deepest level of "Whys" are repositories of identities such as "I want that house because it is in a neighborhood where I have close friends and family members. Why would you want that house?"

This "levels of analysis" approach visually suggests an important feature of identity-based conflict that distinguishes it from the other two. Identity-based conflict contains within it the other two levels of conflict as well. Conceptually moving up the iceberg, a conflict for example over *home* and one's access to and control over it (the root of many community and international identity-based conflicts), will also be about goals (e.g. to accomplish sovereignty and territorial integrity) and resources (e.g. economic and military strength). On the other hand goal conflicts will be primarily about goals and resources (e.g. to establish an independent state in order to be able to gain and control of economic and military resources). Resource conflicts, while also having seeds of goal disputes and even identity issues if they are poorly handled, are fundamentally about the who, when, and how of the control of tangible resources (e.g. gaining access to and control over scarce resources).

With a "levels of analysis" approach, the next step before focusing on solution seeking – in the form of dialogue, negotiation or some problem solving process that seeks to foster collaboration and coordination between conflict parties and reduce destruction and violence – is determining the right kind of approach for which type of issue: a conflict over identities, problems over goals or disputes over resources. Fisher and Keashley were among the first to describe the need for and outlines of a contingency approach to conflict analysis and resolution (1991). In my work it is not so much the scale of conflict (i.e. international versus community) but rather the type (i.e. conflicts, problems or disputes).

...

[A]t the international level, imagine Israelis and Palestinians all seeking an end to the conflict and agreeing in principle about the need for a two-state solution. Next steps might be easy right? Not at all unless it is clear at what level they are operating. Is it about negotiating final status agreements over who gets what resource, when and how (i.e. the nature of a political settlement)? Is it about the nature and purposes of that two-state solution (i.e. is it to be demilitarized? Are Palestinian refugees able to resettle in their old homes within Israel as part of that agreement or not)? Or is it about the values and needs of each community (i.e. for identity, dignity, control over destiny and so forth and ways that state will fulfill or further frustrate such existential needs and values)?

Why is it happening?

Having diagnosed the predominant level at which the conflict resides in a certain context of time and place, interveners and disputants then analyze the causes of the conflict. By asking the appropriate questions (why does this problem matter to you so much? what do you think some of its causes have been?), and utilizing the resulting self diagnosis of conflict, interveners design, or better yet, elicit from the disputants themselves, an approach to address the conflict.

This previously described "Power of Why" process is one in which people are asked to share their personal narrative about why they care about the situation. The deeper the situation, usually the more they care. The process is particularly effective in identity and goal based issues. It can also be useful, however, in a more mechanical way in determining whether concrete issues are at stake.

Step two: how should the issues be addressed?

A hallmark of ARIA is the way it encourages everyone engaged in a specific conflict issue to deal with the same things, in mostly the same way, for largely the same reasons. This is no small task, and perhaps due to the complexity of this effort, it is all too rare. Commonly in conflicts, people are talking about different things, in different ways, for different reasons. So conflicts often protract and worsen as they are surfaced, and the conventional fight-flight response is further encouraged. People involved in the ARIA process develop a single score for all to read from together by getting everyone to share an analysis of the core features or main presenting issues of the conflict and its history. Next, by suggesting different types of intervention strategies and lining them up with the conflict analysis, everyone can start off on the same footing. This is a largely analytic process in which we study the type of situation that emerged in the past – a dispute, a problem or a conflict – and then determine the best path forward to constructively settle, manage or engage it in the future.

The ARIA Acronym

In addition to being a metaphor for creativity (i.e. ARIA is the Italian word for "song"), ARIA is also an acronym for four categories of conflict intervention that align with different conflict types: Antagonism, Resonance, Invention and Action (Rothman 1997).

A– Surfacing of Antagonism: mostly rooted in the past and most clearly in evidence in identity-based conflicts. Some of the conflict intervention processes used in this phase are dialogue, empowerment mediation, confrontation, and facilitation.

R– Narrative excursion in to the Resonance of peoples' hopes, fears, needs and values, is often the starting point for goal-based conflicts. Some of the conflict intervention processes used in this phase are narrative mediation, storytelling, and transformative processes.

I– Invention process of seeking creative ways to foster and promote greater resonance through concrete fulfillment of needs, values and goals. Some of the conflict invention processes used in this phase include interest based bargaining, collaborative visioning, goal setting, and action research.

A– Action planning process of concretely designing and implementing ways to sustain and further creative inventions. Some of the conflict intervention processes used in this phase are negotiation, action planning and techniques drawn from organizational development.

The ARIA Contingency Approach

If the conflict is rooted in identity issues, then intervention processes that safely surface the hurts and indignities of the past – or antagonisms – are often necessary. If the conflict presents mainly at the goal level, then understanding and engaging each side's needs and values, their "resonance," is the suggested starting point. If the conflict is mainly about resources, then proactive processes for inventing mutual gains outcomes, or settling differences amicably, are suggested. The intervention processes suggested by this model move up the iceberg along with the levels of analysis. For example, when starting at the Identity-level, begin with Antagonism and then move upwards to Resonance, then Invention, then Action and so forth.

References

Fisher, R. J., and L. Keashley 1991. "The potential complementarity of mediation and consultation within a contingency model of third party intervention", *Journal of Peace Research* 28(1):29–42.

Rothman, J. (1997) *Resolving Identity-Based Conflicts in Nations, Organizations, and Communities*. San Francisco: Jossey-Bass.

48

Approaches to Community Relations Work

Mari Fitzduff

Mari Fitzduff was the founding director of the Northern Ireland Community Relations Council, which was responsible for funding and promoting many conflict resolution initiatives in Northern Ireland. In this piece, she sets out a typology of community relations work, setting conflict resolution in a broader context of grassroots initiatives to improve inter-community relations. Her book *Community Conflict Skills* has been influential as a source for those grappling with community conflicts. She later became director of the INCORE program and Professor of Conflict Resolution in the University of Ulster, and was the Director of the international MA program in Coexistence and Conflict at Brandeis University, Massachusetts.

* * * *

This typology of community relations work is an attempt to classify the different kinds of work which might validly be called community relations work i.e. work designed specifically to assist the development of understanding, respect and communication between our communities.

The typology offers a brief analysis of the rationale underlying the different kinds of work that are happening, gives examples of programmes and practices pertinent to the particular work, as well as some thoughts about its possible further development.

It is hoped that such a classification can help groups to recognise that there are a variety of approaches to community relations work, all of them useful to the overall objectives of the work, but differing in their focus. It is also hoped that clarifying such a spectrum of approaches can enable groups and organisations to involve themselves in the work at the level required by their own particular concerns and ethos, using the skills available to them, and perhaps moving from one kind of focus to another as their concerns, skills and capacity develop.

The classifications are not intended to be definitive, or limited, but only suggestive, in recognition that we are all of us still defining the boundaries of the work, and continuing to work at new possibilities for its effectiveness, and better methods to evaluate it. Nor does the typology presume to prioritise the differing kinds of work, i.e. indicate that one kind will be more effective than another in achieving the desired goals of community relations work, as our knowledge about the validity of such prioritising is as yet too limited to make such a prioritisation with any certainty.

The typology also includes a brief assessment of the kind of work that needs to happen in parallel to focused community relations work, in order to make it success-ful. This work is called Contextual Work, and it was included in recognition that, by itself, and without progress in these parallel areas, the effect of community relations work will be severely limited. It is believed that the endorsement of such work by agen-cies involved in community relations can also be useful for the overall progress of such work.

The typology was first outlined in 1989. In this, the third edition, the typology has been amended to take account of some of the new approaches and organisations which have sprung up to develop the work over the past few years. The Community Relations Council, set up with the assistance of the Government in 1990, is one such organisation. Its task is to assist in the development of community relations work at whatever level is possible throughout Northern Ireland. The Council have reprinted this typology in the hope that it may assist such development, and be of use to the increasing number of groups who are seeking to involve themselves in community relations work in the belief that, without such work, solutions to our many differences will be much longer in the coming, and much less sustainable.

Cultural Traditions Work

Objectives: Work designed to affirm and develop cultural confidence and an acceptance of cultural diversity.

Rationale and development

Cultural Traditions work is based on the belief that diversity within a society is to be respected and not necessarily to be regarded as a threat. It presumes that different cul-tural and religious perspectives, and even differing preferences for political options, can co-exist within a society and that no one group or community should regard it as their right or duty to dominate or intimidate the other into adopting alternative beliefs and practices. It suggests that arrangements to express such plurality should be devel-oped, and that differing cultural values must be respected in the development of legislation.

It believes that denying a community a distinctive cultural development can contrib-ute to feelings of alienation on the part of many members of that group. It also suggests that the development of cultural confidence work can contribute to the capacity of a community to enter into negotiations with other communities without the excessive defensiveness which can result from insecurity about identity and hence it believes that such work can usefully precede e.g. political options work.

It may be useful to think of cultural traditions work happening through a variety of processes, and in groups of differing composition and pace.

Affirmation

Cultural Traditions work offers a useful way for groups to both affirm and reassess their histories, and feel assured in their identities. Affirmation work concentrates on validating the existence of particular groups, with their differing cultural, social and theological expressions and perspectives. The aim of such work is to increase the confidence of the particular community, affirming their right to be different and ensuring such differences are validated through government and, if necessary, legislative structures.

Reflection

This is work which assumes that a community has developed sufficient confidence to be able to reflect upon, and even challenge possibly simplistic beliefs about its own past and present perspectives which may have contributed to sectarianism. It can provide a safe way to acknowledge contentious historical material which challenges simplified views of allegiances, past and present. This is work which is probably best done on a within-community basis and the aim of such work is to address beliefs which prevent the development of empathy and cross cutting interest between the communities.

Sharing

This is work which continues the type of reflection outlined above, but which is developed on a cross-community basis. Its aim is to permit shared information, reflection upon differing perspectives of similar events and the reasons for such differing perspectives, and facilitate the gradual development of understanding and respect between communities for each other's viewpoints of history.

Pluralism

This is work which concentrates on both legitimising and even celebrating the existence of different cultural traditions. People involved in such work will accept that communities have valid but differing perspectives about their cultural and political hopes for Northern Ireland and that these must all be considered and accommodated in any future negotiations about legal and constitutional structures.

While much of the above work has been happening over the last few years in Northern Ireland, possibilities for its further development would seem to abound. Much of such work can happen through local historical societies. The Federation of Ulster Local Studies has been encouraging the development of networks for furthering contact between groups from different communities through shared meetings, presentations across the divide of research that is informative of differing cultures, and even provocative of reflection upon accepted historical simplicities, and the use of 'dual perspective' presentations on historical events which are seen very differently from each side of the divide.

Community Arts i.e. work which happens through the energies and commitment of local people offers many possibilities for encouraging discussion of an affirming, reflective and challenging nature between communities. Local community projects in particular provide possibilities for communities and individuals to reflect upon their present and past preoccupations and relationships, particularly if allied with parallel discussions upon the dramatic themes.

The development of musical programmes and projects which respect the validity of differing musical traditions has also been significant, as has the promotion of such work through local festivals, and as part of community relations activities.

Many cultural celebrations, particularly at local level now often include marching and other bands from both traditions, and such inclusion can offer a public validation of pluralism in action.

Conflict Resolution Work

Objective: Developing approaches to resolving conflicts at local and regional level which are non-violent, just and effective.

Rationale and development

Since the end of World War II there has been an increasing interest on the part of both academics and practitioner alike in analysing and reviewing the occurrence of conflicts and how they can be resolved, or at least managed more effectively. It is now believed that conflicts do not necessarily have to take place on a 'win/lose' basis and that in many cases 'joint problem solving' i.e. where the problem is seen as a collective one rather than the problem of the other side, can produce mutual gain. Considerable time has been spent analysing the skills needed to achieve such results which have included joint interest identification, structured listening between groups, and the development of creative approaches to local conflict management. Some emphasis has also been placed in such work on the development of the skills of mediation for third parties willing to serve as facilitators between conflicting parties.

Work has already started in Northern Ireland in promoting alternative models of conflict resolution in a variety of areas, particularly within schools, and such work can be usefully encouraged to develop. The development of local mediation and conflict management services has also been developing, either through the informal availability of skilled individuals, or through structured services such as a neighbourhood dispute resolution centre, which can be used as an alternative to the sometimes inappropriate use of e.g. the Housing Executive, the R.U.C., or the paramilitaries to solve disputes. The hope is that such skills can empower people to deal with conflict in a manner that is less aggressive and more widely useful.

Through developing alternative models of conflict, and increasing the skills of people to deal with conflict in their particular communities e.g. in schools, neighbourhoods and work places, it is hoped that this can contribute to their capacity to deal more constructively with conflict at an inter-community or political level.

Those who are developing skills training in conflict resolution at a political level will focus on increasing people's capacities to handle contentious discussions constructively.

Such work will include dealing with prejudice and bigotry, the hurts of history and present day injustices. It will encourage adequate ventilation of fears between groups, empathetic listening between conflicting groups, and the development of scenarios for mutual gain solutions to the political conflict.

The encouragement and training of people to facilitate such work can be developed through some of the many institutions who already provide training e.g. youth, and adult and community education sectors, local community development groups, women's and trade union groups and university training courses.

49

Peacemaking Public and Private

Adam Curle

In this very personal piece, Adam Curle reflects on the importance of the peacemaker nurturing their own awareness and sensitivity. Private peacemaking may be a precondition of public peacemaking, he suggests.

* * * *

Some dedicated and intelligent people believe that we cannot affect human nature until we have altered the society that flawed it, and that we are unlikely to be able to do this without violence. But the habit of violence and the accompanying insensitivity to suffering tend to persist. Thus all too often in history, and we can think of several contemporary examples, a tyranny is overthrown and those ardent lovers of justice who overthrew it become equally tyrannical. If this were not so, there would be many Utopias in our unhappy world. There are, of course, numerous complex reasons for the difficulty of establishing ideal or even relatively decent societies, but the acceptance of violence as a means of achieving ends is certainly one of them. The ends may at first seem good, but with practice we become less discriminating.

This implies particular responsibilities for peacemakers engaged in working towards the establishment of a peaceful society. I have phrased this positively instead of talking about changing or eliminating an unpeaceful one. Peacemakers may indeed devise strategies of social, economic and political change: this is in the public domain of peacemaking, but it is even more important for them to help their collaborators to work on their problems of personal unpeacefulness. This is the private approach, and it is as indispensable as public negotiation in reaching the final goal, not just the cessation of hostilities or the overthrow of a particular regime, but the establishment of a lasting peace, based on justice and non-violence.

...

If it is the common predicament of humanity to be less than half awake, to behave – often violently – like machines, to mask our high potential with misinformation, preconceptions and negative emotions, then the would-be peacemakers must work on themselves as much as or more than on those whose violence they would wish to curb, for they are also violent and violent people cannot create lastingly unviolent situations. Only by learning to control their own malfunctioning can they help others to control theirs, and only thus have a fully human relationship with them rather than a largely mechanical interaction.

First it is necessary to recognise how little real autonomy we have; how much we are dominated by the flow of thoughts, memories, ideas, feelings that flicker across the screen of consciousness; how little we are capable of attention (this is an activity of the whole self as compared with an absorption that can be as automatic as anything else); how, for all our vaunted free will, we cannot choose our feelings or control our thoughts. At the same time we have to recognise that this is the general human condition and that we must not castigate ourselves or forget that below the surface confusion is a deep source of strength. For all our normal lack of complete consciousness, we are not impotent.

Next, we must seek some means of becoming more and more constantly awake. This is an individual matter for each person. Let me, however, mention a few things which I believe to be of general validity. Our normal state is one of inner noise distracting us from reaching the inner parts of the mind. First, therefore, it is necessary to practice quietness. This is not difficult, if we can only remember to do it. It is only necessary to compose ourselves, sitting comfortably but not slouching, for two or three minutes two or three times a day, but preferably between different types of activity. The mind then comes to rest and intruding thoughts ignored or nudged gently aside. During these periods, whatever we are engaged with, we should awake. I mean that we should become conscious of who we are, where we are, what we are doing, what is around us, and particularly what our bodies feel like.

These things are very simple; the only difficulty is in breaking the bad habit of being asleep by the good habit of being awake. If we could be conscious of ourselves the whole time, life would be transformed, including of course, our relationship with others.

50

In the Middle

Adam Curle

Few transcripts of international mediators at work are available, for the very good reason that effective mediation generally depends on confidentiality. To circumvent this problem and give the general reader an idea of what mediation is like, Adam Curle wrote an imaginary transcript, based on his experience of mediation in the Nigerian Civil War. The full transcript is too long to republish here, but we reproduce Curle's introduction, in which he sets out four essential elements in mediation. Later Curle came to take the view that it was for people in the society in conflict to undertake the peacemaking themselves, but he made himself available as a supporter, adviser and confidant of local peace groups, for example in the wars over former Yugoslavia.

*   *   *   *

Mediation

Mediators, as the word implies, are in the middle. This is true in two senses. Firstly they are neither on one side nor the other; secondly they are in the centre of the conflict, deeply involved in it because they are trying to find a satisfactory way out of it.

Although mediation is considered here in the special context of violent conflict, it is a universal human role. All of us, perhaps even the most intractably aggressive, have practised it occasionally. We may not have called it that when we tried to persuade members of our family or friends or colleagues to see each other's point of view and stop bickering about some trivial issue. But mediation it was: we were the people in between those who had fallen out, on fairly good terms with both, not taking sides though often pressured to do so; not personally implicated in the dispute but worried about the situation and hoping to improve it. What mediators do is to try to establish, or re-establish, sufficiently good communications between conflicting parties so that they can talk sensibly to each other without being blinded by such emotions as anger, fear and suspicion. This does not necessarily resolve the conflict; mediation has to be followed-up by skilled negotiation, usually directly between the protagonists, supported by a measure of mutual tolerance and by determination to reach agreement. But it is a good start.

This would apply whether the conflict were between individuals or nations, and irrespective of culture, political ideology, or religion. Although the circumstances of an international dispute, economic, political and strategic, are very different from the emotional tangle of, for example, a marital one, both ultimately focus on human beings who have to make decisions and to act, and whose passions, fears, hopes, rage and guilt are much the same whoever they are. This, at least, has been my experience.

Non-Official Mediation

Within the context of violent conflict, the forms of mediation may differ considerably. Some involve short-term missions having a very specific objective, such as those of Terry Waite to secure the release of captives in various parts of the world, or the shuttle diplomacy of a Henry Kissinger hurrying, often without great success, between one capital and another. There is also the longer-term work of United Nations officials such as Dag Hammarskjöld, Brian Urquhart or Sean McBride, struggling year after year to resolve one bitter quarrel after another.

These and many other patterns may be useful and appropriate. What I shall discuss is mediation usually of long duration, carried out by non-official groups or organisations, churches or other religious organisations, charitable bodies, academic bodies, or concerned individuals without institutional backing (although individuals without such support tend to experience difficulty in launching and maintaining their mission, suffer considerable strain and naturally incur considerable costs). I shall not speak of UN mediation, most valuable though it is; the aegis of a great international organisation creates conditions, occasionally less favourable where there is unilateral distrust of it, different from those pertaining to both governmental and to private or non-official mediation. What I have to say derives from direct experience of mediation initiated by the Quakers who, of the half dozen or so organisations I know of that have worked in the field, have the longest and most varied experience, as well as from efforts which were personal although carried out with much help from others. It is perhaps hardly necessary to emphasise that those engaged in private mediation are never, so far as I know, paid, except for their expenses. Nor do they, being constrained by the need for confidentiality, make money or achieve any ego-enhancement by such means as writing articles or giving interviews. Their mediation is perhaps more appreciated because in no sense influenced by the profit motive; there is no reason why they should submit to considerable trouble and inconvenience except to contribute if possible to the reduction of human misery. In the same vein, I sometimes point out to people that I have been retired for several years and would sooner spend my old age at home than gallivanting around the world. …

The Practice of Mediation

We have seen that would-be mediators have to pass through what might be termed a probationary period, unless of course they have been invited in by the protagonists. However, once they have gained a sufficient measure of acceptance, their work begins to take shape. Although it will obviously change and expand, following the contours of circumstances, it soon becomes possible to identify four aspects of mediation. These are interwoven and overlapping but distinguishable emphases of the unitary task of bringing together those who have been separated by violence.

Building, maintaining and improving communications

By this I mean the mediators' own communications with both groups of protagonists and indeed other involved groups, and – via the mediators – between the protagonists themselves, the second being dependent on the first and both being essential to mediation.

...

Providing information

This means attempting to be aware of facts needed to establish reasonable policies and so as not to be misled by rumour, misinformation or prejudice; peace and negotiation are jeopardised more by ignorance than by truth, however unpalatable. Providing information is, of course, also an aspect of communication, especially because the manner of transmission and the quality of the relationship determines whether it will be heard or understood.

...

Befriending

This refers to the character of the relationship between mediators and those with whom they are dealing. They come essentially as friends, drawn by concern for the suffering of all concerned in the struggle, including the mental anguish of those in power. They play a different part from that of civil servant, diplomat or consultant; they come in a spirit of goodwill to do whatever they can to help the victims of the conflict to escape from the trap of violence. To the extent that their unconditional goodwill is accepted, the relationship of the mediators with leaders and other responsible officials may somewhat diminish the psychological tensions and the possibility of compulsive and unconstructive action.

...

Active mediation

I have coined this term to describe (inadequately) what might be thought of as the more specifically diplomatic activity of mediators. It is not their job, of course, to attempt persuasion or to promote particular approaches to the resolution of a conflict. On the other hand, they do not just passively and impersonally impart information and pass messages; they are not civil servants whose job it is to ensure that their political masters are aware of all the facts necessary for them to decide on wise policies, but who have no part in those decisions. Mediators, of course, attempt to do these things, but they do so with a specific purpose: to remove obstacles on the path to peace, and they argue strongly against the misunderstandings and preconceptions that strengthen those obstacles.

51
Training Manual in Community Mediation Skills

Mediation UK

One of the methods Curle advocates in mediation is active listening. Here, the former umbrella group Mediation UK sets out what active listening is and gives examples of its use in mediation over neighbourhood conflicts.

* * * *

Active Listening (Reflective or Deep Listening)

Active listening is a core foundation skill for mediation and for many applied processes of conflict resolution.

Interpersonal communication skills for active listening fall into two groups:

VERBAL	NON-VERBAL
Encouraging	Body Posture
Empathy	Gestures
Questioning	Eye contact
Reflecting	Physical Space
Acknowledging	Touch
Clarifying	Presence of Others (friendly, unfriendly, supportive, inhibiting)
Summarising	Attentive Silence (Interested)

Active Listening – Why Is It So Important to Develop this Skill?

- In mediation you might be in a situation where you can't take notes, but there is much of information to retain
- So the speaker feels that they are getting complete attention. It is important for them to know that what they have to say has been heard.
- It gives the speaker feedback on what they said, and how it came across
- It creates an environment where the speaker is given confidence to say things, and not be judged
- It helps build a firmer, and more trusting relationship for the future. Some people don't often have the opportunity to be with a good listener (e.g. leaders can't trust

people, competing agendas and self-interest, having information used against them at a later date). This helps avoid misunderstandings, so you can work more effectively with others

Some important elements in active listening

- Listen for the content of what is being said. What are the main points or ideas? What is the context of the conversation (noise, distractions, other elements of external environment)? Can you change it?
- Listen for feelings and emotions and respond to those (acknowledge those that you recognise). What fears and concerns is the speaker expressing?
- Encourage the speaker to explain in some detail
- Don't keep interrupting and talking (you can't listen whilst you are talking), but ask questions at appropriate times (could, for example be used to show you are listening).
- At appropriate times restate or paraphrase what you think you've heard. Be patient with the speaker, move into their domain – don't expect them to move into yours. Use language that they understand.
- Don't fiddle with objects
- Try to practice 'unconditional positive regard' for the speaker. Don't let prejudices and stereotypes influence your listening. Don't filter what you hear to fit in with your world view
- Whilst you are listening try not to keep thinking of what your response is likely to be.
- Be aware of 'door openers' – invitations to get started . . . . . .
  'you seem troubled' . . . .
  'it seems like things went OK' . . . .
  'you sound angry about this'

Active Listening Skills

(*Training Manual in Community Mediation Skills*, Mediation UK, 1995)

- ENCOURAGING
'Tell us some more about. . . .', 'You were saying earlier'

- EMPATHY
'I can understand why you are worried about this' . . . . ., 'I think this situation has been very difficult for you, and you are getting impatient' . . .

- ACKNOWLEDGING
'I understand' . . . .'I see', ...nonverbal signals

- CLARIFICATION
'I'm not sure I understand. Did you say . . . . .'

- QUESTIONING – OPEN AND CLOSED

Open question:

   Could you tell me more about it.....?

   Can you help me understand.......?

   How was that for you......?

Closed question:

   When did you do that....?

   Where did you hear about this.....?

   Why did you take that step.....?

Close ended questions usually begin with are, why, where, did and so on. They often provoke a defensive response.

- REFLECTING

(Somebody says 'I am sick to death of this') – 'You are sick to death? What particularly upsets you?'...

- TONE OF VOICE AND VOLUME

When changing tone or volume do it gently, in stages. Sudden switches will unsettle some speakers.

52

Use of Language by Mediators: Exercises

This exercise is based on the training course run by the Lambeth Mediation Centre in London. In a typical dispute, the mediator brings two disputing neighbours together, hears their accounts, and then puts what they have said into her or his own language in order to help the disputants discuss the issues without being inflamed by the language in which they are expressed. In this exercise there is a series of statements by parties in dispute. Taking the role of a mediator, try to reformulate what has been said in impartial language that accurately reflects the concern and feeling of the speaker, but will not cause offence to the other party.

*   *   *   *

1. Sharing an office
A. "She makes this office unbearable with her filthy cigarettes."
Mediator's response: _____

B. "She's totally unreasonable. It's my office too. I need to smoke while I'm working."
Mediator's response: _____

2. Two sisters
A: "She's always nicking my sweater so it's filthy when I want to wear it."
Mediator's response: _____

B: "She's so mean about her clothes – she'll never lend me anything although I let her borrow my records."
Mediator's response: _____

3. Two neighbours
A: "He's too lazy to put his car in his garage so he leaves it outside my house and I have to park up the road and hump my shopping for miles."
Mediator's response: _____

B: "If you were as busy as I am, in and out all the time, you wouldn't put the car away every time."
Mediator's response: _____

4. Parent and daughter
A. "She uses this house like a hotel. She comes in and out at all hours."
Mediator's response: _____

B. "They nag me all the time. They've never liked my friends. Anyway, I've got my own life to lead."
Mediator's response: _____

5. Boss and worker
A. "He's unreliable and difficult to talk to, and he can't be trusted to carry out orders."
Mediator's response: _____

B: "He's always so chaotic, it's impossible to know what I'm supposed to be doing."
Mediator's response: _____

6. Ethnic conflict
A. "They're breeding like rabbits, they don't work, and they support the terrorists."
Mediator's response: _____

B. "They're abusing our human rights and sending police to burn our homes."
Mediator's response: _____

53

Disputes and Negotiations

Philip Gulliver

This is an anthropologist's account of a dispute between neighbouring farmers in northern Tanzania. It gives a sense of how a dispute over land within a particular African community was handled. The reading shows how the outcome reflected the context, local beliefs and the power balance between the neighbours. The process model of negotiation in Gulliver's book, which there is not space to include here, is an important contribution to the theory of disputes and negotiations. Philip Gulliver has been a research sociologist with the Government of Tanganyika, Professor of Anthropology at the School of Oriental and African Studies, London, and later Professor of Anthropology at Calgary and York University, Canada.

* * * *

A Dispute Between Neighbors in Arusha

Materials for this case were collected during the course of my own field research among the Arusha of northern Tanzania, both by personal observation of the negotiations in a public moot and by discussions with the principal disputants and others before and after the moot. The negotiations took place in 1957.

The emergence of the dispute

Lashiloi and Kinyani were unrelated neighbors. Each was about 50 years old and head of his own autonomous family that included an unmarried, adult son, and other younger children. They were co-members of the age groups then in the age-grade of junior elders, the "executive" age group particularly active in the public affairs of the community ("parish") in which they lived. Thus, both were mature, well-established men. However, neither was an acknowledged "notable"; that is, they were not especially influential among their peers and neighbors (Gulliver 1963:25 ff.).

Each man had undisputedly inherited his farm from his own deceased father. Between their two farms there was a somewhat smaller farm of about $2\frac{1}{2}$ acres, the ownership of which had been in question for a long time. This farm became vacant after the occupying tenant, Ngatio, died and his widow and children went to live in another parish with Ngatio's brother, who made no claim to continue the tenancy. It was generally agreed in the neighborhood that Ngatio was only a tenant and Ngatio himself had never claimed more than that. There was disagreement, however, as to how the tenancy had originally been established and who was now the rightful owner of the newly vacant farm. Some 10 years previously, when Ngatio had inherited the tenancy from his father, Raiyon, at the latter's death, the fathers of Lashiloi and Kinyani had each claimed sole ownership. Although neither had sought to interfere with Ngatio's tenancy at that time, each had demanded recognition as Ngatio's landlord. Negotiations failed to produce any resolution of the matter, and it seems fairly clear (from local informants' accounts) that neither claimant had wished to push the issue to a conclusion that might have endangered otherwise good and valued neighborly relations. Since then and until his recent death, Ngatio had made irregular small gifts of farm produce to both of his neighbor–kinsmen (and later, to their heirs, Lashiloi and Kinyani). Such gifts had indicated his status as a tenant and their acceptance had demonstrated recognition of his good standing. Ownership of the farm had remained undetermined.

During the few months after Ngatio's death, the farm lay vacant. Both Lashiloi and Kinyani grazed their livestock on it and their wives took fruit from the banana grove and did some desultory maintenance work. However, it was apparent that this situation could not persist; good agricultural land was involved and, in Arusha country, land had recently become scarce and valuable as a result of very high population density (about 1000 people per square mile), an inability to expand into new areas, and new cash crop cultivation. Moreover, both Lashiloi and Kinyani were eager to enlarge their existing farms, especially since each had an adult son who would soon marry and require land for a separate homestead.

According to Lashiloi, his grandfather, Loton, had granted the original tenancy to his (Loton's) sister's son, Raiyon, the father of Ngatio. Kinyani claimed that the tenancy had been given by his grandfather, Kosa, to Raiyon, Kosa's daughter's husband (see the genealogy in Figure 1b). Since the event had occurred some 70 years previously, there were no written records nor were there surviving witnesses to the transaction.

Until the time of Ngatio's death, relations between Lashiloi and Kinyani had been friendly and tolerant, with the casual cooperation typical of good neighbors. Any disagreements had been easily dealt with by amicable adjustment. After Ngatio's death, relations gradually deteriorated. Disagreement over the disposition of the vacant farm escalated to the point of open quarreling. In addition, other disagreements developed and were not resolved. Kinyani complained that several times Lashiloi's goats had wandered onto his land and had damaged the growing crop; his demand for compensation was refused. Lashiloi complained that Kinyani had at various times withheld or interrupted the supply of irrigation water to Lashiloi's land, thus endangering his onion crop. Lashiloi also complained that Kinyani had harshly beaten his herdsboy son, but Kinyani counterclaimed that the son had trespassed on his land and, without permission, had operated and damaged the gate that controlled the flow of irrigation water. Lashiloi accused Kinyani of illicitly using supernatural power that threatened severe illness or death to members of Lashiloi's family. The two men had discussed these complaints several times but argument had ended in angry accusations and intransigence, so that relations became effectively cut off.

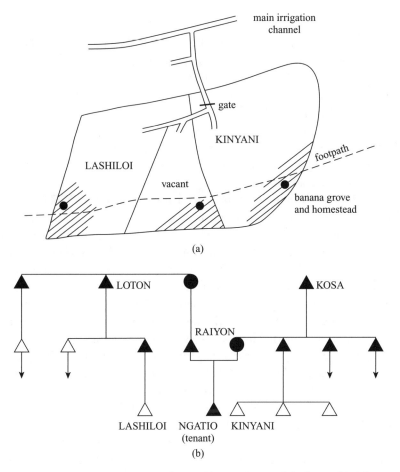

Figure 1 *A dispute between Arusha neighbors: (a) map of the farms; (b) skeleton genealogy*

Negotiating the dispute: phases 1 to 4

Lashiloi forced the crisis that initiated the public dispute. At a meeting of their age-group that had assembled for other purposes, he made a claim to the whole of the vacant farm and demanded that Kinyani refrain from improperly interfering with his irrigation water. Kinyani strongly denied the claim and rejected Lashiloi's demand but he refused to accept offers of mediation by members of the age-group. Afterward, he went to consult with his lineage counsellor,[1] who lived in the same parish. His counsellor agreed to approach the counsellor of Lashiloi's lineage.

Phase 1. The two counsellors, with the consent of Lashiloi and Kinyani, agreed to convene a patrilineal moot. (**C**) There was no real problem in deciding the arena. Kinyani had already made it clear that he did not wish the intervention of co-members of their age-group (apparently apprehensive of their pressures in favor of Lashiloi, the more popular man), and he had shown his preference for a moot by choosing to consult with his lineage counsellor. Lashiloi saw no reason to contest the choice of a moot since he could expect strong support from his patrilineage. Moreover, in so important a matter as land, a moot was often preferred to a purely parish arena (Gulliver 1963:197). The obvious place to hold the moot was the vacant farm itself.

Such a moot posited that each disputant recruit a party of patrilineal supporters composed of members of the inner lineage (the smallest recognized kin group) and those members of the maximal lineage and clan section who lived fairly near and who agreed to participate. Lashiloi's party consisted of 12 men, among whom he, his counsellor, and his father's brother's son were the more prominent speakers in the negotiations. Kinyani's party included 10 men, of whom he, his counsellor, and the counsellor of a collateral lineage were the leading members.

Phase 2. The initial concern of the moot became the establishment and clarification of the issues in dispute. At first, this was not dealt with deliberately. Lashiloi spoke first, giving a list of his allegations and demands in some detail. Kinyani followed in the same way until he referred to a sum of money that Lashiloi allegedly owed him. Lashiloi and his counsellor interrupted. They denied the debt and pointed out that, in any case, it was not a matter under consideration in the moot. (**A**) Kinyani rejected this contention and his counsellor declared that "we are not going to be told what we can talk about by Lashiloi." The counsellor went on to say that the debt was important and long overdue; he added that it was Lashiloi who had raised a petty issue by alleging that Kinyani had slandered him. After some exchanges, it was agreed that each party should be free to introduce any issue that was considered important. (**C**) "This is a dispute between age-mates who are neighbors. If we do not talk about everything they will not be able to live in peace," said one of Kinyani's supporters (the counsellor of the collateral lineage). Silence from both parties signified acceptance of this resolution and then the same counsellor reiterated Lashiloi's complaints. He was followed by Lashiloi's counsellor, who announced Lashiloi's complaints. After a few modifications, these were accepted by both parties. In all, 16 issues were identified. (These are set out summarily in Figure 2, together with the reference symbols used in the following description of the negotiations.)

Phase 3. Kinyani's counsellor then remarked that the important issues were those put forward by his party, whereas those of Lashiloi were petty or false and intended only to cause trouble for Kinyani. (**A**) This comment brought protesting cries from Lashiloi's side and Lashiloi himself came to stand in the open space between the two seated parties. He was allowed to speak at length with little interruption or comment. He began by declaring that his own complaints were the important issues and that Kinyani had so far refused to consider them. Then he repeated his allegations and demands one by one, going into details and justifying his claims. Finally, he referred briefly to Kinyani's demands and rejected all of them, saying that each was too unimportant to call for serious attention. "Kinyani says these things because he is unfriendly, because he dislikes me. Have I not been a good neighbor? Have we not worked together? Have I not helped him? [details of some occasions of this]. He says these things because he wants to take my land [i.e., the vacant farm]. It is not his estate [i.e., inherited property]; it is mine, the estate of my grandfather, Loton, who was the big man here long ago...Kinyani says bad words because he has not good [true, legitimate] ones."

Issues Raised by Both Disputants
I. LAND: Alleged hereditary right to the vacant farm
1. Claimed exclusive ownership of the farm
2. Claimed exclusive use of the land for agricultural and other purposes

Issues Raised by Kinyani
II. TRESPASS: Alleged trespass and damage to crops by Lashiloi's goats
3. Demanded compensation for damages
4. Demanded promise by Lashiloi to control his goats in the future
III. GATE: Alleged damage to his irrigation gate by unauthorized use by Lashiloi's son
5. Demanded payment of costs of repairs
6. Demanded recognition of his sole right to operate the gate
IV. DEBT: Alleged a long-standing debt of money owed to him by Lashiloi
7. Demanded immediate payment in full

Issues Raised by Lashiloi
V. WATER: Alleged interruption and denial irrigation water by Kinyani
8. Demanded acknowledgment of his right to regular supply of water from the main irrigation channel
9. Demanded compensation for damage to crops resulting from interruption of water supply
VI. SUPERNATURAL: Alleged illicit supernatural act by Kinyani on the vacant land, aimed at him and likely to harm him and his family
10. Demanded performance of ritual purification by Kinyani (including provision of sacrificial goat) to lift the threat from supernatural forces
11. Demanded payment of compensation
VII. VIOLENCE: Alleged that his herdsboy son had been severely beaten by Kinyani
12. Demanded apology for illegitimate violence
13. Demanded compensation for injuries to his son
VIII. SLANDER: Alleged public slander of his reputation by Kinyani
14. Demanded recantation
15. Demanded apology
16. Demanded compensation for injury to his reputation

Figure 2 *Summary agenda of the negotiations*

Lashiloi returned to sit with his party and Kinyani came to stand in the central open space. His speech was similar to that of Lashiloi; he set out his complaints in detail and sharply rejected Lashiloi's demands. Kinyani was followed by his counsellor who concentrated on the land issue and gave his version of the history of the tenancy. Although it added little to what Kinyani had already said before and during the negotiations, the counsellor claimed to give it greater validity because he, as a counsellor and a senior elder, knew the facts better than Lashiloi and his supporters. The counsellor then asked two elderly men to affirm his version. One was the oldest surviving member of Kinyani's maximal lineage and the other was the father-in-law of another member. After they did so, Lashiloi's counsellor spoke, apparently in great indignation, though this was largely contrived as a matter of planned tactics.[2] He dismissed the evidence of the two old men: "They are only retired elders. They are feeble. Old men forget." This produced shouts of protest from Kinyani's party but the counsellor ignored them and continued to speak. "I am the spokesman of Loton's lineage. I knew Loton when he was a big man [some details about Loton]. And I remember the things of those days. I am not an old man and my age-group is not that of the old men [i.e., the retired elders]. But you, Oloreng [Kinyani's counsellor], and you, Kinyani, you are still young men who should listen to us, your seniors." From this act of asserting superior status, and thus superior knowledge and experience (quite typical of the behavior of an Arusha toward men of a junior age-group, though not necessarily effective), the counsellor went on to describe the legitimacy of Lashiloi's claim to the land. He ended his speech by accusing Kinyani of deliberately making a false claim because of his greed for land.

When the counsellor returned to his party, Kinyani stood up amid his own party and, ignoring the land issue and the previous speaker, reemphasized his other complaints. He was followed by his brother who went into details about the alleged damage to the irrigation gate (Figure 2, III). He explained that Kinyani, and their father previously, had always controlled the irrigation water.[3] He said that there had never been trouble before and, moreover, that Kinyani was well known to be properly careful in not taking too much water from the main channel, which had to supply many other farms. It was Lashiloi, he said, who was greedy for water because he had begun to cultivate more land than before and was therefore demanding more than his fair share. He concluded with more invidious remarks about Lashiloi.

Exchanges went on in this fashion for some time. Usually a member of one party, then of the other, monopolized the proceedings. Occasionally a witness was called to corroborate some statement or one party cross-examined a speaker from the other. However, there was virtually no attempt to make counteroffers to the opponent's demands. Rather, each speaker simply continued to deny the allegations against their principal and to deprecate the other's demands as grossly exaggerated. Occasionally, one party's interruptions and interjections temporarily interfered with a speaker from the other party, and there were several outbursts of anger. (A+) One of these outbursts, which included a threat that Lashiloi's supporters would go and break up Kinyani's irrigation gate, was quickly suppressed by Lashiloi's counsellor. He declared that, although such violence must not occur, it was Kinyani's actions and continued rejection of Lashiloi's legitimate demands that were responsible for the understandable indignation of Lashiloi's supporters.

Phase 3 to Phase 4. A distinct shift in the nature of the negotiations began rather abruptly when Kinyani's counsellor offered a "package deal": Lashiloi should consent to withdraw issues 9, 12, 13, 14, 15, and 16 and Kinyani would agree to 8 and would withdraw 3 and 4 (Figure 2). Then, added the counsellor, "We can talk about the land."

Lashiloi refused the offer peremptorily. Discussions were renewed on other issues but without proposals for concessions or counteroffers. Then Lashiloi said that he would withdraw the issues relating to the allegation of slander (14, 15, and 16). The slander had been well substantiated by witnesses but Kinyani had merely denied the charge and had made no other response to it. Lashiloi now declared that the matter was "not a big one – a matter of foolish words. We can forget it. We have both spoken many words that are not true when we should have remained silent." (C) Some of Kinyani's supporters made approving noises; Kinyani himself made no response at all and his silence signified his acceptance of Lashiloi's offer. These issues were not referred to again during the negotiations.

Phase 4. Thereafter, as the parties continued to bring up the various issues for discussion, a new orientation became obvious. There were more concentrated exchanges – with direct replies and counterreplies – rather than, as previously, merely a demand by one party and its rejection by the other. There began to be tentative counteroffers and probings for concessions. From this time, there was little personal attack against either principal disputant and the parties concentrated on the issues themselves.

Following Lashiloi's withdrawal of demands relating to slander, the other issues were reintroduced into the negotiations in the following order (reference numbers are to the agenda items summarized in Figure 2). For the sake of simplicity, references are given only to the initiating party in the name of the principal disputant although various members of either party initiated renewed exchanges and discussions (K, Kinyani; L, Lashiloi).

Issue	Initiating Party	Nature of Exchange
1: Land	Kinyani	Exchange of views
10, 11: Supernatural	Lashiloi	Exchange of views; L concentrated on the supernatural danger threatening his family.
5: Gate	Kinyani	Exchange of views
8: Water	Lashiloi	Exchange of views
7: Debt	Kinyani	Exchange of views
10, 11: Supernatural	Lashiloi	L offered to withdraw 11 if K would agree to 10. K rejected this.
1: Land	Lashiloi	Exchange of views
6: Gate	Kinyani	Exchange of views
12, 13: Violence	Lashiloi	Exchange of views
4: Trespass	Kinyani	K insisted that trespass and violence issues were essentially connected; he proposed that L should concede on 12 and 13 (no mention of how much) and then he would "think about" 4 (i.e., possibly offer concession).
13: Violence	Lashiloi	For the first time L named a specific sum of money for compensation. K rejected the demand after discussion.
8: Water	Lashiloi	L insisted that water and violence issues were essentially connected and asked K to make definite offers on these. K refused.
6: Gate	Kinyani	K argued that gate and water issues were essentially connected. He demanded L's acceptance of 6 in return for his acceptance of 8. L refused.
12, 13: Violence	Lashiloi	Exchange of views. L admitted that no real harm had been done to his son (13) and K admitted to his error in chastising another man's son (12). *Issues resolved: 12, 13.*
7: Debt	Kinyani	K agreed to withdraw this issue although reiterating that the unpaid debt still existed. L accepted this. *Issue withdrawn: 7.*

Continued

Issue	Initiating Party	Nature of Exchange
5: Gate	Kinyani	K successively offered minor concessions that
1: Land	Kinyani	were not acceptable to L unless the water
10: Supernatural	Kinyani	issues (8, 9) were dealt with at the same time.
8, 9: Water	Lashiloi	K proposed to accept 8 if L would withdraw 9 and agree to 5. L tentatively agreed on 8 and 9 but not on 5.
6: Gate	Kinyani	K demanded L's acceptance of 6 if K were to concede on 8 and 9. L refused.
1: Land	Lashiloi	Exchange of views but no new proposals.
3, 4: Trespass	Kinyani	L admitted trespass by his goats but held that damage to K's crops was negligible. L offered to make a small "gift" of beer if K would make a similar "gift" for issue 9. K agreed. *Issues resolved: 3, 4, 9.*
5, 6: Gate	Kinyani	Both refused to make requested concessions.
1, 2: Land	Lashiloi	L proposed that he be recognized as owner of the land (1) while there should be a sharing of its use (2). K rejected this.
8: Water	Lashiloi	L insisted that this issue be settled before anything further be considered. K refused.
5, 6: Gate	Kinyani	K insisted that these issues be settled first
8, 10, 11: Water; supernatural	Lashiloi	L reiterated need to settle 8 and also 10 and 11. K rejected this.
6: Gate	Kinyani	K reiterated his earlier insistence. L again refused.
1: Land	Lashiloi	L proposed a division of the land. After exchanges K agreed. Both parties almost immediately agreed to a dividing line where a footpath ran through the middle of the vacant farm. Tacit agreement (no discussion) that each man should have exclusive use of his portion of the land (2). L proposed that, with this division of the land, K should accept L's demand for acknowledgment of his uninterrupted right to irrigation water (8). K agreed. *Issues resolved: 1, 2, 8.*
6: Gate	Kinyani	L rejected K's demand and also K's assertion that this issue was the most important one remaining.
10: Supernatural	Lashiloi	K rejected L's demand and L's similar assertion about issue 10.
5: Gate	Kinyani	L rejected K's demand and made no counteroffer.
11: Supernatural	Lashiloi	K rejected L's demand.

This effectively ended Phase 4, with the obdurate issues now identified. These issues related to the matter of the irrigation gate, raised by Kinyani, and to the allegation of illicit resort to the supernatural, raised by Lashiloi. No substantial concessions or new proposals had been made on these four issues, although all others had been withdrawn or resolved in agreement. (A)

Note

1 A counsellor was selected by the adult males of a maximal lineage to act as their permanent spokesman, advisor, and public representative. (See Gulliver 1963:101 ff.)
2 To make my own position clear: I was friendly with Lashiloi who had become a valued informant and sometimes assistant. Because of this, I was allowed to sit in on the private discussions of Lashiloi's party before the negotiations. During the moot, I sat as a neutral, along with a number of nonparticipating spectators. Kinyani was less well known to me and, as a friend of Lashiloi, I was not privy to his thoughts and plans. My field assistant, however, was able to discuss the dispute with Kinyani, though not with the freedom that I enjoyed with Lashiloi.
3 Because of the lay of the land, water came from the main channel to the men's farms by a takeoff channel. This channel divided into two just inside Kinyani's farm boundary, leading to Kinyani's and Lashiloi's land respectively (see Figure 1(a)). This meant that Kinyani could control the flow to Lashiloi's farm. He had constructed a rough wooden gate that could close the takeoff channel or direct the water to either farm.

Reference

Gulliver, P. H. 1963 *Social control in an African society*. London: Routledge (Boston: Boston University Press).

54

Explaining Conflict Transformation: How Jerusalem Became Negotiable

Cecilia Albin

In this piece, Cecilia Albin offers a review of conflict transformation theory and assesses how far it can help to explain the process that led to Jerusalem becoming negotiable in 2000. Jerusalem lies at the crux of the Israeli-Palestinian conflict and the status of the religious sites on Haram-al-Sharif/the Temple Mount are particularly intractable. The article is suggestive in pointing ways forward, both for the conflict and for conflict transformation theory. Since the article was written, the conflict appears to have turned back to greater intractability, with the completion of the Israeli security wall and extension of Israeli settlements. Cecilia Albin is Professor of Peace and Conflict Research at Uppsala University.

*　*　*　*

At the Camp David talks in July 2000, Israel for the first time ever officially negotiated over the sovereignty of Jerusalem with the Palestinians. It was also the first time since Israel's 1967 capture of East Jerusalem that its government offered to share or divide political rule over the city. For over three decades Israel had insisted that its retention of exclusive sovereignty in Jerusalem was a vital non-negotiable interest of the nation. For just as long, Israel had pursued policies on the ground aimed at cementing the city's unity under exclusive Jewish rule. What had finally rendered the most intractable issue in the entire Israeli-Palestinian conflict negotiable? What had placed Jerusalem at the centre of the bargaining table, after decades of being swept under the rug in Middle East peace talks?

While ever so significant in itself, Jerusalem captures well the features and dynamics of a now widespread and dangerous phenomenon: intractable conflicts. These are long-lasting conflicts that persistently defy attempts at resolution. They are highly intense, and usually violent and destructive. They have many causes – in other words, there are different kinds of intractability. At the core are usually deep-rooted values and needs, linked to ethnicity or other identity issues, which are seen as absolute and too costly to compromise upon. These core concerns tend to colour the entire conflict, so that disputes over land and other material resources assume great symbolic meaning and become seen as indivisible and non-negotiable (Albin 1997a; Coleman 2003). Conflicts are not intractable or irresolvable by nature, however. Some, such as Jerusalem, surely have inherent features that make them far more resistant to resolution than others. But the quality of being intractable ultimately exists in the perceptions and definitions of the parties, and can therefore be changed (Kriesberg et al. 1989).

How then can these long-term conflicts turn into tractable and negotiable ones, after decades of bloodshed and disagreement? What is at play when they do? This question is addressed here using two lenses. The first lens is conceptual, namely the relatively recent literature on so-called 'conflict transformation'. It is founded on a dissatisfaction with the capacity of conventional academic analysis to explain and tackle the reality of intractable conflict, which consistently resists peaceful solutions. This type of conflict is rarely ready for negotiation, mediation or other attempts at resolution. Work on conflict transformation draws on or resembles, to varying degrees, well-established concepts and approaches from the conflict resolution field such as, for instance, 'ripeness' (Zartman 1985), 'problem-solving workshops' (Kelman 1996), 'pre-negotiation' (Gross Stein 1989), and strategic and psychological barriers (Ross 1991). It is not yet sufficiently developed to provide full-fledged theories or to represent its own school of thought. Therefore, conflict transformation and resolution are here seen as complementary and partly overlapping approaches rather than as contrasting ones. The main difference, it is here argued, is one of *emphasis* rather than coverage: in concept and in practice, conflict transformation generally has a distinct – and useful – focus on the context and dynamics of conflict and on conditions favouring tractability.

The second lens is empirical, namely the staggering case of Jerusalem. It is at the heart of the Israeli-Palestinian conflict, the continuation of which breeds much political violence on both sides and has become a top concern on the international agenda. This is a small and poor city: it has some 700,000 inhabitants (Israeli and Palestinian) of which over 40% are reported to live in poverty.[1] Yet it at once holds the key to any durable and comprehensive peace in the Middle East, and threatens to undermine all prospects of such a peace.

…

Transforming Conflict Structures and Relationships

What is actually transformed in the literature labelled 'conflict transformation'? How do we recognise a transformed conflict, and what transforms it? No consistent answers emerge from the collection of work to date, nor from recent assessments of it (Coleman 2004; Mitchell 2002; Miall 2001). A wide range of concepts, approaches, indicators and sources are used which rely to varying degrees on traditional analyses of conflict and conflict resolution. Some aim to provide tools of analysis, and others to give practical guidelines for effective third party intervention (Crocker et al. 2004; Covey et al. 2005). Still others do both. Virtually all seek to discern and explain profound, longer-term transformations that cause a conflict, or the conditions giving rise to it, to completely change dynamics or course. They go beyond the bargaining dynamics in the negotiating room and efforts to resolve specific problems. Virtually all approaches presume that the zero-sum or intractable character of conflicts is perceived and not intrinsic. The focus is on ways in which they may become more malleable, rather than on how they often revert back to intractability. Here the shared features end.

Most striking is the lack of agreement on what changes are in fact so fundamental as to deserve the label 'transformations'. What does conflict transformation towards tractability actually entail or require? Kriesberg (1989) argues for three critical elements: the conflicting parties (their nature and relations, notably degree of internal cohesion and interdependence), the social system in which they are embedded, and conflict issues. Lederach (1995) resonates with two of these by emphasising the need for both personal/relationship change, away from destructive interaction patterns, and change toward justice, equality and non-violent conflict resolution in the overall social system. For Väyrynen (1991) transformation involves four key dimensions: the structure of inter-party relations (i.e. significant changes in their relations, such as the distribution of power, degree of interdependence, and amount of communication), actors (changes in their internal composition or number), rules (changes in any norms guiding relations and behaviour in the conflict) and issues (defined as a significant change in the conflict's political agenda whereby highly controversial issues are reduced in importance in favour of issues where interests overlap). Miall (2001) builds on Väyrynen's typology by elaborating on its four dimensions and adding a fifth: transformations in the context of conflict, meaning the surrounding international or regional environment.

Dimensions commonly distinguished in the literature involve changes in persons, structures and relationships. The term 'structure' is used differently to refer to everything from the basic nature of the international system or environment to the nature of inter-party relations. In one paradigm it consists of a conflict situation (perceptions of incompatible goals among two or more parties), attitudes, and conflict behaviour (Mitchell 1981). Structural transformation is often seen as entailing changes in attitudes, institutions and mechanisms that promote non-violent ways of dealing with conflict (Rupesinghe 1995). Relationships consist of patterns of exchange, and memories and evaluations of those exchanges, which are altered to become more balanced and similar when conflicts undergo transformation (Hinde 1979; Mitchell 2002). More generally, destructive and hostile relationships as the cause of intractable conflict, and improved positive relationships as the means to tackle it, are a recurrent theme especially in the transformation literature that prescribes modes of intervention. In Lederach (1997) reconciliation and empowerment are routes to transformed relationships which mediation can facilitate. Curle (1971) focuses on asymmetric conflicts. He charts the transformation of hostile and unbalanced relationships into peaceful ones based on equality and mutuality through, for example, confrontation, conciliation and bargaining. The most systematic approach to relationship change has been developed by Harold Saunders (e.g. 1999; 2003). His approach engages citizens outside government in 'sustained dialogue' to transform dysfunctional relationships that create conflicts and hinder their resolution. A relationship is defined in terms of specific arenas of interaction and the dialogue process in terms of stages, for analytical and operational purposes. A 'transformed relationship' is one that has changed sufficiently to enable conflicting parties to deal with shared problems in a collaborative way.[2]

What emerges from this very short but reasonably representative overview is a strong emphasis on *structure* and *relationship*. There is no shared view of their relative importance, how they relate to each other, or what exactly each one entails – but generally speaking there is broad agreement on their central role. These two aspects are also here taken to be the most fundamental ones involved in conflict transformation. It is often as a result of profound structural and/or relationship changes that other changes occur; for instance, in the negotiability of issues. The Jerusalem conflict is a case in point. Moreover, one can argue that an emphasis on these two types of change best distinguishes the transformation approach (see Mitchell 2002). While surely allowing for changes in structure and relationship, conventional conflict analysis tends to view these components as the 'givens' within which a solution is sought and found (Rubin and Brown 1975; Raiffa 1982; Kremenyuk 1991). What also emerges from a review of the literature is that factors and forces behind transformations, on the few occasions they are discussed, concern almost exclusively third-party intervention.

Structure and relationship are keys to understanding a complex conflict like Jerusalem: its roots, its development over time, and need for further change. In this analysis, 'structure' refers specifically to the *structure of conflict* – the 'skeleton' and basic components common to all conflicts. It partly reflects the larger context and the environment (political, geographic and normative) in which the conflict is set. Conflict structures tend to persist over long time periods. But structural change, when it finally takes place, can occur abruptly – as with the end of the Cold War, the outbreak of the first Palestinian uprising (the intifada) in the Israeli-occupied territories, and so on. A core part of a conflict structure are *the parties* (direct and any third parties): their number, identities and composition (e.g. ethnic/religious), interests, representation and status (e.g. as a state or a nonstate actor), and power (e.g. physical control over vital resources and the actions of others). Another are *the issues* in dispute, including their number and nature (e.g. whether involving unique and scarce resources, or exchangeable and divisible ones).

The term 'relationship' here refers to how each party perceives the conflict – its own interests and the situation in relation to the other – and then acts based on those perceptions and the other's moves. Two matters are of particular note. The first is each party's *perceptions* (and any misperceptions) of the other side and the distribution of power between them, degree of interdependence and (in)compatibility of goals, and the possibilities of finding a mutually acceptable solution. The second is *the pattern of interaction* which follows from those perceptions; for example, its quality (hostile and competitive vs. friendly and cooperative), intensity (e.g. unilateral vs. joint policies and activities, amount of communication), power balance (e.g. unequal and exploitative vs. roughly equal and reciprocal), and effectiveness (dysfunctional or destructive vs. functional and mutually rewarding). Parties interact at and across many levels, and important relationship changes may develop from shifts within their own teams; for example, in public opinion, domestic leadership, and opposition groups.

A note on the much-debated meaning and relevance of power is in order here. While concerns about power figure prominently in the conflict resolution literature, the conflict transformation approach takes particular interest in how the balance of power changes over time (Väyrynen 1991; Miall 2001; Curle 1971). One notion defines power 'not only as control over superior resources and the actions of others but as the capacity of citizens acting together to influence the course of events without great material resources' (Saunders 2003, p. 87). This article makes a basic distinction between structural and relational power. 'Structural power' refers primarily to physical resources – e.g. military and economic – which enable a party unilaterally to pressurise or coerce another to do something against its will. By controlling resources of this kind the party gains better control over its own destiny and the opponent's actions, and the value of its alternatives to cooperation (its independence) improves. 'Relational power' refers to more intangible resources – e.g. diplomatic, political and social skills – and is acquired and exercised in interaction with others. Put simply, it is the ability to persuade a party to do something it otherwise would not have done, and willingly so (Rummel 1976). Relational power is dynamic and targets the other's will and perceptions of its interests, while structural power more or less bypasses these. Of course, the two are interrelated: excessive reliance on one kind can undermine the other, but used wisely together they can reinforce each other. This recalls arguments about effective influence resulting from a mix of 'hard' and 'soft' power (Nye 2004).

The Intractability of Jerusalem

What has made the Jerusalem conflict so resistant to a negotiated solution? The answer is found in virtually all the elements of 'structure' and 'relationship' described above. Starting with the structure, the battle for Jerusalem is fought by *many parties* at many levels: locally between different groups who live in the city with competing visions of its future; nationally between Israelis and Palestinians; regionally between Israel and Arab states; and internationally between representatives and followers of three world religions. It is at once a major source of conflict itself, and a reflection of the larger conflicts between Israel and the Palestinians, and between Israel and the Arab world.[3] As for party *interests* and *power* endowments, those acquired by Israel following the Six-Day War of 1967 have been particularly influential. Boosted by the capture of East Jerusalem in that war and its new status as occupier, the Israeli government formulated national interests concerning the city which were incompatible with those of its Arab population. They were to extend Israeli rule over Arab East Jerusalem, unite that sector with the western part (to prevent a future redivision) and secure the city's status as solely Israel's capital.

Most fundamental in explaining Jerusalem's intractability are the nature and number of *the issues* involved. It is a conflict over many things: ethnic and spiritual values and symbols (connected to particular religious sites and to the city as a whole), political interests and prestige, scarce resources such as land and housing, and economic concerns. They concern intrinsic features of the city itself, and the meanings given to it by different groups.[4]

At the core are the unique *values* and significance that two peoples and three faiths attach to Jerusalem. For Israeli Jews Jerusalem is historically, politically and spiritually their sole capital as a nation (Kollek 1990). The city as a whole serves as a symbol of these meanings to Jews. The same is true of sacred sites within Jerusalem, notably the Wailing

(Western) Wall, the only remnant of Solomon's (the Second) Temple, and the Temple Mount (Haram al-Sharif) area, and the Cemetery on the Mount of Olives. For Christians, Jerusalem is the historical setting of the preaching and death of Jesus. Within the Old City the Via Dolorosa marks Jesus' route to Golgotha, and the Church of the Holy Sepulchre houses the site of the crucifixion, burial and resurrection of Jesus. On Mount Zion is the site of the Room of the Last Supper, and on the Mount of Olives the site of Jesus' ascension and the Tomb of St Mary. Palestinian Christians, a diminishing group in Jerusalem, are greatly concerned with safeguarding the Christian holy sites and heritage in the city, which they see as being under threat (see Sabella 2000).

For the Islamic world, Al-Quds is the third holy city after Mecca and Medina and sacred for its association with the Prophet Mohammed (Tibawi 1969).[5] The Al-Aksa Mosque, marking the furthest point on the Prophet Mohammed's night journey from Mecca on his horse, and the Dome of the Rock are situated in the Haram al-Sharif (Temple Mount) grounds. The latter shrine houses the rock from which, according to tradition, the Prophet ascended to Paradise. The national awakening of the Palestinian people in the 20th century meant that Jerusalem grew even further in significance, to become for them a political as well as religious centre. For Palestinians today, Muslim and Christian, it is the capital and symbol of their striving for full recognition and independence. For them, there can be no Arab Palestine or West Bank without Jerusalem: it is the political, economic, cultural and spiritual centre of life for Palestinians striving to have their own state (Khalidi 1978).

Both Israelis and Palestinians thus view Jerusalem as an integral part and symbol of their history, ethnic-religious identity and nationhood. Both peoples link the city to the preservation or achievement of full recognition, control over their destiny, and justice. The absolute value attached to sovereignty in Jerusalem as a means to fulfil these needs is reflected in each party's willingness to make concessions on most other matters, such as access to the holy sites and cultural-religious autonomy. Palestinians specifically have come to regard sovereignty as the only means to retain land in the city, and preserve its Arabic and Christian–Islamic heritage and character. At the micro-level, the indivisible and highly symbolic features of the problem are notably reflected in the conflicting Jewish and Muslim claims to the Temple Mount/Haram al-Sharif area.

The relational aspects also explain Jerusalem's intractability. Following the occupation of East Jerusalem in 1967, Israel's *perceptions* of the conflict became clearer than ever. It came to regard its own aspirations in the city as irreconcilable with those of the Palestinians, and as attainable by unilateral means. In particular, the city's physical indivisibility became equated with political indivisibility: concessions on exclusive Israeli sovereignty were portrayed and became seen as an invitation to a return to the situation of the 1948–67 period when Jerusalem was physically divided and freedom of access to its holy sites severely limited (Kollek 1990).

...

Turning Points in the Transformation of Jerusalem

After the outbreak of the Palestinian uprising in 1987, the Jerusalem conflict started to change toward tractability. Three major turning points can be distinguished, particularly at the official governmental and international levels, in the period from 1993 to 2000: the placement of Jerusalem on the bargaining table, the recognition of the issue of sovereignty over the city as a central negotiable issue, and international endorsement of dual capitals there.

...

Explaining Progress Toward Tractability: The Role of Structure and Relationship

Jerusalem has thus become negotiable. Sovereignty as the core issue and dual Israeli and Palestinian capitals as the basis of a solution have won widespread agreement. Genuine disagreement is focused on sovereignty over the Temple Mount/Haram al-Sharif, and is now often seen as the only remaining issue to be resolved (Amirav 2003). How do we explain this significant progress? How illuminating is the conflict transformation approach in this regard? We return to the concepts of structure and relationship discussed at the outset.

Structural change: in party representation, agenda issues and the balance of power

The structure of the Jerusalem conflict has been transformed dramatically over time since 1967, and provides a key to understanding its turn toward tractability. A most important change is the Palestinians' success in achieving greater control over their future, including in Jerusalem. At the time of the Israeli capture of East Jerusalem in 1967, the Palestinians were viewed as a humanitarian refugee issue. A shift occurred with the 1974 Rabat declaration by Arab states that the PLO was the sole legitimate representative of the Palestinian people. This decision, in turn, put in practice the issue of an independent Palestinian state on the agenda for negotiations (Saunders and Albin 1993). At the same time East Jerusalem had begun to experience a 'Palestinisation' under Israeli rule. These developments inevitably weakened King Hussein's claim to sovereignty over East Jerusalem and the West Bank, and culminated with the 1988 Jordanian declaration of disengagement from these territories. Three matters had become clear. Any occupied territory from which Israel withdrew was to be set aside for a Palestinian solution. Moreover, this solution had to be reached in negotiations with the Palestinians themselves. Finally, the Palestinians would claim a right to statehood with a capital in Jerusalem.

   The overall impact of changes in the balance of power is less clear-cut. Both structural and relational elements of power, as defined earlier, have been influential. On the one hand, Israel's capture of East Jerusalem in 1967 and the subsequent policies pursued to consolidate its rule there have changed the map of the city and hence permanently the parameters of a realistic solution. On the other, despite an overwhelming military advantage, Israel proved incapable of winning Palestinian acceptance of this rule or controlling Palestinian political action. While the Palestinians lost sovereign control over many resources such as land, water and housing, their national identity and political life in East Jerusalem started to flourish under occupation. Fully aware of Israel's intention to retain exclusive rule, the Palestinians took the opportunity to assert their claims and presence in the city through institution building and diplomatic initiatives. Despite periodic Israeli interference, Arab East Jerusalem emerged in many ways as the de facto Palestinian capital particularly from late 1980 onwards. East Jerusalem became the base of the political leadership of the first Palestinian uprising, which broke out in late 1987, and then the centre of Palestinian diplomatic activity when the Middle East peace process was revitalised around 1991 (Albin 1997b). Thus, although of a very different nature, the Palestinians like the Israelis established 'facts on the ground' for their own capital in the city.

Relationship change: in party perceptions of the conflict and patterns of interaction

Israel's policies in Jerusalem, put in place following the 1967 war, were long predicated on the assumption that unilateral action could secure the city's future under sole Jewish sovereignty. The first Palestinian uprising shattered this perception in the eyes of many Israelis and the international community. Its strategies of resistance and separation had a greater effect in Jerusalem than anywhere else. They clarified that two decades of 'unification' policies had failed to reach some of Israel's most essential goals. Jerusalem was redivided, politically and psychologically rather than physically, but in many ways these divisions had a similar impact to the wall that existed in the period from 1948 to 1967. In the words of an Israeli policymaker, 'the *intifada* put a border of fear in the middle of the city which we didn't have before...and divided the city'.[6] A Palestinian spokesman in East Jerusalem referred to this new Green Line as 'a political wall dividing ruler from ruled, occupier from occupied, victor from vanquished' and as a 'steel barrier' between the two parts of the city which the uprising reinforced and which still exists (Nusseibeh 1990). Violence arising from the political situation kept escalating to new, unprecedented levels. Thus the uprising increased and clarified the costs associated with Jerusalem's de facto division. It put the two sides on a more equal footing in that the latent state of warfare constrained the daily lives of both communities. It clarified the failure of each to gain control over the other's space in the city by unilateral action. The Palestinians had always depended on negotiations with Israel to secure their interests in Jerusalem, and had no real alternative in the long term. Now Israel gained a sense of real dependency as well on negotiation – to end the de facto division of the city, achieve international recognition of Jerusalem as its capital, and make a resolution of the overall conflict possible.
...

Reverting to Intractability? A Concluding Note on Conflict Transformation

Recent developments suggest that Jerusalem, and the overall Israeli–Palestinian conflict, may become intractable again. It is too early to conclude whether these constitute a trend that will take root; that is, whether the conflict has entered a new area of long-term intractability. Some analysts argue that the Camp David summit in 2000 marks a turning point, when Jerusalem started to be cast increasingly in religious and non-negotiable terms and less as a political–national dispute open to compromise (e.g. Telhami 2001). More definite setbacks for the peace process followed shortly thereafter. The outbreak of the second Palestinian uprising in September 2000 marked the beginning of a period of escalating violence and terrorist incidents in the city. Reliable statistics are scarce but suggest that the number of casualties in the Jerusalem area from 2000 to 2003 was nearly as high as in the entire 1967–1999 period.[7] In 2002 came Israel's dramatic decision, under Prime Minister Sharon, to build the fence in the West Bank as a security buffer against the infiltration of terrorists and other threats. In Jerusalem it largely follows the present municipal border, and thus physically separates Arab East Jerusalem and its inhabitants from the rest of the West Bank. The new walls and barbed wire dividing the city area are intensively disputed from the local to the international level. So are their likely long-term effects, including on Israel's own security. The fence may well end up having the greatest long-term impact on the conflict of all recent developments to date.

This turn of events points to a first significant area in which the conflict transformation approach needs to be developed. Clearly, it usefully emphasises longer-term developments toward tractability and helps to explain breakthroughs and turning points over time and in specific situations. The focus on long-term dynamics complements many standard analyses of negotiation and conflict resolution. There is a substantial gap, however, concerning causes and factors behind conflict transformations. As it now stands, the approach focuses heavily on different aspects of change rather than the driving forces behind them. An exception is the discussion of various forms of third-party intervention as a tool that can promote tractability, as for example in the relationship between parties. The approach needs to be expanded to take account of a much wider range of explanatory factors. Jerusalem points to two key factors in intractable conflicts whose roles under different conditions deserve more careful investigation: values and force. The unique value attached to Jerusalem has led Israelis and Palestinians alike to resort to force, and unilateral action held in place by force, and this has shaped the city's fate extensively to date. The great value attached to Jerusalem by the Palestinians also has played a role in forcing the Israelis, step by step, to the negotiating table and into bargaining over the issue.

A second concern is that the approach focuses almost entirely on positive transformations toward tractability. It says very little about processes reverting conflicts to intractability. Are they just a progression through the various dimensions of change toward tractability, in the opposite direction? Are the causes and factors behind transformations in both directions the same? This is a serious problem that conceptualisations of conflict dynamics and transformation should cover. Apart from filling a theoretical gap, this could result in better guidelines for effective intervention. Working toward peace in Jerusalem continues to be a pressing international issue, and an enormous challenge, which definitely will require strong third-party roles. And beyond Jerusalem there are 'transformed' conflicts that time and again appear to relapse into intractability for reasons that conflict analysts still cannot explain adequately.

Notes

1 Statistics for 2002, reported in Choshen (2004).
2 Personal communication with Harold H. Saunders, Director of International Affairs at the Kettering Foundation, 6 July 2004.
3 In-depth studies of the many levels at which the struggle for Jerusalem is fought include Friedland and Hecht (1996) and Wasserstein (2001).
4 The points and text that follow draw on earlier writings (Albin 1997a; 1997b), where they are discussed more fully.
5 And interview with Sheik Abdel Hamid Es-Saaih, Spokesman for the Palestine National Council, Amman, and Member of the Royal Academy for Islamic Civilization Research (Al Albait Foundation), in Amman, 2 January 1991; and interview with Sheik Jamal, high-ranking Muslim leader, Jerusalem, 10 November 1990.
6 Personal communication with Moshe Amirav, at the time a member of the Jerusalem Municipal Council and Secretary-General of the Shinui Party, in Palo Alto, CA, 27–28 April 1992.
7 Statistics published in Choshen (2004), p. 17.

References

Albin, C. (1997a) 'Negotiating Intractable Conflicts: On the Future of Jerusalem', *Cooperation and Conflict*, 32(1), pp. 29–77.
Albin, C. (1997b) 'Securing the Peace of Jerusalem: On the Politics of Unifying and Dividing', *Review of International Studies*, 23(2), pp. 117–42.
Amirav, M. (2003) *The Palestinian Struggle for Jerusalem* (Jerusalem, Jerusalem Institute for Israel Studies).
Choshen, M. (Ed.) (2004) *Statistical Yearbook of Jerusalem, No. 20, 2002–2003* (Jerusalem, Jerusalem Institute for Israel Studies).
Coleman, P. (2003) 'Characteristics of Protracted, Intractable Conflict: Towards the Development of a Meta-framework – I', *Peace and Conflict*, 9(1), pp. 1–37.
Coleman, P. (2004) 'Paradigmatic Framing of Protracted, Intractable Conflict: Towards the Development of a Meta-framework – II', *Peace and Conflict*, 10(3), pp. 197–235.
Covey, J., Dziedzic, M. and Hawley, L. (Eds) (2005) *The Quest for Viable Peace. International Intervention and Strategies for Conflict Transformation* (Washington, United States Institute of Peace Press).
Crocker, C., Hampson, F.O. and Aall, P. (2004) *Taming Intractable Conflicts: Mediation in the Hardest Cases* (Washington, United States Institute of Peace Press).
Curle, A. (1971) *Making Peace* (London, Tavistock).
Friedland, R. and Hecht, R. (1996) *To Rule Jerusalem* (Cambridge, England, Cambridge University Press).
Gross Stein, J. (Ed.) (1989) *Getting to the Table: The Processes of International Prenegotiation* (Baltimore, Johns Hopkins University Press).
Hinde, R. (1979) *Towards Understanding Relationships* (New York, Academic Press).
Kelman, H. (1996) 'Negotiation as Interactive Problem Solving', *International Negotiation*, 1(1), pp. 99–123.
Khalidi, W. (1978) 'Thinking the Unthinkable: A Sovereign Palestinian State', *Foreign Affairs*, 56, pp. 695–713.
Kollek, T. (1990) 'Jews Cannot Be Exclusive Masters', *Jerusalem Report*, 25 October.

Kremenyuk, V. (Ed.) (1991) *International Negotiation: Analysis, Approaches, Issues* (San Francisco, Jossey-Bass).

Kriesberg, L. (1989) 'Conclusion: Research and Policy Implications', in: L. Kriesberg, T. Northrup and S. Thorson (Eds), *Intractable Conflicts and Their Transformation* (Syracuse, NY, Syracuse University Press).

Kriesberg, L., Northrup, T. and Thorson, S. (Eds) (1989) *Intractable Conflicts and Their Transformation* (Syracuse, NY, Syracuse University Press).

Lederach, J.P. (1995) *Preparing for Peace: Conflict Transformation across Cultures* (Syracuse, NY, Syracuse University Press).

Lederach, J.P. (1997) *Building Peace: Sustainable Reconciliation in Divided Societies* (Washington, United States Institute of Peace Press).

Miall, H. (2001) 'Conflict Transformation: A Multi-dimensional Task', in: D. Bloomfield, M. Fischer and B. Schmelzle (Eds) *Berghof Handbook for Conflict Transformation* (Berlin, Berghof Research Center for Constructive Conflict Management).

Mitchell, C. (1981) *The Structure of International Conflict* (London, Macmillan Press).

Mitchell, C. (2002) 'Beyond Resolution: What Does Conflict Transformation Actually Transform?', *Peace and Conflict Studies*, 9(1).

Nusseibeh, S. (1990) 'Whose Jerusalem?', *New Outlook*, January/February, pp. 19, 21.

Nye, J. (2004) *Soft Power: The Means to Success in World Politics* (New York, Public Affairs).

Raiffa, H. (1982) *The Art and Science of Negotiation* (Cambridge, MA, Harvard University Press).

Ross, L. (1991) 'Barriers to Conflict Resolution', *Negotiation Journal*, 7(4), pp. 389–404.

Rubin, J. and Brown, B. (1975) *The Social Psychology of Bargaining and Negotiation* (New York and London, Academic Press).

Rummel, R.J. (1976) *Understanding Conflict and War. Volume 2: The Conflict Helix* (Beverly Hills, CA, Sage).

Rupesinghe, K. (1995) 'Conflict Transformation', in: K. Rupesinghe (Ed.), *Conflict Transformation* (London, Macmillan).

Sabella, B. (2000) 'Jerusalem: A Christian Perspective', in: B. Sabella et al. (Eds), *Jerusalem: Religious Aspects*, 2nd edn (Jerusalem, Palestinian Academic Society for the Study of International Affairs).

Saunders, H. (1999) *A Public Peace Process: Sustained Dialogue to Transform Racial and Ethnic Conflicts* (New York, St Martin's Press).

Saunders, H. (2003) 'Sustained Dialogue in Managing Intractable Conflict', *Negotiation Journal*, January, pp. 85–95.

Saunders, H. and Albin, C. (1993) *Sinai II: The Politics of International Mediation, 1974–1975* (Washington, Johns Hopkins Foreign Policy Institute).

Telhami, S. (2001) 'Camp David II: Assumptions and Consequences', *Current History*, January, pp. 10–14.

Tibawi, A.L. (1969) *Jerusalem. Its Place in Islam and Arab History* (Beirut, Institute for Palestine Studies).

Väyrynen, R. (1991) 'To Settle or to Transform? Perspectives on the Resolution of National and International Conflicts', in: R. Väyrynen (Ed.), *New Directions in Conflict Theory: Conflict Resolution and Conflict Transformation* (London, Sage).

Wasserstein, B. (2001) *Divided Jerusalem: The Struggle for the Holy City* (New Haven, Yale University Press).

Zartman, I.W. (1985) *Ripe for Resolution: Conflict and Intervention in Africa* (New York and Oxford, Oxford University Press).

55

The Dayton Agreement. The General Framework Agreement for Peace in Bosnia and Herzegovina

The Dayton Agreement runs to more than 100 pages. Its military provisions are particularly lengthy. This short extract sets out the kernel of the treaty, but should be read in conjunction with the Annexes to gain a full picture. The parties agreed to a new constitution, which retained Bosnia-Herzegovina as a unitary federation composed of two entities, the Federation of Bosnia-Herzegovina and Republika Srpska. The treaty provided for a territorial demarcation, a NATO-led implementation force, and a European High Representative empowered to oversee civil administration.

*   *   *   *

General Framework Agreement for Peace in Bosnia and Herzegovina

The Republic of Bosnia and Herzegovina, the Republic of Croatia and the Federal Republic of Yugoslavia (the "Parties"),

Recognizing the need for a comprehensive settlement to bring an end to the tragic conflict in the region,

Desiring to contribute toward that end and to promote an enduring peace and stability,

Affirming their commitment to the Agreed Basic Principles issued on September 8, 1995, the Further Agreed Basic Principles issued on September 26, 1995, and the cease-fire agreements of September 14 and October 5, 1995,

Noting the agreement of August 29, 1995, which authorized the delegation of the Federal Republic of Yugoslavia to sign, on behalf of the Republika Srpska, the parts of the peace plan concerning it, with the obligation to implement the agreement that is reached strictly and consequently,

Have agreed as follows:

Article I

The Parties shall conduct their relations in accordance with the principles set forth in the United Nations Charter, as well as the Helsinki Final Act and other documents of the

Organization for Security and Cooperation in Europe. In particular, the Parties shall fully respect the sovereign equality of one another, shall settle disputes by peaceful means, and shall refrain from any action, by threat or use of force or otherwise, against the territorial integrity or political independence of Bosnia and Herzegovina or any other State.

Article II

The Parties welcome and endorse the arrangements that have been made concerning the military aspects of the peace settlement and aspects of regional stabilization, as set forth in the Agreements at Annex 1-A and Annex 1-B. The Parties shall fully respect and promote fulfillment of the commitments made in Annex 1-A, and shall comply fully with their commitments as set forth in Annex 1-B.

Article III

The Parties welcome and endorse the arrangements that have been made concerning the boundary demarcation between the two Entities, the Federation of Bosnia and Herzegovina and Republika Srpska, as set forth in the Agreement at Annex 2. The Parties shall fully respect and promote fulfillment of the commitments made therein.

Article IV

The Parties welcome and endorse the elections program for Bosnia and Herzegovina as set forth in Annex 3. The Parties shall fully respect and promote fulfillment of that program.

Article V

The Parties welcome and endorse the arrangements that have been made concerning the Constitution of Bosnia and Herzegovina, as set forth in Annex 4. The Parties shall fully respect and promote fulfillment of the commitments made therein.

Article VI

The Parties welcome and endorse the arrangements that have been made concerning the establishment of an arbitration tribunal, a Commission on Human Rights, a Commission on Refugees and Displaced Persons, a Commission to Preserve National Monuments, and Bosnia and Herzegovina Public Corporations, as set forth in the Agreements at Annexes 5-9. The Parties shall fully respect and promote fulfillment of the commitments made therein.

Article VII

Recognizing that the observance of human rights and the protection of refugees and displaced persons are of vital importance in achieving a lasting peace, the Parties agree to and shall comply fully with the provisions concerning human rights set forth in Chapter One of the Agreement at Annex 6, as well as the provisions concerning refugees and displaced persons set forth in Chapter One of the Agreement at Annex 7.

Article VIII

The Parties welcome and endorse the arrangements that have been made concerning the implementation of this peace settlement, including in particular those pertaining to the civilian (non-military) implementation, as set forth in the Agreement at Annex 10, and the international police task force, as set forth in the Agreement at Annex 11. The Parties shall fully respect and promote fulfillment of the commitments made therein.

Article IX

The Parties shall cooperate fully with all entities involved in implementation of this peace settlement, as described in the Annexes to this Agreement, or which are otherwise authorized by the United Nations Security Council, pursuant to the obligation of all Parties to cooperate in the investigation and prosecution of war crimes and other violations of international humanitarian law.

Article X

The Federal Republic of Yugoslavia and the Republic of Bosnia and Herzegovina recognize each other as sovereign independent States within their international borders. Further aspects of their mutual recognition will be subject to subsequent discussions.

Article XI

This Agreement shall enter into force upon signature.

DONE at Paris, this [21st] day of [November], 1995, in the Bosnian, Croatian, English and Serbian languages, each text being equally authentic.

For the Republic of Bosnia and Herzegovina

For the Republic of Croatia

For the Federal Republic of Yugoslavia

Witnessed by:

European Union Special Negotiator

For the French Republic

For the Federal Republic of Germany

For the Russian Federation

56
Northern Ireland Documents

This sequence of documents from Northern Ireland illustrates how peace processes frequently involve learning and reformulation of earlier agreements which failed to stop the fighting. The Hume–Adams agreement was a result of secret talks between John Hume, the leader of the Social Democratic and Labour Party, and Gerry Adams, the leader of Sinn Fein. It set out a carefully balanced set of commitments that the Irish Taoiseach and the British Prime Minister were expected to make. The British would accept the principle of self-determination for the people of Ireland, and the Irish would accept that the right of self-determination of the people of Ireland must be exercised with the consent of the people of Northern Ireland and in accordance with the civil rights of both communities. These formulas were reiterated with minor variations in the May 1993 agreed document between the governments and in the Downing Street Declaration jointly made by John Major, the British Prime Minister, and Albert Reynolds, the Irish Taoiseach, on 15 December 1993. The Framework Agreement of December 1995 developed these understandings further, outlining three strands of institutions: devolved bodies for Northern Ireland, a North–South body to promote cooperation between the peoples of Ireland, north and south, and an East–West body to promote cooperation between Ireland and the UK. These understandings on self-determination and institutional structures were carried over into the text of the Belfast Agreement, which also re-emphasized the point that the status of Northern Ireland could not be changed without the consent of its people. The Belfast Agreement, signed on Good Friday, 10 April 1998, is generally taken to mark the end of the conflict, although sporadic violence has continued by groups who remain opposed to the settlement.

* * * *

June 1992 Sinn Fein Draft (also Known as 'Hume–Adams')

Draft of a declaration which Sinn Fein suggests should be made jointly by the British and Dublin Governments

1   The Taoiseach and the Prime Minister acknowledge that the most urgent and important issue facing the people of Ireland, north and south, and the British and Irish governments together, is to remove the causes of conflict, to overcome the legacy of history and to heal the divisions which have resulted, recognising that past failures to settle relationships between the people of both islands satisfactorily has led to continuing tragedy and suffering.

2 They consider that the development of European Union fundamentally changes the nature and the context of British-Irish relationships and will progressively remove the basis of the historic conflict still taking place in Northern Ireland. The challenges and opportunities of European Union will, of themselves, require new approaches to serve interests common to both parts of Ireland.

3 The Taoiseach and the Prime Minister are convinced of the inestimable value to both their peoples of healing divisions in Ireland and of ending a conflict which has been so manifestly to the detriment of all. Both recognise that the ending of divisions can come about only through the agreement and cooperation of the people, North and South, representing both traditions in Ireland. They therefore make a solemn commitment to promote cooperation at all levels. It is their aim to foster agreement and reconciliation, leading to a new political framework founded on consent and encompassing the whole island.

4 The British Prime Minister reiterates, on behalf of the British Government, that they have no selfish, strategic, political or economic interest in Northern Ireland, and that their sole interest is to see peace, stability and reconciliation established by agreement among the people who inhabit the island. The British Government accepts the principle that the Irish people have the right collectively to self-determination, and that the exercise of this right could take the form of agreed independent structures for the island as a whole. They affirm their readiness to introduce the measures to give legislative effect on their side to this right (within a specified period to be agreed) and allowing sufficient time for the building of consent and the beginning of a process of national reconciliation. The British Government will use all its influence and energy to win the consent of a majority in Northern Ireland for these measures. They acknowledge that it is the wish of the people of Britain to see the people of Ireland live together in unity and harmony, with respect for their diverse traditions, independent, but with full recognition of the special links and the unique relationship which exists between the peoples of Britain and Ireland.

5 The Taoiseach, on behalf of the Irish Government, considers that the lessons of Irish history, and especially of Northern Ireland, show that stability and well-being will not be found under any political system which is refused allegiance or rejected on grounds of identity by a significant minority of those governed by it. He accepts, on behalf of the Irish Government, that the democratic right of self-determination by the people of Ireland as a whole must be achieved and exercised with the agreement and consent of the people of Northern Ireland and must, consistent with justice and equity, respect the democratic dignity and the civil rights of both communities.

6 The Irish Government accordingly commits itself to working in the spirit and on the basis of the Report of the New Ireland Forum, to create institutions and structures which, while respecting the diversity of the peoples of Ireland, would enable them to work together in all areas of common interest. This will help to build the trust necessary to end past divisions, leading to an agreed and peaceful future. Such structures would, of course, include institutional recognition of the special links that exist between the peoples of Britain and Ireland as part of the totality of relationships, while taking account of newly forged links with the rest of Europe.

7 In light of their joint commitment to promote the foregoing objectives, the Taoiseach has indicated to the Prime Minister his intention of establishing a permanent Irish Convention to consult and advise on the steps required to remove the barriers of distrust which at present divide the people of Ireland and which stand in the way of the exercise in common by them of self-determination on a basis of equality. It will be open to the Convention to make recommendations on ways in which agreement, as defined in the Forum Report, and respect for the rights and identities of both traditions in Ireland, can be promoted and established. The convention will be governed by the authority of Bunreacht na hEireann, and the institutions established under it. It will be a fundamental guiding principle of the Convention that all differences between the Irish people relating in the exercise in common of the right to self-determination will be resolved exclusively by peaceful, political means.

8 The convention will be open to all democratically mandated political parties in Ireland which abide exclusively by the democratic process and wish to share in dialogue about Ireland's political future and the welfare of all its people.

Extract from May 1993 Agreed Document

The British Prime Minister reiterates, on behalf of the British Government, that they have no selfish, strategic, political or economic interest in Northern Ireland, and that their sole interest is to see peace, stability and reconciliation established by agreement among the people who inhabit the island. The British Government accept the principle that the Irish people have the right collectively to self-determination, and that the exercise of this right could take the form of agreed independent structures for the island as a whole. They affirm their readiness to introduce the measures to give legislative effect on their side to this right over a period and according to procedures to be agreed by both Governments and allowing sufficient time for the building of consent and the beginning of a process of national reconciliation. The British Government will use all their influence and energy to win the consent of a majority in Northern Ireland for these measures. They acknowledge that it is the wish of the people of Britain to see the people of Ireland live together in unity and harmony, with respect for their diverse traditions, independent, but with full recognition of the special links and the unique relationship which exists between the peoples of Britain and Ireland.

Extract from Paragraph 4 of the Downing Street Declaration, 15 December 1993

The British government agree that it is for the people of the island of Ireland alone, by agreement between the two parts respectively, to exercise their right of self-determination on the basis of consent, freely and concurrently given, North and South, to bring about a united Ireland, if that is their wish.

The Framework Documents, 22 February 1995

A New Framework For Agreement: A shared understanding between the British and Irish Governments to assist discussion and negotiation involving the Northern Ireland parties.

1. The Joint Declaration acknowledges that the most urgent and important issue facing the people of Ireland, North and South, and the British and Irish Governments together, is to remove the causes of conflict, to overcome the legacy of history and to heal the divisions which have resulted.

2. Both Governments recognise that there is much for deep regret on all sides in the long and often tragic history of Anglo-Irish relations, and of relations in Ireland. They believe it is now time to lay aside, with dignity and forbearance, the mistakes of the past. A collective effort is needed to create, through agreement and reconciliation, a new beginning founded on consent, for relationships within Northern Ireland, within the island of Ireland and between the peoples of these islands. The Joint Declaration itself represents an important step towards this goal, offering the people of Ireland, North and South, whatever their tradition, the basis to agree that from now on their differences can be negotiated and resolved exclusively by peaceful political means.

3. The announcements made by the Irish Republican Army on 31 August 1994 and the Combined Loyalist Military Command on 13 October 1994 are a welcome response to the profound desire of people throughout these islands for a permanent end to the violence which caused such immense suffering and waste and served only to reinforce the barriers of fear and hatred, impeding the search for agreement.

4. A climate of peace enables the process of healing to begin. It transforms the prospects for political progress, building on that already made in the Talks process. Everyone now has a role to play in moving irreversibly beyond the failures of the past and creating new relationships capable of perpetuating peace with freedom and justice.

5. In the Joint Declaration both Governments set themselves the aim of fostering agreement and reconciliation, leading to a new political framework founded on consent. A vital dimension of this three-stranded process is the search, through dialogue with the relevant Northern Ireland parties, for new institutions and structures to take account of the totality of relationships and to enable the people of Ireland to work together in all areas of common interest while fully respecting their diversity.

6. Both Governments are conscious of the widespread desire, throughout both islands and more widely, to see negotiations underway as soon as possible. They also acknowledge the many requests, from parties in Northern Ireland and elsewhere, for both Governments to set out their views on how agreement might be reached on relationships within the island of Ireland and between the peoples of these islands.

7. In this Framework Document both Governments therefore describe a shared understanding reached between them on the parameters of a possible outcome to the Talks process, consistent with the Joint Declaration and the statement of 26 March 1991.

Through this they hope to give impetus and direction to the process and to show that a fair and honourable accommodation can be envisaged across all the relationships, which would enable people to work constructively for their mutual benefit, without compromising the essential principles or the long-term aspirations or interests of either tradition or of either community.

8. Both Governments are aware that the approach in this document presents challenges to strongly-held positions on all sides. However, a new beginning in relationships means addressing fundamental issues in a new way and inevitably requires significant movement from all sides. This document is not a rigid blueprint to be imposed but both Governments believe it sets out a realistic and balanced framework for agreement which could be achieved, with flexibility and goodwill on all sides, in comprehensive negotiations with the relevant political parties in Northern Ireland. In this spirit, both Governments offer this document for consideration and accordingly strongly commend it to the parties, the people in the island of Ireland and more widely.

9. The primary objective of both Governments in their approach to Northern Ireland is to promote and establish agreement among the people of the island of Ireland, building on the Joint Declaration. To this end they will both deploy their political resources with the aim of securing a new and comprehensive agreement involving the relevant political parties in Northern Ireland and commanding the widest possible support.

10. They take as guiding principles for their co-operation in search of this agreement:
    (i)   the principle of self-determination, as set out in the Joint Declaration;
    (ii) that the consent of the governed is an essential ingredient for stability in any political arrangement;
    (iii) that agreement must be pursued and established by exclusively democratic, peaceful means, without resort to violence or coercion;
    (iv) that any new political arrangements must be based on full respect for, and protection and expression of, the rights and identities of both traditions in Ireland and even-handedly afford both communities in Northern Ireland parity of esteem and treatment, including equality of opportunity and advantage.

11. They acknowledge that in Northern Ireland, unlike the situation which prevails elsewhere throughout both islands, there is a fundamental absence of consensus about constitutional issues. There are deep divisions between the members of the two main traditions living there over their respective senses of identity and allegiance, their views on the present status of Northern Ireland and their vision of future relationships in Ireland and between the two islands. However, the two Governments also recognise that the large majority of people, in both parts of Ireland, are at one in their commitment to the democratic process and in their desire to resolve political differences by peaceful means.

12. In their search for political agreement, based on consent, the two Governments are determined to address in a fresh way all of the relationships involved. Their aim is to overcome the legacy of division by reconciling the rights of both traditions in the fullest and most equitable manner. They will continue to work towards and encour-

age the achievement of agreement, so as to realise the goal set out in the statement of 26 March 1991 of "a new beginning for relationships within Northern Ireland, within the island of Ireland and between the peoples of these islands".

13. The two Governments will work together with the parties to achieve a comprehensive accommodation, the implementation of which would include interlocking and mutually supportive institutions across the three strands, including:

    (a) Structures within Northern Ireland (paragraphs 22 and 23) – to enable elected representatives in Northern Ireland to exercise shared administrative and legislative control over all those matters that can be agreed across both communities and which can most effectively and appropriately be dealt with at that level;

    (b) North/South institutions (paragraphs 24–38) – with clear identity and purpose, to enable representatives of democratic institutions, North and South, to enter into new, co-operative and constructive relationships; to promote agreement among the people of the island of Ireland; to carry out on a democratically accountable basis delegated executive, harmonising and consultative functions over a range of designated matters to be agreed; and to serve to acknowledge and reconcile the rights, identities and aspirations of the two major traditions;

    (c) East-West structures (paragraphs 39–49) – to enhance the existing basis for co-operation between the two Governments, and to promote, support and underwrite the fair and effective operation of the new arrangements.

Extract from the Belfast (Good Friday) Agreement, 10 April 1998

Constitutional Issues

1. The participants endorse the commitment made by the British and Irish Governments that, in a new British-Irish Agreement replacing the Anglo-Irish Agreement, they will:

    (i) recognise the legitimacy of whatever choice is freely exercised by a majority of the people of Northern Ireland with regard to its status, whether they prefer to continue to support the Union with Great Britain or a sovereign united Ireland;

    (ii) recognise that it is for the people of the island of Ireland alone, by agreement between the two parts respectively and without external impediment, to exercise their right of self-determination on the basis of consent, freely and concurrently given, North and South, to bring about a united Ireland, if that is their wish, accepting that this right must be achieved and exercised with and subject to the agreement and consent of a majority of the people of Northern Ireland;

    (iii) acknowledge that while a substantial section of the people in Northern Ireland share the legitimate wish of a majority of the people of the island of Ireland for a united Ireland, the present wish of a majority of the people of Northern Ireland, freely exercised and legitimate, is to maintain the Union and, accordingly, that Northern Ireland's status as part of the United Kingdom reflects and relies upon that wish; and that it would be wrong to make any change in the status of Northern Ireland save with the consent of a majority of its people;

(iv) affirm that if, in the future, the people of the island of Ireland exercise their right of self-determination on the basis set out in sections (i) and (ii) above to bring about a united Ireland, it will be a binding obligation on both Governments to introduce and support in their respective Parliaments legislation to give effect to that wish;

(v) affirm that whatever choice is freely exercised by a majority of the people of Northern Ireland, the power of the sovereign government with jurisdiction there shall be exercised with rigorous impartiality on behalf of all the people in the diversity of their identities and traditions and shall be founded on the principles of full respect for, and equality of, civil, political, social and cultural rights, of freedom from discrimination for all citizens, and of parity of esteem and of just and equal treatment for the identity, ethos, and aspirations of both communities;

(vi) recognise the birthright of all the people of Northern Ireland to identify themselves and be accepted as Irish or British, or both, as they may so choose, and accordingly confirm that their right to hold both British and Irish citizenship is accepted by both Governments and would not be affected by any future change in the status of Northern Ireland.

2. The participants also note that the two Governments have accordingly undertaken in the context of this comprehensive political agreement, to propose and support changes in, respectively, the Constitution of Ireland and in British legislation relating to the constitutional status of Northern Ireland.

Toolbox

When mediators and negotiators are successful, the desired outcome is a comprehensive peace agreement. Peace agreements form an essential bridge to move beyond conflict towards reconciliation and transitional justice. The Transitional Justice Institute at the University of Ulster in Northern Ireland has produced a Peace Agreement Database which provides details of more than 640 peace agreements signed since 1990, addressing conflicts that affect over 85 jurisdictions. It is available at http://www.transitionaljustice.ulster.ac.uk/peace_agreements_database.html. Another comprehensive database has been developed at the University of Notre Dame in the USA, the Peace Accords Matrix at https://peaceaccords.nd.edu/.

An unrivalled resource and toolkit is provided by the United Nations. Its UN Peacemaker site at http://peacemaker.un.org/ is an online mediation support tool developed by the UN Department of Political Affairs. Intended for peacemaking professionals, it includes an extensive database of peace agreements, guidance material and information on the UN's mediation support services.

Part V
Praxis (3) Peacebuilding

The theme of this part is the extraordinary experiment conducted in international peacebuilding interventions in internal conflicts in order to reconstruct conflict-riven societies and to convert fragile ceasefires into lasting peace. Such experiments have been mounted – sometimes under the aegis of the United Nations, sometimes not – since the end of the Cold War. *Peacebuilding* addresses the deep political, economic, social and psychological roots of conflict, in contrast to *peacemaking* between conflict parties, and *peacekeeping* that aims to prevent a relapse into war.

Although in the early 1990s most of these 'peace operations' were postwar 'peace support' interventions to consolidate political agreements (Nicaragua, Angola, El Salvador, Cambodia, Mozambique), the field expanded to cover interventions to expedite transition from colonial control (Namibia, East Timor), interventions to restore democratic government (Haiti, Sierra Leone), humanitarian interventions (Somalia, Kosovo), and even, it was claimed, interventions to promote regime change (Afghanistan, Iraq).

This colossal laboratory of case studies has tested the efficacy and legitimacy of postwar peacebuilding to the limit. As many as six *reflective pieces* have been chosen here in order to help readers orient themselves to what is at stake in this highly complex and controversial field. These are followed by one *guide to practice* piece and two *case studies*. Readers can easily look up further guides to practice and case studies via the Toolbox section at the end.

The main challenge for readers is to understand what Roland Paris and Timothy Sisk call the 'dilemmas' inherent in postwar peacebuilding interventions, but may in some cases be better seen as 'trade-offs' – for example, between intervention and dependency, between the use of military force (peacekeeping) and nonviolent peacebuilding, between peace and justice and between short-term order and long-term transformation. Beyond this lie critiques of the entire concept and practice of imposing a 'liberal peace' – Western models of democracy and the free market – on non-Western societies. Many in the conflict resolution field are unhappy about the fact that it is always the powerful states that intervene in conflicts in the less powerful states, never the other way round, and that these interventions in the end serve the interests of the interveners (and the world order that protects them), not those of the populations in whose name they are carried out. Others are less dismissive, recognize the difficult dilemmas, believe that past failures can be remedied and consider international peacebuilding which aims to convert 'negative peace' – the cessation of direct violence – into 'positive peace' – autonomy, reconciliation, development, justice – to be a noble enterprise that should be improved not abandoned.

Further exposition of these issues can be found throughout *Contemporary Conflict Resolution*, particularly in the chapters on postwar reconstruction, peacebuilding and the ethics of intervention. On the issue of the evaluation of peacebuilding interventions – whose evaluation? judged by what criteria? in whose interest? – see the chapter 'Peacebuilding' in *Contemporary Conflict Resolution* and the resources in the Toolbox section below.

57

Understanding the Contradictions of Postwar Peacebuilding

Roland Paris and Timothy Sisk

Roland Paris, University Research Chair in International Security and Governance at the University of Ottawa, and Timothy Sisk, Professor and Associate Dean at the Josef Korbel School of International Studies at the University of Denver, have been prominent in recent years in their constructive criticism of postwar peacebuilding operations. In this reading they identify some of the dilemmas and contradictions inherent in the gigantic post-Cold War international experiment in liberal interventionism into fragile states. Their central argument is that these tensions and trade-offs should be recognized and factored in from the outset – as was not the case in interventions in the early 1990s which were over-ambitious and relied on 'quick fixes' that were often unsustainable. Above all, since democratic and economic liberalization are inherently destabilizing in fragile postwar states, the immediate emphasis in postwar peacebuilding should be on statebuilding – the prior construction of legitimate governmental institutions capable of delivering all these other public goods. In Paris's phrase, 'institutionalisation before liberalisation' (2004).

*   *   *   *

Since the end of the Cold War, an enormous international experiment has been underway. A shifting constellation of international and regional organizations, national governments, and non-governmental organizations has conducted a series of complex "peacebuilding" operations aimed at stabilizing countries just emerging from periods of internal war. From Namibia in 1989 to Darfur in 2007, more than 20 major multilateral peacebuilding missions were deployed to post-conflict societies with the goal of preventing the resumption of violence (see Table 1). Nor is the demand for these operations likely to abate in the near future, given the increased tendency of armed conflicts to end in negotiated settlements rather than military victory.[1]

Why characterize these missions as an experiment? For one thing, there is still no reliable formula for transforming a fragile ceasefire into a stable and lasting peace. Nor should this observation come as a surprise. It is difficult to imagine a more complex or demanding task than post-conflict peacebuilding, which combines three separate yet

Table 1 Major post-civil conflict peacebuilding operations, 1989–2007

Location	Duration (military component)
Namibia	1989–1990
Nicaragua	1989–1992
Angola	1991–1997
Cambodia	1991–1993
El Salvador	1991–1995
Mozambique	1992–1994
Liberia	1992–1997
Rwanda	1993–1997
Bosnia	1995–present
Croatia (E. Slavonia)	1995–1998
Guatemala	1997
Timor Leste	1999–2002
Sierra Leone	1999–2005
Kosovo	1999–present
DR Congo	1999–present
Afghanistan	2002–present
Liberia	2003–present
Burundi	2004–present
Côte d'Ivoire	2004–present
Sudan (Southern)	2005–present
Sudan (Darfur)	2007–present

Note: Excludes missions with fewer than 200 military personnel (e.g., Georgia) and those not following an armed conflict (e.g., Haiti).

simultaneous transitions, each posing its own tremendous challenges: a social transition from internecine fighting to peace; a political transition from wartime government (or the absence of government) to postwar government; and an economic transition from war-warped accumulation and distribution to equitable, transparent postwar development that in turn reinforces peace. Peacebuilding also resembles an experiment in the sense that its methods have been evolving over the past two decades in response to the perceived lessons – and shortcomings – of preceding missions. Much of this policy evolution has occurred within sectoral or "micro" areas of peacebuilding, such as specific techniques for organizing and administering elections, but there has also been policy evolution at the "macro" level of the missions as a whole, and in the broad approaches they pursue.

One of the most important macro-level shifts in peacebuilding strategy occurred in the late 1990s and early 2000s, when major peacebuilding agencies began emphasizing the construction or strengthening of legitimate governmental institutions in countries emerging from civil conflict, or what we call "statebuilding" in this book. Statebuilding is a particular approach to peacebuilding, premised on the recognition that achieving security and development in societies emerging from civil war partly depends on the existence of capable, autonomous and legitimate governmental institutions. One of the lessons from the preceding years was that peacebuilding operations tended to rely on quick fixes, such as rapid elections and bursts of economic privatization, while paying too little attention to constructing the institutional foundations for functioning postwar governments and markets. Without mechanisms such as pre-election power-sharing pacts and institutions to uphold election results, for example, balloting initially served as a catalyst for renewed conflict in Angola in 1992. Without arrangements to ensure that newly elected officials would themselves respect the rule of law, autocratic elites reverted to despotic forms of rule in Cambodia during the 1990s and in Liberia after 1997. Without institutions to govern the market, economic reform initiatives were diverted by powerful black marketers in Bosnia in the years following the negotiation of the 1995 Dayton Accords. In response to these and other lessons, international agencies such as the United Nations (UN) began to reorient their peacebuilding strategies towards the construction of effective, legitimate governmental institutions in transitional states. Because such institutional reform required more time, moreover, missions began to be deployed for longer periods, including in Timor Leste, Kosovo, and Sierra Leone.

Increased attention on statebuilding as a foundation for peacebuilding made good sense. The assumption that political and economic liberalization could be achieved in the absence of functioning, legitimate institutions – an assumption that implicitly underpinned the design and conduct of peacebuilding in its early years – was deeply flawed (Paris 2004). In other development-related fields, too, weak governance was increasingly recognized as a contributing factor to a range of social ills: from poverty[2] and famine[3] to disease.[4] Institutional strengthening, alone, would not produce peace and prosperity, but without adequate attention to the statebuilding requirements of peacebuilding, war-torn states would be less likely to escape the multiple and mutually reinforcing "traps" of violence and underdevelopment.

As the mandates and time-frames of postconflict missions expanded, however, the problematic aspects of externally-assisted statebuilding became more apparent. Longer-term international deployments, for instance, risked being perceived by local actors as foreign intrusions in domestic affairs. How could international actors promote the goals of statebuilding without creating real or perceived "neo-trusteeship" arrangements over the host state? How could "local ownership" be achieved in the presence of powerful external actors? What about the danger of creating dependency on foreign actors or resources? How could international agencies promote statebuilding in a manner that respected local traditions and expectations in political, social and economic life? What were the long-run effects of different statebuilding strategies, including different electoral systems? How could postwar constitutions be designed to keep the peace in the short term and to lay the foundation for an effective, legitimate state in the longer-term? Postwar statebuilding is rife with these – and many other – vexing dilemmas.

To be sure, practitioners of statebuilding in the United Nations and other international organizations have been aware of many of these challenges. Issues such as coordination and coherence, local ownership, legitimacy, capacity-building, dependency, accountability, and exit are now commonly discussed in meetings of the new UN Peacebuilding Commission and elsewhere. But one of the arguments of this book is that such official discussions still tend to superficial, relying more on catch phrases than substance.[5] Meanwhile, the underlying sources of statebuilding's problems are rarely explored – or even directly acknowledged.

We believe that the time has come for a closer examination of the dilemmas and contradictions that lurk beneath the more visible, day-to-day challenges of statebuilding. Fundamental and unresolved tensions in the idea of externally-assisted statebuilding have given rise to a recurring series of policy problems facing peacebuilding actors in the field. Directly acknowledging and confronting these problems is crucial to the future success of the international community's peacebuilding efforts. The principal objective of this book is to investigate these contradictions and the policy dilemmas they generate.

...

Whither Statebuilding? Retreat, Reinvest, Reorganize or Rethink?

Today, the future of postwar peacebuilding and statebuilding is uncertain, for several reasons. First, the record of these missions since 1989 has been mixed.[6] Most of the countries that have hosted these missions have not reverted to war, but the durability of peace even in the most "successful" cases is less clear. How should we judge, for example, the outcome of peacebuilding in Central America where missions did little to address deep socio-economic inequalities, which have arguably been among the root causes of the region's violent past? What about the utter failure of peacebuilding in Rwanda prior to the 1994 genocide, or the on-again, off-again progress in Angola or Sierra Leone? And what should we make of the burst of renewed fighting in Timor Leste in 2006, in a country that was widely touted as one of the most notable peacebuilding successes? Such outcomes have raised doubts about prospects for peacebuilding and statebuilding even in relatively favorable settings. Although most experts hold that these operations have, on the whole, done considerably more good than harm, serious doubts persist about the ability of international agencies to create the conditions for sustainable peace.

Second, the movement toward statebuilding – with its emphasis on longer-lasting missions and institutional strengthening – has raised additional concerns for some observers, including the charge that such missions represent a new form of colonial control over the territory of the war-torn state. The strongest versions of this critique portray statebuilding as a form of neo-imperial or capitalist exploitation of vulnerable societies.[7] Less extreme versions highlight the dangers of fostering a "culture of dependency" in the host society due to the international community's extended and seemingly intrusive role, which is contrary to the goal of promoting sustainable self-rule built on domestic governing capacities.[8] Whatever one may think of these critiques, the difficulties faced, for example, by the continued presence of international peacebuilders in

Bosnia, well over a decade after their initial deployment, raises doubts about whether statebuilding efforts open a Pandora's Box of perpetual deployments and unending dependency.

Third, in the post-9/11 period – and particularly since the 2003 invasion of Iraq – it has become increasingly difficult to separate discussions of statebuilding in war-torn states from the ill-fated attempt to stabilize post-invasion Iraq. In fact, the circumstances of peacebuilding in Iraq (and Afghanistan) are profoundly different from those of most statebuilding operations: almost all of these operations have been deployed after civil wars (not external invasions) and at the request of local parties who have sought international assistance to help implement peace settlements. However, this distinction between post-invasion and post-settlement statebuilding is often unrecognized or deliberately blurred. As a result, exasperation over the deterioration of conditions in Iraq can spill over into skepticism about the potential effectiveness or desirability of *any* kind of post-conflict statebuilding operation.

…

The Next Challenge for Statebuilding: Sustainability

Designing and conducting statebuilding missions based on greater understanding of these contractions and dilemmas is a crucial and immediate need, but over the longer-term international actors should focus more attention on tackling the problem of "sustainability" in peacebuilding and statebuilding. The idea of sustainability is two-fold. First and most obviously, it means sustaining international attention and resources on states that are currently hosting (or have recently hosted) peacebuilding missions. (This is one of the laudable goals of the UN Peacebuilding Commission.) However, sustainability also implies developing mission strategies with longer-term results in mind. Today's peacebuilding approaches still tend to be rooted in short-term thinking and needs, focusing on the initial period following the termination of a conflict. For these strategies and missions to produce more sustainable results, they need to be viewed not simply as "post-conflict" operations, but rather as the first of many phases of international engagement in recovering countries, most of which will remain fragile long after the formal termination of the initial mission. For example, threats to a postwar democratization process can manifest themselves over many years, not only in the first or second electoral contests.

Subsequent phases of statebuilding may be conceived as "successive missions" aimed at the gradual stabilization of political and economic conditions within the country. This does not necessarily mean open-ended military or security deployments. Rather, once initial transitional tasks are completed – such as disarmament, demobilization, return of refugees, interim government, and elections – the international role should gradually shift towards a more "ordinary" international development and monitoring presence. Further analysis is required to evaluate what different types of successive missions (involving fewer military deployments but still providing for security and credible commitment to peace agreements and protection to vulnerable UN and other international staff) are best deployed to fill the gap between the full-scale peace operation and a "normal" development presence.

The idea of successive missions also calls into question the usefulness and appropriateness of thinking about "exit strategies" for statebuilding operations. As Dominik Zaum (2007) writes, "Exit should best be seen as a process, not an event, and therefore does not mean disengagement." Rather than "exiting," external actors should explicitly remain involved in promoting (and to some extent overseeing) the statebuilding process in progressively less intrusive ways. These might involve long-term international police missions, deployment of significant numbers of UN civilian personnel, further security-sector reform activities, rule of law and judicial reform, working with parliament and political parties, training for future elections observers, building civil-society or community-level conflict resiliency, and developing the capacity and dispute resolution skills of electoral management bodies. A key challenge for international statebuilders is to incorporate planning for these subsequent phases directly into the initial design of the mission, thereby reducing some of the contradictions between short-term and long-term statebuilding needs.

Notes

1 Human Security Centre 2008.
2 Keefer and Knack 1997.
3 Sen 1999.
4 Menon-Johansson 2005.
5 For example, see the Security Council's discussion of peacebuilding in S/PV.5895 and S/PV.5895 (Resumption 1), May 20, 2008.
6 See Doyle and Sambanis 2000, and Paris 2004.
7 For example, Bendaña 2005.
8 For example, Chandler 2006, chap. 6.

References

Bendaña, Alejandro (2005). 'From Peacebuilding to Statebuilding: One Step Forward and Two Steps Back?' *Development* 48(3): 5–15.

Chandler, David (2006). *Empire in Denial: The Politics of Statebuilding*. London: Pluto Press.

Doyle, Michael and Nicholas Sambanis (2000). 'International Peacebuilding: A Theoretical and Quantitative Analysis.' *American Political Science Review* 94(4): 779–801.

Human Security Centre (2008). 'Human Security Brief 2007.' Simon Fraser University, http://www.humansecuritybrief.info.

Keefer, Philip and Stephen Knack (1997). 'Why don't poor countries catch up? A cross-national test of institutionalist explanation.' *Economic Inquiry* 35(3) (July): 590–602.

Menon-Johansson, Anatole S. (2005). 'Good governance and good health. The role of societal structures in the human immunodeficiency virus pandemic.' *BMC International Health and Human Rights* 5(4) (April) http://www.biomedcentral.com/content/pdf/1472-698X-5-4.pdf.

Paris, Roland (2004). *At War's End: Building Peace After Civil Conflict*. Cambridge: Cambridge University Press.

Sen, Amaryta (1999). *Development as Freedom*. New York: Anchor Books.

Zaum, D. (2007) *The Sovereignty Paradox: The Norms and Politics of International Statebuilding*. Oxford: Oxford University Press.

58

The US and UN Roles in Nation-Building

James Dobbins et al.

As a complement to reading 57, this set of two extracts from the comparative evaluation of US-led and UN-led 'nation-building' interventions, conducted by the RAND Corporation, look at much the same data but from a different angle. James Dobbins was US Ambassador to the EU at the time of the UN peacebuilding experiments in the early 1990s and was later US envoy to Kosovo, Bosnia, Haiti and Somalia; he led negotiations that resulted in the 2001 Bonn Agreement in Afghanistan. Readers may like to consider whether like is being compared to like here in the US/UN comparison, and also what criteria for success and failure are being used. The US model for postwar peacebuilding (called 'nation-building' in these extracts) is post-1945 Germany and Japan – that is what US planners originally hoped to emulate in Iraq in 2003. From this perspective, UN-led efforts, from the Congo intervention in the early 1960s onwards, are often seen to have been ineffective. The relatively favourable assessment of UN-led operations in this study may, therefore, come as something of a surprise.

* * * *

The US Role in Nation-Building: From Germany to Iraq

The German and Japanese occupations set standards for postconflict transformation that have not since been equaled. One of the most important questions an inquiry such as this must address, therefore, is why those two operations succeeded so well while all subsequent efforts have fallen short to one degree or another. The easiest answer is that Germany and Japan were already highly developed, economically advanced societies. This certainly explains why it was easier to reconstruct the German and Japanese economies than it was to make fundamental reforms to the economies in the other five case studies. However, economics is not a sufficient answer. Nation-building is not principally about economic reconstruction; rather, it is about political transformation. The spread of democracy in Latin America, Asia, and parts of Africa suggests that this form of government is not unique to Western culture or to advanced industrial economies. Democracy can, indeed, take root in circumstances where neither exists.

No postconflict program of reconstruction could turn Somalia, Haiti, or Afghanistan into thriving centers of prosperity. But the failure of US-led interventions to install viable democracies in these countries has more than purely economic explanations. All three societies are divided ethnically, socioeconomically, or tribally in ways that Germany and Japan were not. Thus, homogeneity helps. But it is not a necessary condition. The kind of communal hatreds that mark Somalia, Haiti, and Afghanistan are even more marked in Bosnia and Kosovo, where the process of democratization has nevertheless made some progress.

…[W]hat principally distinguishes Germany, Japan, Bosnia, and Kosovo from Somalia, Haiti, and Afghanistan are not their levels of Western culture, economic development, or cultural homogeneity. Rather it is the level of effort the United States and the international community put into their democratic transformations. Nation-building, as this study illustrates, is a time- and resource-consuming effort. The United States and its allies have put 25 times more money and 50 times more troops, on a per capita basis, into postconflict Kosovo than into postconflict Afghanistan. This higher level of input accounts in significant measure for the higher level of output measured in the development of democratic institutions and economic growth.

Japan, one of the two undoubted successes, fully meets these criteria, at least in terms of the amount of time spent on its transformation. On the other hand, Japan received considerably less external economic assistance per capita than did Germany, Bosnia, or Kosovo. Indeed, it received less than Haiti and about the same as Afghanistan. Japan's postconflict economic growth rate was correspondingly low. U.S. spending on the Korean War, however, spurred Japan's economic growth during the 1950s, which subsequently helped consolidate public support for the democratic reforms that had been instituted soon after the war. As with the German economic miracle of the 1950s, this experience suggests that rising economic prosperity is not so much a necessary precursor for political reform as a highly desirable follow-up and legitimizer.

The stabilization (or, as it was then termed, occupation) force in Japan was also smaller in proportion to population than those in Germany, Bosnia, or Kosovo, although it was larger than those in Haiti and Afghanistan. The willing collaboration of the existing power structures and the homogeneity of the population undoubtedly enhanced the ability to secure Japan with a comparatively small force. But the very scale of Japan's defeat was also important. Years of total war had wrought devastation, including the firebombing of Japanese cities and, finally, two nuclear attacks. As a result, the surviving population was weary of conflict and disinclined to contest defeat. When conflicts have ended less conclusively and destructively (or not terminated at all) – as in Somalia, Afghanistan, and, most recently, Iraq – the postconflict security challenges are more difficult. Indeed, it seems that the more swift and bloodless the military victory, the more difficult postconflict stabilization can be.

Throughout the 1990s, the United States wrestled with the problem of how to achieve wider participation in its nation-building endeavors while also preserving adequate unity of command. In Somalia and Haiti, the United States experimented with sequential arrangements in which it organized, led, and largely manned and funded the initial phase of each operation but then quickly turned responsibility over to a more broadly representative and more widely funded UN-led force. These efforts were not successful, although the operation in Haiti was better organized than that in Somalia. In Bosnia, the United States succeeded in achieving unity of command and broad participation on the military side of the operation through the North Atlantic Treaty Organization (NATO) but resisted the logic of achieving a comparable and cohesive arrangement on the civil side. In Kosovo, the United States achieved unity of command and broad participation on both the military and civil sides through NATO and the UN, respectively. While the military and civil aspects of the Kosovo operation remained under different management, the United States ensured that the mandates and capabilities of the two functional entities, the Kosovo Force (KFOR) and the UN Interim Administration in Kosovo (UNMIK), overlapped sufficiently to prevent a gap from opening between them.

None of these models proved entirely satisfactory. Arrangements in Kosovo, however, do seem to have provided the best amalgam to date of US leadership, European participation, broad financial burden-sharing, and strong unity of command. Every international official in Kosovo works ultimately for either the NATO commander or the Special Representative of the Secretary General. Neither of these is an American, but by virtue of the United States' credibility in the region and its influence in NATO and the UN Security Council, the United States has been able to maintain a satisfactory leadership role while paying only 16 percent of the reconstruction costs and fielding only 16 percent of the peacekeeping troops.

The efficacy of the Kosovo and Bosnian models for managing a large-scale nation-building operation depends heavily on the ability of the United States and its principal allies to attain a common vision of the enterprise's objectives and then to shape the response of the relevant institutions – principally NATO, the European Union, and the UN – to the agreed purposes. When the principal participants in a nation building exercise have such a common vision, the Balkan models offer a viable amalgam of burden-sharing and unity of command.

In Afghanistan, the United States opted for parallel arrangements on the military side and even greater variety on the civil side. An international force, with no US participation, operates in Kabul, while a national, mostly US force, operates everywhere else. The UN is responsible for promoting political transformation, while individual donors coordinate economic reconstruction – or, more often, fail to do so. This arrangement is a marginal improvement over Somalia, since the separate US and international forces are at least not operating in the same physical territory, but it represents a clear regression from what was achieved in Haiti, Bosnia, or, in particular, Kosovo. By the same token, the overall results achieved to date in Afghanistan are better than those in Somalia, not yet better than those in Haiti, and not as good as those in Bosnia or Kosovo. However, the operation in Afghanistan is a good deal less expensive.

Duration

Another aspect in which these seven cases differ is in duration. Some began with clear departure deadlines that were adhered to, such as Haiti. Some began with very short time lines but saw those amended, such as Germany, Japan, Somalia, and Bosnia. And some began without any expectation of an early exit, such as Kosovo and Afghanistan. The record suggests that, while staying long does not guarantee success, leaving early ensures failure. To date, no effort at enforced democratization has taken hold in less than five years. And if democratization takes hold, does that provide the ultimate exit strategy? As these case studies suggest, not necessarily. US forces have left clear failures behind, such as Somalia and Haiti, but remain present in every successful or still-pending case: Germany, Japan, Bosnia, Kosovo, and Afghanistan. These five interventions were motivated by regional or global geopolitical concerns. Democratization alone did not fully address such concerns. Germany and Japan were disarmed and consequently required US help in providing for their external security long after they became reliable democracies, fully capable of looking after their own internal affairs. Bosnia, Kosovo, and Afghanistan may also require assistance with their external security long after internal peace has been established. Whether this help will take the form of an external troop presence, an external security guarantee, or external leadership in forging new regional security arrangements remains to be seen. But some security relationship is likely to continue long after the democratic transformation is completed. Indeed, if Germany and Japan are any guide, the more thorough the democratic transformation the more deeply forged the residual links may be. The record suggests that nation-building creates ties of affection and dependency that persist for a substantial amount of time.

The UN's Role in Nation-Building: From the Congo to Iraq

For the United States, post-Cold War nation-building had distant precursors in the American occupations of Germany and Japan in the aftermath of World War II and its role in fostering the emergence of democratic regimes there. For the United Nations, the comparable precursor was in the early 1960s in the newly independent Belgian Congo.

The Republic of the Congo failed almost from the moment of its birth. Within days of the Congo's independence its army mutinied, the remaining white administrators fled, the administration and the economy collapsed, Belgian paratroops invaded, and the mineral-rich province of Katanga seceded. These developments cast a serious shadow over the prospects for the successful and peaceful completion of Africa's decolonization, at that point just gathering momentum. On July 14, 1960, acting with unusual speed, the Security Council passed the first of a series of resolutions authorizing the deployment of UN-led military forces to assist the Republic of the Congo in restoring order and, eventually, in suppressing the rebellion in Katanga.

Given the unprecedented nature of its mission and the consequent lack of prior experience, existing doctrine, designated staff, or administrative structure to underpin the operation, the United Nations performed remarkably well in the Congo. Significant forces began to arrive within days of the Security Council's authorization – performance matched in few subsequent UN peacekeeping missions. The United Nations was quickly able to secure the removal of Belgian forces. Over the next three years, UN troops forced the removal of foreign mercenaries and suppressed the Katangan secession while civil elements of the mission provided a wide range of humanitarian, economic, and civil assistance to the new Congolese regime. Measured against the bottom-line requirements of the international community – that decolonization proceed, colonial and mercenary troops depart, and the Congo remain intact – the United Nations was largely successful.

Democracy did not figure heavily in the various Congo resolutions passed by the UN Security Council; there was, in any case, no agreement during the Cold War on the definition of that term. The Congo never became a functioning democracy, but large-scale civil conflict was averted for more than a decade following the United Nations' departure, and the country more or less held together for two more decades, albeit under a corrupt and incompetent dictatorship.

UN achievements in the Congo came at considerable cost in men lost, money spent, and controversy raised. For many people, the United Nations' apparent complicity in the apprehension and later execution of Prime Minister Patrice Lumumba overshadowed its considerable accomplishments. As a result of these costs and controversies, neither the United Nations' leadership nor its member nations were eager to repeat the experience. For the next 25 years the United Nations restricted its military interventions to interpositional peacekeeping, policing ceasefires, and patrolling disengagement zones in circumstances where all parties invited its presence and armed force was to be used by UN troops only in self-defense.

Healing Cold War wounds

The conclusion of the Cold War ended this hiatus in nation-building and presented the United Nations with new opportunities and new challenges. By the end of the 1980s, the United States and the Soviet Union had begun to disengage from proxy wars in Latin America, Africa, and Asia and were finally prepared to work together in pressing former clients to resolve their outstanding differences.

The early post–Cold War UN-led operations in Namibia, Cambodia, El Salvador, and Mozambique followed a similar pattern. The international community, with US and Soviet backing, first brokered a peace accord. The Security Council then dispatched a UN peacekeeping force to oversee its implementation. In each case, the UN mission's responsibilities included initiating an expeditious process of disarmament, demobilization, and reintegration; encouraging political reconciliation; holding democratic elections; and overseeing the inauguration of a new national government. Operations in each of these countries were greatly facilitated by war-weary populations, great-power support, and the cooperation of neighboring countries. The United Nations became adept at overseeing the disarmament and demobilization of willing parties. The reintegration of former combatants was everywhere more problematic, for nowhere did the international community provide the necessary resources. Economic growth accelerated in most cases, largely as a result of the cessation of fighting. Peace, growth, and democracy were often accompanied by an increase in common crime, as old repressive security services were dismantled and demobilized former combatants were left without a livelihood.

All four of these operations culminated in reasonably free and fair elections. All four resulted in sustained periods of civil peace that endured after the United Nations withdrawal. Cambodia enjoyed the least successful democratic transformation and experienced the greatest renewal of civil strife, although at nothing like the level that preceded the UN intervention. Cambodia was also the first instance in which the United Nations became responsible for helping govern a state in transition from conflict to peace and democracy. The United Nations was ill prepared to assume such a role. For its part, the government of Cambodia, although it had agreed to UN administrative oversight as part of the peace accord, was unwilling to cede effective authority. As a result, UN control over Cambodia's civil administration was largely nominal.

Despite the successes of these early post-Cold War operations, a number of weaknesses in the United Nations' performance emerged that would cripple later missions launched in more difficult circumstances. Deficiencies included

- the slow arrival of military units
- the even slower deployment of police and civil administrators
- the uneven quality of military components
- the even greater unevenness of police and civil administrators
- the United Nations' dependence on voluntary funding to pay for such mission-essential functions as reintegration of combatants and capacity building in local administrations
- the frequent mismatches between ambitious mandates and modest means
- the premature withdrawal of missions, often following immediately after the successful conclusion of a first democratic election.

Coping with failed states

During the early 1990s, the United Nations enjoyed a series of successes. This winning streak and a consequent optimism about the task of nation-building came to an abrupt end in Somalia and were further diminished by events in the former Yugoslavia. In both instances, UN-led peacekeeping forces were inserted into societies where there was no peace to keep. In both cases, UN forces eventually had to be replaced by larger, more robust American-led peace enforcement missions.

Although the Cold War divided some societies, it provided the glue that held others together. Even as former East-West battlegrounds, such as Namibia, Cambodia, El Salvador, and Mozambique, were able to emerge as viable nation states with UN assistance, other divided societies, such as Somalia, Yugoslavia, and Afghanistan – which had been held together by one superpower or the other, and sometimes by both – began to disintegrate as external supports and pressures were removed. Not surprisingly, the United Nations had a harder time holding together collapsing states than brokering reconciliation in coalescing ones.

The original UN mission in Somalia was undermanned and overmatched by warring Somali clan militias. The US-led multinational force that replaced it was built on a core of 20,000 American soldiers and marines. This force was quickly able to overawe local resistance and secure the delivery of famine relief supplies, its principal mission. Washington then chose to withdraw all but 2,000 troops. The United States passed overall responsibility back to the United Nations and supported a radical expansion of the UN's mandate. The previous UN and US forces had confined their mission to securing humanitarian relief activities. Even as the United States withdrew 90 percent of its combat forces and saw them replaced by a smaller number of less well equipped UN troops, it joined in extending the mission of those remaining forces to the introduction of grass-roots democracy, a process which would put the United Nations at cross purposes with every warlord in the country. The result was a resurgence of violence to levels that residual US and UN troops proved unable to handle. Insuperable difficulties also arose in the former Yugoslavia, where UN peacekeepers were again deployed to an ongoing civil war without the mandate, influence, or firepower needed to end the fighting. UN deficiencies contributed to the failure of its efforts in Bosnia, as they had in Somalia, but at least equal responsibility lies with its principal member governments: with Russia, for its stubborn partisanship on behalf of Serbia; with the United States, for its refusal to commit American forces or to support the peacemaking initiatives of those governments that had; and with Britain and France, the principal troop contributors, for failing to enforce the mandate they had accepted to protect the innocent civilians entrusted to their care.

The failure of UN missions in both Somalia and Bosnia, when contrasted with the more robust American-led multinational efforts that succeeded them, led to a general conclusion that, although the United Nations might be up to peacekeeping, peace enforcement was beyond its capacity. This conclusion, not uncongenial to the United Nations' own leadership, is belied by that organization's performance 30 years earlier in the former Belgian Congo. Its subsequent conduct of small, but highly successful peace enforcement missions in Eastern Slavonia from 1996 to 1998 and in East Timor beginning in 1999, suggested that the United Nations was capable of executing a robust peace enforcement mandate in circumstances where the scale was modest, the force included a core of capable First World troops, and the venture had strong international backing.

Eastern Slavonia was the last Serb-held area of Croatia at the end of the conflict between these two former Yugoslav republics. The United Nations once again became responsible for governing a territory in transition, in this case from Serb to Croat control. The UN operation in Eastern Slavonia was generously manned, well led, abundantly resourced, and strongly supported by the major powers, whose influence ensured the cooperation of neighboring states. Not surprisingly, given these advantages, the UN peace enforcement mission in Eastern Slavonia was highly successful. American-led multinational missions in Somalia and Bosnia contrasted positively with the UN missions that had preceded them, primarily because they were better resourced and more determined in the employment of those larger capabilities. Had the United States been willing to provide a military commander and 20,000 American troops to the UN-led operations in Somalia or Bosnia, those earlier efforts would likely have fared better, perhaps obviating the need for the subsequent multinational interventions.

Nation-building in the new decade

In the closing months of 1999, the United Nations found itself charged with governing both Kosovo and East Timor. The latter operation proved an ideal showcase for UN capabilities. Like Eastern Slavonia, East Timor was small in both territory and population. International resources, in terms of military manpower and economic assistance, were unusually abundant. Major power influence secured the cooperation of neighboring states. A multinational coalition, in this case led by Australia, secured initial control of the territory and then quickly turned the operation over to UN management. Remaining combatants were disarmed, new security forces established, a local administration created, elections held, and a democratically elected government inaugurated in less than three years.

Even this showcase operation exhibited certain chronic UN deficiencies. International police and civil administrators were slow to arrive and of variable quality. Once ensconced, UN administrators were a trifle slow to turn power back to local authorities. These were minor blemishes, however, on a generally successful operation.

In less benign circumstances, such weaknesses continued to threaten the success of UN operations. In Sierra Leone, inadequate UN forces were inserted in 1999 as part of the United Nations Mission in Sierra Leone (UNAMSIL) under unduly optimistic assumptions. They encountered early reverses and eventually suffered the ultimate humiliation of being captured and held hostage in large numbers. Poised on the verge of collapse, the Sierra Leone operation was rescued by the United Kingdom and turned around thanks in large measure to extraordinary personal efforts by the UN Secretary-General. British forces arrived, extricated UN hostages, intimidated insurgent forces, and began to train a more competent local military. The United States threw its logistic and diplomatic weight behind the operation. The regime in neighboring Liberia, highly complicit in Sierra Leone's civil war, was displaced. Additional manpower and economic resources were secured. Thus bolstered, the United Nations was able to oversee a process of disarmament and demobilization and hold reasonably free elections.

Comparative Conclusions

Size of mission

UN missions have normally fielded much smaller contingents than American-led operations, both in absolute numbers and in relation to the local population. The largest UN mission we studied is smaller than the smallest US mission studied.

Duration

UN forces have tended to remain in post-conflict countries for shorter periods of time than have US forces. In the early 1990s, both US and UN-led operations tended to be terminated rather quickly, often immediately following the completion of an initial democratic election and the inauguration of a new government. By the end of the decade, both UN- and US-led operations became more extended and peacekeeping forces were drawn down more slowly, rather than exiting en masse following the first national election.

Peace

Peace is the most essential product of nation-building. Of the eight US-led cases, four are at peace; four are not – or not yet – at peace.

Conclusion

UN-led nation-building missions tend to be smaller than American operations, to take place in less demanding circumstances, to be more frequent and therefore more numerous, to have more circumspectly defined objectives, and – at least among the missions studied – to enjoy a higher success rate than US-led efforts.

The UN success rate among missions studied – seven out of eight societies left peaceful, six out of eight left democratic – substantiates the view that nation-building can be an effective means of terminating conflicts, insuring against their reoccurrence, and promoting democracy. In fact, despite the daily dosage of horrific violence displayed in Iraq and Afghanistan, the world has not become a more violent place within the past decade. Rather, the reverse is true. International peacekeeping and nation-building have contributed to this reduced death rate.

59

Hybrid Peace: The Interaction between Top-Down and Bottom-Up Peace

Roger Mac Ginty

This analysis of international peacebuilding interventions by Roger Mac Ginty, Professor of Peace and Conflict Studies at the Humanitarian and Conflict Response Institute, University of Manchester, is in sharp contrast to Reading 58 – and also in many ways to Reading 57. It is a good example of the influential and powerful critique of the 'top-down' approach of 'liberal interventionism' that is widespread in conflict resolution circles, as noted in the introduction to this part. Mac Ginty refers here to Oliver Richmond, who has also been influential in arguing that the 'bottom-up' principles of indigenous legitimacy should shape all postwar peacebuilding interventions, that these should be emancipatory and rest on the consent of local actors, and that the resulting peace should be seen as a hybrid construct – a 'variable geometry' of local–international engagement – rather than a rigid external imposition.[1]

Note

1 O. Richmond, *Peace in International Relations*. London: Routledge, 2008.

*   *   *   *

The Liberal Peace

Given the dominance of Western states, institutions and technologies in contemporary peacemaking, peace accord implementation and development, it is legitimate to use the liberal peace as the principal reference frame for an account of how international and local forms of peacemaking combine to produce a hybridized peace. The term has been popularized in a number of, largely critical, accounts of contemporary peacemaking, peacebuilding, postwar reconstruction and development literature (Chandler, 2004; Fanthorpe, 2006; Richmond & Franks, 2007; Mac Ginty & Richmond, 2007; Petersen, 2009). The liberal peace is taken to mean the dominant form of internationally supported peacemaking and peacebuilding that is promoted by leading states, leading international organizations and international financial institutions. These peace interventions and peacebuilding strategies are justified using liberal rhetoric. The concept of the liberal peace is a broad umbrella, as it takes account of the ideology of peacemaking, the socio-cultural norms of peacemaking, the structural factors that enable and constrain it, its principal actors and clients, and its manifestations. The term seeks to capture the totality of internationally sponsored peace support interventions, and so the way in which the term is used in this context is very different from its usage in some econometric studies that interrogate datasets in the hope of finding correlations between trade statistics and the propensity of states going to war. Crucially for this work, the liberal peace offers a comparative lens enabling the examination of multiple peacemaking interventions in the contemporary era.

According to its critics, it reflects the practical and ideological interests of the global north. It draws on the Wilsonian tradition and deploys liberal rhetoric to justify peacemaking interventions. In its proponents' view, liberalism is the 'ideology upon which life, culture, society, prosperity and politics are assumed to rest' (Mac Ginty & Richmond, 2007: 493). While 'there is no canonical description of liberalism' (Doyle, 1983: 206), it is possible to identify core liberal values that are found with regularity in justifications of peace interventions. Thus there has been the repeated invocation of, and peacebuilding strategies to reflect, the primacy of the individual, the belief in the reformability of individuals and institutions, pluralism and toleration, the rule of law, and the protection of property. Eric Herring (2008: 48) gives a good summary of liberalism as operationalized in the contemporary world: 'a formal and informal commitment to principles and practices of individual rights and responsibility in the context of equality of opportunity, the rule of law, freedom of expression and association, a mainly market economy and governments chosen in multi-party free elections'.

Liberalism is capable of constructing a beguiling and attractive rationale for its own promotion. Thus it speaks of 'responsibility', 'development', 'common interests' and, above all, intervention (Williams, 2007: 543). Sometimes called 'liberal interventionism' or 'liberal internationalism', the liberal peace is most visible in societies undergoing Western-backed peace support interventions in the aftermath of civil war. But many of the tools of the liberal peace, particularly in disciplining societies, governments and economies, are also at work in developing states that have not experienced war in the recent past. In non-postwar environments, these interventions are often covered by the terms 'good governance', 'poverty reduction strategy papers' and 'reform' (Abrahamsen, 2004; Craig & Porter, 2003). The rationale for intervention based on liberalism stems from the belief – shared by many governments in the global north and international organizations – that liberalism is intrinsically peace-promoting. Through the 'democratic peace' thesis (or the 'liberal peace' thesis), advocates of liberal interventionism have posited links between the type of economic and political organization within a state and liberal outcomes (Doyle, 1995: 84). This strain of thought attests that since liberal states do not go to war with each other, then the 'solution' to international aggression is to export liberal forms of state-building.

Liberalism has provided the intellectual underpinning for a series of post-Cold War international interventions (Cooper, 2002). Indeed, Williams (2006: 2) has identified the development of a 'new liberal militancy' in the wake of 9/11. Thus, liberalism has encouraged states and international organizations to express concern with the condition of citizens within. Allied with the liberal belief in the reformability of individuals and institutions is an equally confident belief in the superiority of liberal ideas (and a consequent denigration of 'non-liberal' ideas). As Williams (2006: 5) observed, liberals believe 'quite sincerely in the creation of a better world and that they are the exemplars of what that world should look like'. All of this combines to create a predisposition towards intervention and particular types of liberal prescriptions. In short, in the post-Cold War period, a number of states and international actors have displayed an exuberant confidence in the abilities of their anointed version of liberalism to save the world. Liberal remedies offered salvation against war, poverty, disease and 'terrorism'. Liberalism had become a kind of magic dust that, if spread within states and economies, would produce harmony and prosperity at the international level.

Critics of the liberal peace point to its central irony: that it often uses illiberal means in its promotion of liberal values (Williams, 2005). They contend that it is an essentially conservative and realist philosophy that reinforces the position of power-holders (national, regional, international elites and their private-sector allies), while doing little to emancipate the general population (Jacoby, 2007: 536–537; Mayall, 2006: 96). In this view, the liberal peace is equated with negative peace, or forms of peace that address conflict manifestations but avoid structural change. The liberal peace is criticized for its alleged ethnocentrism – its promotion of essentially Western values and its belief in the universalism of liberal goals. Critics also point to the unbending belief in the liberating abilities of the free market shown by the international financial institutions and leading states in their postwar reconstruction strategies. In a sense, the liberal peace becomes a neoliberal peace and engages in 'aggressive social engineering', whereby the private sector is privileged over notions of the common good, often with profound human consequences (Pugh, 2006a: 153). As Pugh (2006b: 271) observes, 'peace operations can be considered an integral part of the world ordering project that has accompanied projects for stabilising capitalism'. According to the critique, liberal interventionism uses state-building as its principal vehicle of reform, promoting Western-style governance and electoral processes (Sriram, 2008: 35–37). Advocates of the liberal peace are accused of attempting to replicate Western democratic, economic and social processes to the extent that observers pithily referred to the enterprise as 'getting to Denmark', a byword for a generic 'any state' with a functioning bureaucracy, developed economy and compliant foreign policy (Pritchett & Woolcock, 2004: 191–212). Darby & Mac Ginty (2008: 4–6) highlight the deeply compromised, poor-quality peace that often results from liberal peace interventions characterized by technocratic 'solutions' that fail to deal with the affective dimensions of grievances that can linger across generations.

Proponents of liberal peace interventions (who – like the critics – by no means comprise a homogenous bloc) suggest that the core elements of the liberal peace (security and stabilization, reinforcing states, democratic governance, and marketization) bring the ability to emancipate people. They do not see liberal interventionism as part of a large-power aggrandizement project. Instead, they note that only international processes organized by capable states or international organizations are able to mobilize the resources necessary for the large-scale state rebuilding (Cooper, 2003). Often this involves difficult choices. As Quinn & Cox (2007: 517) note:

> While a liberal peace of a more home-grown, or even 'emancipatory' kind might well be desirable in the abstract, in most situations where the issue arises, the international community and the United States find themselves facing a choice between imposing peace from the outside, with some aspiration to grafting liberal institutions on to such an imposed order at a later stage, or simply allowing the forces already pushing a society into violence to run their bloody course.

Post-civil war contexts may necessitate difficult trade-offs, particularly concerning the 'order versus liberty' dilemma. Proponents of the liberal peace would argue that security is a necessary prerequisite for liberty (as articulated by the 'institutionalization before liberalization' formulation associated with Roland Paris [2004]). They also question the degree to which critics have feasible alternatives.

The extent to which liberal ideas have influenced contemporary peace and reconstruction interventions is not in doubt. This is an era dominated by the liberal peace. Yet, there is a risk of overestimating the power and coherence of the liberal peace. As will be discussed in later sections, local actors can have considerable agency, which results in a hybridized peace. It is also important to underscore the power of regional and international powers (such as China and Russia) to provide alternative sources of coercion, incentives and tutelage.

In summary, the liberal peace is the dominant mode of peacemaking, peacebuilding, reconstruction and development favoured by powerful actors from the global north. Underpinned by specific interpretations of liberal ideas, the liberal peace is the 'software' that drives the 'hardware' of many international organizations, states and international nongovernmental organizations (INGOs). It has helped shape the international norms (for example, international human rights laws or the Millennium Development Goals) that dominate the landscape of international peace and development. Leading states from the global north, and the international institutions that they control, constitute the principal agents of the liberal peace. These are joined by a series of other agents, such as national governments, municipalities and INGOs, who often operate in the society emerging from conflict. The liberal peace can thus be conceived as a top-down transmission chain of peacemaking ideas, language and practice. The principal agents are able to coerce and incentivize some degree of compliance. As will become clear in later sections, the principal liberal peace agents are unable to construct neat silos of compliance. Liberal peace agents and structures are fallible, prone to distraction, and suffer from limitations in budgets and capabilities. Richmond's (2005: 217) 'graduations of the liberal peace model' is useful in helping to illustrate the variety of liberal peaces on offer: hyper-conservatism, conservative, orthodox and emancipatory.

Despite its limitations, the liberal peace is pervasive, shaping international structures and the language of peacemaking, and amassing immense material power in service of its preferred notions of peace and development. Given the pervasive nature of liberal peacemaking and the internationalized nature of civil war, it is difficult to conceive of actors completely outside of the liberal peace ambit. To some extent, virtually all actors involved in peacemaking and peacebuilding have to take cognizance of structures, principles and laws shaped by the liberal peace. Finally, it is important not to make an exclusive equation between liberalism (and linked notions of pluralism and toleration) and the global north. Instead, it is worth bearing in mind the rich traditions of pluralism and toleration found in the global south.

Conceptualizing Hybridity

In many ways, the concept of hybridity defies neat categorization. Much of the literature on hybridity descends into discussions of relativity from which it is difficult to gain bearings. To caricature some of this literature: everything is the result of hybridity, everything is a hybrid, there can be no certainty, and all discussions must be smothered in caveats (McEwan, 2008: 77). This article seeks to move beyond such discussions to examine hybridization, or hybridity as a process. Specifically, it is interested in the processes whereby hybrid peace comes about. It seeks to conceptualize the 'variable geometry' of peace whereby different actors coalesce and conflict to different extents on different issues to produce a fusion peace. In the context of a peace-implementation environment, for example, we might see how local mores hold sway on issues of reconciliation, while international norms and practices prevail in relation to the structure of the economy. The result is a hybridized peace that is in constant flux, as different actors and processes cooperate and compete on different issue agendas.

...

The Compliance Powers of the Liberal Peace

Promoters of the liberal peace are able to mobilize a formidable suite of compliance mechanisms to encourage conformity and to discipline attempts at deviance. The obvious compliance tool is force or the threat of force, such as attempts to 'install democracy at gunpoint' in Afghanistan (MacGregor, 2009). But other compliance mechanisms abound, most notably the globalized free market that simultaneously offers both opportunities and constraints. In order to access reconstruction resources (often loans and assistance from international financial institutions), states emerging from civil war must conform to the strictures of the international financial system (Brynen, 2000). Thus the economy must be marketized, the public sector pared, new governance regimes instituted, and any semblance of state financial sovereignty sacrificed to the demands of international and transnational economic flows. In many cases, the liberal peace has become a series of binding relationships predicated on Western economic and governance norms. Although many of its key transmission agents may be local actors (government ministries and national elites, municipalities, NGOs, etc), the DNA is Western and may have profound implications for the host society and culture. The rhetoric of 'participation', 'local ownership' and 'partnership' may do little to mask power relations in which the conception, design, funding, timetable, execution and evaluation of programmes and projects are conducted according to Western agendas (Cooke & Kothari, 2002). The cooption of local actors as agents of the liberal peace (for example, the national government or municipalities) means that a hierarchy of compliance is constructed and maintained. In many cases, the management of compliance is devolved from the international to the national to the local.

Perhaps the most insidious compliance tool operating in favour of the liberal peace is the notion that the liberal peace is the 'only deal in town'. The genius of many commercial monopolies is in persuading the consumer that there is really only one choice. The liberal peace, because of the strength of its chief proponents and the resources they can mobilize, has had considerable success in promoting the notion that there is one acceptable version of peace and that other versions do not constitute 'peace'. In other words, the proponents of the liberal peace have been able to mobilize massive psychological resources to set the boundaries of acceptable and unacceptable peace. The 'moral authority' of the liberal peace stems from the power of its promoters, the intellectual heritage they deploy in justifying their peace support interventions, and the co-option of major international organizations and international NGOs in the service of this version of peace. The power of precedence also comes into play: the liberal peace has been road-tested in many locations and many aspects of it have been seen to work, particularly in relation to the delivery of humanitarian and development assistance.

...

The Incentivizing Powers of the Liberal Peace

The variable geometry of the liberal peace means that it is able to combine coercive elements with gentler, persuasive incentives. Certainly the supportive rhetoric of the liberal peace is replete with potential for the individual, the community and the state. While the core elements of the liberal peace (security and stabilization, reinforcing statehood, democratic governance, and the extension of the free market) can have negative consequences, they also hold out positive potential. Security and stabilization can be restrained, targeted and cognizant of the need to protect human rights and minorities. In the context of post-civil war and deeply divided societies, security (and particularly demobilization) is often a necessary prerequisite not only for a peace accord but also for the range of state-building, peacebuilding and reconstruction tasks that often facilitate the implementation of a peace accord (Stedman, 2002: 668). Through a positive lens, reinforcing statehood can enable widespread social improvement: protecting and promoting human rights, ensuring the widespread provision of public goods, and establishing a bureaucracy capable of managing democratic transitions. Democratic governance can help promote responsibility and the civic virtues that may prevent conflict recidivism. It is, in US President George W. Bush's (2008) phrase, 'the beauty of democracy'. Potentially, the free market can be liberating and emancipating: rewarding creativity and offering independence and the opportunity for self-improvement. Deudney & Ikenberry (1999: 190) observe the political ambitions of the promotion of open economies: 'liberal states have pursued economic openness for political ends, using free trade as an instrument to alter and maintain the preferences and features of other states that are politically and strategically congenial'. In this sense, free markets are politically pacifying, in that they bind states and citizens (remodelled as consumers, producers, regulators and enablers) into a series of mutual ties.

...

The Ability of Local Actors to Resist, Ignore or Adapt Liberal Peace Interventions

The third factor that influences the extent to which peace might be hybridized concerns the ability of actors, networks and structures in host states to resist, ignore, subvert or adapt liberal peace interventions. This factor is important in that it reminds us of the agency of actors in host societies. Rather than being mere passive actors (victims, recipients, beneficiaries, etc.), local actors may be capable of considerable autonomous action. By pushing back against 'the echoes of colonialism', local actors may have power to hybridize peace (Richmond, 2009). Of course, this power to resist will vary according to context, and in some contexts exogenous actors, networks and structures will dominate, leaving minimal room for local agency. In other contexts, liberal internationalism may be promoted in a half-hearted way or in a more relaxed format, allowing local actors more freedom to exert their influence. Crucial here will be the extent to which traditional or indigenous structures and norms (themselves hybrids) are intact (Mac Ginty, 2008). Often they may have been severely eroded by conflict. Respect for village elders in a rural African context, for example, may have been reduced by the dislocation of conflict, rural–urban migration and the dissipation of moral authority caused by long-term social change. But, in other cases, norms and practices based on kinship or an understanding of the local ecology may survive and hold local legitimacy.

…

The Ability of Local Actors, Structures and Networks to Present and Maintain Alternative Forms of Peace and Peacemaking

The final factor in the construction of hybrid peace concerns the ability of local actors to promote alternative forms of peace. As already mentioned, the hegemonic ambitions of the liberal peace mean that it attempts, often successfully, to minimize the space for alternative versions of peace, development, security and governance. It often succeeds in promoting the perception that it is 'the only game in town' and that locally inspired alternatives that do not ape approved models from the global north are somehow illiberal or illegitimate. Quite simply, in many cases the liberal peace *has* unrivalled coercive and economic power and so is able to overshadow, outbid or outgun alternatives.

Local forms of dispute resolution and reconciliation that draw on traditional, indigenous or customary norms and practices exist in many societies (Mac Ginty, 2008: 139–163). Often these are most apparent at the local level, or on the margins (perhaps in geographically isolated areas of a large state where the reach of liberal peace agents is weak, or among constituencies deemed marginal). Yet, customary practice can also operate at the national elite level, for example in the formation of a coalition government in which power is shared on the basis of kinship and clan as well as some sort of democratic formula. These may not conform to perceptions of legitimate peacemaking or peacebuilding according to the liberal peace perspective, but they may have cultural purchase in the host society.

References

Abrahamsen, Rita, 2004. 'Poverty Reduction or Adjustment by Another Name?', *Review of African Political Economy* 31(99): 184–187.

Brynen, Rex, 2000. *A Very Political Reconstruction: Peacebuilding and Foreign Aid in the West Bank and Gaza*. Washington, DC: USIP Press.

Chandler, David, 2004. 'Responsibility To Protect? Imposing the "Liberal Peace"', *International Peacekeeping* 11(1): 59–81.

Cooke, William & Uma Kothari, eds, 2002. *Participation: The New Tyranny?* London: Zed.

Cooper, Robert, 2002. 'Why We Still Need Empires', *Observer*, 7 April.

Cooper, Robert, 2003. *The Breaking of Nations: Order and Chaos in the Twenty-First Century*. London: Atlantic.

Craig, David & Doug Porter, 2003. 'Poverty Reduction Strategy Papers: A New Convergence', *World Development* 31(1): 53–69.

Darby, John & Roger Mac Ginty, 2008. 'What Peace, What Process?', in John Darby & Roger Mac Ginty, eds, *Contemporary Peacemaking: Conflict, Peace Processes and Post-War Reconstruction*. Basingstoke: Palgrave (1–8).

Deudney, Daniel & John Ikenberry, 1999. 'The Nature and Sources of Liberal International Order', *Review of International Studies* 25(2): 179–196.

Doyle, Michael, 1983. 'Kant, Liberal Legacies, and Foreign Affairs: Part I', *Philosophy and Public Affairs* 12(3): 205–235.

Doyle, Michael, 1995. 'Liberalism and World Politics Revisited', in Charles W. Kegley, ed., *Controversies in International Relations Theory: Realism and the Neoliberal Challenge*. Basingstoke: Palgrave Macmillan (86–103).

Fanthorpe, Richard, 2006. 'On the Limits of Liberal Peace: Chiefs and Democratic Centralization in Post-War Sierra Leone', *African Affairs* 105(418): 27–49.

Herring, Eric, 2008. 'Neoliberalism Versus Peacebuilding in Iraq', in Michael Pugh, Neil Cooper & Mandy Turner, eds, *Whose Peace? Critical Perspectives on the Political Economy of Peacebuilding*. Basingstoke: Palgrave Macmillan (47–64).

Jacoby, Tim, 2007. 'Hegemony, Modernisation and Post-War Reconstruction', *Global Society* 21(4): 521–537.

McEwan, Cheryl, 2008. *Postcolonialism and Development*. Abingdon: Routledge.

Mac Ginty, Roger, 2008. 'Indigenous Peacemaking Versus the Liberal Peace', *Cooperation and Conflict* 43(2): 139–163.

Mac Ginty, Roger & Oliver Richmond, 2007. 'Myth or Reality: Opposing Views on the Liberal Peace and Post-War Reconstruction', *Global Society* 21(4): 491–497.

MacGregor, Douglas, 2009. 'Refusing Battle: The Alternative to Persistent Warfare', *Armed Forces Journal*, April; available at http://www.afji.com/2009/04/3901424 (accessed 5 May 2010).

Mayall, James, 2006. 'Security and Self-Determination', in William Bain, ed., *The Empire of Security and the Safety of the People*. Abingdon: Routledge.

Paris, Roland, 2004. *At War's End: Building Peace After Civil Conflict*. Cambridge: Cambridge University Press.

Petersen, Jenny, 2009. '"Rule of Law" Initiatives and the Liberal Peace: The Impact of Politicised Reform in Post-Conflict States', *Disasters* 34(1): 15–39.

Pritchett, Lant & Michael Woolcock, 2004. 'Solutions When the Solution Is the Problem: Arraying the Disarray in Development', *World Development* 32(2): 191–212.

Pugh, Michael, 2006a. 'Transformation in the Political Economy of Bosnia Since Dayton', in David Chandler, ed., *Peace Without Politics? Ten Years of International State-Building in Bosnia*. Abingdon: Routledge (142–156).

Pugh, Michael, 2006b. 'Post-War Economies and the New York Dissensus', *Conflict, Security and Development* 6(3): 269–289.

Quinn, Adam & Michael Cox, 2007. 'For Better, For Worse: How America's Foreign Policy Became Wedded to Universal Liberalism', *Global Society* 21(4): 499–519.

Richmond, Oliver, 2005. *The Transformation of Peace*. Basingstoke: Palgrave.

Richmond, Oliver, 2009. 'Liberal Peace Transitions: A Rethink Is Urgent', OpenDemocracy, 19 November; available at http://www.opendemocracy.net/oliver-p-richmond/liber-al-peace-transitions-rethink-is-urgent (accessed 6 April 2010).

Richmond, Oliver & Jason Franks, 2007. 'Liberal Hubris? Virtual Peace in Cambodia', *Security Dialogue* 38(1): 27–48.

Sriram, Chandra Lekha, 2008. *Peace as Governance: Power-Sharing, Armed Groups and Contemporary Peace Negotiations*. Basingstoke: Palgrave.

Stedman, Stephen, 2002. 'Policy Implications', in Stephen Stedman, Donald Rothchild & Elizabeth Cousens, eds, *Ending Civil Wars: The Implementation of Peace Agreements*. Boulder, CO: Lynne Rienner (663–671).

Williams, Andrew, 2005. 'What's So Peaceful About Liberals?', paper prepared for the 47th Annual Convention of the International Studies Association, San Diego, CA, 22–25 March; available at http://www.st-andrews.ac.uk/intrel/media/Williams_what_is_so_peaceful_about_liberals.pdf (accessed 12 December 2005).

Williams, Andrew, 2006. *Liberalism and War: The Victors and the Vanquished*. Abingdon: Routledge.

Williams, Andrew, 2007. 'Reconstruction: The Bringing of Peace and Plenty or Occult Imperialism?', *Global Society: Journal of Interdisciplinary International Relations* 21(4): 539–551.

60

Transitional Justice and Reconciliation: Theory and Practice

Martina Fischer

In this reading, Martina Fischer, Programme Director Southeast Europe and co-editor of the *Berghof Handbook for Conflict Transformation*, Berghof Foundation, Berlin, offers an insightful critical account of the 'transitional justice' component of postwar peacebuilding. This is a major element in Dan Smith's 'peacebuilding palette' (see Reading 61) and can serve to illustrate some of the 'dilemmas' referred to by Paris and Sisk (Reading 57) – for example the 'peace versus justice' and 'truth versus justice' dichotomies. A good account is given here of the influential contribution made by Alex Boraine, based on the South Africa experience, with his emphasis on a 'holistic' approach that combines retributive and restorative justice.[1] Particularly impressive in this piece is the emphasis placed on the importance of adding 'gender justice' to the transitional justice agenda.[2]

Notes

1 A. Boraine, 'Transitional Justice: A Holistic Interpretation', *International Affairs* 60/1 (2006): 17–27.
2 D. Pankhurst, ed., *Gendered Peace: Women's Struggles for Post-War Justice and Reconciliation*. London: Routledge, 2008.

* * * *

Transitional Justice: The Emergence of a Paradigm

The concept of transitional justice stems from the international human rights movement. At first, it referred to the judicial process of addressing human rights violations committed by dictatorial or repressive regimes in the course of democratic transition. Later on, the term also came to be used for processing war crimes and massive human rights abuses committed in violent conflicts (Kritz 1995; Minow 1998, 2002; Teitel 2000). The concept has increasingly gained in importance, and has been widely discussed by peacebuilding agencies engaged in war-torn societies during the past two decades. Along the way, it has gradually extended its meaning. Today it covers the establishment of tribunals, truth commissions, lustration of state administrations, settlement on reparations, and also political and societal initiatives devoted to fact-finding, reconciliation and cultures of remembrance.

2.1 Focus on accountability: international criminal justice and truth commissions

For a long time, the TJ literature has principally been the province of legal scholars, human rights activists and individuals who have served as judges, prosecutors or policy-makers in official capacities. Most attention has been given to the moral-philosophical and jurisprudential apects, and in particular to the institutional design and implementation of tribunals. International law experts have extensively published on the development, capacities and legal procedures of international, hybrid or domestic courts dealing with gross human rights violations. Many studies focus on the international courts that have been established to prosecute war crimes, such as the Tribunals for the former Yugoslavia, Rwanda, Sierra Leone and Lebanon, including the International Criminal Court (ICC).

As the International Criminal Tribunal for the former Yugoslavia (ICTY) represents the first court implemented under the auspices of the UN, much research has been focused on its relevance for international law and legal procedures. Many authors consider the ICTY to be an innovative tool in the context of civilising international relations. Analysis of its impact on the societies in question is not so abundant and very few empirical studies exist on these issues (Meernik 2005; Nettelfield 2006; Orentlicher 2008). The question of whether the ICTY has contributed to the "restoration of peace and reconciliation", as was stated in UN Resolution 1534 and promoted by high-ranking representatives of the Tribunal, is still the subject of controversy (Meernik 2003; Mertus 2004; Hazan 2006). This example illustrates both the variety of opinions on the potential and limits of prosecution by international criminal courts and the difficulty of assessing the impact of tribunals on war-torn societies (see Box 1).

Some scholars argue that the idea that the ICTY would contribute to reconciliation between former warring groups has proved unrealistic, and that expanding expectations beyond its legal mandate might "undermine the important contributions that international trials can make to post-conflict societies" (Fletcher/Weinstein 2004, 30). Moreover, it has become obvious that a final and comprehensive assessment can only be determined in the long run. As Pierre Hazan has outlined, the Nuremberg trials after World War II were regarded as victors' justice by part of the German population, and did not have an immediate effect in terms of initiating debates in the 1950s. But their archives became an important point of reference for the following generations 25 years later, and thus contributed to informing German society once initiatives for facing the past had begun to develop on a larger scale (Hazan 2007, 11).

A relevant part of the TJ literature has centred on the dichotomy of peace vs. justice and truth vs. justice (Thoms et al. 2008, 18–19; Biggar 2001). In the *peace vs. justice debate*, advocates of the legalist approach have emphasised criminal justice as a means to deter future human rights violations and to support peacebuilding. Another argument is that criminal justice will stigmatise the elites who perpetuate conflict, and help separate individual from collective guilt, breaking the cycle of violence (Minow 1998; Bell 2000). Sceptics doubt that criminal justice can achieve all of this. Some have criticised international criminal justice in particular and argued for domestic prosecutions based on the

Box 1 Ambivalent assessments – the International Criminal Tribunal for the former Yugoslavia (ICTY)

The ICTY, established in The Hague in 1993, has taken the lead in prosecuting war crimes and crimes against humanity and in documenting facts surrounding the recent wars in the Western Balkans. It has indicted 161 persons for serious violations of international humanitarian law committed in the territory of former Yugoslavia: 83 cases (117 accusations) have been concluded. To date, proceedings are ongoing against 44 accused and two suspects are still at large. Several cases have been referred to war crimes chambers at domestic courts (mostly to Bosnia-Herzegovina), and the ICTY and international donors have also set up capacity-building programmes for domestic judiciaries in the countries of former Yugoslavia. In order to establish closer cooperation with the societies in the region, the ICTY has set up regional offices in Sarajevo, Belgrade and Zagreb. However, the legitimacy of the Hague Tribunal is seen as controversial in the region itself. In particular, parts of the population in Serbia and the Bosnian Republika Srpska have regarded the ICTY from its outset as being biased – a kind of "justice of the victors" (although there is no evidence to support this view, as Meernik 2003 concludes), or at least as a distant mechanism imposed from the outside (Arzt 2006; Spoerri/Freyberg-Inan 2008; McMahon/ Forsythe 2008). There are controversial assessments of the reasons for the lack of acceptance and legitimacy granted to the ICTY. Distorted media reporting was an important factor for this dynamic (Sajkas 2007; Allcock 2009). However, other problems seem to be related to the Tribunal's own procedures, a lack of clarity regarding its purposes and the issue of communication between the ICTY and its local publics (Hodzic 2007; Mertus 2007). Trials and public declarations were published exclusively in English during the first years of the ICTY's existence. It was also argued that the ICTY lacked credibility, as NATO forces had not managed to detain some of the most high-profile accused (Kerr 2005, 325).

The Hague Tribunal has been accused by human rights and women's organisations of focusing too strongly or exclusively on the perpetrators and protecting their personal rights, thereby neglecting the needs of the victims. The lack of formal procedural law for victims and groups of victims came in for heavy criticism, as did the fact that those affected could only be heard as witnesses. The main problem highlighted was the use of Anglo-American legal traditions, such as the practice of cross-examination (Franke 2006, 818). There has also been criticism that the work of the Hague Tribunal is not complemented by mechanisms that would provide compensation for the victims. This deficit was raised in October 2009 by the president of the ICTY, Patrick Robinson, who suggested establishing a "claims commission", through which victims would be able to lodge compensation claims. Scholars' assessments of the Hague Tribunal's impact on the respective societies are equally ambivalent. It has been argued that the Tribunal is an important motor for public discussions in the Western Balkans. Nevertheless, there are also clear indicators that it has fuelled nationalist discourses about the war (Allcock 2009, 367) and hostilities in local communities. James Meernik has analysed the dynamics of conflict and cooperation among the principal ethnic groups in Bosnia-Herzegovina based on aggregated, statistical data from 1996–2003 and found little evidence to support the notion that the ICTY was having a positive impact on societal peace in Bosnia: "In fact, in more instances the effect was the opposite of that intended [...]. More often than not, ethnic groups responded with increased hostility towards one another after an arrest or judgement" (Meernik 2005, 287). At the same time, it is also widely acknowledged that the ICTY has helped to set up important archives of facts about the massacres and atrocities.

conviction that justice should follow rather than precede the consolidation of peace. In earlier debates bargains and amnesties, rather than prosecutions, were often seen as the best ways to achieve peace because of the need to contain 'spoilers' in many post-conflict regions. Since then, most advocates of transitional justice have come to reject the idea of impunity and emphasise that amnesties, if applied at all, should be introduced as partial and conditional (Hayner 2009).

The *truth vs. justice debate* has balanced the merits of trials against other accountability mechanisms. The 1990s in particular were marked by this dichotomy, due to the almost simultaneous creation of the South African Truth and Reconciliation Commission (TRC) and the ICTY, which became emblematic of this discussion (Hazan 2006, 20). Truth commissions have been promoted as alternatives to prosecutions and as important mechanisms for counteracting cultures of denial. It has been argued that public and official exposure of truth provides redress for victims and may contribute to individual and social healing and reconciliation (Hayner 1994, 2001). Divided societies in particular need truth-seeking and truth-telling mechanisms. Given that nationalist myth-making, based on historical distortion, has fuelled both interstate and intrastate wars, efforts to prevent the instrumentalisation of facts and history are needed to prevent a return to violent conflict (Mendeloff 2004, 356–357). Especially after violent conflicts between ethnic and religious groups, who remain living next to each other while maintaining their distinct identities, extremists are eager to tie responsibility for past crimes and human rights violations to their ethnic or religious adversaries. In order to counteract such tendencies, a truth commission is considered as a means "to engage and confront all of society in a painful national dialogue, with serious soul-searching, and attempt to look at the ills within society that make abuses possible"; furthermore "civil society produces a sense of public ownership in this process, so that this dialogue actually leads to something. Otherwise, a country has merely a nice history lesson, destined for the bookshelf" (Kritz 2009, 18). An important policy recommendation stems from these reflections, arguing that truth and reconciliation commissions should be established "only where…a robust civil society remains intact. Where such conditions do not exist, the commission's mandate should be narrowly focused on documenting the truth along the lines of some earlier commissions rather than on the broader reconciliation goals established more recently. In a context that lacks a civil society altogether, a more top-down approach may be appropriate" (ibid.). However, research on truth commissions has also revealed enormous shortcomings and it has become clear that – apart from a strong civil society – there is a need for reliable alliance partners in parliaments, governments and administrations who are willing to engage in institutional reforms and establish the rule of law.

In the 1990s, overly high expectations were raised regarding the potential that truth commissions may have. Having seen the early truth commissions in Latin America as major advances in terms of accountability, the human rights community has meanwhile come to view these instruments much more sceptically. An important aspect of this disillusionment was the "enormous chasm" between the commissions' mandates to develop detailed recommendations on societal reforms and the non-implementation of these proposals by the governments that received them. It has therefore been recommended that international donors might think about strategies of tying aid to the implementation of truth commission recommendations (Kritz 2009, 17; Laplante 2008). Clear warnings have also been expressed that establishing truth commissions has become an almost routine and standard practice without analysing the context. It seems that many countries in transition decide to have truth commissions without any clear understanding of what such endeavours are about, and these policy decisions are "usually based not on research but on instinct" (Kritz 2009, 17). Disillusionment about truth commissions has contributed to broadening the discourse and to overcoming the fixation on dichotomies between "truth vs. justice" or "justice vs. peace" [see also Michelle Parlevliet in this volume].

2.2 *The call for a holistic interpretation: focusing on different levels and dimensions and addressing gender justice*

As the discourse has moved on, many more authors agree that societies recovering from oppression or violent conflict need both legal and restorative approaches, addressing different levels and dimensions of truth and justice. Alexander Boraine (former member of the South African TRC and founder of the International Center for Transitional Justice, ICTJ) has made an important contribution to this discussion by suggesting that retributive justice should be complemented with restorative justice. He strongly advocates a holistic interpretation based on five key pillars, including accountability, truth recovery, reparations, institutional reform and reconciliation (Boraine 2006, 19–25).

Accountability derives from the fact that no society can claim to be free or democratic without strict adherence to the rule of law; there are mass atrocities and crimes that have been so devastating that civilisation cannot tolerate their being ignored. Yet in cases of large-scale human rights violations such as in the former Yugoslavia, Rwanda or Sierra Leone, it is impossible to prosecute everyone. Given the limits to the law and prosecution, and although criminal justice is important, additional activities are needed that focus on documenting the truth about the past. Within *truth recovery*, four different notions are covered: objective or forensic truth (evidence and facts about human rights violations and missing persons), narrative truth (storytelling by victims and perpetrators and communicating personal truths and multi-layered experiences to a wider public), social or dialogical truth (truth of experience that is established by interaction, discussion and debate) and healing or restorative truth (documentation of facts and acknowledgement to give dignity to the victims and survivors). *Reparations* play an important role, as they belong to the few efforts undertaken directly on behalf of the victims. Nevertheless, reparations need to be closely connected to other processes aiming at documenting and acknowledging truth; otherwise they could be interpreted as being insincere. *Institutional reforms* form a prerequisite for truth and reconciliation. There has been criticism that in many cases truth commissions have chosen to focus almost entirely on individual hearings. Instead, Boraine argues, they need to focus on institutional settings in order to call to account those institutions directly responsible for the breakdown of a state, repression or human rights violations.

Reconciliation must be accompanied by acknowledgement of the past, the acceptance of responsibility and steps towards (re-)building trust. It is a long-term process and identifying suitable starting points depends on the specific situation in a society. Although the concept is ambivalent (and regarded with scepticism, due to its Christian connotation), Boraine sees a need to achieve "at least a measure of reconciliation" in a deeply divided society by creating a "common memory that can be acknowledged by those who created and implemented an unjust system, those who fought against it, and the many more who were in the middle and claimed not to know what was happening in their country" (Boraine 2006, 22).

Combining retributive and restorative elements sounds convincing, however, developing a holistic approach requires us furthermore to apply a "gender lens". The ICTJ has, therefore, added gender justice to its agenda, alongside criminal prosecutions, truth commissions, reparations programmes, security system reform and memorialisation efforts.

Given the experience of the systematic rape of women as part of warfare in the Balkans and other regions, researchers and women's rights activists have documented gender-specific violence and pushed forward the debate on gender-specific war crimes (Allen 1996; Kohn 1995; Korac 1994; Stiglmayer 1992). Researchers, human rights and peace activists have argued that a better understanding of gender, culture and power structures is needed to appropriately analyse the causes, dynamics and consequences of conflict and violence (Jalusic 2004; Slapsak 2000, 2004; Zarkov 1995; Djuric-Kuzmanovic et al. 2008).

Feminist research has also increasingly focused on transitional justice (Pankhurst 2008) and revealed that, as a consequence of campaigns to end impunity for violence against women, legal standards have been modified. Gender-based violence in armed conflict has been recognised as a war crime in international law and prosecutions have been secured. Furthermore, courtroom procedures have been reformed in order to ensure that victims of sexual violence are not re-traumatised by adversarial legal processes. The ICTY, for instance, has introduced changes to the procedures of investigation and to the rules regarding evidence, limiting the extent to which consent can be presented as a defence for sexual assault and prohibiting the use of evidence of a victim's past sexual conduct (Bell/O'Rourke 2007, 27). Following criticism of gaps in ICTY practice, women's organisations' appeals to respect the rights, needs and inclusion of victims were taken into account when the International Tribunal for Lebanon and the International Criminal Court were set up, and these courts have introduced procedural law for victims. There is now also greater representation of women on the staff of the international tribunals. However, in feminist debates several scholars have questioned whether punitive justice in the form of tribunals is an appropriate means of dealing with gender-based violence at all, due to the negative experiences of adversarial processes (Mertus 2004; Campbell 2004; O'Connell 2005). The feminist discourse has argued that truth commissions offer space "to move beyond the rather masculine discourse of crime and punishment towards a notion of repairing relationships" (Bell/O'Rourke 2007, 40). Truth commissions might also be a better alternative to trials as they give space to individual narratives, can address needs for public acknowledgement and seem to be more accessible to women due to the greater flexibility of their processes (Ni Aolain/Turner 2007).

Some commissions, indeed, have also responded to the need to find appropriate ways of addressing gender-based violence. In Haiti, Sierra Leone and East Timor, gender or sexual violence was explicitly incorporated into the mandates; other commissions have held gender hearings (South Africa) or established gender units (Peru). However, it has also been argued that placing emphasis on post-conflict restoration or calls for reconciliation without challenging uneven gender power relations can contribute to women losing equality gains that they made through the war and subordinating them in unjust relationships. Christine Bell and Catherine O'Rourke have therefore suggested analysing the gender implications of TJ mechanisms and discussing these in terms of their value for a larger political project of securing substantial material gains for women in transitional processes (2007, 44). The International Center for Transitional Justice (ICTJ) calls for increased consultation of women in the design of TJ mechanisms, in order to make sure that these mechanisms strengthen women in independent roles and to enable them to participate in the political transformation process. It makes a strong case for structuring post-war societal programmes, especially programmes of compensation, in a gender-sensitive way. The British NGO International Alert has also adopted the term gender justice in its "Women Building Peace" campaign, begun in 2004. Some international peace and human rights organisations insist that development cooperation measures must recognise gender justice as being an integral part of social justice (Barth et al. 2004). They argue that reconstruction programmes should be geared more towards the specific needs of women, and that demobilisation and reintegration initiatives for former combatants require particular attention to gender perspectives. Measures must be implemented together with local communities, including women, to avoid injustices and prevent those guilty of war crimes from going unpunished or otherwise benefiting from the situation (Farr 2003). For this not only runs counter to the principle of justice, but is also making processes of reconciliation more difficult.

References

Allcock, John B. 2009. The International Criminal Tribunal for the Former Yugoslavia, in: Charles Ingrao and Thomas A. Emmert (eds.). *Confronting the Yugoslav Controversies. A Scholars' Initiative.* West Lafayette, IN: Purdue University Press, 347–389.

Allen, Beverly 1996. *Rape Warfare. The Hidden Genocide in Bosnia-Herzegovina and Croatia.* Minneapolis: University of Minnesota Press.

Arzt, Donna E. 2006. Views on the Ground. The Local Perception of International Criminal Tribunals in the Former Yugoslavia and Sierra Leone, in: *Annals, American Academy of Political and Social Science,* 603, 226–239.

Barth, Elise Fredrikke, Karen Hostens and Inger Skjelsbæk 2004. *Gender Aspects of Conflict Interventions: Intended and Unintended Consequences.* Report to the Ministry of Foreign Affairs, Oslo.

Bell, Christine 2000. *Peace Agreements and Human Rights.* Oxford: Oxford University Press.

Bell, Christine and Catherine O'Rourke 2007. Does Feminism Need a Theory of Transitional Justice?, in: *International Journal of Transitional Justice* 1, 1, 23–44.

Biggar, Nigel (ed.) 2001. *Burying the Past. Making Peace and Doing Justice after Civil Conflict.* Washington DC: Georgetown University Press.

Boraine, Alexander 2006. Transitional Justice. A Holistic Interpretation, in: *Journal of International Affairs* 60, 1, 17–27.

Campbell, Kirsten 2004. The Trauma of Justice. Sexual Violence, Crimes against Humanity and the International Criminal Tribunal for the Former Yugoslavia, in: *Social and Legal Studies* 13, 3, 329–350.

Djuric-Kuzmanovic, Tanja, Rada Drezgic and Dubravka Zarkov 2008. Gendered War, Gendered Peace: Violent Conflicts in the Balkans and Their Consequences, in: Donna Pankhurst (ed.). *Gendered Peace. Women's Struggles for Post-War Justice and Reconciliation.* New York/London: Routledge, 265–291.

Farr, Vanessa 2003. The Importance of a Gender Perspective to Successful Disarmament, Demobilization and Reintegration Processes, in: *Disarmament Forum,* 4/2003, 25–36.

Fletcher, Laurel E. and Harvey M. Weinstein 2004. A World unto Itself? The Application of International Justice in Former Yugoslavia, in: Eric Stover and Harvey M. Weinstein (eds.). *My Neighbour, My Enemy. Justice and Community in the Aftermath of Mass Atrocity*. Cambridge, UK: Cambridge University Press, 29–48.

Franke, Katherine M. 2006. Gendered Subjects of Transitional Justice, in: *Columbia Journal of Gender and Law* 15, 3, 813–828.

Hayner, Priscilla 2009. *Negotiating Justice: Guidance for Mediators*. Geneva: Humanitarian Dialogue Centre. Available at www.hdcentre.org/files/negotiating%20justice%20report.pdf.

Hayner, Priscilla 1994. Fifteen Truth Commissions – 1974–1994: A Comparative Study, in: *Human Rights Quarterly* 16, 4, 597–655.

Hazan, Pierre 2007. Das neue Mantra der Gerechtigkeit. Vom beschränkten Erfolg international verordneter Vergangenheitsbewältigung, in: *Der Überblick* 43, 1–2, 10–22.

Hazan, Pierre 2006. Measuring the Impact of Punishment and Forgiveness. A Framework for Evaluating Transitional Justice, in: *International Review of the Red Cross* 88, 861, 19–47.

Hodzic, Refik 2007. *Bosnia and Herzegovina – Legitimacy in Transition*. Paper presented at the conference Building a Future on Peace and Justice, Nuremberg, 25–27 June 2007. Available at www.peace-justice-conference.info/download/Hodzic_Expert%20Paper.pdf.

Jalusic, Vlasta 2004. Gender and Victimization of the Nation as Pre- and Post-War Identity Discourse, in: Ruth Seifert (ed.). *Gender, Identität und kriegerischer Konflikt. Das Beispiel des ehemaligen Jugoslawien*. Münster: Lit-Verlag, 40–67.

Kerr, Rachel 2005. The Road from Dayton to Brussels? The ICTY and the Politics of War Crimes in Bosnia, in: *European Security* 14, 3, 319–337.

Kohn, Elizabeth 1995. Rape as a Weapon for War. Women's Human Rights during the Dissolution of Yugoslavia, in: *Golden Gate University Law Review* 25, 1, 199–221.

Korac, Maja 1994. Representation of Mass Rape in Ethnic Conflicts in What Was Yugoslavia, in: *Sociologija* 6, 4, 495–514.

Kritz, Neil J. 2009. Policy Implications of Empirical Research on Transitional Justice, in: Hugo van der Merwe, Victoria Baxter and Audrey R. Chapman (eds.). *Assessing the Impact of Transitional Justice. Challenges for Empirical Research*. Washington DC: USIP, 13–22.

Kritz, Neil J. (ed.) 1995. *Transitional Justice. How Emerging Democracies Reckon with Former Regimes*. 3 volumes. Washington DC: USIP.

Laplante, Lisa J. 2008. Transitional Justice and Peace Building: Diagnosing and Addressing Socioeconomic Roots of Violence through a Human Rights Framework, in: *International Journal of Transitional Justice* 2, 3, 331–355.

McMahon, Patrice C. and David P. Forsythe 2008. The ICTY's Impact on Serbia. Judicial Romanticism Meets Network Politics, in: *Human Rights Quarterly* 30, 2, 412–435.

Meernik, James 2005. Justice and Peace? How the International Criminal Tribunal Affects Societal Peace in Bosnia, in: *Journal of Peace Research* 43, 3, 271–287.

Meernik, James 2003. Victor's Justice or the Law? Judging and Punishing at the ICTY. in: *Journal of Conflict Resolution* 47, 2, 140–162.

Mendeloff, David 2004. Truth-Seeking, Truth-Telling, and Post-Conflict Peacebuilding. Curb the Enthusiasm?, in: *International Studies Review* 6, 3, 355–380.

Mertus, Julie 2007. Findings from Focus Group Research on Public Perceptions of the ICTY, in: *Südosteuropa* 55, 1, 107–117.

Mertus, Julie 2004. *Women's Participation in the International Criminal Tribunal for the Former Yugoslavia (ICTY). Transitional Justice for Bosnia and Herzegovina*. Cambridge, MA: Women Waging Peace Policy Commission.

Minow, Martha (ed.) 2002. *Breaking the Cycles of Hatred. Memory, Law and Repair*. Princeton, NJ: Princeton University Press.

Minow, Martha 1998. *Between Vengeance and Forgiveness. Facing History after Genocide and Mass Violence*. Boston: Beacon Press.

Nettelfield, Lara J. 2006. Courting Democracy. *The Hague Tribunal's Impact in Bosnia-Herzegovina*. Columbia University, New York. [PhD dissertation.]

Ni Aolain, Fionnuala and Catherine Turner 2007. Gender, Truth and Transition, in: *UCLA Women's Law Journal* 16, 229–279.

O'Connell, Jamie 2005. Gambling with the Psyche. Does Prosecuting Human Rights Violators Console their Victims?, in: *Harvard International Law Journal* 46, 2, 295–345.

Orentlicher, Diane 2008. *Shrinking the Space for Denial: The Impact of the ICTY in Serbia*. New York: Open Society Institute.

Pankhurst, Donna (ed.) 2008. *Gendered Peace. Women's Struggles for Post-War Justice and Reconciliation*. New York/London: Routledge.

Sajkas, Marija 2007. *Transitional Justice and the Role of the Media in the Balkans*. Discussion paper. New York: ICTJ. Available at www.ictj.org/images/content/8/3/833.pdf.

Slapsak, Svetlana 2000. *Women's Discourse / War Discourse. Essays and Case Studies from Yugoslavia and Russia*. Ljubljana: Topas & Graduate School of Humanities Ljubljana.

Slapsak, Svetlana 2004. Gender and War in the Post-Socialist World, in: Ruth Seifert (ed.). *Gender, Identität und kriegerischer Konflikt. Das Beispiel des ehemaligen Jugoslawien*. Münster: Lit-Verlag, 26–39.

Spoerri, Marlene and Annette Freyberg-Inan 2008. From Prosecution to Persecution. Perceptions of the International Criminal Tribunal for the Former Yugoslavia (ICTY) in Serbian Domestic Politics, in: *Journal of International Relations and Development* 11, 4, 350–384.

Stiglmayer, Alexandra (ed.) 1992. *Mass Rape. The War Against Women in Bosnia-Herzegovina*. Lincoln: University of Nebraska Press.

Teitel, Ruti G. 2000. *Transitional Justice*. New York: Oxford University Press.

Thoms, Oskar N. T., James Ron and Roland Paris 2008. The Effects of Transitional Justice Mechanisms. A Summary of Empirical Research Findings and Implications for Analysts and Practitioners. Working paper. Centre for International Policy Studies, University of Ottawa.

Zarkov, Dubravka 1995. Gender, Orientalism and Ethnic Hatred in Former Yugoslavia, in: Helma Lutz, Ann Phoenix and Nira Yuval-Davis (eds.). *Crossfires: Nationalism, Racism and Gender in Europe*. London: Pluto, 105–120.

61

Towards a Strategic Framework for Peacebuilding: Getting Their Act Together

Dan Smith

Dan Smith is Secretary-General of International Alert. In this short piece, reflecting on the recent track records of the British, Dutch, German and Norwegian governments in peacebuilding, Smith suggests that, rather than the usual image of a toolbox, it would be better to envisage the range of sectoral tasks facing postwar peacebuilders as a 'palette' of colours which need to be 'mixed' in appropriate ways. For example, the topic of Reading 60, 'transitional justice', comes in the fourth colour range (reconciliation and justice), whereas the topic of Reading 65, 'territorial self-governance', comes in the second colour range (political framework). These overlapping – and sometimes contradictory – sectoral tasks then have to be further related to the nature of the conflicts and the conflict phases in question – see Reading 62.

* * * *

3 Working in and on Conflict

Within the field of development cooperation, the options have been identified of working *around* conflict, *in* conflict and *on* conflict.[1] Peacebuilding always means working on conflict (i.e., targeting and attempting to remove the causes of armed conflict), and sometimes means working in conflict (i.e., implementing assistance programmes amidst conditions of armed conflict).

3.1 Assessing the context

How does the context of war – looming, current or recent – affect the development activities carried out for peacebuilding? A World Bank study sees civil war as "development in reverse."[2] Does this mean that peacebuilding is simply development going forward? Yes, but with this defining difference – the context of crisis and war.

The differences the context makes are many and fundamental, starting with the stakes and risks both for the beneficiaries and the personnel of peacebuilding. The aim of peacebuilding interventions is to save life, but interventions into crisis situations can and do also cost lives, often because aid ends up in the wrong hands. Even when this does not directly cost lives, it may hamper the work of peacebuilding. The diversion of funds by conflict parties – and the basic fact that, since conflict is about control of resources, the injection of resources into a conflict country inevitably means involvement in the conflict – was already highlighted in 1997 by the OECD DAC guidelines.[3] Even when misappropriation of funds is not part of the problem, peacebuilding assistance must be worked out in the knowledge that some of the standard operating procedures of development cooperation are inappropriate. The World Bank study argues that post-war development assistance needs to be calibrated differently from normal circumstances – "social policy is relatively more important and macroeconomic policy is relatively less important in post conflict situations".[4] Equally, it can be questioned whether it is right or possible to carry out programmes for private sector investment when there is no stable peace, which means instability in the operating environment and arbitrariness in the legal framework.

Thus, to say that peacebuilding is development in a war-defined context does not mean it is the same old development routine with marginal variations. The difference is fundamental and the logic of peacebuilding differs in important respects from the logic of development assistance.

3.2 The complexity of peacebuilding

Commenting on peacebuilding in Kosovo and East Timor, the most demanding peace operations the UN had ever taken on, the Brahimi report says,

> "These operations face challenges and responsibilities that are unique among United Nations field operations. No other operation must set and enforce the law, establish customs services and regulations, set and collect business and personal taxes, attract foreign investment, adjudicate property disputes and liabilities for war damage, reconstruct and operate all public utilities, create a banking system, run schools and pay teachers and collect the garbage – in a war-damaged society, using voluntary contributions, because the assessed mission budget, even for such "transitional administration" missions, does not fund local administration itself. In addition to such tasks, these missions must also try to rebuild civil society and promote respect for human rights, in places where grievance is widespread and grudges run deep."[5]

It is not clear that all those involved in peacebuilding projects always share this nuanced understanding of the demanding complexity of their tasks. Many international field staff are out of their depth, especially those on short-term secondments to IGOs. With six-month assignments, they may have only a brief period of effective work shortly before they leave. The experience for locals is often disillusioning and demoralising. There are, of course, many exceptions both in IGOs and NGOs – people who know more to begin with and stay for longer – but often their task is made more difficult by others who are less knowledgeable and leave quicker.

Another part of the problem is a failure to confront mentally the realities of the context. Consider the implications of the hypothesis put forward in an NGO publication: "Good peacebuilding is about being good human beings and embodying and reflecting personal and organizational integrity. The focus should be kept on one's own and others' humanity and the partnerships, relationships and trust that are central to this work."[6]

Perhaps if the statement were more qualified ("One focus," for example, rather than "The focus") it would work better. It is a good thought about good peacebuilding yet somehow ignores elements such as greed, rapacity, deceit and hunger for power, which are part of the contextual reality and part of the reason that a peacebuilding intervention is necessary.

The problem seems to be an approach that is shaped by the idea of serving beneficiaries, focusing on those who have suffered, and assuming that those who have suffered are both needy and deserving. These concerns have to be balanced by recognising that some people perpetrated the violence from which others suffered, that they are still around, may not reveal themselves, and may try to get their hands on some of the aid – and that some who suffered were also perpetrators and likely to be part of the problem, not the solution.

3.3 Local ownership

In similar vein, Jan Egeland, former State Secretary in the Ministry of Foreign Affairs in Norway, warns of the need for hard-headedness among peacemakers and peacebuilders:

> "A third party should not naively believe the stated intentions of the leaders involved. In the ten conflict resolution efforts in which I have been involved, *all* the leaders at all times claimed their goal was "to end the suffering of our peoples." In reality, there were always influential political, military, or economic warlords who had their personal and professional interests tied to continued conflict."[7]

This must place some question marks around local ownership, which is now an axiomatic goal in development cooperation, including among the *Utstein* group as reflected in its statement of principles. A failure to recognise the reality of the conflict context might make a simple commitment to local ownership almost fatal to hopes of successful peacebuilding. This is true not only of the governments of partner countries, which are likely themselves to be conflict parties, but also of local project partners. There needs to be very careful research about the identity and background of project partners, and recognition that it will be best to attempt to increase the degree of local ownership slowly and carefully as experience offers a growing basis of trust. Otherwise, local ownership risks being a code for working with the most powerful and most opportunistic sectors of society. The lines of division that led to conflict escalation normally survive the peace process: if war is continuation of politics by other means, peace is generally the resumption of the same politics, often by the same pre-war means. Groups with the capacity to own projects are usually connected to those political divisions or active parts of them. For donors, in short, devotion to local ownership needs to be nuanced by attention to local realities.

3.4 The peacebuilding palette

To help develop the structural conditions, attitudes and modes of political behaviour that may permit peaceful, stable and prosperous social and economic development, peacebuilding uses a wide range of policy instruments. Some of these instruments are activities undertaken as projects – discreet, chronologically limited activities, implemented by partner organisations; there are other policy instruments, including diplomatic initiatives and military operations.

The survey looked at project activities under four headings – security, establishing the socioeconomic foundations, establishing the political framework, and generating reconciliation, a healing of the wounds of war and justice. Figure 1 sets out the types of activities of peacebuilding under these four general headings.[8]

It is common to refer to these policy instruments as "tools" and to the full range of them as a "toolbox."[9] The point of this terminology is to emphasise that the policy actor makes a selection of which policy instruments to use and how to use them – just as if fixing a car. For those who understand internal combustion, the metaphor emphasises

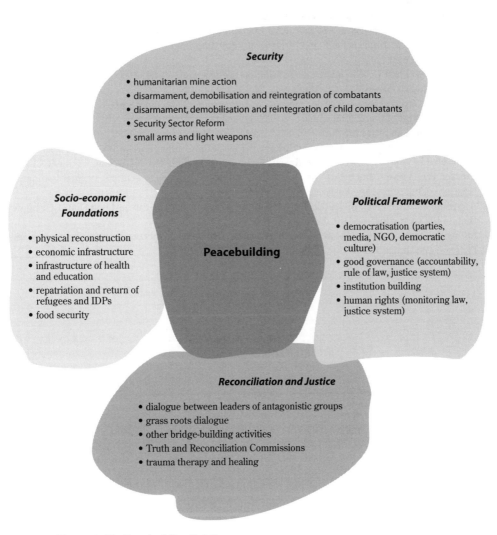

Security

- humanitarian mine action
- disarmament, demobilisation and reintegration of combatants
- disarmament, demobilisation and reintegration of child combatants
- Security Sector Reform
- small arms and light weapons

Socio-economic Foundations

- physical reconstruction
- economic infrastructure
- infrastructure of health and education
- repatriation and return of refugees and IDPs
- food security

Peacebuilding

Political Framework

- democratisation (parties, media, NGO, democratic culture)
- good governance (accountability, rule of law, justice system)
- institution building
- human rights (monitoring law, justice system)

Reconciliation and Justice

- dialogue between leaders of antagonistic groups
- grass roots dialogue
- other bridge-building activities
- Truth and Reconciliation Commissions
- trauma therapy and healing

Figure 1 *The Peacebuilding Palette*

the inter-linkages and inter-dependence between the different elements in the process – the importance of the harmonious working of the different components in the machine. The interplay between the different elements of peacebuilding, however, both goes beyond the purely mechanical and is harder to predict than the toolbox metaphor implies. Moreover, the possibilities for optimising and multiplying the effect by combining different kinds of activities are richer and more varied. Accordingly, the term "palette" is preferred here, because one of the interesting things about peacebuilding "tools" is that they can be combined together in ways that are specific to the country, region and conflict in question, for greater effect – like mixing paints.

Notes

1. Jonathan Goodhand, *Violent Conflict, Poverty and Chronic Poverty*, CPRC Working Paper 6 (Manchester, Chronic Poverty Research Centre, May 2001) pp. 5 and 30–3.
2. Paul Collier, VL Elliott, Håvard Hegre, Anke Hoeffler, Marte Reynal-Querol and Nicholas Sambanis, *Breaking the Conflict Trap: Civil War and Development Policy* (Washington, DC, World Bank & Oxford University Press, 2003).
3. "Conflict, Peace and Development Co-operation on the Threshold of the 21st Century, 1997," *The DAC Guidelines: Helping Prevent Violent Conflict* (Paris, OECD, 2001) p.109.
4. Collier et al, *Breaking the Conflict Trap: Civil War and Development Policy*, pp. 154–5.
5. *Report of the Panel on United Nations Peace Operations*, para 77.
6. Anneke Galama and Paul van Tongeren, eds, *Towards better Peacebuilding Practice: On Lessons Learned, Evaluation Practices and Aid & Conflict* (Utrecht, European Centre for Conflict Prevention, 2002) p.23.
7. Jan Egeland, "The Oslo Accord: Multiparty Facilitation through the Norwegian Channel," in CA Crocker, FO Hampson and P Aall, eds, *Herding cats: Multiparty Mediation in a Complex World* (Washington, DC, United States Institute for Peace, 1999) p.544.
8. As a result of the research in the project surveys, the number of activity categories in Figure 2 is higher than in the survey instructions in Annex 3.
9. Influential in setting this fashion was Michael S Lund, *Preventing Violent Conflicts: A Strategy for Preventive Diplomacy* (Washington, DC, United States Institute for Peace, 1996).

62

The Potential Complementarity of Mediation and Consultation within a Contingency Model of Third-Party Intervention

Ronald Fisher and Loraleigh Keashly

This article by Ronald Fisher, Professor of International Peace and Conflict Resolution, American University, Washington, DC, and Loraleigh Keashly, Associate Professor, Department of Communication, Wayne State University, Michigan, is a classic text in the conflict resolution field. It established the conceptual framework for relating different types of third-party intervention to the nature and phases of the conflicts in question. 'Contingency' refers to the aim of fitting different types of intervention to different aspects of the conflict situation. 'Complementarity' refers to the importance of seeing that these different types of intervention are mutually reinforcing and do not duplicate each other. Fisher and Keashley's model applies to all levels of conflict. But at the level of the large-scale international peacebuilding interventions ('peace operations') that are the main topic of this reading, this evidently makes very heavy demands on the numerous, highly diverse agencies involved, as noted in the introduction to this part.

*　　*　　*　　*

Drawing on these various contributions, particularly the work of Glasl, it is possible to develop a stage model of conflict escalation which will serve as the prerequisite to the contingency model of third party intervention. The present stage model identifies four stages of conflict escalation: (1) Discussion, (2) Polarization, (3) Segregation, and (4) Destruction. The stages are distinguished by significant changes in the nature of communication between the parties, their perceptions and images of each other and their relationship, the overt issues at the fore of the dispute, the perceived possible outcomes and the preferred strategy for handling the conflict. Described in these terms, the reverse order of the stages provides for the occurrence of de-escalation, although other elements specific to de-escalation may need to be added for a fully comprehensive description. Briefly, as intergroup and international conflict escalates, communication and interaction move from discussion and debate (Stage 1) to a reliance on the interpretation (often the misinterpretation) of actions with less direct interchange (2), to the use of threats

(3), and finally to an absence of direct communication combined with attacks of violence on the adversary (4). With respect to perceptions and images, these change from being relatively accurate, or at least benign (l), to rigid and simplified negative stereotypes (2) which become cast in terms of good versus evil (3), to an ultimate view of the other party as non-human (4). Concurrently, the relationship moves from one of trust, respect and commitment (l), to one wherein the other party is still seen as important in its own right (2), to one of mistrust and disrespect (3), to one of complete hopelessness in terms of any possible improvements (4). In terms of issues fuelling the conflict, the emphasis shifts from substantive interests and related positions (l), to concerns regarding the relationship (2), to fundamental needs or core values such as identity and security (3), to the question of the ultimate survival of one or both parties (4). In concert with these changes, the perceived possible outcomes begin with joint gain or win-win options (l), move to mutual compromise (2), then to win-lose possibilities (3), and finally to lose-lose alternatives wherein the objective is to minimize one's own losses while inflicting maximum costs on the other party (4). In attempting to achieve these kinds of outcomes, the parties' preferred methods on conflict management shift from joint decision-making (l), to negotiation (2), to defensive competition (3), to outright attempts at destruction (4).

To the extent that this stage model represents a valid, albeit simplified, picture of the escalation process, it is immediately apparent that different management or intervention strategies would be appropriate and effective at different points. In fact, it is likely that one of the reasons for the 'failure' of particular interventions in particular conflicts may be inappropriate application with regard to the stage of escalation. Given that most intervenors rely predominantly or solely on one type of intervention and attempt to apply it to a variety of conflicts at different stages of escalation, it is not surprising that frustration and failure are often the result. An additional reason for failure in the longer term may be the lack of coordinated follow-up interventions to deal with elements not addressed by the initial intervention.

The overall strategy of the contingency approach is to intervene with the appropriate third party method at the appropriate time in order to de-escalate the conflict back down through the stages identified above. This is potentially accomplished by initially matching a particular intervention to a specific stage and then by combining further interventions, if necessary, in appropriate sequences to further de-escalate the conflict. The initial contingency model which relates the stage of conflict to the prescribed intervention sequence is given in Figure 1.

In stage 1, the key dimension of concern is the quality of communication between the parties, since the relationship is still in relatively good shape in terms of trust and commitment and perceptions and images are relatively accurate and positive. The primary issues derive from substantive concern and the parties believe that joint gain is possible. However, for whatever reasons, communication difficulties may occur as the interaction moves from discussion to a debate involving adversarial behaviour. Particularly if the parties are having difficulty talking constructively or directly about the issues in dispute, the intervention of a third party might be useful. The prescribed intervention would be that of conciliation, in order to facilitate clear and open communication on interests and related positions. The hope would be that this would clear the way toward direct

Intervention Sequence

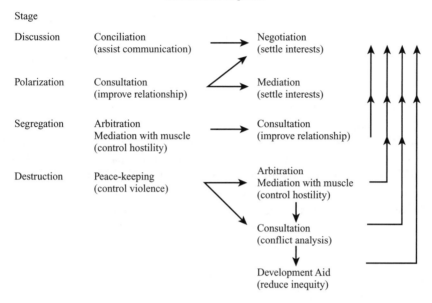

Reprinted by permission of Fisher & Keashly (1990), p. 237

Figure 1 *A Contingency Model of Third Party Intervention*

negotiations between the parties which would settle the dispute before any damage was done to the underlying relationship.

In the second stage of conflict escalation, relationship issues become the focus of concern as trust and respect are threatened and distorted perceptions and simplified images in the form of negative stereotypes begin to emerge. At this point, consultation is the most appropriate intervention, since it uniquely deals with relationship issues such as mistrust, distorted perceptions and negative attitudes. Once these issues are addressed and a cooperative relationship is established or re-established, the parties are in a more efficacious position to handle the substantive issues in the dispute. Thus, consultation could pave the way for direct negotiation between the parties. However, given that the particular substantive issues led to escalation of the conflict in the first instance, it is likely that they are contentious and difficult and not readily settled by direct negotiation. It is in this instance that mediation in its pure form becomes the preferred third party intervention to follow consultation. Rather than having to work around relationship issues, as is typical in mediation practice, the mediator would be in the relatively advantageous position of focusing on substantive issues without the typical interference of distorted perceptions, negative attitudes, considerable mistrust, and so on. It is of course also possible that successful mediation may restore trust, build more positive attitudes, and improve other important qualities of the relationship. It should be noted, however, that there is very little empirical evidence for the positive influence of successful mediation on relationship variables, and in fact some recent evidence from a complex laboratory simulation of intergroup conflict indicates that mediation does not have these effects (Keashly et al., 1989).

Thus, the first point of potential complementarity between consultation and mediation is that the former may be able to serve a very useful 'pre-mediation' function. This is similar to the emerging realization that problem-solving workshops may be able to serve as an important technology in the pre-negotiation phase of conflict management (Fisher, 1989). This linkage is provided for in the contingency model where consultation is successfully followed by direct negotiation between the parties (see Figure 1).

Pre-negotiation as an emerging focus in the study of international conflict management is defined as the process which begins when one or more parties considers negotiation as an option and communicates this intention to other parties; pre-negotiation ends when one party abandons negotiation as a policy option or when the parties agree to formal negotiations (Stein, 1989). In addition to providing a constructive forum to work on relationship issues, consultation in the form of problem-solving workshops provides the parties with a low risk opportunity to evaluate the feasibility of and to create a conducive atmosphere for negotiations as well as establishing a framework for negotiations (Kelman & Cohen, 1986).

In recent work on a prescriptive theory of pre-negotiation, Rothman (1989) identifies three stages of pre-negotiation: the diagnostic, the procedural and agenda setting. In the diagnostic phase, parties are encouraged to jointly articulate their underlying concerns (such as basic needs for security, identity and so on) along with the substantive issues (such as territory, economic resources, and so on) in order to move toward a shared definition and analysis of the conflict. The procedural phase then provides a bridge for moving these two sets of issues into the agenda-setting process. The third party intervention appropriate to the diagnostic phase of pre-negotiation is that of consultation, again primarily in the form of problem-solving workshops. Indeed, linking consultation to negotiation in this direct manner may help overcome one of the central issues in consultation, that of transferring the effects of workshops back to the decision-making process, in this case, that of negotiation.

To return to the contingency model, the prescription is that consultation has a useful role to play during 'pre-mediation' in which the parties are going through a decision-making process very similar to that of pre-negotiation. Used in this way, consultation would allow the parties to work on relationship issues (that are not the focus in mediation) and would provide the parties with a low risk forum in which to consider the merits of and the potential agenda for mediation. The desired outcome would be that mediation would have a much greater chance of success if the parties chose to move in that direction. It is apparent that this scenario is at odds with existing practice and reality in contemporary conflict management, where consultation is not readily available and not seriously considered by parties to disputes. Mediation is typically the third party intervention of choice when the parties have exhausted the possibilities of negotiation as well as themselves. Unfortunately, this may be one of the prime reasons why mediation is as likely to fail as to succeed – the relationship between the parties has deteriorated significantly, interests are often interfused with needs and appear non-negotiable, and the respective positions have become intransigent through a series of past commitments. By suggesting consultation as the lead intervention in moderately escalated conflict, the contingency model may provide an avenue for significantly increasing the success rate of mediation. This form of 'preventative consultation' has occurred at times in industrial relations (e.g. Birnbaum, 1984; Brett et al., 1980), but appears to occur only informally and partially, if at all, in international relations. The appeal of utilizing consultation in this manner is that it may prevent the conflict from escalating further and rendering future efforts at resolution, including third party interventions, much more difficult. In line with the contingency model, successful mediation would then de-escalate the conflict back down to stage one, wherein the parties could handle future disputes through bilateral interaction.

In the third stage of conflict escalation, defensive competition and hostility become main themes. More importantly, the conflict is now seen as threatening basic needs such as those for security and identity. Therefore, some form of immediate control is necessary to halt the spiral and to show the parties that agreement is still possible on substantive issues. Thus, in situations where it is appropriate, arbitration would be the third party intervention of choice. A second alternative, which can be seen as midway between arbitration and pure mediation, is mediation with muscle or power mediation. In this form of intervention, the third party has 'muscle' (Stein, 1985) or 'leverage' (Touval & Zartman, 1985), that is, the power to influence the parties toward agreement through inducing costs, present or future, or providing positive inducements such as military or development aid. The result of this power is that the mediator is able to go beyond persuasion to coerce the parties toward a settlement that will temporarily halt the escalatory spiral. This creates the second point of complementarity between mediation and consultation, in that the latter intervention could immediately be used to improve the relationship between the parties and de-escalate the conflict to stage 2 (where pure mediation could be instituted to deal with further substantive issues – the first point of complementarity noted above) or to stage 1 (where the parties could negotiate directly – the pre-negotiation function of consultation). Thus, consultation, typically in the form of problem-solving workshops, could serve as a potential follow-up intervention to power mediation, rather than assuming that settlement of substantive issues will by itself improve the relationship between the parties.

In the fourth stage, the conflict has escalated to the point where the parties attempt to destroy each other through the use of various forms of violence, expressed as war at the international level. The third party strategy of choice at this point is that of peacekeeping, a power intervention designed to assist in the separation of the parties and the control of violence. This pacific and impartial intervention typically follows a diplomatic agreement on a ceasefire, and provides for the monitoring of the ceasefire and the restoration of some normalcy of living by forces under the control of the third party, most commonly the United Nations. When the interaction between the parties can be stabilized and some initial commitment to joint effort can be obtained, the path is cleared for other third party interventions, depending on the receptivity of the parties and their sense of the critical issues. In line with other elements of the contingency model, the first possibility is that arbitration or mediation with muscle might be implemented to further control hostility and demonstrate that at least a partial agreement is possible. As in stage three, this could be followed by consultation to improve the relationship, but more broadly to provide a full analysis of the conflict and its escalation. This recognizes that it will be more difficult to de-escalate the conflict from stage four than stage three, and therefore a more intensive and comprehensive problem-solving effort will be required. It is also conceivable that this form of consultation could follow peace-keeping directly in order to identify key elements and issues in the conflict, some of which might be handled by pure mediation and some of which by continuing consultation. Finally, the provision of development aid by third parties could be one outcome of consultation. This form of intervention could be designed to deal with the structural inequalities that are often part and parcel of protracted intercommunal and international conflict. The need and focus for such efforts would be identified in the consultation process through dealing with basic needs relating to equality and justice. Thus, combined efforts on a number of fronts would be required to eventually de-escalate a stage four conflict back down to a manageable and productive relationship. The role and utility of third party interventions in this process could be maximized through the matching, coordination and sequencing envisaged in the contingency model.

References

Birnbaum, Robert, 1984. 'The Effects of a Neutral Third Party on Academic Bargaining Relationships and Campus Climate', *Journal of Higher Education*, vol. 55, no. 6, pp. 719–734.

Brett, Jeanne M.; Steven B. Goldberg & William Ury, 1980. 'Mediation and Organization Development', pp. 195–202, *Proceedings of the Thirty-Third Annual Meeting of the Industrial Relations Association*. Madison, WI: Industrial Relations Research Associates.

Fisher, Ronald J., 1989. 'Pre-negotiation Problem-solving Discussions: Enhancing the Potential for Successful Negotiation', *International Journal*, vol. 64, Spring, pp. 442–474.

Fisher, Ronald J. & Loraleigh Keashly, 1990. 'Third Party Consultation as a Method of Intergroup and International Conflict Resolution', pp. 211–238 in Ronald J. Fisher, *The Social Psychology of Intergroup and International Conflict Resolution*. New York: Springer.

Keashly, Loraleigh, Ronald J. Fisher & Peter R. Grant, 1989. 'The Comparative Effectiveness of Third Party Consultation versus Mediation within a Complex Simulation of Intergroup Conflict', manuscript under review.

Keashly, Loraleigh & Ronald J. Fisher, 1989. *Toward a Contingency Approach to Third Party Intervention in Regional Conflict*. Paper presented at the Conference on Managing Regional Conflict: Regimes and Third Party Mediators, Canadian Institute for International Peace and Security, Ottawa, Canada, January.

Kelman, Herbert C. & Stephen P. Cohen, 1986. 'Resolution of International Conflict: An Interactional Approach', pp. 323–342 in Stephen Worchel & William G. Austin, eds, *The Psychology of Intergroup Relations*. Second ed. Chicago, IL: Nelson-Hall.

Rothman, Jay, 1989. 'Developing Pre-negotiation Theory and Practice', Policy Studies, no. 29. The Hebrew University of Jerusalem: The Leonard Davis Institute for International Relations.

Stein, Janice Gross, 1985. 'Structures, Strategies and Tactics of Mediation: Kissinger and Carter in the Middle East', *Negotiation Journal*, vol. 1, no. 4, October, pp. 331–347.

Stein, Janice Gross, ed., 1989. *Getting to the Table: The Processes of International Prenegotiation*. Baltimore, MD: Johns Hopkins University Press.

Touval, Saadia & I. William Zartman, eds., 1985. *International Mediation in Theory and Practice*. Boulder, CO: Westview.

63

Code of Conduct for Conflict Transformation

International Alert

International Alert was set up in 1985 as a nongovernmental organization committed to 'the just and peaceful transformation of violent conflict', and is taken here as representative of conflict resolution NGOs in general. The Guiding Principles included in this reading come from the 1998 International Alert Code of Conduct, described as an 'ethical framework' for conflict transformation interventions. As a result of constant self-examination under these guiding principles, the organization hopes to be able to continue to adapt creatively and ethically in the light of 'lessons learned' and 'experience acquired'. Also included here is further guidance on the key issue of impartiality. Readers may like to consider the relationship between self-descriptions of impartiality by interveners of this kind, and how these are likely to be viewed by different conflict parties at various times in the crucible of intense political conflict.

* * * *

Guiding Principles for Conflict Transformation Work

A. Principles

1. **Primacy of People in Transforming Conflicts**
   We believe that genuine conflict transformation is only possible with the participation and involvement of those most affected by the conflict.

2. **Humanitarian Concern**
   Our primary motivation is the alleviation of human suffering and our engagement in situations of violent conflict is driven principally by concern for the societies and peoples at risk from such conflicts.

3. **Human Rights and Humanitarian Law & Principles**
   We are committed to the principle and practice of promoting human rights in our work in situations of violent internal conflict. We urge compliance with international humanitarian law & principles and respect for human rights amongst all parties to the conflict.

4. **Respect for Gender and Cultural Diversity**

   We respect the dignity and cultural diversity of all peoples and we make no discrimination on grounds of nationality, race, class or gender or religious, cultural or political beliefs. We recognise and endeavour to build upon the capacities of people to resolve their own conflicts and we support the distinctive peacemaking roles of women in societies affected by violent conflict.

5. **Impartiality**

   We endeavour to be inclusive in our work, seeking access to the relevant parties to the conflict. We do not take sides in conflicts and we derive guidance from our adherence to the principles outlined in this Code which we strive to advance in appropriate ways at all times.

6. **Independence**

   We are an independent organisation, free to formulate policies and operational strategies in accordance with our legally registered aims and the principles expressed in this Code.

7. **Accountability**

   We are morally responsible to those whom we seek to assist and accountable to those with whom we work. We are bound by UK Charity Law through our trustees and accountable through regular reporting mechanisms to our donors. As a means of enhancing accountability, we endeavour to be open and transparent in our work.

8. **Confidentiality**

   Whilst endeavouring to be open and transparent, we are committed to maintaining confidentiality in situations where the effectiveness of our programmes or the security of our staff and partners may be at risk. Furthermore, we believe that, in most cases, conflict transformation work is best done discreetly.

9. **Partnerships**

   We are committed to working in collaboration and complementarity with individuals, organisations, governments and other institutions which can contribute to the prevention and resolution of conflict. In particular, we believe sustainable conflict transformation is dependent upon effective co-operation with individuals and organisations within conflict-affected societies.

10. **Institutional Learning**

    We are committed to building up our collective pool of knowledge, institutional memory and experience through undertaking regular reviews and evaluations of our work and developing the skills of all our staff. Furthermore, we endeavour to share the lessons we learn with relevant individuals and organisations who may benefit from them and, in turn, learn from the experiences and knowledge of others.

B. Commentary

Peace is not merely the absence of war. In developing ways of contributing to the transformation of violent internal conflict, we are committed to pursuing a just and

lasting settlement through wholly peaceful means recognising that non-violent conflicts can be a constructive force for change. We work towards empowering people to make peace by supporting local efforts, helping to develop and strengthen local capacities and, more generally, building peace constituencies. Further, we seek to create spaces for dialogue at different levels and sectors within societies in conflict and work in collaboration and complementarity with organisations, governments and other institutions.

Ultimately, building sustainable peace involves transforming situations characterised by violence and fear, thereby creating an environment in which peace, respect for human rights and participative democracy can take root and where differences and disputes can be settled non-violently. The process towards a just peace requires sustainable reconciliation among the different parties to the conflict. Such a process demands time, patience and protracted engagement in efforts leading to constructive medium and long-term change.

1. **Primacy of People in Transforming Conflicts**

   We recognise the capacities of people to resolve their own conflicts and we believe that the people whom they affect should be the primary actors in, and the driving force behind, their successful transformation. Indeed, effective conflict transformation is only possible with the consent and participation of those most affected by the conflict and we are committed to strengthening the capacities of local actors and organisations to contribute to peacemaking and peace-building within their societies.

2. **Humanitarian Concern**

   Our primary motivation is the alleviation of human suffering and our engagement in situations of violent conflict is driven principally by concern for the societies and peoples at risk from such conflicts. As part of the humanitarian and human rights community, we strive to protect the most fundamental human right of all – the right to life – by addressing the root causes of conflicts and contributing to their peaceful and just transformation.

3. **Human Rights and Humanitarian Law & Principles**

   We are committed to the principle and practice of promoting individual and collective human rights in our work in situations of violent internal conflict. The Universal Declaration of Human Rights serves as our basic frame of reference and we seek to promote the observance of the fundamental principles enshrined therein. Furthermore, we are committed to encouraging observance amongst all parties of minimum standards of human rights and humanitarian principles contained in Common Article 3 of the Geneva Conventions and Protocol II. We are committed to pressing for international human rights standards to be recognised and incorporated in settlement agreements and for the establishment and development of effective institutions for the protection, promotion and implementation of civil, political, economic, social and cultural rights. We are also committed to supporting measures which address the problems of impunity and injustice, historical truth and compensation for victims.

4. **Respect for Gender and Cultural Diversity**

We endeavour to respect the dignity and cultural diversity of all peoples and we make no discrimination on grounds of nationality, race, class, gender, or religious, cultural or political beliefs. Furthermore, in designing and implementing programmes and activities, we strive to ensure sensitivity to local cultures and respect for traditional methods and customs of conflict resolution as well as recognising the primacy of local actors in bringing about the transformation of the conflict.

We explicitly recognise the particular and distinctive peacemaking roles played by women in communities afflicted by violent conflict. We endeavour to ensure that this potential is supported not diminished by our programmes and we are committed to strengthening the capacities of women's organisations to contribute to sustainable peace.

5. **Impartiality**

The principle of impartiality is strictly adhered to at all times. We therefore endeavour to be inclusive in our work, seeking access to relevant parties to the conflict. By impartiality we mean not to take sides in conflicts. It is a commitment to serve all parties, discriminating against none. Although impartial in as far as we conduct our work among different conflict parties, we are not neutral in terms of the principles and values we adhere to which we must in appropriate ways work to advance at all times.

In our work, we frequently come into contact with parties suspected of, and responsible for, grievous human rights abuses. Indeed, such contact may be a requirement of successful conflict transformation work. However, it in no way implies agreement with, or support for, the views or objectives of those parties. Equally, it does not signal acceptance of, or approval for, the activities or methods employed by such groups in pursuing their particular agendas.

Our engagement in situations of internal conflict is dictated only by our capacity to assist positively in moving the peace process forward and is conditional upon an invitation to engage by interested parties, sectors or institutions within civil society or by relevant national or international actors. Our adherence to the principle of impartiality precludes us from engaging in any activity which furthers the personal or collective ambitions of any individual or group in so far as those ambitions conflict with the primary goal of transforming the conflict.

6. **Independence**

We are an independent organisation seeking to contribute to the transformation of violent internal conflicts. Whilst we welcome and solicit advice from our partners, donors and other interested organisations, we are free to determine policies and operational strategies in accordance with our legally registered aims and the principles expressed in this Code.

In endeavouring to fulfil its aims and objectives, the organisation does not allow itself to be used by governments or other bodies in ways which conflict with or contradict those objectives or the principles which inform them. Likewise, the assistance we receive and offer will be used strictly in accordance with the principles, aims and needs identified in our programmes and not to further the interests, political or otherwise, of any particular donor, government or party to the conflict.

7. **Accountability**

We are morally responsible to those whom we seek to assist and accountable to those with whom we work. We are bound by UK Charity Law through our trustees and accountable through regular reporting mechanisms to our donors. We endeavour to be open and transparent in our work by communicating our mission, objectives, policies, operational practices, methods and activities, and management and decision-making procedures to relevant parties so as to ensure the continued good faith and trust of our partners, donors and the general public.

8. **Confidentiality**

As an organisation engaged in sensitive and sometimes dangerous work, we recognise the potential risks to staff and those with whom we work. Accordingly, we endeavour to take every precaution to ensure those risks are minimised and we do not divulge information which might endanger their security. Equally, when the trust of those with whom we work is dependent upon confidentiality, we do not publish, disseminate or otherwise divulge information which might prejudice or undermine the work we are engaged in. We believe that conflict transformation work is often most effective when conducted in a low-profile manner.

9. **Partnerships**

We believe that progress in conflict transformation is best made through a process of co-operation in which responsibilities are shared and roles clearly identified. An essential element of our work is to foster and promote the capacities and abilities of local organisations, peacemakers and peace advocates. This may be through developing effective relationships, participating in relevant NGO consortia and networks, both locally and internationally, and avoiding actions which might cause rivalry or competition with or among our partners.

10. **Institutional Learning**

We believe in building up our collective pool of knowledge, institutional memory and experience through fostering and developing the skills of all our staff. We also acknowledge the importance of drawing lessons from conflicts around the world, sharing them with relevant individuals and organisations and learning from the experiences of others. Furthermore, we are committed to pursuing a long-term approach to our conflict transformation work and in the interests of continual improvement, we are also committed to undertaking regular reviews and evaluations of the different programmes. These reviews will be used to inform our planning and will provide the basis for material reflecting best practice in the field.

Impartiality in Conflict Transformation Work

A. *Basic position*

Based on its experience in diverse conflict situations, IA understands impartiality to mean endeavouring to be inclusive in its work and seeking access to relevant parties to the conflict. It means not taking sides in conflict situations while deriving guidance from its adherence to the principles expressed in its Code of Conduct. It implies

acquiring the capacity to work with relevant parties to the conflict without discrimination or bias, adhering to internationally-recognised standards while aiming to address or alleviate human suffering.

Impartiality is thus understood to be both a guiding principle and a means to achieve the organisation's aim of helping to bring about a just and sustainable peace. Adhering to this approach ensures not only that conflict transformation work remains credible but also that the organisation maintains the trust of the parties to the conflict.

Although impartial in as far as it conducts its work among different conflict parties, IA is committed to principles and not neutral in terms of the values it subscribes to which it must in appropriate ways work to advance at all times. Thus, the term: principled impartiality which indicates a position that is bound to international standards of human rights and humanitarian law while maintaining an inclusive and even-handed approach with regard to the parties to the conflict. (To express this idea IA has previously used the term committed neutrality: "IA maintains a position of committed neutrality strictly bound to international standards of human rights and humanitarian law, and impartiality with regard to the parties in any conflict." Annual Report, 1995.)

B. *Guidelines on impartiality*

The following are proposed guidelines on implementing the principle of impartiality in conflict transformation work undertaken by International Alert:

1. **Understanding the Conflict**

   Understanding the conflict by means of a thorough and balanced attempt to document and analyse the conflict, mapping out its causes and consequences, as well as exploring alternative options is a precondition for conflict transformation work. Likewise, identifying the different players, their profiles, roles, interests and objectives, possibilities and limitations is equally necessary.

2. **A Principled Framework**

   To help maintain impartiality, IA's work is informed by a clear framework of principles and values. This framework is based on internationally-recognised standards such as the Universal Declaration of Human Rights, Common Article 3 of the Geneva Conventions and Protocol II.

3. **Consent and Impartial Contact with the Parties**

   The organisation respects the principle of consent whereby work in a particular situation is generally subject to the consent of the parties. However, those affected by the conflict such as members of civil society and their organisations can request assistance. Responding to an invitation or exploring contact with one of the parties does not imply neglect of the others. Bridge-building at the earliest possible stages is indispensable to pursuing an even-handed approach and maintaining a delicate balance. Ensuring where possible that observations, analysis and strategy development are tested against the experience and insights of other relevant parties or organisations can prove invaluable in developing best practice.

4. **Confidentiality and Discretion**

   To enhance reliability and credibility, it is crucial that confidentiality is maintained when and where it is required. Earning the trust and the confidence of relevant parties in conflict situations requires discretion and tact, patience and respect, and contributes to the practice of impartial conduct in the work of transforming situations of violence.

5. **Consistency and Creativity**

   Consistency and coherence in the organisation's ways of working generate trustworthiness. To maintain access to parties with different perspectives requires a consistent and balanced approach to the work and the sensitivity to nurture and support the process of relationship-building. At the same time, creativity throughout the process encourages openness to new options and opportunities. Keeping a balance between consistency and creativity helps maintain impartiality.

6. **Communication and Transparency**

   Communication is essential to the practice of impartiality. It must be clear, timely, and directed to all relevant parties leading to transparency as far as possible without compromising the requirements of confidentiality. Misunderstandings which do arise have to be dealt with in a timely and appropriate manner. At the same time, potential difficulties can be identified so that alternative ways of dealing with them may be properly explored.

7. **Consultation and Co-operation with Others**

   In complex situations of violent conflict with diverse demands and different actors, consultation with relevant parties and co-operation with others are essential. This approach implies shared responsibilities. It likewise contributes to empowering those engaged in the common endeavour and results in more constructive complementarity.

8. **Sustained Support**

   The practice of impartiality in difficult situations on the ground is best supplemented by effective back-up systems to support field persons, so that individual efforts are sustained and properly serviced in the short, medium and long-terms. Whenever necessary, advisory or support groups can be set up to ensure that efforts are sustained. Efforts for peace involve an understanding and a commitment to long-term processes.

9. **Regular Evaluation**

   To ensure that the principle of impartiality is maintained in the course of conflict transformation work, a systematic and regular evaluation of the programme is important. Internal and external reviews done rigorously and periodically with a team can provide insights from a broad range of experiences and perspectives so that any shortcomings in the practice of impartiality can be detected early on and practice revised as called for.

10. **Institutional Learning**
To ensure that the practice of impartiality in conflict transformation work is constantly improved it is important to build up institutional knowledge. Institutional learning requires harnessing the experience and recording the reflections that could be useful for the efforts of others within the organisation. A systematic approach to the organisation's planning ensures that the principle of impartiality becomes part of comprehensive and coherent peace efforts.

64

Women Take the Peace Lead in Pastoral Kenya

This reading tells the remarkable story of the emergence of the Wajir Peace and Development Committee in northeast Kenya in the mid-1990s and its subsequent work. It gives a vivid example of what Roger Mac Ginty calls 'hybrid' peacebuilding in Reading 59 – in this case, the way in which the spontaneous action of local women 'reviving basic methods of conflict resolution used in pre-colonial times' subsequently inspired extraordinary positive change at higher levels. In her account of the women's initiative, Dekha Ibrahim Abdi shows the potential for linking deep local mediation and peacebuilding traditions with more formal national and international structures in addressing not just the social, but also the political, economic – and even military – aspects of the conflict as well. The reading also illustrates the capacity of indigenous initiatives to deliver the basis for what Martina Fischer calls 'gendered justice' in Reading 60. Dekha Ibrahim Abdi was awarded the Right Livelihood Award in 2007. She was killed in a car accident in 2011 and was widely mourned within the international peace community.

*   *   *   *

Back to the Future

In the early 1990s, a group of women were having a good time at a wedding in Wajir district, a remote and violent area in Kenya. 'We looked around,' recalls Fatuma Sheikh Abdulkadir, 'and realized that a cross-section of all the clans had attended the wedding and we were feeling good. But outside this small compound, the happiness and the mixing was not there. So we discussed at length – what is happening with our society?'

In the remote regions of Africa over which they roam, the weather sets the pattern of the nomadic pastoralists' movement: rainfall dictates the pace of life. Movement is constant. Pasture must be sought.

Past conflicts have left a legacy of suspicion. The blocking of access to an animal water pan, or a problem between market vendors, can be like a match applied to dry leaves. Political interference by outsiders doesn't help.

In Wajir, the second largest district in Kenya, rainfall averages just 200 mm per year. Some 275,000 people occupy 56,600 square kilometers of largely barren landscape bordering Ethiopia and Somalia. This is a recipe for conflict. So too is the composition of the population. Three major clans – Ogaden, Ajuran and Degodia – and several smaller clans, battle to make a living. Eighty percent of them have a source of livelihood from herding camels, sheep and goats.

In 1992, there was yet another drought. Most of pastoralist families had little or no access to essential services. Childhood immunization was 23 percent compared to 71 nationally in Kenya. There was inadequate healthcare. Low livestock immunization. Seventy percent of cattle and thirty percent of camels were lost.

Violence became the order of the day. Deaths followed incidents between the Ogaden and Degodia clans over alleged land encroachment and violation of political space. In one, near Lagbogol, over 20 people lost their lives. Homes were destroyed and livestock taken. Members of the security forces were killed. Refugees and weapons were shifted across the border from conflict-ridden Ethiopia and Somalia. Thieves went on the rampage. There were hijackings, looting and arson, rape, murder.

But there were still normal things. Like weddings.

It was after a wedding that the Wajir Peace Group was born. One thing led to another. Discussions began, first at the workplace and in the homes of other women and men.

The violence continued. At Wagalla, a small trading center outside Wajir town, two herders from the Degodia clan were killed. Women from that clan refused to sell or buy from women of the Ajuran clan, and would not allow them entry to the market. More fighting. More injury. More police in action. Heightened tension.

These incidents provided a major test for the nascent peace group.

When they encountered more police indifference, the women went to see the District Commissioner. They asked for his co-operation. The District Commissioner approved their plan to intervene and asked for feedback as to the outcome. Meetings were held with professional women from all the clans. They were informed about the problems and of the group's intention to bring the key women leaders together.

Contact was made with other women from different strata. Sixty people attended one of the meetings arising out of this overture. After a freeflowing discussion, they agreed to form a Joint Committee of the clans. This group would act as a kind of vigilante body, defusing tension and reporting incidents to the police.

'The formation of the committee helped a lot to put off the fire before it spread far,' says Dekha Ibrahim Abdi, one of the founders of the Peace Group.

In essence, the Wajir peace initiative has taken the region back to the future, by reviving basic methods of conflict resolution used in pre-colonial times to encourage the equitable sharing of the region's limited resources. Under the old Somali clan system, what appears on the surface to be a recipe for problems over access to land and water was regulated in a basic way, even during times of drought.

Within five years, the Peace Group has touched almost everyone in this remote region; its basic approach – community involvement, and the use of dialogue as a counterpoint to conflict. Participation was eventually widened to include young men working with NGOs, government departments and schoolboys. Elders were approached. Seventy of them attended a meeting on August 13, 1993.

They agreed to the setting up of a standing committee of forty, with ten elders from each of the three major clans, and ten from minority groups. The decision of the forty to agree to a peacemaking role marked a new stage for the initiative.

Breakdown of the Pastoral System

During British colonial rule, and continuing into Kenyan independence, the pastoral lifestyle of Wajir's people – and the traditional system underpinning it – were undermined by setting of administrative boundaries leading to fresh conflict over access to natural and political resources. In the two world wars of this century, Somalis were pitted against Somalis, fighting on the sides of warring European powers. More bitterness and artificial rivalries were instilled. An attempt to secede from Kenya led to the Shifta War (1963–69). Negative feelings against the people of the Northeast were reinforced in 'down country' Kenya, and remain strong even today. Clan boundary disputes, inter-clan conflicts, and violence based on electoral politics wracked Wajir district during the post-independence period. A state of emergency was kept in place until 1992. The authorities used powers of arbitrary arrest to keep the Somalis in check. All ethnic Somalis were required to have special ID cards. Neighbourhood wars (Ethiopia-Somalia) and internal conflicts in the two countries spilled over into the region. Refugees, weapons and fighters realigned clan alliances and caused further instability.

A further effort was made to deepen the peace and reconciliation process with the convening of talks between the Christian and Muslim religions. It was about that time that Unicef's compound in Wajir was attacked. The upshot: Wajir was declared an unsafe zone by the international community. Several NGOs moved out, though basic humanitarian services were maintained after intensive lobbying efforts by the women's peace group.

In the meantime, at the urging of Member of Parliament, Ahmed Khalif, all the Wajir elders who had joined the Wajir Peace Group attended a major conference in Wajir town. They agreed to form a 28-member committee comprising representatives of various clans. A declaration was issued, taking stock of the increasing intensity of inter clan fighting. Condemnation was made of the murder of the Unicef pilot and serious injury to a staff member. It was acknowledged that banditry and clan clashes posed a danger to the whole district.

Twenty-five leaders from the major clans and five from two other clans met to deliberate on the cause of the continuing internecine strife. A cessation was urged to the inter-clan fighting and stock theft. Agreement on a cease-fire, to take effect on September 29, 1993, was among a 14-point resolution passed by what has become known as the Al Fatah conference.

Thereafter, the peace initiative took on a brisk momentum. Infrastructure support was provided with help from the donor community. Public meetings and discussions involved a full range of community leaders. A new, more consultative atmosphere prevailed. Workshops delved into the roots of conflict, and how it related to the actual economic conditions facing the people of the region.

Referees' Rapid Response – An Example

In July 1998, while a continent away, in France, nations battled towards the final stages of the football World Cup in France, the north-eastern region of Kenya was wrapped in tension of a different kind. A fragile peace, painstakingly forged and monitored, was in danger of breaking down.

Quickly, the Wajir Peace and Development Committee sprang into action. Two clans were involved in the conflict that erupted on July 6 – Degodia Fai and Murrulle clan. The Committee activated its equivalent of a football referee to blow the whistle on the two groups and find a middle-ground. The Rapid Response Team comprised three elders, two women and two government representatives. Travelling 90 miles to the village where the dispute had developed over access to an animal water pan, they sat down, prayed and listened.

Those blocking access of the animals to the water – the Fai clan – said there was no 'clan problem', as such; the camels of the complainants were sick and could not be allowed access to a common animal pan. After talking to members of the nomadic family whose herd had been at the center of the dispute, the team asked one of its members – a trained veterinarian – to investigate the condition of the camels. They were found to be healthy. A second opinion was sought from the secretary of the Wajir Peace and Development Committee, Mrs Nuria Abdullahi, also a qualified vet. She also found no signs of surra, the disease mentioned. When that failed to satisfy the Fai clan, resolution strategies were activated. Each group was invited to sit separately, discuss the problem, and to find a solution. Out of this exercise came an initiative from the Murrulle family members themselves – that of moving their 'sick' animals out of the area within four days, with provision for family members to receive water during the period they were in-transit, and that they be protected from physical attacks as they depart.

This agreed, the Rapid Response Team members also suggested that, in the interest of future peace, a member of the minority Murrulle clan be added to the Water and Peace committee, thus making them feel part and parcel of the area, Ber Janai. Then details of the measures to resolve the conflict, and avoid the community scoring an own goal, were announced to the public.

By 1994, the atmosphere had healed sufficiently for discussions to move to a new stage. To ensure the peace was not a temporary affair, the Wajir Peace and Development Committee was established. It comprised Members of Parliament, religious leaders, businessmen, NGO workers, the security committee, women and clan elders. Its key instrument is the Rapid Response Team, made up of community leaders – elders, religious leaders, and security officers.

Charged with moving into any part of the district to diffuse tension and mediate in case of conflict or violence, the Rapid Response Team's fire-fighting role buttresses measures taken to go beyond just keeping the peace. In other words, economic and education deprivation are seen as part of the underlying reason for conflict.

Extensive research into ways of achieving permanent peace in the district led to another initiative. When elections approached, the peace group organized discussions involving elders, chiefs, parliamentarians and candidates, so as to reduce the tension normally associated with campaigning. Attention was paid to youth training schemes. Workshops were held. There were peace festivals. Peace Days. Preventive measures were instituted. At the core of the group's activities was an effort to improve the underlying causes of conflict, which were mainly economic, having to do with the sharing of resources.

Thus, by 1996, what had begun as an attempt to give form to throwaway comments, made at a wedding, had evolved to a new stage. Analysis of drought monitoring data concluded that the next one would be particularly severe in Wajir South and East. By September 1996, food was distributed to the affected area.

As Dekha puts it: 'Drought is one of the major contributors to poverty, and poverty is also one of the contributors to the escalation of conflict to violence. Anticipating the drought and early intervention has saved lives and also livelihood of the people affected.'

This story has largely been based on an article by Dekha Ibrahim Abdi: 'Citizen's Peace – Peacebuilding in Wajir, North Eastern Kenya'.

65

Governing (in) Kirkuk: Resolving the Status of a Disputed Territory in Post-American Iraq

Stefan Wolff

The second case study presented here, by Stefan Wolff, Professor of International Security at the University of Birmingham, is in marked contrast to the first. It uses the example of the highly complex situation in Kirkuk, contested by Arabs, Kurds and Turkmen, to illustrate the importance of – but also the difficulties associated with – attempts to use the many varieties of 'territorial self-governance' (TSG) – for example confederation, federation, autonomy, devolution – to build lasting peace from fragile ceasefires in bitterly contested territorial struggles in divided societies. This also serves to illustrate the 'political framework' component of Dan Smith's peacebuilding palette (Reading 61). Erbil, mentioned in the text, is the capital of the Kurdistan region of Iraq.

Wolff then analyses the grievances, demands and power balance of the three communities in Kirkuk, in relation to the wider struggle between Erbil and Baghdad. Taking account of the scope for a solution offered by the Iraqi Constitution of 2005 and the UN Assistance Mission for Iraq report of 2009, he concludes that the most feasible way forward is an interim settlement based on local power-sharing arrangements and a special status for Kirkuk. The context has changed dramatically since this article was published, but the general principles of power-sharing in disputed territories remain important.

Although this case study and the case study presented above (Reading 64) appear to lie at entirely different ends of the international peacebuilding spectrum, the logic of much recent analytical work in the field, as illustrated in the 'reflective pieces' at the beginning of this part, is that the long-term success of the venture depends on somehow being able to encompass both. Readers may like to discuss what this implies.

*   *   *   *

Kirkuk has been among Iraq's most intractable problems. A diverse province and city with three main ethnic groups – Arabs, Kurds and Turkmen – all of whom have different tales of suffering and entitlements to tell, Kirkuk is also beset by problems well beyond the control of its citizens and their representatives. Controlling Kirkuk, which supposedly sits on approximately 10 per cent of Iraq's oil and gas reserves, or preventing someone else from doing so, has major resource implications. Control of Kirkuk is also symbolically important for all three of its main ethnic groups, but especially so for Kurds who have come to see Kirkuk as 'their Jerusalem'. Politically, the future of Kirkuk is, like that of the other internally disputed territories of Iraq, tied up with the full implementation of Iraq's 2005 constitution, which, in its article 140, stipulates normalization (i.e. reversal of Arabization), a census and a referendum 'in Kirkuk and other disputed territories to determine the will of their citizens' (concerning the status of these territories in other words, whether they are to become part of the Kurdistan Region). The future status of Kirkuk has thus become a major bone of contention between Kurds and Arabs in Iraq as a whole, and has become entangled in two other disputes, over a federal hydrocarbons law and over constitutional reform. Beyond Iraq, Kirkuk matters to Turkey,[1] which allegedly fears that a Kirkuk that is part of the Kurdistan Region would further encourage Kurdish separatism in Iraq and the region as a whole,[2] including Turkey. Being seen, rightly or wrongly, as having significant potential for igniting an all-out civil war between Arabs and Kurds, the future of Kirkuk also matters to the international coalition forces in Iraq, and especially to the US, which cannot afford for Kirkuk to derail its plans now that combat forces have been withdrawn.

Local, national, regional and international factors and dynamics thus combine in a near-perfect storm of conflicting interests, mismatched capabilities and diverging agendas. In all this, the fate of local Kirkukis has become a peripheral distraction at best and an unwelcome inconvenience at worst. This is all the more unfortunate as local initiatives over the past three years have shown some promise in preventing Kirkuk from becoming engulfed in sectarian warfare. In December 2007 an agreement was reached between political representatives of Kirkuk on governance arrangements; they committed themselves further to genuine cooperation and power sharing in the Dead Sea Declaration of December 2008 and again in the Berlin Accords of April 2009, the latter including a specific agreement on the distribution of senior posts in the provincial administration as mandated under article 23 of the Elections Law of the Provincial, Districts, and Sub-Districts Councils (Law36/2008, henceforth Provincial Elections Law). While these agreements remain essentially unimplemented, and while local governance arrangements are at best part of a broader solution of the problems of Kirkuk, they are nonetheless significant indicators that Kirkuk need not remain an intractable problem, let alone become the fatal wound to a democratic Iraq.

...

Disputed Territories: Conceptualizing Stakes and Remedies

Territorial disputes occur principally in three different forms: between sovereign states; between the government of a sovereign state and a domestic challenger; and between established entities within a sovereign state. Territorial disputes between sovereign states normally involve a threat to the territorial integrity of one of the disputants: examples are Nazi German claims to the Sudetenland in interwar Czechoslovakia, Argentinian claims to the Falkland Islands and Spanish claims to Gibraltar. In the latter two cases, the state with sovereign title to the disputed territory has staunchly, and so far successfully, defended the status quo, including by military means, whereas in the former case an international arrangement – the so-called Munich Agreement – between the Great Powers of the day (Germany, Italy, France and the United Kingdom) annexed the disputed territory to the challenger state.

The territorial integrity of a state may also be endangered by a domestic challenger, as is evident from cases in which territorially based self-determination movements demand independence: examples include past and present conflicts in Sri Lanka, Sudan, Quebec, Kosovo, and Abkhazia and South Ossetia. Here, too, outcomes have differed. Sri Lanka eventually defeated the Tamil Tigers militarily; in Sudan, North and South agreed on an interim solution providing autonomy to the South for a period of time after which a referendum on its future status would be conducted whose result both parties vowed to accept. In Quebec, a referendum on independence was narrowly defeated and the province continues to exist as a federal entity within Canada. Kosovo, after a period of almost ten years of international administration by the UN, gained independence and (especially western) recognition, while in Abkhazia and South Ossetia, military confrontation between Georgia and Russia created the conditions in which the two separatist entities were able to further consolidate their separate status and achieve a modicum of international recognition of their sovereignty.

However, often enough what is at stake is not outright independence, but rather an enhanced degree of self-governance that the self-determination movement seeks to exercise in the territory it considers its homeland. In such cases, territorial self-governance arrangements within the boundaries of an existing sovereign state are accepted as a compromise by the disputants, as for example in Crimea, Gagauzia or Aceh. Disputes between states and between states and domestic challengers can also overlap when territorially based self-determination movements seek not independent statehood but unification with what they consider their ancestral homeland or kin-state. In some cases, for example in the Åland Islands, South Tyrol, Northern Ireland and Republika Srpska, compromise solutions have been found, occasionally with heavy-handed international mediation, that maintain the territorial integrity of the challenged state while providing for a high degree of territorial self-governance and privileged cross-border relations with the kin-state for the self-determination movement. In others, notably the Saarland in 1935 and 1956, the disputed territory was allowed to reunite with its kin-state.

Territorial disputes between entities within a sovereign state are relatively rare, but nonetheless of significant import. For illustrative purposes, consider the cases of Brčko in Bosnia and Herzegovina, and of Abyei in Sudan. The District of Brčko was disputed between the Federation of Bosnia and Herzegovina (the Bosniak–Croat entity of the Bosnian state) and Republika Srpska, both of which claimed the district as part of their territory. Eventually, international arbitration ruled that Brčko be held in condominium, thus 'belonging' simultaneously to the two entities (Republika Srpska and the Federation of Bosnia and Herzegovina), but be self-governing as a unitary territory in which neither entity exercises any authority. In the case of Abyei, North and South Sudan struggled for years to find a compromise over the boundaries of an area that holds some of Sudan's most significant oil reserves. Eventually, both sides submitted their dispute to the Permanent Court of Arbitration in The Hague, which defined the area geographically in a ruling of July 2009. The thus demarcated territory of Abyei was subsequently given the right to hold a referendum in 2011 (alongside the referendum in the South) on whether it wishes to remain with the North or join the South, a potentially independent state. Until then, the territory is governed jointly by North and South, with a Southerner appointed as head of the interim administration in August 2008 and a Northerner as his deputy.

This last category is the one that best fits the situation in Kirkuk. Here we have an internal territorial dispute that, while clearly not secessionist in nature and therefore not threatening the territorial integrity of Iraq as such, nonetheless has a distinct external dimension to it inasmuch as its resolution (the settlement of Kirkuk's future status) is perceived to have regional implications beyond Iraq. The empowering of the Kurdistan Region in Iraq that would accompany 'winning' the territorial dispute over Kirkuk, and the political and economic prize that this would deliver, is considered by some of Iraq's neighbours, particularly Turkey, as a significant threat because of its alleged impact on the Kurdish question in the Middle East as a whole and on the relations between each of the states (Iran, Syria and Turkey) with relatively large Kurdish communities and the Kurds within its borders. The Kirkuk territorial dispute thus occurs on three levels and has two dimensions. It is a dispute among Kirkuk's communities (principally Arabs, Kurds and Turkmen), a dispute between Baghdad and Erbil, and a dispute that draws in regional powers (principally Turkey). At stake are the territorial–political status of Kirkuk in Iraq and the internal governance arrangements in Kirkuk.

Kirkuk, in other words, falls into a category of territorial disputes that are essentially about territorial control which the disputants seek for themselves (Baghdad, Erbil, local Kirkuk communities) or seek to prevent others from obtaining (Turkey) for a variety of reasons ranging from strategic value (e.g. control of major transport and communication arteries, access to the open sea, military defensibility) and economic gain (e.g. the natural resources located in the disputed territory, and the tax revenue, goods and services generated there) to political significance (e.g. the precedent of how dealing with one specific territorial dispute will affect the likelihood and outcome of others) and cultural importance (e.g. territory as an ancient homeland, mythical place of origin, site of events defining group identity, etc.). These things constitute, individually and collectively, what is at stake for the disputants. The higher the stakes, the more likely it is that disputants' positions will become firmly entrenched and the more difficult it will be to find mutually acceptable compromises – despite the fact that, conceptually, it is relatively easy to find remedies for territorial disputes.

The most prominent way in which the existing literature on conflict resolution engages with territorial disputes is through the framework of territorial self-governance (TSG), which can be defined as the legally entrenched power of territorially delimited entities within the internationally recognized boundaries of existing states to exercise public policy functions independently of other sources of authority in this state, but subject to its overall legal order. Conceptually, this definition of TSG applies its meaning as a tool of statecraft to the specific context of conflict resolution in divided societies and encompasses five distinct governance arrangements – confederation, federation, autonomy, devolution and decentralization. One of the shortcomings of current theoretical engagements with TSG as a mechanism for conflict resolution in divided societies is a focus on just the territorial dimension of conflict settlement. Only rarely do scholars look beyond the territorial dimension and towards a more complete package of institutions within which TSG is but one, albeit a central, element. Caroline Hartzell and Matthew Hoddie, for example, argue that conflict settlements (after civil war) are the more stable the more they institutionalize power sharing across four dimensions – political, economic, military and territorial.[3] Ulrich Schneckener reaches similar conclusions in a study that is focused on European consociational democracies.[4] Arend Lijphart established such specific conceptual and empirical links between consociation and federation as long as three decades ago, noting two crucial principles, namely that 'the component units [must] enjoy a secure autonomy in organizing their internal affairs… [and] that they *all* participate in decision-making at the central level of government'.[5] John McGarry and Brendan O'Leary also note that 'some successful cases of territorial pluralism suggest that, at least with sizable nationalities, autonomy should be accompanied by consociational power sharing within central or federal institutions. Such arrangements prevent majoritarianism by the dominant nationality, and make it more likely that minorities have a stake in the state.'[6] This is in line with conclusions reached by Marc Weller and Stefan Wolff, who argue that 'autonomy can only serve in the stabilization of states facing self-determination conflicts if it is part of a well-balanced approach that draws on elements of consociational techniques, moderated by integrative policies, and tempered by a wider regional outlook'.[7]

This phenomenon of TSG arrangements occurring in combination with other conflict resolution mechanisms has been identified by several authors over the past few years.[8] Analytically, it is possible to explain both why such multidimensional institutional arrangements emerge and why they might have a greater chance of success than purely territorially based solutions. Empirically, there is some evidence of their sustainability, as well as a relatively large number of more recent cases in which such arrangements have been the outcome of negotiated settlements, even though they are too recent for their longer-term success to be assessed.

Leaving aside the rather more trivial condition that TSG is of real benefit only to minorities that live in territorially concentrated communities,[9] two characteristics are particularly important in determining the likelihood of a combination of TSG arrangements with power-sharing institutions at the local and/or central levels of government: the degree of ethnic heterogeneity in the territorial entities to which powers and competences of self-governance are to be assigned; and their significance relative to the rest of the state. Thus, it can be expected that the settlement for a territorial entity characterized by ethnic (or another identity-based form of) heterogeneity would include local power-sharing institutions, whereas a more homogeneous one might not – compare Brussels to the Flemish region, the Federation of Bosnia and Herzegovina to Republika Srpska, or Northern Ireland to the Åland Islands. The institution of local power-sharing mechanisms (i.e. within the self-governing entity) also addresses one frequent criticism and potential flaw of TSG arrangements – that they empower a local majority to the disadvantage of one or more local minorities, either creating new conflict within the entity or, if the local minority is a state-wide dominant group, destabilizing the TSG arrangement as the central government (out of concern for its ethnic or religious kin) might want to abrogate or delimit the powers of the TSG entity, seeing them as being abused to discriminate against other population groups.

As far as power-sharing at the level of the central government is concerned, the most likely structural predictor here is the significance of the self-governing territory (or territories) relative to the rest of the state. Such significance can arise from geographical and population size, natural resource availability, strategic location and/or cultural importance. Power-sharing institutions at the centre, then, are a reflection of the bargaining position that a given self-determination movement has – the greater that is, the more it can assert its position at the centre. Yet elements of a carefully designed set of power-sharing institutions at the centre can also address a frequently mentioned reservation about TSG arrangements, namely that they empower self-determination movements while weakening the central government: in other words, that they create an asymmetric power relationship that privileges separatists. This is because power-sharing institutions, for their own success, also need to involve agreed dispute resolution mechanisms, which in turn can contribute to regulating ongoing bargaining processes between central government and the self-governing entity in ways that maintain a political process of dispute management (rather than resurgence of violence) and enable state- and TSG-preserving outcomes (rather than state breakups or abrogation of TSG arrangements). Consociational power sharing in the Belgian federation, combined with the so-called 'alarm-bell mechanism', is one example of this. Belgium is also an instructive illustration of the notion of 'significance'. The country has three linguistic groups – French-speakers, Dutch-speakers and German-speakers – but only the former two are large enough to warrant inclusion in central power-sharing arrangements. In the UK, none of the four devolution settlements (London, Northern Ireland, Scotland and Wales) provides for central-level power sharing, given the predominance of England within the UK. On the other hand, the comprehensive peace agreement for Sudan and Iraq's 2005 constitution both provide consociational institutions to include, respectively, the SPLA/M and the Kurds into decision-making at the centre, and both offer dispute resolution mechanisms, including judicial arbitration and joint committees and implementation bodies.

Applying such a conflict resolution perspective to Kirkuk enables a focus on the political–institutional relationship between Kirkuk on the one hand and Baghdad and Erbil on the other. Such a relationship is determined through governance arrangements and secured in domestic and, occasionally, international law. In this context, governance arrangements have two dimensions: where which powers are exercised (i.e. determining the levels of governance and the relationship and distribution of powers between them) and who makes what decisions and how (the institutions and mechanisms of governance). Framed in the kind of conflict resolution perspective elaborated above, resolving the kind of territorial dispute that confronts the parties in Kirkuk is about determining the form of *territorial construction of the overall state*, with options for self-governance ranging from confederation to federation, federacy, devolution and decentralization; and it is further about deciding the *distribution of powers* between the centre and the disputed territory as a self-governing entity, within the framework defined by the way in which the overall state is territorially constructed, according to principles of subsidiarity, proportionality, economic efficiency and administrative capacity. Resolving such territorial disputes also concerns the establishment of *power-sharing arrangements* both within the disputed territory (in this case, between the communities in Kirkuk) and possibly at the centre or, if applicable, the next level of governance (Baghdad or Kurdistan Region). Finally, to achieve effective and efficient government and a functioning, predictable and stable political process it is essential that the overall set of institutional arrangements agreed by the immediate disputants also incorporates a range of *mechanisms for policy coordination and future dispute resolution*. These four dimensions of such territorial dispute settlements need to be properly entrenched in domestic (constitutional) law, and possibly, albeit not necessarily in the case of Kirkuk, in international law.

If it is possible to make any general empirical observation about the outcomes of territorial dispute settlement processes – that is, the nature of the political–institutional relationship achieved along these four dimensions and the nature of its legal entrenchment – it is that they are, unsurprisingly, highly context-dependent. What the disputants have at stake is informed by their grievances and in turn shapes their demands. The ability to realize these demands is a function of the balance of power between the disputants, which is determined partly by the extent to which they are backed by third parties and partly by their ability to present a united front. Balance of power, however, is also a matter of structural factors, such as demography (e.g. how numerically large a particular group is and how concentrated its members are) and geography (e.g. how clearly defined and unfragmented the disputed territory is). Structural factors, in turn, also shape disputants' preferences, expressed in their demands. For example, a large, compact group will not only seek as much control as possible over the disputed territory, it will also demand a share of power at the centre as it will have a significant stake in the political process of the whole state (as do, for example, Serbs in Bosnia and Herzegovina or Kurds in Iraq). A smaller group that does not constitute a majority even in the disputed territory will want to ensure it has a say at the local level and can retain a maximum amount of control over its own affairs through forms of corporate (or cultural) autonomy and power sharing in order to make territorial self-governance meaningful rather than its becoming another instance of majority control (e.g. Nationalists and Republicans in Northern Ireland).

It is important to bear in mind that the process of settlement itself – its format, structure and participants – also co-determines its outcome. Face-to-face negotiations create a different dynamic from shuttle diplomacy; well-resourced, outcome-driven international mediation biased against secession enables and constrains parties to a conflict in different ways from talks between such parties facilitated by under-resourced yet impartial NGOs; negotiations which involve only one principal negotiator on each side offer different opportunities for settlement from negotiations in which one or both parties are highly fragmented and consist of essentially self-interested individuals with little or no commonality of purpose. Agreements put to a popular vote either within specific constituencies (e.g. a political party congress) or in the disputed territory as a whole (e.g. a referendum) add a further dimension to the settlement process that more often than not puts a constraint on what the parties feel they are able to agree upon at the negotiating table.

Notes

1 On the role of Turkey see, among others, Bülent Aras, 'Turkey, northern Iraq and Kirkuk', *Foreign Policy Bulletin* 5, 2007, pp. 6–9; Philip Giraldi, 'Turkey and the threat of Kurdish nationalism', *Mediterranean Quarterly* 19: 1, 2008, pp. 33–41; International Crisis Group, *Turkey and Iraqi Kurds: conflict or cooperation?*, Middle East report 81 (Brussels: ICG, 2008); Robert Olson, 'Relations among Turkey, Iraq, Kurdistan-Iraq, the wider Middle East, and Iran', *Mediterranean Quarterly* 17: 4, 2006, pp. 13–45; Robert Olson, 'Turkey's policies toward Kurdistan-Iraq and Iraq: nationalism, capitalism, and state formation', *Mediterranean Quarterly* 17: 1, 2006, pp. 48–72; Thanos Veremis, 'The transformation of Turkey's security considerations', *International Spectator: Italian Journal of International Affairs* 40: 2, 2005, pp. 75–84.

2 See Ted Galen Carpenter, 'Middle East vortex: an unstable Iraq and its implications for the region', *Mediterranean Quarterly* 20: 4, 2009, pp. 22–31.

3 C. Hartzell and M. Hoddie, 'Institutionalizing peace: powersharing and post-civil war conflict management', *American Journal of Political Science* 47: 2, 2003, pp. 318–32; C. Hartzell and M. Hoddie, *Crafting peace: power-sharing institutions and the negotiated settlement of civil wars* (University Park, PA: Pennsylvania State University Press, 2007).

4 U. Schneckener, 'Making powersharing work: lessons from successes and failures in ethnic conflict regulation', *Journal of Peace Research* 39: 2, pp. 203–28.

5 A. Lijphart, 'Consociation and federation: conceptual and empirical links', *Canadian Journal of Political Science* 12: 3, 1979, pp. 499–515 at p. 506.

6 J. McGarry and B. O'Leary, 'Territorial approaches to ethnic conflict settlement', in K. Cordell and S. Wolff, eds, *The Routledge handbook of ethnic conflict* (London: Routledge, 2010, pp. 249–65).

7 M. Weller and S. Wolff, 'Recent trends in autonomy and state construction', in *Weller and Wolff, Autonomy, self-governance and conflict resolution*, pp. 262–70 at p. 269.

8 See C. Kettley, J. Sullivan and J. Fyfe, 'Self-determination disputes and complex powersharing arrangements: a background paper for debate', Centre of International Studies, Cambridge, 2001, http://www.intstudies.cam.ac.uk/centre/cps/download/background1.pdf, accessed 4 March 2009; M. Weller, 'Settling self-determination conflicts: an introduction', in M. Weller and B. Metzger, eds, *Settling self-determination disputes: complex powersharing in theory and practice* (Leiden: Nijhoff, 2008), pp. xii–xvii; S. Wolff, 'Complex power-sharing and the centrality of territorial self-governance in contemporary conflict settlements', *Ethnopolitics* 8:1, 2009, pp. 27–45; S. Wolff, 'Peace by design? Towards complex powersharing', in R. Taylor, ed., *Consociational theory: McGarry and O'Leary and the Northern Ireland conflict* (London: Routledge, 2009), pp. 110–21.

9 See e.g. D. Brancati, *Peace by design: managing intrastate conflict through decentralization* (Oxford: Oxford University Press, 2009); J. McGarry, B. O'Leary and R. Simeon, 'Integration or accommodation? The enduring debate in conflict regulation', in S. Choudhry, ed., *Constitutional design for divided societies: integration or accommodation?* (Oxford: Oxford University Press, 2008), pp. 41–88; D. Treisman, *The architecture of government: rethinking political decentralization* (Cambridge: Cambridge University Press, 2007); Wolff, 'Peace by design?'.

Toolbox

When peace agreements are made, the challenge is to sustain them by robust pro-grammes of peacebuilding. The term 'peacebuilding' first emerged in the work of one of our pioneers, Johan Galtung, in the 1970s. The strategic framework within which peacebuilding is set was first outlined comprehensively in UN Secretary General Boutros-Ghali's Agenda for Peace in 1992, and more recently the UN has established its Peace-building Commission. The Agenda for Peace and other resources for peacebuilding can be accessed at the UN Peacebuilding Support Office at http://www.un.org/en/peacebuild-ing/pbso/pbun.shtml.

Methods for the monitoring and evaluation of peacebuilding have also been developed by many agencies. The UN Peacebuilding Support Office has a Learning Portal for Design Monitoring and Evaluation of peacebuilding projects, providing resources to share evalu-ation reports and data, methodologies and tools, and best and emerging practices, at http://www.dmeforpeace.org/. The diversity of roles that practitioners can adopt to support peacebuilding can be explored at the Third Sider Project page at http://www.thirdside.org/. The NGO 'Responding to Conflict' has made a series of films on local peacebuilding. For example, 'The Story of Wajir' (available on YouTube) illustrates Reading 64. Peacekeeping has become an important element of peacebuilding. Excellent data and resources are available at the United Nations Department of Peacekeeping Operations website, at http://www.un.org/en/peacekeeping/about/dpko/. Also at the Centre for International Peace Operations Berlin (ZIF), at http://www.zif-berlin.org/en/.

Part VI

Challenges and Future Directions

In this final part, we revisit some of the themes set out in the Introduction. Readers are once again invited to see themselves as fellow-participants in a joint venture that no one person, organization, culture, gender or part of the world can claim as its own. There is no expertise or body of knowledge that exhausts this topic. We are all students.

In particular, evaluating success and failure is bound to be controversial (see the Toolbox resources in Part V). Given the deep complexity of human conflicts, and the multiplicity of their social, political, psychological and cultural roots, we should follow Jay Rothman in seeing failure as normal.[1] Failure can be regarded as opportunity rather than defeat as long as lessons are learnt and creative alternatives found. These then become what Rothman calls 'successful failures' – growth points for future development, examples of what in the introduction we referred to as 'second-order social learning'.

There is also always something 'left out' of any analysis – some blindness in understanding, some 'gap' in practice. In a selection of readings like this – with editors who represent only a minute fragment of humanity – most voices are left out. We are very aware of that, and invite readers to identify these gaps and silences, and if possible to think of ways in which the field can be improved by remedying this. In this spirit, we end the book with four questions:

1 Have levels of violent conflict gone down since the Second World War?
2 If so, has this had anything to do with a greater level of international endorsement of the aim of conflict resolution – to transform actually or potentially violent conflict into nonviolent processes of change – and expertise in bringing this about?
3 Where are the continuing 'frontiers of failure'?
4 How are these now being addressed, and what more needs to be done?

Have Levels of Violent Conflict Gone Down Since the Second World War?

With this question, we plunge into the complex and contested realm of 'statistics of deadly conflicts', to use the title of Lewis Fry Richardson's seminal work (see Reading 3).

We cannot do justice in this book to what are now highly sophisticated attempts to measure both 'violence' and 'peaceful change' statistically. In the chapter of *Contemporary Conflict Resolution* entitled 'The Statistics of Deadly Quarrels', we conclude that incidents of direct violence have indeed gone down during this period – contrary to many popular perceptions. Reading 66 gives a summarizing extract from Steven Pinker's argument to the same effect.

Does Conflict Resolution Deserve Some of the Credit?

Many of the factors considered in Pinker's study of the decline of violence over recent millennia can be seen to have nothing to do with conflict resolution. But some of them do. Readers may like to distinguish between the two. There are, of course, alternative explanations for an absence of war – for example, the realist argument that direct major armed conflict was prevented between the superpowers during the Cold War because of mutual nuclear deterrence. These are 'counterfactual' discussions: what might or might not have happened had such-and-such factors been present or absent? In the social and political sciences, we cannot, as in classical physics, rerun the experiment with single factors altered. In the chapter entitled 'Towards Cosmopolitan Conflict Resolution' and in the second part of the chapter 'Conflict Resolution and the Future' in *Contemporary Conflict Resolution*, the claim is made that a measure of credit for apparently declining levels of violent conflict does indeed go to improved international capacities to prevent and mitigate large scale conflict – and to a whole host of varied interlocking efforts at other levels.

Where are the Frontiers of Failure Today?

But will this continue into the future? The enterprise of conflict resolution is evidently still in its infancy. It is not hard to point to examples where attempts at settlement and transformation so far do not work. These are the intractable conflicts, which have been a focus of attention in the field at least since the 1989 study by Kriesberg et al.[2] See also the Conflict Information Consortium website referenced in the Toolbox at the end of this part, and Peter Coleman's book *The Five Percent* (2011).[3]

In the final chapter of *Contemporary Conflict Resolution*, we consider threats of future armed violence from a 'hybrid mixture' of local, regional, interstate and global levels of conflict that we call 'transnational' conflict. This includes future *interstate* conflict between states, *ethnonational* conflict to determine the geographical identity of states, *ideological conflict* to decide the nature of states, *economic-factional* conflict to control the resources of states – and mixtures of these. We also consider as yet untamed underlying 'drivers' of conflict, such as the *north–south economic divide*, *environmental change*, the *absence of adequate transnational forms of accountable governance*, and the continuing development and spread of *lethal weaponry*.

In this part, we illustrate only one of these (Reading 67): the possible future link between environmental change and human conflict (see also the chapter entitled 'Environmental Conflict Resolution' in *Contemporary Conflict Resolution*).

So far as concerns challenges to the field of conflict resolution itself, its greater prominence since the end of the Cold War has led to criticism from a number of diverse quarters. These are summarized and responded to in the chapter 'Theories and Critiques' in *Contemporary Conflict Resolution*. For traditional *realists*, in a world where irreconcilable interests compete for power, 'soft' conflict resolution approaches are dismissed as ineffective and dangerous. What possible answer can conflict resolution have to the lethal combination of rogue states, globalized crime, the proliferation of weapons of mass destruction, and the fanatical ideologues of international terrorism? For *critical theorist* inheritors of the Marxist mantle, in the structurally unequal world of late capitalism, 'problem-solving' conflict resolution approaches are seen to reinforce existing imbalances and to fail to address the need for underlying change. For *poststructuralists* conflict resolution discourse about cosmopolitan values are permeated by unwarranted universalizing assumptions about truth and reality. Beyond this lie even broader assaults, such as Paul Salem's 'critique of western conflict resolution from a non-western perspective'.[4] Here again we offer only one illustration. This is Vivienne Jabri's critique of what she sees as the continuing 'positivist' assumptions behind mainstream conflict resolution, together with the damaging deficiencies that attend such a 'de-politicization' of the topic (see Reading 68).

How Are These Being Addressed?

It is hoped that the conflict resolution response is to acknowledge the silences, failures and conceptual limitations of the field shown up in practical set-backs and informed criticism, and to learn and adapt accordingly. The central motive for those who work in conflict resolution is the perception that the human future depends on our capacity to do this. In the chapter 'Origins, Foundations and Development of the Field' in *Contemporary Conflict Resolution*, we report on current efforts to address the *systemic complexity* of many contemporary conflicts (see Reading 28), the *intractability* of conflicts that so far resist attempts at positive engagement, settlement and transformation as noted above, and the *asymmetry* of some of the most obdurate conflicts, as well as the importance of closer coordination between conflict resolution and *nonviolent direct action* (see Reading 32). We end the book with a selection of examples of parallel tasks to be addressed.

Notes

1 *International Journal of Conflict Engagement and Resolution* 2/1 (2014).

2 L. Kriesberg, A. Northrup and S. Thorson, eds, *Intractable Conflicts and Their Transformation*. Syracuse, NY: Syracuse University Press, 1989.

3 P. Coleman, *The Five Percent: Finding Solutions to Seemingly Impossible Conflicts*. New York: Public Affairs, Perseus Books, 2011.

4 P. Salem, 'In Theory: A Critique of Western Conflict Resolution from a Non-Western Perspective', *Negotiation Journal* 9/4 (1993): 361–369.

66

The Better Angels of Our Nature: Why Violence Has Declined

Steven Pinker

Steven Pinker is the Johnstone Family Professor at Harvard University. He became influential in the conflict resolution field through his argument from evolutionary psychology against the 'central dogma of a secular faith' that the mind is a benign 'blank slate' and his acceptance of the fact that violence is inherent in human nature, pointing to human bodies and minds for 'direct signs of human aggression'.[1] Nevertheless, because the mind is a 'combinatorial recursive system' (we not only have thoughts, but thoughts about thoughts etc), we can learn and adapt to changed circumstances and 'advances in human conflict resolution' are 'dependent on this ability'.

Note

1 S. Pinker, *The Blank Slate: The Modern Denial of Human Nature*. London: Penguin, 2002.

*   *   *   *

This book is about what may be the most important thing that has ever happened in human history. Believe it or not – and I know that most people do not – violence has declined over long stretches of time, and today we may be living in the most peaceable era in our species' existence. The decline, to be sure, has not been smooth; it has not brought violence down to zero; and it is not guaranteed to continue. But it is an unmistakable development, visible on scales from millennia to years, from the waging of wars to the spanking of children.

...

A large part of the book will explore the psychology of violence and non-violence. The theory of mind that I will invoke is the synthesis of cognitive science, affective and cognitive neuroscience, social and evolutionary psychology, and other sciences of human nature that I explored in How the Mind Works, The Blank Slate, and The Stuff of Thought. According to this understanding, the mind is a complex system of cognitive and emotional faculties implemented in the brain which owe their basic design to the processes of evolution. Some of these faculties incline us toward various kinds of violence. Others – "the better angels of our nature," in Abraham Lincoln's words – incline us toward cooperation and peace. The way to explain the decline of violence is to identify the changes in our cultural and material milieu that have given our peaceable motives the upper hand.

Finally, I need to show how our history has engaged our psychology. Everything in human affairs is connected to everything else, and that is especially true of violence. Across time and space, the more peaceable societies also tend to be richer, healthier, better educated, better governed, more respectful of their women, and more likely to engage in trade. It's not easy to tell which of these happy traits got the virtuous circle started and which went along for the ride, and it's tempting to resign oneself to unsatisfying circularities, such as that violence declined because the culture got less violent. Social scientists distinguish "endogenous" variables – those that are inside the system, where they may be affected by the very phenomenon they are trying to explain – from the "exogenous" ones – those that are set in motion by forces from the outside. Exogenous forces can originate in the practical realm, such as changes in technology, demographics, and the mechanisms of commerce and governance. But they can also originate in the intellectual realm, as new ideas are conceived and disseminated and take on a life of their own. The most satisfying explanation of a historical change is one that identifies an exogenous trigger. To the best that the data allow it, I will try to identify exogenous forces that have engaged our mental faculties in different ways at different times and that thereby can be said to have caused the declines in violence.

The discussions that try to do justice to these questions add up to a big book – big enough that it won't spoil the story if I preview its major conclusions. *The Better Angels of Our Nature* is a tale of six trends, five inner demons, four better angels, and five historical forces.

Six Trends (chapters 2 through 7). To give some coherence to the many developments that make up our species' retreat from violence, I group them into six major trends.

The first, which took place on the scale of millennia, was the transition from the anarchy of the hunting, gathering, and horticultural societies in which our species spent most of its evolutionary history to the first agricultural civilizations with cities and governments, beginning around five thousand years ago. With that change came a reduction in the chronic raiding and feuding that characterized life in a state of nature and a more or less fivefold decrease in rates of violent death. I call this imposition of peace the Pacification Process.

The second transition spanned more than half a millennium and is best documented in Europe. Between the late Middle Ages and the 20th century, European countries saw a tenfold-to-fiftyfold decline in their rates of homicide. In his classic book *The Civilizing Process*, the sociologist Norbert Elias attributed this surprising decline to the consolidation of a patchwork of feudal territories into large kingdoms with centralized authority and an infrastructure of commerce. With a nod to Elias, I call this trend the Civilizing Process.

The third transition unfolded on the scale of centuries and took off around the time of the Age of Reason and the European Enlightenment in the 17th and 18th centuries (though it had antecedents in classical Greece and the Renaissance, and parallels elsewhere in the world). It saw the first organized movements to abolish socially sanctioned forms of violence like despotism, slavery, dueling, judicial torture, superstitious killing, sadistic punishment, and cruelty to animals, together with the first stirrings of systematic pacifism. Historians sometimes call this transition the Humanitarian Revolution.

The fourth major transition took place after the end of World War II. The two-thirds of a century since then have been witness to a historically unprecedented development: the great powers, and developed states in general, have stopped waging war on one another. Historians have called this blessed state of affairs 'the Long Peace.'

The fifth trend is also about armed combat but is more tenuous. Though it may be hard for news readers to believe, since the end of the Cold War in 1989, organized conflicts of all kinds – civil wars, genocides, repression by autocratic governments, and terrorist attacks – have declined throughout the world. In recognition of the tentative nature of this happy development, I will call it the New Peace.

Finally, the postwar era, symbolically inaugurated by the Universal Declaration of Human Rights in 1948, has seen a growing revulsion against aggression on smaller scales, including violence against ethnic minorities, women, children, homosexuals, and animals. These spin-offs from the concept of human rights – civil rights, women's rights, children's rights, gay rights, and animal rights – were asserted in a cascade of movements from the late 1950s to the present day which I will call the Rights Revolutions.

Five Inner Demons (chapter 8). Many people implicitly believe in the Hydraulic Theory of Violence: that humans harbor an inner drive toward aggression (a death instinct or thirst for blood), which builds up inside us and must periodically be discharged. Nothing could be further from a contemporary scientific understanding of the psychology of violence. Aggression is not a single motive, let alone a mounting urge. It is the output of several psychological systems that differ in their environmental triggers, their internal logic, their neurobiological basis, and their social distribution. Chapter 8 is devoted to explaining five of them. *Predatory or instrumental* violence is simply violence deployed as a practical means to an end. *Dominance* is the urge for authority, prestige, glory, and power, whether it takes the form of macho posturing among individuals or contests for supremacy among racial, ethnic, religious, or national groups. *Revenge* fuels the moralistic urge toward retribution, punishment, and justice. *Sadism* is pleasure taken in another's suffering. And *ideology* is a shared belief system, usually involving a vision of utopia, that justifies unlimited violence in pursuit of unlimited good.

Four Better Angels (chapter 9). Humans are not innately good (just as they are not innately evil), but they come equipped with motives that can orient them away from violence and toward cooperation and altruism. *Empathy* (particularly in the sense of sympathetic concern) prompts us to feel the pain of others and to align their interests with our own. Self-control allows us to anticipate the consequences of acting on our impulses and to inhibit them accordingly. The *moral sense* sanctifies a set of norms and taboos that govern the interactions among people in a culture, sometimes in ways that decrease violence, though often (when the norms are tribal, authoritarian, or puritanical) in ways that increase it. And the faculty of *reason* allows us to extricate ourselves from our parochial vantage points, to reflect on the ways in which we live our lives, to deduce ways in which we could be better off, and to guide the application of the other better angels of our nature. In one section I will also examine the possibility that in recent history *Homo sapiens* has literally evolved to become less violent in the biologist's technical sense of a change in our genome. But the focus of the book is on transformations that are strictly environmental: changes in historical circumstances that engage a fixed human nature in different ways.

Five Historical Forces (chapter 10). In the final chapter I try to bring the psychology and history back together by identifying exogenous forces that favor our peaceable motives and that have driven the multiple declines in violence.

The Leviathan, a state and judiciary with a monopoly on the legitimate use of force, can defuse the temptation of exploitative attack, inhibit the impulse for revenge, and circumvent the self-serving biases that make all parties believe they are on the side of the angels. *Commerce* is a positive-sum game in which everybody can win; as technological progress allows the exchange of goods and ideas over longer distances and among larger groups of trading partners, other people become more valuable alive than dead, and they are less likely to become targets of demonization and dehumanization. *Feminization* is the process in which cultures have increasingly respected the interests and values of women. Since violence is largely a male pastime, cultures that empower women tend to move away from the glorification of violence and are less likely to breed dangerous subcultures of rootless young men. The forces of *cosmopolitanism* such as literacy, mobility, and mass media can prompt people to take the perspective of people unlike themselves and to expand their circle of sympathy to embrace them. Finally, an intensifying application of knowledge and rationality to human affairs – the *escalator of reason* – can force people to recognize the futility of cycles of violence, to ramp down the privileging of their own interests over others', and to reframe violence as a problem to be solved rather than a contest to be won.

As one becomes aware of the decline of violence, the world begins to look different. The past seems less innocent; the present less sinister....Instead of asking, "Why is there war?", we might ask, "Why is there peace?" We can obsess not just over what we have been doing wrong but also over what we have been doing right. Because we have been doing something right, and it would be good to know what, exactly, it is.

67

Climate Change and Armed Conflict

James Lee

James Lee is a pioneer in the field of research on conflict and environmental issues. In 1997 he initiated a project called the Inventory of Conflict and Environment (ICE), to stimulate discussion and research on climate change as a driver of conflict. The book from which this reading is taken was published in the Routledge series 'Studies in Peace and Conflict Resolution'.[1] The issue of climate change as a future challenge for conflict resolution is dealt with briefly in the final chapter of *Contemporary Conflict Resolution* and is more fully elaborated here. In this extract, Lee presents six future cases or scenarios where climate change is likely and where it will influence the emergence of new forms of conflict. Lee argues that new policy responses are needed to anticipate these conflicts and there is a challenge to the conflict resolution field to enhance its theory and practice in relating to this potentially new conflict domain.

Note

1 Information on this series can be accessed at http://www.routledge.com/books/series/rspcr/.

*   *   *   *

Five Conclusions

Think about the unfolding of climate change in terms of the financial crisis as it erupted in 2008. The seeds to the crisis were sown many years ago, and the slow rise of market risk began well before 2008. However, once it hit a tipping point the entire system began to unravel. The problem became so widespread that the original source of the problem, risky mortgages, had undermined global systems of credit and put into peril municipal projects, education endeavors, and the entire US auto industry, to name but a few examples.

Would climate change act out in this fashion and produce similar sets of cascading phenomena? Would it start to reduce livelihoods, imperil social safety, sap economic productivity, and cause desperate leaders to take even greater risk by resorting to conflict to acquire resources?

> How would increased fire risks and other derivative effects of acute water scarcity [due to climate change] affect the job market or the real estate market? ... And what would happen to the banking

system if banks become suddenly saddled with a huge increase in unsalable properties possessed through foreclosure? With no cushion and no buyers, foreclosures would quickly propagate back up through the financial system. Because mortgages have been sliced and diced into so many derivatives, the crisis could quickly become systematic as investors fled markets. (Linden 2006: 254)

This section has five parts that bring together the major findings of the research and implications that arise from them. First, there needs to be a historic perspective on climate change and conflict. Second, there is a clear trajectory that will be difficult to alter which gives the future cases some degree of potential inevitability. Third, there will be very different pathways from climate change to conflict, and thus the modes and types of responses will be dramatically different. Fourth, there is tremendous value in recognizing and advancing scientific understanding of the relationship as a means to cope with or possibly preclude climate-induced conflict. Fifth, this knowledge, rather than politics, should guide actionable policy tools relevant to climate change and conflict issues.

The Need for a Historic Perspective on Climate Change and Conflict

People will need to re-contextualize themselves to understand and respond to the challenge of climate change and conflict. They will need to see themselves not only as supra-biological beings, but also as instinctive creatures in a natural world.

The natural forces behind the end of the Ice Age starting 50,000 years ago brought about the ascendance of human beings. The addition of the human to the climate equation also began a dynamic process where anthropogenic forces intermingled with and ultimately superseded nature in determining the course of climate's direction. Some of today's warming trends are a continuation of natural processes. Today's great acceleration, however, is driven by human behavior. The changing climate has always been a factor in the rise and fall of peoples and civilizations. This phenomenon is often accompanied by conflict, insofar as such periods of ascent and descent are inherently unstable as relative power changes. It could also push people to adjust, and develop new technologies or lifestyles that allow for survival and in some way improve humans over the long term. Changing climate pushed humans out of Africa, but it also led to their worldwide spread. It brought people into conflict with other species over food sources, especially other predators, but also other advanced primates.

Conflict is driven in part by a changing climate, as peoples are pushed from and pulled to other habitats. Conflict is often intrinsic to acquiring basic biological needs, and applies to humans and many other species. Climate change and conflict is essentially a socio-biological response that occurs when two species overlap in range.

People today often come into conflict when their "ranges" overlap. The varied interactions between climate change and conflict over time is reflected in cases involving Neanderthals, Aryans, Mayans, Vikings, or Anasazi. It is clear that at times the interaction of natural and human forces was very significant in determining the evolutionary path of peoples, and indeed their very survival. The evidence is that today's and tomorrow's conflict from climate change represents continuity rather than a new phenomenon.

Thus, climate change as a cause of conflict is not a revolutionary idea – it is evolutionary.

Believing in the Future Cases

The future cases are not wild possibilities or attempts at science fiction. They are instances where climate change is highly likely, and conflict emergence a clear possibility. Trends point to geopolitical realignments that are likely to interact, to some degree, with physical realignments. The six future cases are premised on a general trajectory that is unavoidable, where causal factors will intermingle, and where human factors tend to deepen the problem.

1 There will be extreme warming in the world's polar areas and opportunities for resource access in a time coupled with an increasing demand for land and sea resources.
2 The loss of most of the world's great forests and the relation to human livelihoods will be both a cause and a consequence of conflict.
3 The increase of deserts around the Equator, along with the existence of populations that currently exceed water replenishment levels, will aggravate already high levels of tension.
4 Further desertification and deforestation in Africa, coupled with human growth rates and increasing levels of poverty, will push peoples into structural violence.
5 The extreme warming of the central Asian plateau and its role in providing the headwaters for most major rivers in Asia, on whose waters billions of people depend, will be a fact of geopolitical importance.
6 The inevitable rise of the world's ocean levels due to extreme warming will threaten both island states and billions of people living along coastlines.

How these scenarios unfold will lead to a multitude of paths to conflict or peace. From a global perspective, limiting the conflict to political or diplomatic venues must be preferred to those paths that will emerge as violent, armed conflict.

How the Very Different Pathways from Climate Change to Conflict will Emerge

The historic and future cases show continuity in the types of convergences between climate change and conflict. This continuity is especially driven by changes in temperature and its impact on people's livelihoods. Temperature changes in turn impact precipitation patterns and water retention in soil. These general changes in climate, however, translate differently around the planet. The patterns impact developed and developing countries, though in differing mixtures that are both direct and indirect.

There are clearly regional and local microclimates that may react in a variety of ways to climate change. There are two types of habitat that are driven by temperature and precipitation patterns. Cold temperature climates become more habitable and exploitable by humans when temperatures increase. Hot temperature climates become more habitable and exploitable by humans when temperatures decrease. A decline in tempera-ture leads to less evaporation and make habitats more suitable to human habitation.

Cold areas are generally economically developed countries, and hot areas are generally developing countries. Cold and hot economies, along with the differing types of climate impact, produce two very different types of behavior. The paths can lead to wars of expansion and wars of contraction. In some places, those of expansion and contraction will overlap. Conflict among developed countries might lead to concentrated fatalities, while those in developing countries might lead to conflict that is more diffuse.

There are two aspects of modern trends that differ from those of the past. The past cases represent thousands of years of history, within which natural patterns produced periods of extremely slow change. This pace of change is accelerating in two ways.

First, today's rate of climate change is comparable only to the historic end of large-scale glaciations in the Northern Hemisphere roughly 20,000 years ago. No interim period or conflict intersection since the Neanderthal case is even remotely as dramatic in terms of the rate of climate change. Understanding this unique aspect of the context underlines the potential severity. Second, societies at that time lived in times of great isolation. There was of course trade between early humans, but these were not of bulk items, only specialty crafts and new technologies (mostly tools). Bulk trade was impos-sible without domesticated animals. Modern societies are, however, quite economically interdependent.

The difference is that "losers" from climate change will have strong economic linkages to other countries that may be in the middle ground between winning and losing. Their geographic or economic connection to a "loser" may start a chain reaction, where con-flict from climate change spreads across national boundaries through natural or human forces in a domino-like effect. The problem is thus to identify how the onset of armed conflict caused by climate change spreads to other countries, and what the nature of the "infection" is. When conflict is confined to a single country, solutions and approaches are quite different from in cases that involve more than one country. There is also the danger of spread to the entire global system.

Building a Scientific Understanding of the Relationship Between Climate Change and Conflict

Social predictions have long been prey to political interests. Over time, however, good science needs to win out in order to make good policy on climate change and conflict. Scientific understanding will need to examine both the macro- (national interests) and the micro-issues (individual and local interests) in the relationship. Rapid climate change is now undeniable.

It is comfortable to believe that lifestyles, which drive national interests, will simply adjust to meet the challenge of climate change and conflict, but that is wishful thinking. The developed countries have stored resources, and can survive economic pressures more easily than a poor family in Africa that lives year to year. Either case can end in armed conflict, with the only difference being how long it takes. There is a need to push the understanding of climate change and conflict to the forefront of scientific investigation.

It is inevitable that the two will develop linkages, and possible theories of behavior need to emerge.

Is it possible to incorporate into Global Climate Models data and research assumptions about causal relationships related to conflict? Basic conflict data and models do exist. There would need to be at least three common ground rules for these models in order for them to correspond. First, there is the need for a common unit of analysis. The IPCC approach includes regional climate models, and there needs to be a correspondence table that translates conflict from a national level to a regional one.

The second need is for relevant assumptions on how climate change translates into conflict. Some pathways have been proposed here, but a more definitive model would need the assistance of existing data, theories, and algorithms on the causes of conflict and where climate change fits in. There will need to be further work in order to glean any statistical reliability and appropriate parameters. A third need is an evolving sense of what the picture looks like in a dynamic fashion. With assumptions built into models, what impact on conflict will likely occur? How will conflict rise and subside over this long time horizon? Could conflict actually produce some feedback that dynamically adds to climate change? A short-term examination could focus on burning oil wells, as in the Kuwait War and a long-term examination on the burning of forests for land appropriation and settlement in Kalimantan on Borneo. There, migrants from Java began to arrive in large numbers and needed land for agriculture. The forests are also claimed by the indigenous Dayaks, who are largely hunter-gatherers. Burning the forests meant claiming the land.

The patterns of conflict need to be understood alongside the patterns of climate change. The macro-wars in the twentieth century may give way to micro-wars in the twenty-first century. There are clearly other derivative modes of interaction between macro- and micro-trends in climate, just as there are in conflict.

Making Policy Tools Relevant to Climate Change and Conflict Issues

The long historical relationship between climate change and conflict means that policy makers need to embrace long-term commitments to solving the problem. This change in outlook will require the adoption of new thinking about treaties. The Kyoto Protocol shows the difficulty in getting to the long timeframe required to alter the climate side of the equation. The protocol was adopted in December 1997, but did not enter into force (needing a minimum quota of signatories) until February 2005. This first commitment period of the protocol will expire in 2012, meaning that it will be in effect for only seven years. It is obviously only an interim agreement, but one would imagine the commitment periods to increase over time.

Negotiations on a post-Kyoto framework are slowly underway. Will this process be continuous or discontinuous? Will the agreements that follow be essentially new agreements that are negotiated anew each time, or will agreement follow the progressive pattern of the GATT/WTO, where rounds of negotiations amend and broaden the original agreement? The idea behind these agreements is based on the Bicycle Theory: one either keeps going forward or risks falling off the bike.

Treaties covering conflict are unlike climate treaties, and they are long-standing in construct and usually without temporal limitations. Conflict treaties are often very forward-looking. Not long after space exploration began, in 1967 United States and the Soviet Union signed the Treaty on Principles Covering the Activities of States in the Exploration and Use of outer Space, Including the Moon and other Celestial Bodies. (Most countries signed it then, like Burkina Faso and the Holy See, but only the two Super powers had any space presence at this time.) The treaty was a preventative non-armament model, built on principles set out in the 1959 Antarctic Treaty that came into force in 1961. Both treaties stand today. Contrast this record to the very short-term horizon of the Kyoto Treaty.

The need for overlap between the two treaty types is manifest in two ways. The first is the need for timeframes that have greater alignment for stability. Conflict treaties have long-term stability as a built-in factor. Climate treaties should also have more long-term commitments.

The second area of overlap is that the threat of climate change can be a justification for a preventative war in at least three ways. First, it can be a reason to stop another country from taking harmful environmental actions that impact another, such as pollution that can cross borders. Second, it might be used to prevent countries from depriving others of their fair share of environmental resources (such as water in clouds). Third, some may resort to it in order to acquire basic resources such as food, when state survival or a humanitarian catastrophe looms. It may also turn out that climate change can be a justification for conflict, even if that connection is quite remote. In either case, climate change will be a growing fact in the calculus of conflict.

Even if current forecasts turn out different from the ones shown here, there is a salience to the issue of climate change and conflict. It does not matter whether the climate is warming or cooling, if it is moderate or high, or if humans are responsible. In whatever configuration, climate change has been and will continue to be a source of conflict. Understanding this relationship is more important now, because the degree of warming will be the highest in recorded human history and because the world has become so globalized and interdependent.

Reference

Linden, Eugene (2006). *The Winds of Change: Climate Weather, and the Destruction of Civilization*. New York: Simon and Schuster.

68

Revisiting Change and Conflict: On Underlying Assumptions and the De-Politicisation of Conflict Resolution

Vivienne Jabri

Vivienne Jabri is Professor of International Politics at King's College London. She has been a major contributor to the conflict resolution field since her seminal 1996 book *Discourses on Violence*, which cited work by Anthony Giddens and Jürgen Habermas to mount a critical reassessment of the field. Mark Hoffman, Assistant Professor at the London School of Economics and Political Science, is another conflict resolution specialist who has done a great deal to enrich the field in this way.[1] Readers may like to discuss what practical difference Jabri's critique would make to some of the conflict resolution approaches illustrated elsewhere in this book.

Notes

1 M. Hoffman, 'Critical Theory and the Inter-Paradigm Debate', *Millennium* 16/2 (1987): 234–262.

* * * *

The De-politicisation of Conflict Analysis and Resolution

Conflict analysis has historically sought to somehow extract itself from social and political theory, so that its language is rendered neutral, a management consultant's toolkit, ready for use in any context wherein conflict might emerge. There is here an underlying assumption of rationality, even as there is a recognition that such rationality might, at times of crisis, be subject to distortion. Nevertheless, the image of the actors involved is one that assumes the capacity for cost/ benefit evaluation, even as the agent of conflict resolution might intervene to somehow influence how costs are calculated and what benefits might accrue through suggested courses of action. A third party aiming for the resolution of a protracted conflict, for example, the Israeli-Palestinian, might seek to influence how the parties articulate their identities so these are no longer conceived in zero-sum terms; that mutual recognition accrues mutual benefit. The interaction necessarily relies on a conception of agency that is rational to the core; it remains reliant upon cost/benefit evaluations and the only problem that concerns the third party is achieving change in how such costs and benefits are defined, or re-defined, by the parties.

There is, at first sight, absolutely nothing that is wrong with the above aspiration; mutual recognition, especially in the example I highlight above, is desirable not just for those immediately involved, but for the world as a whole, given that the world is now experiencing the consequences of the absence of resolution to this conflict. What then is the problem in the above formulation? The problem, as I reiterate here, is not the ambition to achieve mutual recognition. The problem lies in the extraction of the con-flict resolution setting from its social and political context. This, in conflict resolution speak, is always portrayed as simply dealing with the constituency problem "back home". The frames of reference utilised in the conflict resolution process are assumed to be independent of, though possibly constrained by, the context of the conflict, so that the aspiration is to transcend such constraints, enabling the parties thereby to move beyond the present and towards some positive future.

The extraction of conflict from its socio-political setting constitutes the de-politicising move. This happens on a number of fronts. Firstly, the third-party resolutionary is assumed to possess a language that is managerial to the core, aiming to solve the problem at hand, and hence not implicated. However, we know that the language of analysis is not simply a mirror-image of the world "out there", but actively constructs the world, in its choice of parties to a conflict, its understanding of the issues, the historical trajectory to a conflict, and its conception of desirable interventions and outcomes. Just to return to the above example: mutual recognition is desirable indeed; however, the content of such recognition, its institutional manifestation on the ground, is ultimately what matters. Secondly, the language of conflict analysis is subject itself to the linguistic repertoires that surround and constitute a particular conflict. When the question of identity, for example, is reduced to the "ancient hatreds" formulation, or indeed a majority-minority construction, conflict analysis and resolution do no more than simply reiterate the lan-guage of leaderships bent on such exclusionary frameworks and the practices they seek to legitimise.[1] If the Bosnian conflict, for example, was so represented, as it indeed was, then the language of Milosevic, Karadjic, Mladic, and Tudjman was simply taken as given, interpolating the populations involved in the ethnic terms that these leaders, all in one way or another implicated in war crimes, sought in their efforts to create ethnically defined, supremacist political entities. It is in this sense that conflict analysis, even in its most "sanitised" form, is always somehow implicated, always situated politically, even where it seeks to modify taken-for-granted constructions of a conflict.

A more crucial consequence of the extraction of conflict analysis and resolution from its worldly location is that its conception of agency comes to be limited to that of the rational actor model, wherein complexity is once again reduced to the capacity to be neutral, consistent and systematic. Mitchell's classification of third parties and their capacities to realise change towards conflict resolution suffers from its conception of agency in terms of role. These range from "monitors" to "enskillers", "facilitators", "implementers", and so on. Each has their designated role, each aiming to transform a conflict in very specific ways. All, however, are assumed to be engaged in a process that culminates in a negotiated outcome. Once again, each is provided with a toolkit from which they might draw as they enact their role. Again, there is no problem with the classification scheme per se. Rather, it is its formulaic representation, one that extracts the substantive content of each role in the specificities of a distinct conflict, that is at issue. There is no way that this analysis can, for example, inform on the consequences or desirability of these roles and their applications.

In the final section of this response, I want to provide a different understanding of agency, one that acknowledges that the agencies involved in conflict analysis and resolution are always located in a mutually constitutive relationship with the structural continuities of social and political life, so that far from seeking the extraction of conflict resolution from politics, it is actively re-located in politics.

Re-locating Conflict and Change in Politics (and Ethics)

It is necessary first of all to rethink agency by way of a return to the social sciences, their epistemologies (modes of justification of knowledge) and ontologies (assumptions relating to social entities). As is shown in the hermeneutic tradition (that knowledge is based on interpretative understanding), human action and human society possess their own distinctiveness that cannot be reduced to the terms of the natural sciences. When this tradition is taken further into critical thought, knowledge is understood as always situated in relation to interests (Habermas 1972) and power (Foucault 1980), so that its frameworks of understanding are unavoidably located in society and implicated in the constitution of its relations of power. Understood in this way, knowledge about conflict may be judged, not in terms of the criteria of science, but in terms of the interests that constitute particular frameworks of knowledge and in terms that reveal the complicities of different modes of understanding in relations of power.

The second element relates to conceptions of agency, structure, and their relationship. Drawing on critical social and political thought, Giddens provides a way of thinking about agency that is not dualistically related to structure, but constituted in relation to structure (Giddens 1979). Agency understood in this sense is not simply reduced to particular roles, but is conceived in relation to the discursive and institutional continuities of social systems. These continuities are not simply constraining, but enable actors to make sense of the world.[2] Agents are hence always positioned in relation to symbolic orders, frameworks of meaning and structures of domination, drawing upon such continuities both consciously and unconsciously in social interaction. Even that most transformative of actions, dissent, is only meaningful in relation to existing linguistic frameworks and relations of power.

The implications for conflict analysis and resolution are profound, for these forms of agency come to be re-located in the social and political context, so that it is no longer possible simply to adhere to a toolkit approach, acknowledging that any intervention in conflict has political as well as ethical consequences, even when these are constructed in discourse in purely managerial and instrumental forms.

Conflict and change must hence be explored in relation to the specificities of context and not in generic terms. These specificities emerge in the distinctiveness of forms of struggle and contestation in relation to the discursive and institutional context of a conflict. Conflicts of the late modern period are no longer isolated occurrences, but take place in a globalised arena, drawing on the resources that this arena provides while being subject in turn to its differential enablements and constraints. Any critical approach to conflict and its resolution takes these differentiations seriously, revealing in turn the exclusionary practices that enable some while constraining the many, inequalities of access that in themselves are at the heart of the most serious and deadly conflicts of our age. Mitchell is aware of all of this; his analysis, however, conceals its political and ethical implications.

The implications for conflict resolution relate primarily to a shift away from a toolkit approach to the subject. Intervention is understood in political and ethical terms and not simply in terms that seek to divorce the procedural from the substantive. Conflict analysis is recognised as a "practice", and, in the critical vein, as one that reveals the underlying relationships of power that differentially give voice or confer legitimacy, as well as its own complicity in such relationships. Practices of conflict resolution are themselves subjected to close scrutiny, located in relation to, for example, their complicity in contributing variously towards the pacification of the weaker side, the perpetuation of exclusionary practices, and the legitimisation of discourses and institutions that are the root causes of violence. This re-formulation suggests that practices relating to conflict resolution are always distinctly political practices, and as such, always subject to contestation.

Notes

1 For an excellent investigation into the complicities of diplomatic engagement in the Bosnian conflict, see Campbell 1998.
2 For the application of critical social and political thought, including Giddens's structuration theory, to the analysis of conflict, see Jabri 1996, where the agency-structure problematique in the context of war and peace is explored.

References

Campbell, David 1998. *National Deconstruction: Violence, Identity and Justice in Bosnia*. Minneapolis: University of Minnesota Press.

Foucault, Michel 1980. Truth and Power, in: *Power/Knowledge*, edited by Colin Gordon. New York and London: Prentice Hall, 109–133.

Giddens, Anthony 1979. *Central Problems in Social Theory*. London: Macmillan.

Habermas, Jürgen 1972. *Knowledge and Human Interests*. Boston: Beacon Press.

Jabri, Vivienne 1996. *Discourses on Violence: Conflict Analysis Reconsidered*. Manchester and New York: Manchester University Press.

69

From Pacification to Peacebuilding: A Call to Global Transformation

Diana Francis

In this brief but eloquent piece, Diana Francis sums up a major subtheme of this book. Her points about the negative impact that 'gender mainstreaming' can have, and the tension that she notes between gender and culture, are increasingly recognized as complications that need attention. Her central insistence that 'dominant models of masculinity' and 'male–female identities and relationships' still need to be re-examined and reconsidered remains a major future task for the field.

* * * *

I heard a heartbreaking story from an African woman colleague who described the village group that had begun the work in which she was now involved. No-one had a degree, no-one was used to handling money, but their work was vital, and they were in control of it. Then someone put them in touch with a donor, who was keen to support the work but had stipulated qualified staff and professional accounting as a precondition. Now not one of the original women was involved.

Women, gender and power

Since in many societies girls are often excluded from education, or have fewer and poorer educational opportunities, such professionalisation is liable to have a disproportionate effect on women, who in those societies are also the regular victims of daily violence – often sanctioned by law – and are largely excluded from power and public participation. This hidden war, covering a large part of the globe, needs to be seen as such and addressed at least as seriously as other, localised wars.

Of course 'gender' and 'women' are two different things. But in the current gender dispensation women, the numerical majority, are a power minority, and are often assigned the roles of servants and victims. Of course there are differences in this respect between one society and another, but when we talk about the great progress that has been made over the last century in terms of gender equality, we should not forget that, for many of the world's women, nothing has changed. Nor should we ignore the role of sexual violence in war, or the particular ways in which war and its consequences are experienced by women.[1]

The Islamophobia that has grown since 9/11 and the wars subsequently launched by the West have fed extreme, repressive forms (or perversions) of Islam, and have added political sensitivities and complications to women's work and its profile in affected societies. They have strengthened the forces of religious and cultural patriarchy and have left women caught between concern for their own rights and freedoms and the wish not to be out of solidarity with their own 'side' in relation to Western bullying and disrespect.

In some places the lot of women improved for a while, only to deteriorate again as one dominating, controlling system was challenged by another, and women became – as so often in war – the emblems and victims of the struggle for mastery. This has happened in Iraq and in Palestine, where women's freedom has been greatly curtailed and violence against them has risen sharply. Rape continues to be a weapon of internal war – for instance in Sudan and in north-east India. News of sexual crimes against women by UN troops in the Democratic Republic of Congo caused some apparent shock, but rape has always been one of the hallmarks of military violence.

Although women far outnumber men in peace work, the pattern of male dominance in key positions often prevails in organisations. But that may be changing. Moreover, many women's organisations have been established. UN Resolution 1325 has provided a lever for women to insist on having a voice, and has helped them to win funding for mobilisation. There are some excellent programmes to support this work and to help them access funds.

I do, however, hear disturbing accounts of the negative impact of 'gender mainstreaming', which is meant to ensure that the gender dimension of all work is explored and addressed as a matter of routine. The danger is that, in practice, it may mean no more than the ticking of boxes in strategic planning frameworks and funding applications. And since the funds no longer get earmarked for gender work or for women's use, some work that might previously have been supported no longer is. It seems also that, in general, more funds are allocated to work in the 'security' and 'institution-building' sectors, and less to the kind of community-based work in which women often take the lead.

We are faced here with the dilemma already referred to: that, in efforts to escape from the immediate violence of war, it is hard to avoid privileging the power of male-led violence, by virtue of the attention those leaders receive. This is reflected in the relative absence of women, whether as parties or third parties, from top- or high-level negotiation processes, despite the progress made in building civil society's role (including that of women) in wider peace processes. And when it comes to the third-party roles of NGOs in peace processes, here too most of the work that is done with political and military leaders (who are almost always men) remains male-dominated. There is a largely unspoken assumption (probably correct) that men will take other men more seriously. It is crucial that work be done on rethinking gender constructions and relationships, not only in women's groups but also in mixed and men-only settings, so that dominant models of masculinity are re-examined and male-female identities and relationships reconsidered. A shift in understanding on masculinity is central to a shift away from the culture of war.

Gender and culture are inextricably linked, but special pleading about culture that excuses violence against women and the wanton constriction of their lives has no moral basis and denies their full humanity. We all bear responsibility for our cultures, not as we have received them but as we choose to live in them. We can perpetuate them or we can change them. All of us, women as well as men, need to pinpoint and then to break the cultural link between constructions of masculinity and the idea of dominance, expressed in men's 'conquest' of women and their glorification through military violence: the notion that the archetype of manhood is the warrior hero, whether he is armed with a spear, toting a machine gun or piloting a B52 bomber. Until we break this link and unmask war, finally, as the brutal, inhumane and destructive institution that it is, any progress we make will be limited and fitful and all of us, male as well as female, will suffer.

Note

1 For moving examples of these, see L. Vušković and Z. Trifunović (eds), *Women's Side of War*, Belgrade: Women in Black, 2008.

70

Culture and Conflict Resolution

Kevin Avruch

Kevin Avruch is Henry Hart Professor of Conflict Resolution at the School for Conflict Analysis and Resolution at George Mason University, Virginia. Together with Peter Black, he took a lead in the 1990s in offering a critique of 'generic' conflict resolution approaches that were 'culture blind' and insisted that what he called 'ethnoconflict theory and practice' should be integral to all aspects of conflict resolution. In these extracts, taken from his influential 1998 book *Culture and Conflict Resolution*, he applies a nuanced understanding of culture to two aspects of the field.

Two brief extracts are given here. The first points to the importance of deconstructing the misuse – and sometimes gross abuse – of these erroneous concepts by conflict parties. The reference to Matthew Arnold is to his *Culture and Anarchy* (1867–9) in which the Victorian poet and critic defined culture as 'the best that has been thought and said'. The second extract draws conclusions about how culture-awareness can best inform conflict resolution theory and practice in general. In this case the reference is to 'problem-solving'. It begins by contrasting John Burton's more generic and prescriptive approach (see Reading 5) with John Paul Lederach's more contextualized and elicitive approach (see Reading 22).

In *Culture and Conflict Resolution*, Avruch first looks critically at the concept of 'culture' and contrasts 'older approaches' which treat culture as if it is homogeneous, timeless and uniformly distributed among groups such as tribes, races and nations with a more nuanced understanding that individuals may have more than one culture, that these are likely to contain inner tensions and contradictions, and that such patterns can and do fluctuate in complex ways in response to a changing environment: 'This means (contrary to the reified or stable or homogeneous view of culture) that culture is to some extent always situational, flexible, and responsive to the exigencies of the worlds that individuals confront' (1998: 20). Avruch then moves on to consider conflict resolution responses in the light of these 'inadequate ideas': 'These ... inadequate ideas about culture are related and mutually reinforcing. Using them, we argue, greatly diminishes the utility of the culture concept as an analytic tool for understanding social action, in this case, conflict and conflict resolution' (1998: 16).

*   *   *   *

[T]he whole issue of culture's analytical utility and of these inadequate ideas is complicated by the fact that *each of these inadequate ideas is routinely invoked in what we have called the Matthew Arnold sense of culture* [original italics]. This happens when culture is objectified by actors and used in politically charged – usually nationalistic, racialistic or ethnic – discourses. Many of these discourses go way beyond the injuries inflicted by Arnold's snobbery, or even the class system of nineteenth-century England. As Rwanda, Burundi, Bosnia, and before them Nazi Germany all demonstrate, they are capable of provoking genocide. In fact, we have now identified one way in which one version of the culture concept, used as an ideological resource by contestants – is itself a source – or accelerant – of social conflict. One strategy for conflict resolution immediately presents itself: the proactive deconstruction, in the sense of debunking or unmasking, of these inadequate ideas.

...

If Burton's conception of the role of the third party represents one pole – highly directive and prescriptive – then surely Lederach's conception represents the other. Addressing practitioners and trainers in intercultural conflict resolution, Lederach counterposes the prescriptive model of practice and training with what he calls the elicitive model. In the prescriptive model, one's own (typically North American and middle-class) presumptions about conflict and third-party roles are elevated to the status of expert system. The elicitive model aims to get at what Avruch and Black call ethnoconflict theory and practice, discovering, in the words of Lederach, the "models that emerge from the resources present in a particular setting and responding to needs in that context."[1]

Which brings us full circle back to the analytical, interactive, collaborative, problem-solving workshops. When they work, it is not just because a conflict has been broken down dispassionately into its component parts, costs and benefits arrayed on a balance sheet for all participants to compute. Rather, if they succeed, it is undoubtedly because, as Kelman and Rouhana write, the workshops "enable the parties to penetrate each other's perspective, gaining insight into each other's concerns, priorities and constraints."[2] It is hard to imagine a better description of the exercise of an ethnographic imagination – or of a cultural analysis. We would go further, arguing that in *intercultural conflict resolution a cultural analysis is an irreducible part of problem-solving.*

In this reframing of the problem-solving workshop, cultural analysis is part and parcel of analytical problem-solving. But beyond that, what goes on in the course of conflict resolution (with the help of a third party or not) is the emergence of something like a new culture – a culture genesis. The new culture is a metaculture of shared schemas and ideational encodements, of understandings and symbols, by means of which the parties achieve a new image of their world and, as Kelman and Rouhana phrase it, a new "sense of possibility ... that a peaceful solution is attainable" (ibid.). Of course, such a metaculture is fragile in the extreme, vulnerable to the stronger, better entrenched, and "traditionalized" old cultures – the cultures of conflict – shared by the participants' home communities and constituencies. That is why, virtually all practitioners agree, the problem of reentry for participants after *successful* workshops is so fateful. And this is why, we would argue, for conflict resolution theory and practice to ignore cultural dynamics is to invite failure, for problem-solving workshops and beyond.

Notes

1 J. P. Lederach, *Preparing for Peace*. New York: Syracuse University Press, 1995, p. 55.
2 H. Kelman and N. Rouhana, 'Promoting Joint Thinking in International Conflicts', *Journal of Social Issues* 50, no. 1 (1994): 174.

71

Peace Studies: A Cultural Perspective

Wolfgang Dietrich et al.

These short extracts from Wolfgang Dietrich's edited volume on cultural perspectives on peace and conflict are indicative of the rich potential for drawing from different global value systems to underpin the normative aspirations of conflict resolution. As presented here, this may seem something of a 'wish list'. But Dietrich and his fellow authors are well aware of what Scott Appleby famously called 'the ambivalence of the sacred'[1] – the capacity of world religions and cultures to foster both 'violence' and 'reconciliation'[2] – and they discuss this in the main body of the book. These fierce debates within world cultures are clearly crucial sites for advancing the agenda argued for by Avruch in Reading 70.

Notes

1 R. Appleby, *The Ambivalence of the Sacred: Religion, Violence and Reconciliation.* Lanham, MD: Rowman & Littlefield, 2000.
2 M. Gopin, *Between Eden and Armageddon: The Future of World Religions, Violence and Peacemaking.* Oxford: Oxford University Press, 2000; M. Juergensmeyer, *Terror in the Mind of God: The Global Rise of Religious Violence.* Berkeley: University of California Press, 2000.

* * * *

Section 1   Peace Concepts in Europe

Peace: The European Narrative
Karlheinz Koppe

In this time, ideas of peace always ran the risk of not being heard. This is what happened, for example, to the first peace researcher of the newer history, Desiderius Erasmus of Rotterdam (1466–1536). In 1516 he received the commission of the Duke of Burgundy (later Emperor Charles V) – who at that time was only fifteen years old – to produce a study on the keeping of the peace. According to tradition he clad his investigation in allegorical clothing by letting peace itself appear as a person and complaining about his fate: Querela Pacis (The Complaint of Peace). The work was finished in 1517. It says:

> Almost no peace is so unjust that it would not be preferable to the seemingly most just war. Consider at first the different circumstances which war necessitates or brings with it, and you will see, what gain you have accomplished. ... You have seen so far, that nothing has been achieved with alliances, that neither marriage and relation by marriage, nor violence and lust for revenge have helped. Now, confronted with this danger, show what reconciliation and benefaction can achieve. One war sows the next, revenge begets revenge. May now one friendship give birth to the other and one benefaction attract the other. (Erasmus, 1917)

This study was intended as a preparation for the first international peace conference and signified the first important document in which peace was formulated for humanity's sake and every kind of war was clearly refused. Translated into the language of modern peace research, Erasmus argued that military violence would not be an appropriate means to regulate disputes between princes and states, because it would harm the welfare of the state and its citizens more than it would benefit them.

Section 2   Peace Concepts in the Middle East

Salaam: A Muslim Perspective
Aurangzeb Haneef

Islam is the system of Salaam. Many scholars consider Islam to extend beyond submission to God's will, to define Islam as 'the making of peace' (Abu-Nimer, 2003, p. 45). 'The paths of righteousness and virtue that lead to God are also called subul al-salam or paths of peace (Qur'an, 5: 16). Hence, the Qur'an calls Heaven as Dar al-Salam, which is the home of peace and perfection (Qur'an, 10: 25)' (Siddiqi, 2001). Maulana Wahiduddin Khan (1999, p. 45) cites a verse from the Qur'an to deduce that attaining a state of peace in the soul is the spiritual goal of Islam: 'O tranquil soul, return to your Lord, well pleased and well-pleasing Him' (Qur'an, 89: 27–28). The daily greeting of Muslims is Assalaam-o-alaikum (may peace be upon you) that is also derived from the Qur'an (10: 10). Siddiqi (2001) further explains: 'Salam is an active and dynamic involvement to keep and to restore the right order. Salam is both an individual quest for peace and harmony for one's self and it includes the concern for the well-being of all people regardless of their races, colors or genders.' According to Siddiqi (2001), 'there are three major components in the concept of peace (Salam) in Islam.' These are:

- Inner peace and harmony in the life of every individual;
- Social cohesion in the community;
- Treatment of tensions and conflicts.

Thus, Salaam begins from the individual peace, expands to the harmony in the immediate community and encompasses conflict resolution at all levels. It aims for the peaceful whole.

Section 3   Peace Concepts in South and East Asia

He Ping: A Confucian Perspective
Kam-por Yu

The Confucian tradition has been very consistent in holding that the function of governance is three-fold, all aspects directed towards the people: (1) survival, (2) prosperity and (3) education. The first and foremost duty of the government is to guarantee the survival of the people. The next stage is to enable the people not only to survive, but also to have a decent livelihood. Finally, it is to renew the people – to make them become civilized human beings.[1]

With regards to interstate relation, Confucius believes that there is some minimal ethics that is valid across culture: 'If in word you are conscientious and trustworthy and in deed single-minded and reverent, then even in the lands of the barbarians you will go forward without obstruction' (*Analects* 15.6 [trans. by Lau 1992, p. 149]). Confucius opposes the use of military force to coerce, but holds instead that a state should demonstrate its superiority to charm people in other states. When Confucius was asked about government, he replied: 'Ensure that those who are near are pleased and those who are far away are attracted' (*Analects* 13.16 [trans. by Lau 1992, p. 26]).

Section 4   Maori and Native American Peace Concepts

Thaq: 'Peace' in the Andean–Amazonian Culture. The Andean Conception of Peace
Grimaldo Rengifo V

In the Andean–Amazonian culture, there are words that evoke a kind of peace that is understood as a state of serenity and tranquility. In the Quechua tongue of Lircay, Huancavelica, they speak about *hawkalla*, a word related to calm and tranquility. *Hawqa* (or *Qawka*, both are read *jauqa*) is said of a tranquil person who respects and does not disturb the community, celebration or ritual. *Hawqa yachay* means knowing how to live in tranquility without fostering conflicts in the community. It is common, for example, for people to say *Hawqalla kawsasun* ('We will live in tranquility'). In Auquilla, Ayacucho, the same as in the Quechua (or Quichua) of Ecuador, the word for someone who is tranquil, peaceful, who does not look for trouble, who is not a provoker and who gladly receives and assumes his or her commitments is *Kasilla*, so that *kasilla kawsay* means 'to live in tranquility.' In Agato, Ecuador, *fangalla* is said of a light, tranquil person. In general, the Quechua words *kasilla* or *hawqalla* are associated with the Quechua word *kawsay*, and they mean 'to live in a tranquil and relaxed manner.' The expression *allin kawsay* means 'to live well,' and better still if you add the adjective *sumaq* – nice, pleasing – to the expressions *hawqalla kawsay* and *allin kawsay*. In this case, these phrases would mean 'to live in harmony, nicely, without problems or difficulties.' In the Quechua of Ancash, in northern Peru, there is the expression *mana ajanashqa*, which means 'without difficulty, to be well, without conflict.' Alternatively, there is another: *Mana piñashqa, mana chikinakushqa,* which is translated as 'We are not in situations of bitterness, wrath or hatred, we are tranquil.'

Thaq, a Quechua word from Cuzco, in southern Peru, is another Andean expression that can be related to peace. In English, among other aspects it means 'tranquil; to be well, serene, sharing what you know, in peace, just living nicely,' for example *thaq kunanka tiyaychi* ('now live in tranquility, in peace'), *thaq kani* ('I am in peace, tranquil'), or *thak kay*, which means 'in tranquility.' In the Aymara tongue, to be tranquil in peace can be said with the expression *ph'ajtata* or *phajtatawa*, and to say that everything is tranquil, in calm, in peace, you would say *Ph'ajtatakiwa*. Ms. Victoria Panti Espillico (2007), from the village of Queruma, Juli, in Puno, says, for example, *Yapu irnaqawita juttha chuymaja wali phajtatawa* ('My heart is tranquil because I have finished harvesting in my entire farm').

This feeling of calm, serenity, tranquility and joy can be observed when, during the celebration of carnival, the *comunero* (joint holder of a tenure of lands) appraises his crops in full bloom, when the fruits have been gathered, when there is food for everyone (in Quechua expressed by *mikuylla kachunqa thakllan tiyakusun*, 'We will live in tranquility if there is food'). Also, these circumstances are experienced when the corn is softly caressed by the wind, or when the sunset is windless and tranquil, the morning is sunny, when there is an intense experience of being at the moment of a ritual, or in the calmness of the countryside after a storm.

Section V   Peace Concepts in Africa

Asomdwoe: A West African Perspective
Kofi Asare Opoku

Peace and community

Though there are many diverse societies and cultures on the African continent, a careful and meticulous examination reveals a striking commonality that characterizes them all, and that is the emphasis on community and communal living. This emphasis stems from an awareness of the limitation or lack of self-sufficiency on the part of each person and the consequent need to overcome this by cooperating with others in order to realize each person's full potential. A lesson from the human body provides imaginative insights into this matter in the form of an African proverb: 'The left hand washes the right and the right hand washes the left' (Opoku, 1997, p. 17). Each hand has a limitation in the sense that it cannot wash itself, but when the hands wash each other they become clean. In the same manner, each person has a limitation in the sense that he/she cannot meet all his/her basic needs single-handedly, but requires the assistance of others. Through cooperation and mutual helpfulness, individual limitations are overcome and human welfare is enhanced, and each person can fulfil his or her potential.

Society exists to promote life in its fullest dimension, which can be described as a state of being at peace, but this cannot be achieved without the cooperation of others and therefore cooperation and mutual helpfulness are necessary to bring about peace. Communal living is based on the harmonious interrelationships between the members of the community, as its sine qua non, for in the African understanding life is not possible without community. Society is the context of human existence and the Akan of Ghana say: 'When a person descends from the heavens, he/she descends into a town inhabited by human beings' (Akan proverb), which means human society. But this society is understood to include not only the visible members, but also invisible members: the Overlord of the community, the Great Spirit or Supreme Being; the ancestors, who are forbears and predecessors of the community; the divinities, regarded as agents of the Supreme Being; and those who are yet to be born. The society also includes animals and nature, regarded as an integral part of humankind's world order; and life is at its best and peace is attained when a state of equilibrium prevails, and when there is a state of undisturbed, harmonious relations between humans, the spirit world, animals and nature.

A way to create peace is sharing, and common etiquette demands that strangers be welcomed into homes. As Malidoma says, 'It is the task of him who is not a stranger to turn the potential enemy in the stranger into a friend' (1994, p. 96). The Ibo (Nigeria) do this in their communities through the ritual of splitting kola, praying over it and sharing it with the guest and those present, to indicate that the guest is genially welcome. Likewise, in Akan communities, guests are given Bresuo, literally water against weariness; since tiredness is one of the most common signs of dehydration, the guest is cooled by the water, which is shared with him and prevents him from becoming mentally fuzzy and enables the guest to feel at ease and welcome.

The community is based on peace as its inescapable foundation and the moral obligations imposed on members of the community have as their goal the securing of a state of peaceful living so that each person can live his/her life fully. This goal is achieved through education.

Note

1 *Analects* 13.9 and *Mencius* 3A3 illustrate this point well.

References

Abu-Nimer, M. (2003) *Nonviolence and Peacebuilding in Islam: Theory and Practice* (Gainesville: University Press of Florida).

Erasmus De Rotterdam (1917) *Querela Pacis: The Complaint of Peace* (Chicago: Open Court).

Espillico, V. et al. (2007) 'Violencia en el mundo andino.' Presented at Minga on International Education and Sustainable Research, Juli, May 2007.

Khan, M.W. (1999) *Islam and Peace* (New Delhi: Goodword Books/Al-Risala).

Lau, D.C. (tr.) (1992) *The Analects* (Hong Kong: Chinese University Press).

Malidoma, P.S. (1994) *Of Water and the Spirit: Ritual, Magic and Initiation in the Life of an African Shaman* (New York: Penguin/Arkana).

Opoku, K.A. (1997) *Hearing and Keeping* (Pretoria: UNISA Press).

Siddiqi, M.H. (2001) 'Islam is Peace,' http://www.pakistanlink.com/religion/2001/1102.html, date accessed October 15, 2004.

72

Ushahidi: From Crisis Mapping in Kenya to Mapping the Globe

This reading illustrates several 'growth points' in the conflict resolution field – the global nature of the enterprise, the role that initially small-scale local initiatives can play at other levels and, above all, the new 'frontier' opened up by the internet for conflict resolution in the age of cybertechnology – the opportunity to develop 'cyberpeace' as a counterpart to 'cyberwar'. The global information networks opened up by the World Wide Web, and by the horizontal social media communication platforms such as Twitter and Facebook, are creating opportunities and spaces for real time virtual-digital data and analysis to the point that we can begin to talk about cyber-conflict resolution. These opportunities and technologies are creating exciting tools which younger and digitally literate conflict resolvers are mastering. There are many examples, from the online Global Peace Index produced annually by Vision of Humanity at http://www.visionofhumanity.org/#/page/indexes/mexico-peace-index, to the Facebook Peace page at https://www.facebook.com/peace/.

In the example we have selected here, we have used the Ushahidi conflict mapping platform, which developed its approach to crisis mapping using crowdsourcing methods in Kenya following electoral violence there in 2007. Since then the method has been developed as an open source tool to enable people to design their own early warning and crisis mapping systems around the world. The Ushahidi system is still in its infancy, but with its real time data gathering, it promises to provide more power and speed of analysis and response than static systems such as the mapping tools shown in Part II. However these tools also embody an analytic sophistication that may in future enhance even more the power and reliability of Ushahidi-style digital systems.

* * * *

Vision and Motivation

Waves of violence unfolding across the country. Communities in fear of rioting, armed gangs and a government-imposed shoot-to-kill policy. Disorder and destruction continuing unchecked without an idea of when it would end. This was Kenya following the 2007 presidential elections. Incumbent President Mwai Kibaki was announced the winner on December 30; however, leading opposition candidate Raila Odinga claimed that ballots were rigged.[1] Members of Odinga's Luo tribe were infuriated, setting off decades-old tensions with Kibaki's Kikuyu tribe. The initial outburst of chaos ushered in a turbulent period in Kenyan history, prompting Kenyan activist Ory Okolloh to send out a plea on her blog *Kenyan Pundit*: "Any techies out there willing to do a mashup of where the violence and destruction is occurring using Google Maps?"[2] Okolloh's simple query on January 3, 2008 inspired a group of bloggers to collaborate over the weekend to turn her dream into a reality. On January 9, Ushahidi, meaning 'witness or testimony' in Swahili, was born, enabling Kenyans, and people around the world, to report and map incidents of violence via SMS or the web.

Goals and Objectives

Okolloh had been covering the elections from inside Kenya but chose to leave once the violence started. The disconnect between local media coverage and information she received directly from her sources sparked the call for Ushahidi. She saw the need for those still inside the country to have information-sharing technology to communicate with each other and those seeking to help victims. For the release of Ushahidi, Okolloh announced on her blog, "We believe that the number of deaths being reported by the government, police, and media is grossly underreported. We also don't think we have a true picture of what is really going on – reports that all of us have heard from family and friends in affected areas suggests that things are much worse than what we have heard in the media."[3]

Ushahidi allowed Kenyans to create a more accurate picture of the violence occurring. The platform is simple. As events occur in the field, witnesses send SMS messages to a designated phone number or submit a report online. Ushahidi administrators can view the reports, which are stored in a secure database. Administrators prioritize urgent messages, fact-check and confirm each submission before posting it in near real time. Each report is posted with a title, description, and most importantly, exact GPS coordinates onto an interactive Google map. Each report is categorized by type of incident – for example, fire, rape, or looting. The Ushahidi platform compiles full analytical reports and alerts that identify areas with high levels of activity. In addition, the platform can compile a full timeline of events. NGOs, relief workers and civic activists can easily access data to identify where assistance is needed and what type of response is required.

Leadership

Ushahidi was made possible by a group of Kenyan activists and tech experts who wouldn't stand by idly as a crisis engulfed their country. Okolloh was born and raised in an impoverished, rural area of Kenya. According to her, "For most Africans today, where you live, or where you were born, and the circumstances under which you were born, determine the rest of your life. I would like to see that change, and the change starts with us … as Africans, we need to take responsibility for our continent!"[4] Okolloh studied in the United States at the University of Pittsburgh for her undergraduate degree and then Harvard Law School for her JD. Following her law school graduation in 2005, she returned to Africa and established herself as a prominent blogger on Kenyan politics. In 2006, she co-founded *Mzalendo: Eye on Kenyan Parliament*. Mzalendo, which means 'patriot' in Swahili, is a volunteer-run watchdog site that posts information and articles on members of Kenya's parliament.

Okolloh's civic activism tied her in to a strong network of tech experts and Kenyan activists, including those who helped start Ushahidi. Erik Hersman, who grew up in Kenya and Sudan, is a technologist and author of the *White African* blog. In addition to Ushahidi, he has founded *AfriGadget*, a site which showcases creative tech solutions to problems in Africa. Co-founder and *AfroMusing* author Juliana Rotich grew up in Kenya and studied information technology in the United States before helping develop Ushahidi. David Kobia, despite being thousands of miles away in the United States, also contributed his expertise in software development to Ushahidi.[5] According to Hersman, although the mapping technology was already about three years old, the Ushahidi team put it to a new, more dynamic, ground-breaking use.[6]

Civic Environment

The bloodshed that prompted Ushahidi resulted from decades-old ethnic tensions in Kenya over land ownership and governance.[7] Following independence from the British in 1963, land was left mostly in the hands of government trusts and political allies, not the original, pre-colonial owners.[8] The unfair allocation of land, in addition to allegations of rampant corruption within Kenya's post-colonial government, created rifts between the ethnic communities who benefited from their political connections and those who did not. Land ownership and governance were central issues in Kenya's multiparty elections, the first of which was held in 1992. The 2007 elections were expected to be a close race between the two candidates, but no one had predicted that a post-election crisis would leave 1,000 Kenyans dead and 500,000 others displaced.[9]

Freedom of religion, education, assembly and press are provided for in the Kenyan constitution, and in 2007, Kenya boasted one of the most open media environments in Africa, with six private television stations, two FM radio stations and unrestricted internet access.[10] However, when the presidential election results were announced, the government swiftly banned live TV and radio coverage of the ensuing chaos. Journalists covering the election were threatened with tear gas attacks and intimidated at polling stations. The ban presented an opportunity for non-traditional media to play a greater role in election coverage.

Although Internet penetration in Kenya was estimated at only 8%,[11] there was already a rich blogging tradition in the country.[12] The *Kenyan Blogs Webring*, founded in 2004, supports Kenyan citizen and grassroots media by aggregating over 800 Kenyan blogs on a host of topics from politics to civil society to technology to personal experiences. Because internet content in Kenya was unfettered, the online community had an opportunity to step in and challenge the mainstream media's narrative of political developments and the growing violence.[13]

Message and Audience

Ushahidi's developers envisioned the platform as an easy-to-use tool to empower and connect the general public. According to cofounder David Kobia, the platform is "an opportunity for everyone to create the narrative."[14] In 2007, over 40% of Kenyans owned mobile phones, which were the only tool necessary to submit a report of violence.[15] The developers coordinated a grassroots communications strategy to reach a wide audience. As established bloggers, each of the developers had their own following to spread the word. In addition to the Internet, the Ushahidi developers utilized the country's flourishing independent radio network to broadcast information on how to submit reports of violence. Combining radio and internet outreach expanded the project's potential audience from less than 10% to 95% of the population.[16] During the post-election crisis, Ushahidi had over 45,000 Kenyan users.[17]

Guest Ushahidi blogger Jason Nickerson highlighted the value of Ushahidi beyond map-making: "Beyond collecting and analyzing the data, there's a need to ensure action is taken to address the issues Ushahidi identifies. Interactions with the search and rescue community during past events have demonstrated the value of the platform for meeting their needs."[18]

Organizations such as MMC Outreach were able to identify affected communities in need of hot meals and clothing.[19] Peace Caravan, a local organization, used Ushahidi to identify areas where its peacebuilding efforts were most needed. Peace Caravan, run by Rachel Kung'u, is a project to promote development and education through the formation of youth community groups. Kung'u spoke about the usefulness of Ushahidi's communication and information for Peace Caravan: "It gave us the updates, the people sharing the information from various communities on what is happening. Then we were able to get the right information and use it to run the caravan."[20] Meanwhile, international and Kenyan diaspora organizations could use the platform to determine appropriate funding for relief efforts.

Outreach Activities

Once the post-election violence calmed down, the Ushahidi team worked to expand the platform's reach. In May 2008, Ushahidi was awarded first place in a NetSquared Challenge for innovative mashup projects using Web and mobile-based technologies focused on social change. The award money provided enough funding to create Ushahidi 2.0, an open-source version of the original platform.[21] The open-source platform allows anyone to adapt Ushahidi to meet their local needs. The platform has been utilized around the world for a variety of causes. In fact, by 2011, the platform had been deployed over 11,000 times.[22] In India and Mexico, the platform has been used to monitor elections. Ushahidi enabled relief organizations to organize rescue efforts during floods in Thailand and Pakistan and after the devastating 2010 earthquake in Haiti. In Egypt, activists have developed HarassMap, a system of monitoring sexual harassment and violence against women. Indonesian activists are using the platform to track crime in the capital city of Jakarta.

The Ushahidi site provides users with deployment toolkits with comprehensive instructions on how to utilize the platform. One of the major challenges of crowd-sourced information is data authenticity. Ushahidi has developed a verification guide to coach users on authenticating reports. Additionally, Ushahidi has launched a new platform,

Swift River, which can quickly analyze and verify large amounts of crowd-sourced data. Swift River is intended to make it even easier for NGOs and humanitarian organizations to respond in emergency situations. Ushahidi also hosts Crowd Map, a version of the Ushahidi platform that doesn't require downloading and can be deployed within minutes to monitor elections or map a crisis. Ushahidi has attracted partnerships and funding from diverse and powerful organizations such as Google, Mozilla Foundation, Knight Foundation, Digital Democracy and the United States Institute for Peace. Although Ushahidi began as an ad-hoc group of bloggers reacting to a local crisis, it has grown into a full-fledged non-profit tech organization helping people across the globe.

Notes

1 Gettleman, Jeffrey. "Fighting Intensifies After Election in Kenya." *New York Times*. 1 January 2008.
2 Okolloh, Ory. "Update Jan 3 1100pm" Kenyan Pundit. 3 January 2008.
3 Okolloh, Ory. "Ushahidi.com" Kenyan Pundit. 9 January 2008.
4 "Ory Okolloh on Becoming an Activist." Ted. January 2007.
5 Greenwald, Ted. "David Kobia, 32." *Technology Review*. 2010.
6 Hersman, Erik. "Creating a New Narrative" Ushahidi. 5 January 2011.
7 "Ballots to Bullets: Organized Political Violence and Kenya's Crisis of Government." Human Rights Watch. March 2008.11.
8 "Ballots to Bullets." 12.
9 Ibid. 2.
10 "Kenya – Freedom in the World." Freedom House. 2008.
11 "ITU ICT EYE." International Telecommunications Union. Accessed 23 May 2012.
12 Goldstein, Joshua and Juliana Rotich. "Digitally Networked Technology in Kenya's 2007–2008 Post-Election Crisis." The Berkman Center for Internet and Society at Harvard University. September 2008.
13 Goldstein and Rotich.
14 Hersman, Erik. "Creating a New Narrative" Ushahidi. 5 January 2011.
15 "ITU ICT EYE."
16 Goldstein and Rotich.
17 "About Us: Press Kit." Ushahidi. Accessed 20 May 2012.
18 Nickerman, Jason. "The Crowdsourced Tipping Point: Knowing When to React".
19 Hersman, Erik. "Rachel's Peace Caravan in Kenya" Ushahidi. 11 August 2008.
20 Hersman, Erik. "Rachel Kungu Talks About Ushahidi." Ushahidi. 1 September 2008.
21 Hersman, Erik. "Some Ushahidi Updates." Ushahidi. 5 May 2008.
22 George, Sarah. "Ushahidi Key Deployment Report 2008 to 2011" Ushahidi. 21 March 2011.

73

Cosmopolitanism after 9/11

David Held

Our final reading comes from David Held, Professor of Politics and International Relations at the University of Durham. One of the greatest challenges from the passing of Western hegemony in world politics is that the entire venture of conflict resolution, together with the values that underpin it, may be seen as a merely Western construct rather than a truly global undertaking. This is greatly enhanced by continuing economic, political and military imbalances in world politics – embodied in the preponderant international financial and legal institutions that still reflect past and present inequalities. In this reading, Held argues eloquently that, in the end, it is only a genuinely cosmopolitan future that can underpin the gains already made in fields such as conflict resolution. In our words, this must be the broad direction in which what we call the 'arrow of history' needs to move 'if the worst of up-coming dangers are to be averted and the human family as a whole is to be able to look ahead to the future with hope – the prerequisite for community – and not despair – the incubator of violence'.[1]

Note

1 O. Ramsbotham, T. Woodhouse and H. Miall, *Contemporary Conflict Resolution*, 3rd ed. Cambridge: Polity, 2011, p. 414.

*   *   *   *

Thinking about the future of humankind on the basis of the early years of the twenty-first century does not give grounds for optimism. From 9/11 to the 2006 war in the Middle East, terrorism, conflict, territorial struggle and the clash of identities appear to define the moment. The wars in Afghanistan, Iraq, Israel/Lebanon and elsewhere suggest that political violence is an irreducible feature of our age. Perversely, globalization seems to have dramatized the significance of differences between peoples; far from the globalization of communications easing understanding and the translation of ideas, it seems to have highlighted what it is that people do not have in common and find dislikeable about each other (Bull, 1977). Moreover, the contemporary drivers of political nationalism – self-determination, secure borders, geo-political and geo-economic advantage – place an emphasis on the pursuit of the national interest above concerns with what it is that humans might have in common.

...

From the foundation of UN system to the EU, from changes to the laws of war to the entrenchment of human rights, from the emergence of international environmental regimes to the establishment of the International Criminal Court, people have sought to reframe human activity and embed it in law, rights and responsibilities. Many of these developments were initiated against the background of formidable threats to human-kind – above all, Nazism, fascism and Stalinism. Those involved in them affirmed the importance of universal principles, human rights and the rule of law in the face of strong temptations to simply put up the shutters and defend the position of only some coun-tries and nations. They rejected the view of national and moral particularists that belong-ing to a given community limits and determines the moral worth of individuals and the nature of their freedom, and they defended the irreducible moral status of each and every person. At the centre of such thinking is the cosmopolitan view that human well-being is not defined by geographical or cultural locations, that national or ethnic or gendered boundaries should not determine the limits of rights or responsibilities for the satisfaction of basic human needs, and that all human beings require equal moral respect and concern. The principles of equal respect, equal concern and the priority of the vital needs of all human beings are not principles for some remote utopia, for they are at the centre of significant post-Second World War legal and political developments.

What does 'cosmopolitan' mean in this context? (see Held, 2002). In the first instance, cosmopolitanism refers to those basic values that set down standards or boundaries that no agent, whether a representative of a global body, state or civil association, should be able to violate. Focused on the claims of each person as an individual, these values espouse the idea that human beings are, in a fundamental sense, equal, and that they deserve equal political treatment; that is, treatment based upon the equal care and consideration of their agency, irrespective of the community in which they were born or brought up. After over 200 years of nationalism, sustained nation-state formation and seemingly endless conflicts over territory and resources, such values could be thought of as out of place. But such values are already enshrined in the law of war, human rights law, the statute of the ICC, among many other international rules and legal arrangements.

Second, cosmopolitanism can be taken to refer to those forms of political regulation and law-making that create powers, rights and constraints that go beyond the claims of nation-states and that have far-reaching consequences, in principle, for the nature and form of political power. These regulatory forms can be found in the domain between national and international law and regulation – the space between domestic law that regulates the relations between a state and its citizens, and traditional international law, which applies primarily to states and interstate relations. This space is already filled by a host of legal regulation, from the legal instruments of the EU and the international human rights regime as a global framework for promoting rights to the diverse agree-ments of the arms control system and environmental regimes. Within Europe, the Euro-pean Convention for the Protection of Human Rights and Fundamental Freedoms and the EU create new institutions and layers of law and governance which have divided political authority; any assumption that sovereignty is an indivisible, illimitable, exclusive and perpetual form of public power – entrenched within an individual state – is now defunct (Held, 1995, pp. 107–113). Within the wider international community, rules governing war, weapons systems, war crimes, human rights and the environment, among other areas, have transformed and delimited the order of states, embedding national polities in new forms and layers of accountability and governance. Accordingly, the boundaries between states, nations and societies can no longer claim the deep legal and moral significance they once had in the era of classic sovereignty. Cosmopolitanism is not made up of political ideals for another age, but is embedded in rule systems and institutions that have already altered state sovereignty in distinct ways, and in societies of diverse faiths....

If 9/11 was not a defining moment in human history, it certainly made, among other things, today's generation less secure. The terrorist attacks on the World Trade Center and the Pentagon were an atrocity of immense proportions. Yet, after 9/11, the United States and its allies could have decided that the most important things to do were to enforce international law, to strengthen international rules in the face of global terrorist threats, and to enhance the role of multilateral institutions. They could have decided it was important that no single power or group should act as judge, jury and executioner. They could have decided that global hotspots like the Middle East that help feed global terrorism should be the main centre of international attention. They could have decided to be tough on terrorism and tough on the conditions that lead people to imagine (falsely) that Al-Qaeda and similar groups are agents of justice in the modern world. But they systematically failed to pursue this agenda. In general, the world after 9/11 became more polarized, international law weaker, and multilateral institutions more vulnerable.

...

An alternative approach existed, let's call it a cosmopolitan security agenda. This agenda requires three things of governments and international institutions (Held and Kaldor, 2001). First, there must be a commitment to the rule of law and the development of multilateral institutions – not the prosecution of war as the first response. Civilians of all faiths and nationalities need protection. Terrorists and all those who systematically violate the sanctity of life and human rights must be brought before an international criminal court that commands cross-national support. This does not preclude internationally sanctioned military action to arrest suspects, dismantle terrorist networks and deal with aggressive rogue states (see Hoffmann, 2003). But such action should always be understood as a robust form of international law enforcement – above all as a way, as Mary Kaldor has most clearly put it, of protecting civilians and bringing suspects to trial (1998). In short, if justice is to be dispensed impartially, no power can arrogate to itself the global role of setting standards, weighing risks and meting out justice. What is needed is momentum towards global, not American or Russian or Chinese or British or French, justice. We must act together to sustain and strengthen a world based on common principles and rules (Solana, 2003).

Second, a sustained effort has to be undertaken to generate new forms of global political legitimacy for international institutions involved in security and peace-making. This must include the condemnation of systematic human rights violations wherever they occur, and the establishment of new forms of political accountability. This cannot be equated with an occasional or one-off effort to create a new momentum for peace and the protection of human rights, as is all too typical.

And, finally, there must be a head-on acknowledgement that the global polarization of wealth, income and power, and with them the huge asymmetries of life chances, cannot be left to markets to resolve alone. Those who are poorest and most vulnerable, linked into geo-political situations where their economic and political claims have been neglected for generations, may provide fertile ground for terrorist recruiters. The project of economic globalization has to be connected to manifest principles of social justice; the latter need to frame global market activity (see, Held, 2004).

References

Bull, H. (1977) *The Anarchical Society*. London: Macmillan.

Held, D. (1995) *Democracy and the Global Order: From the Modern State to Cosmopolitan Governance*. Cambridge: Polity.

Held, D. (2002) Law of states, law of peoples: Three models of sovereignty. *Legal Theory* 8(1): 1–44.

Held, D. (2004) *Global Covenant: The Social Democratic Alternative to the Washington Consensus*. Cambridge: Polity.

Held, D. and Kaldor, M. (2001) What hope for the future? http://www.lse.ac.uk/depts/global/maryheld.htm, accessed 8 December 2008.

Hoffmann, S. (2003) America goes backward. *New York Review of Books* 50(10): 74–80.

Kaldor, M. (1998) *New and Old Wars*. Cambridge: Polity Press.

Solana, J. (2003) The future of transatlantic relations. *Progressive Politics* 2(2), http://www.policy-network.net/uploadedFiles/Publications/Publications/pp2.2%2060-67_SOLANA.pdf.

Toolbox

The internet has already had a significant impact on conflict resolution and will continue to do so. Like all other walks of life, the World Wide Web is transforming the ways in which knowledge is formed and distributed. We deal with this issue in the section of *Contemporary Conflict Resolution* on 'Conflict Resolution in the Age of Cybertechnology'.

The Conflict Information Consortium supports efforts to use rapidly advancing information technologies to provide citizens in all walks of life with the information that they need to deal with conflicts more constructively. It is available at http://www.crinfo.org/.

In this final part, we provided an extract describing the Ushahidi project to use social media and mobile phone technology for real time tracking of conflicts. Ushahidi is a non-profit tech company that specializes in developing free and open source software for information collection, visualization and interactive mapping. It is available at http://www.ushahidi.com.

This part looked at future challenges and developments in the conflict resolution field. One powerful tool to explore this is by using the Future Imaging Workshop idea first proposed by one of the founders of the field, Elise Boulding. The methodology can be found at http://www.gmu.edu/programs/icar/pcs/EB83PCS.htm.

Index